100 PHOTOS

THAT CHANGED THE WORLD

Project Editor
VALERIA MANFERTO DE FABIANIS

Editorial Coordination
LAURA ACCOMAZZO, GIORGIO FERRERO

Graphic Design
MARIA CUCCHI

Editorial Staff
CHIARA SCHIAVANO, CARLO BATÀ (ICEIGEO, Milano)

Text by FRANCESCO BISELLI, MICHELE BUZZI, CLAUDIA GALAL,
GIULIA GATTI, ILARIA GHISLETTI, MARGHERITA GIACOSA, LORENZO MARSILI,
GIANNI MORELLI, ROBERTO MOTTADELLI, PAOLO PACI, PAOLA PAUDICE,
ELENA ROSSI, MARCO SANTINI, CHIARA SCHIAVANO, LARISSA SOFFIENTINI.

100 PHOTOS

THAT CHANGED THE WORLD

Edited by

MARGHERITA GIACOSA
ROBERTO MOTTADELLI
GIANNI MORELLI

whitestar·

Contents

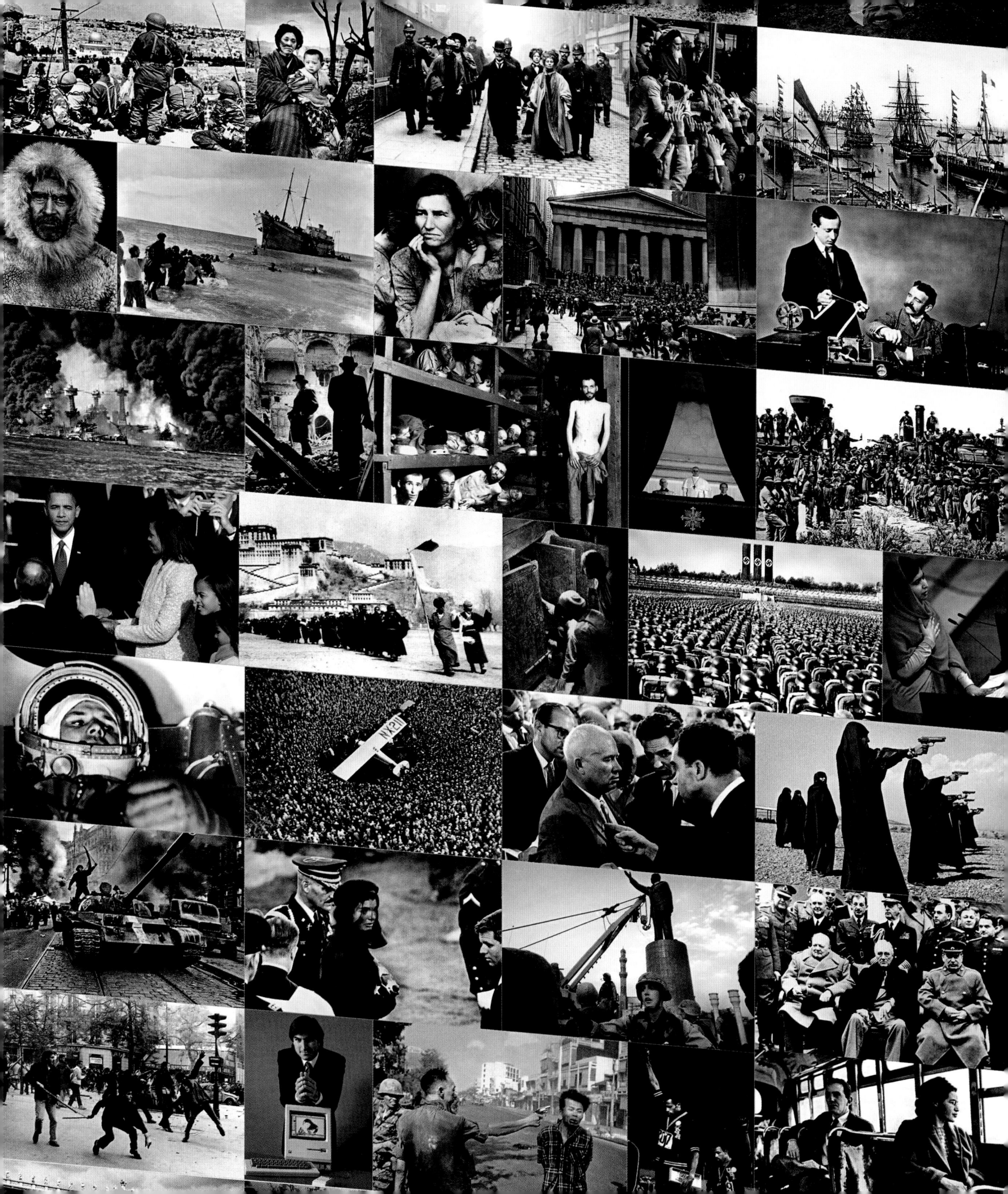

Introduction

by Roberto Mottadelli

The twentieth century had not yet begun, and already humanity was ready to welcome it, investigate it, and immortalize it with a camera. The instrument was still young, and yet so pervasive and effective that it would change forever our way of experiencing and reporting history: both private history – of individuals and families of every social background, who could leave for posterity tangible evidence of their existence – and history with a capital "H," which is inevitably marked by fewer but grander figures and events.

The history books relate that the history of photography began in 1839, when the prestigious Académie des Sciences de l'Institut de France and the Académie des Beaux-Arts recognized the new daguerreotype technique, invented by Louis Daguerre, a man of multifaceted brilliance. In reality the unofficial history had begun at least twelve years before, when Joseph Nicéphore Niépce obtained the first, unstable image "drawn with light." He then began a close collaboration with Daguerre. As often happens with great inventions, there are many disputes and "counter-histories" regarding the invention of photography. For example, the French pair, Niépce-Daguerre, is often opposed to two British scientists, Thomas Wedgwood and William Henry Fox Talbot. What is certain is that the new technique originated in France and Britain in the first half of the nineteenth century and that, from then on, it crossed borders and continents with remarkable speed.

We can identify two dates as watersheds in the transition of photography as a pastime for the wealthy, or as an activity requiring technical skill and training, to its spreading everywhere. The first is 1867, with the founding of Aktiengesellschaft für Anilinfabrikation (or Agfa, as it was later

Steve McCurry, Afghan Girl, 1984 *Sharbat Gula was only 12 years old when she met Steve McCurry in a refugee camp in Peshawar, in an Afghanistan enduring a bloody Soviet invasion. She was brave. She chose not to hide, not even behind a smile. She challenges the camera with a gaze which is magnetic and yet difficult to hold. Without saying a word, she told of her pain and the dignity of her people, who for thirty years have suffered too many wars and still seek peace.*

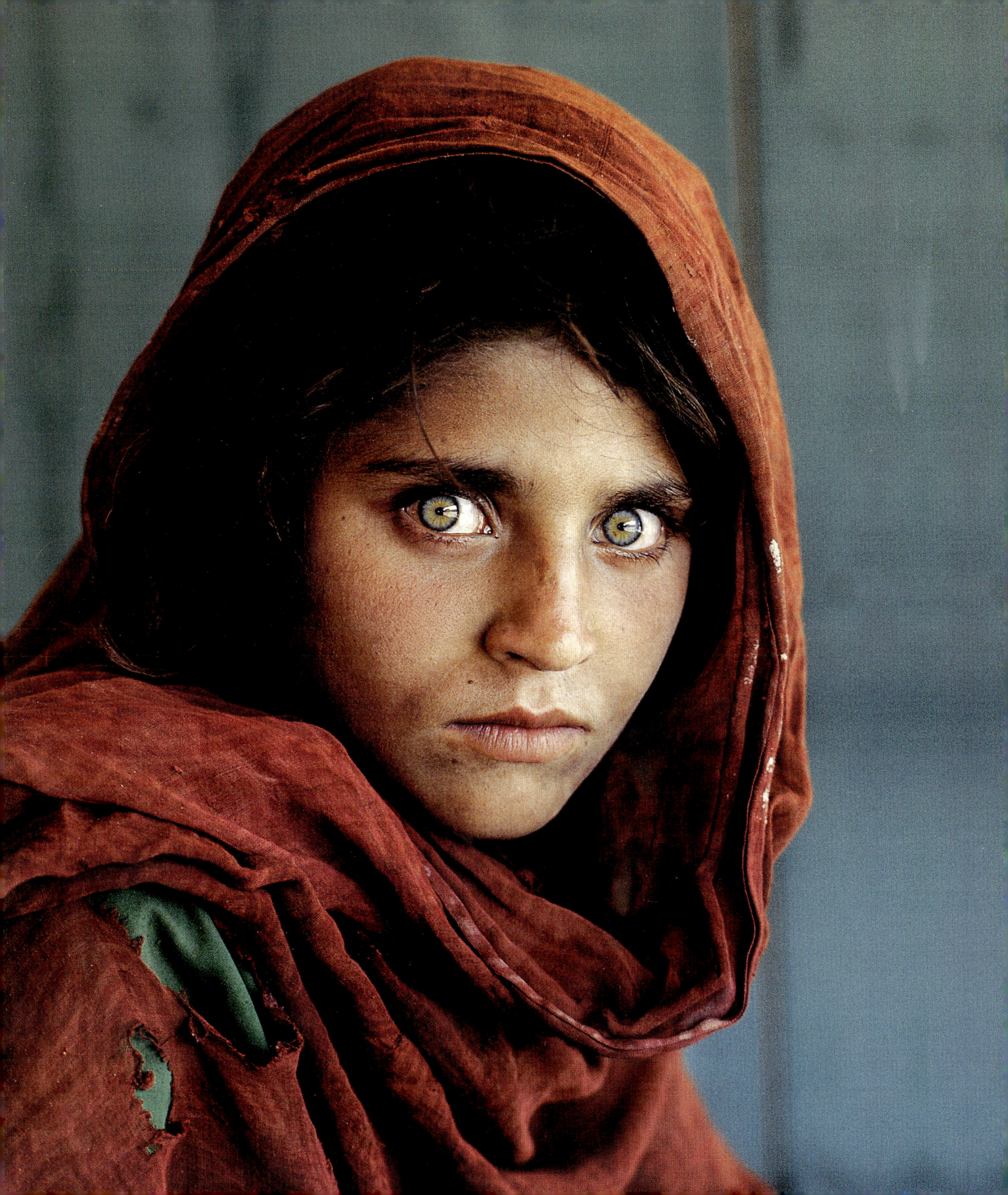

Introduction

known) in Berlin, the company specialized in the production of photographic equipment. The second date is 1888, when the just-founded Kodak put on the market a small box camera that was relatively cheap and extremely simple to use: the model No. 1. From this moment on, there would always be a lens ready to immortalize practically every episode, every figure capable of making a more or less glorious, or at least significant, mark in the progress of humanity.

What started as an exciting phenomenon, at the beginning of the twentieth century, soon became an overwhelming rush. This revolution was completely unforeseen by those who, in the last decades of the nineteenth century, immortalized the opening of the Suez Canal, the building of the great railroads, and the construction of the Eiffel Tower over a Paris that was all optimism and *Belle Époque* elegance. It seemed that the fate of the planet could only be splendid and progressive, due to, above all, science and engineering. And photography, so modern and accessible, appeared to be more consistent with the *fin-de-siècle Zeitgeist* than painting and drawing, which for centuries had held a monopoly on the visual documentation of events. Photographs also seemed honest and sincere, and by their nature faithful to the reality of events: "It's true! The camera can't lie." But soon we discovered that this is a shaky truth, and that photography can lie, too. And it was a still greater disappointment when we understood that the twentieth century had at least two faces. It was not only a *crescendo* of prodigious inventions and scientific discoveries (from telegraphic communication between Europe and America to the World Wide Web) and of social progress (from the battles for votes for women, to those for equality between whites and blacks, to the courage of Malala Yousafzai). Nor was it only an era of conquests, of challenges to the eternal snows of the poles, of reaching the stars. The latter began with the jerky flight of the Wright brothers, overcame accidents like that of the airship Hindenburg, only to reach ever higher, up to the mysterious red soil of Mars, where NASA has sent a rover that is able to communicate with Earth, and, of course, to take pictures. The twentieth century was also a dreadful sequence of wars, conducted on immense scales and with ever more deadly weapons: tools of death which epitomize the dark side of progress. Chemical research laid the foundations for the use of asphyxiating gases in the First World War. Discoveries in physics were a step toward the use of atomic bombs in Japan. The great ideologies, as well, have required a tribute in blood. Only a few years after the taking of the Winter Palace, the Communist dream degenerated into the repression of every form of opposition, as the tanks advancing on Prague demonstrated. On the other hand, the so-called "export of democracy," which drove the United States to invade Vietnam, had tragic consequences. And then there was the Berlin Wall, and the Cold War. Since September 11th, 2001, the world has changed. A pandemic held the entire world hostage for months, Russia's invasion of Ukraine has undermined Europe's security, and climate change looms over the future of humanity.

We dedicate the volume you are reading to 100 photographs that document these and other key moments of the last century and a half. Thus it is not a history of photography, but a volume of photographs of history. Collected here are snapshots of events and figures who are very distant and different, and yet essential to form a picture of an era that was so full of promise and contradiction. They have often become icons, more effective than every other testimony, in a century marked by the power of the image over the written word. There are examples of manipulated or forged photographs, starting from the one portraying a famous speech by Lenin, which was "purged" by Stalin's censorship; or of constructed photographs presented as reality, perhaps with good intentions, as in the shot that Major Tracy dedicated to the effects of asphyxiating gases.

Among the photographers selected are some giants, like Henri Cartier-Bresson, Robert Capa, Dorothea Lange and Cecil Beaton; great reporters and eye-witnesses with flair and courage, from Elliott Erwitt to Abbas Attar, from Eugene Smith to Kevin Carter, to Larry Burrows; But we owe many images to the honest artisans of photography and to amateurs, who sometimes remained nameless, and who had the good fortune to be in the right place at the right time, because history is not always predictable. The important thing, when it knocks on your door, is to have a camera in your hands, and to be ready to capture the moment.

The Transcontinental Railroad

May 10, 1869 - Promontory, Utah, United States

On May 10th, 1869, a large crowd waited at Promontory Summit, Utah, for the historic meeting between the locomotives Jupiter, of the Central Pacific line, and the 119, of the Union Pacific, which completed the first American transcontinental railroad (the only transcontinental line prior to this was the Panama Railway, but it was only 48 miles long). The two locomotives arrived and approached each other until the engineers managed to make them touch, then they shook hands and each broke a bottle of champagne on the locomotive of the other. A Golden Spike was driven with a silver hammer to symbolically weld together the rails of the two lines.

We owe this famous shot to Andrew J. Russell, a photographer who had already documented the American Civil War and had followed, in the previous years, the progress of the Transcontinental. In a composition typical of the commemorative photo, we see the workers framing the two locomotives and the handshake between the presidents of the two companies in the center of the shot.

Construction on the railroad linking the Atlantic and Pacific coasts was set in 1862, with the Pacific Railroad Act, signed by President Lincoln. It was entrusted to two companies, which would each have to complete part of the route until they met in the middle of the country.

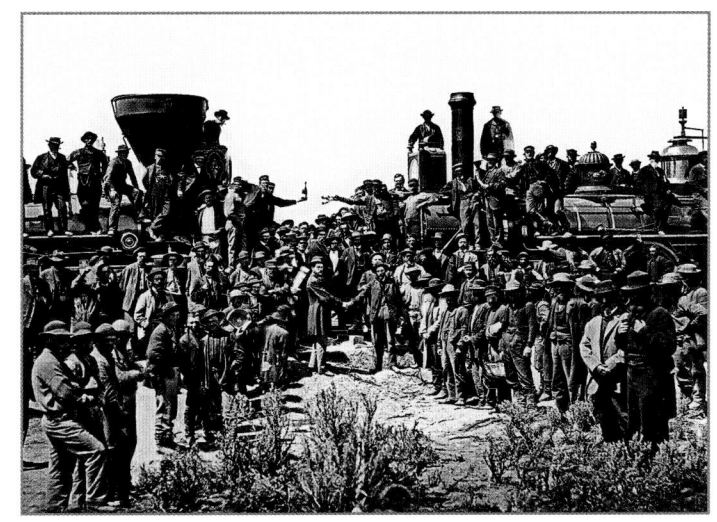

Photograph by Andrew J. Russell

Work began in the following year and went quickly despite innumerable difficulties, above all on the section which was to cross the mountains of the Sierra Nevada. To finance the construction, the companies received economic support and the ownership of a strip of land along the future railroad, which would soon gain a considerable market value. Central Pacific had many German, Irish, and Italian immigrants as workers, while most of the labor force for Union Pacific was Chinese.

The route envisaged crossing the hunting reserves of the Native American peoples. Feeling threatened by the invasion of their territories, they watched the advance of the railroad and on various occasions they ambushed and violently attacked the workers.

"Done!" announced briefly a telegram from Leland Stanford, one of the financiers of Central Pacific, to President Grant, who had just begun his first term in office, to inform him of the success of the endeavor.

The completion of the railroad enabled people to accomplish in only seven days a journey that until then had required weeks, if not months, by stagecoach or by sea. Furthermore, it opened the territories of the West to massive colonization, which also led to the end of Native American civilization.

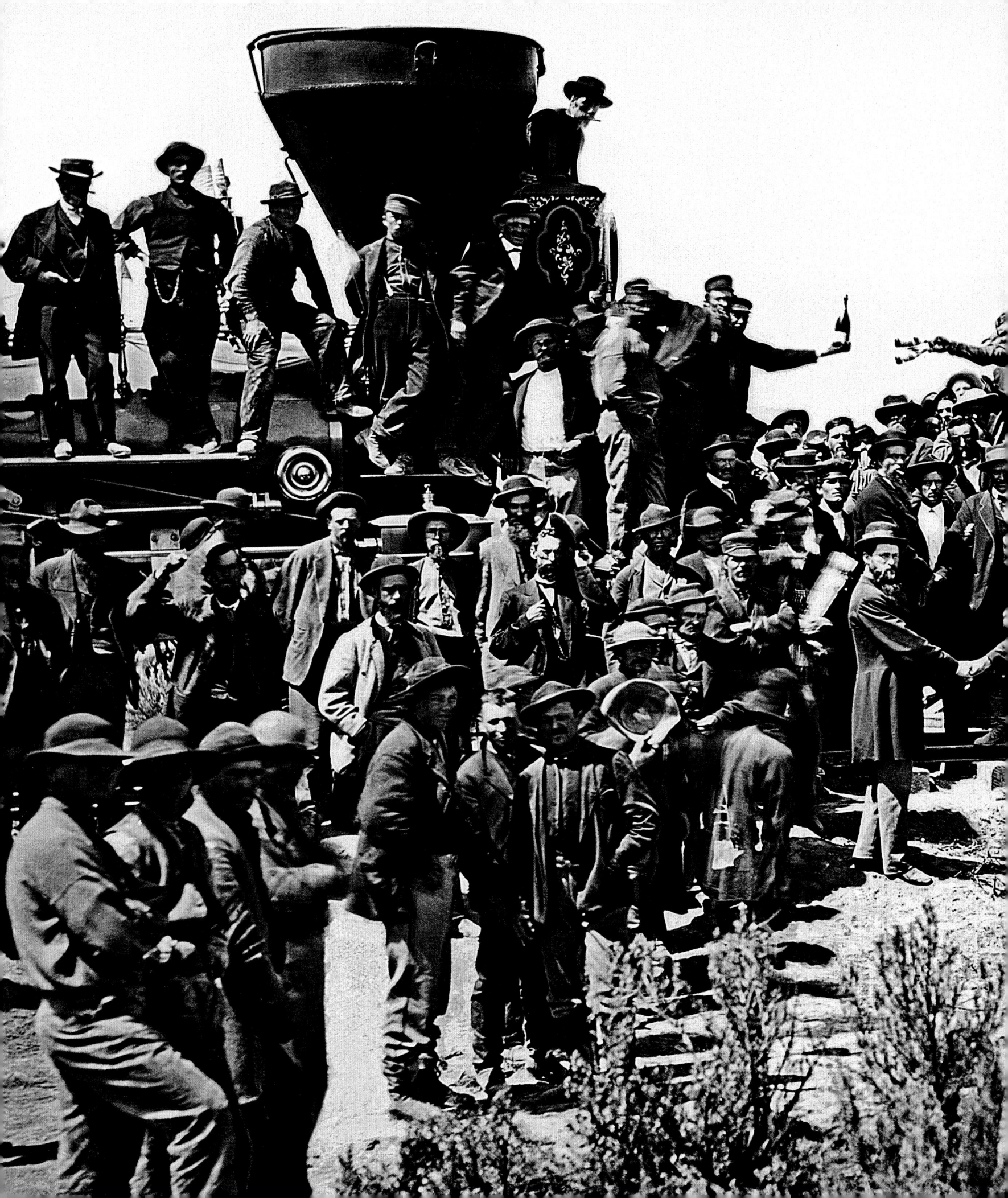

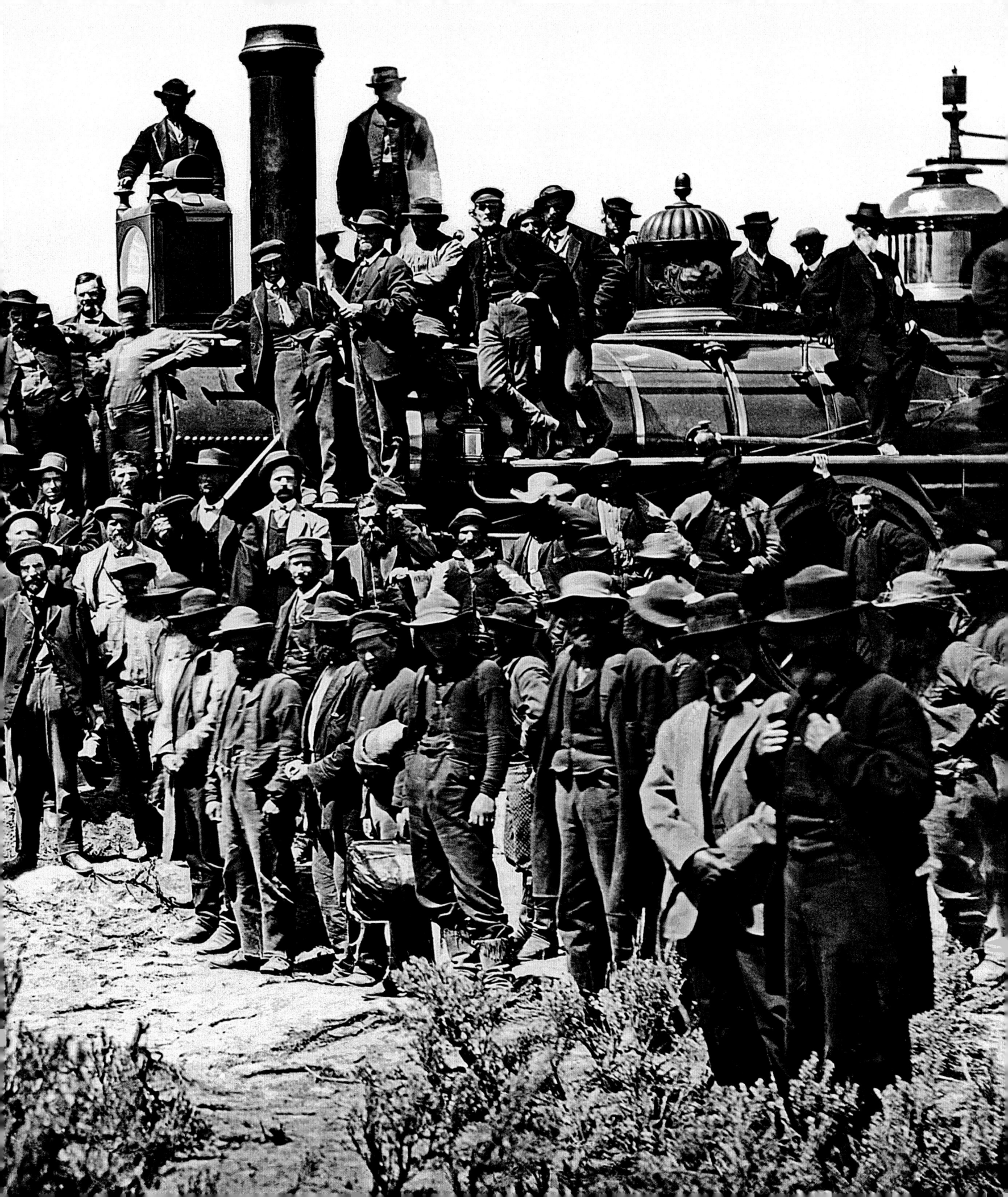

The Eiffel Tower and the Expo

1889 - Paris, France

In 1889, Paris is the center of the world. *Belle Époque* elegance intensifies the secular rite of the World's Fair, a hymn to progress and, for France, a celebration of the hundredth anniversary of the Revolution. For the occasion, an engineer with a revolutionary's soul, Gustave Eiffel, has designed a tower destined to change the history of the city and of architecture. Some people already love it, while most still have to get used to its presence. They need time to take in a structure that is so huge and bulky, but at the same time innovative. Perhaps the Eiffel Tower has gone up too quickly: only two years, two months, and five days have elapsed between the opening of the construction site and the tower's inauguration, on March 31st, 1889. When work on the tower begins, Henri Roger-Viollet is still in his teens. Born in 1869, he studies engineering, and loves photography. He enjoys creating photomontages before these are commonplace, often changing the proportions of the objects and the people he portrays. No one more than Roger-Viollet – with his young mind, engineering training, and creative spirit – can appreciate Eiffel's genius. With his camera, he documents every phase of the construction, which rises day after day, from the first to the 324th meter (986th foot). Yet in this shot Roger-Viollet chooses not to pay homage to the verticality of the structure. He concentrates on its enormous base, which frames the Central Dome, the heart of the fair. The contrast of forms, and especially dimensions, between the powerful architectonic structure and the little figures moving beneath it, is disorienting. It is as if an astronaut had stepped out of one of Jules Verne's novels and landed in an impressionist painting. Before Eiffel decided to challenge the heavens, such images could only appear in photomontages.

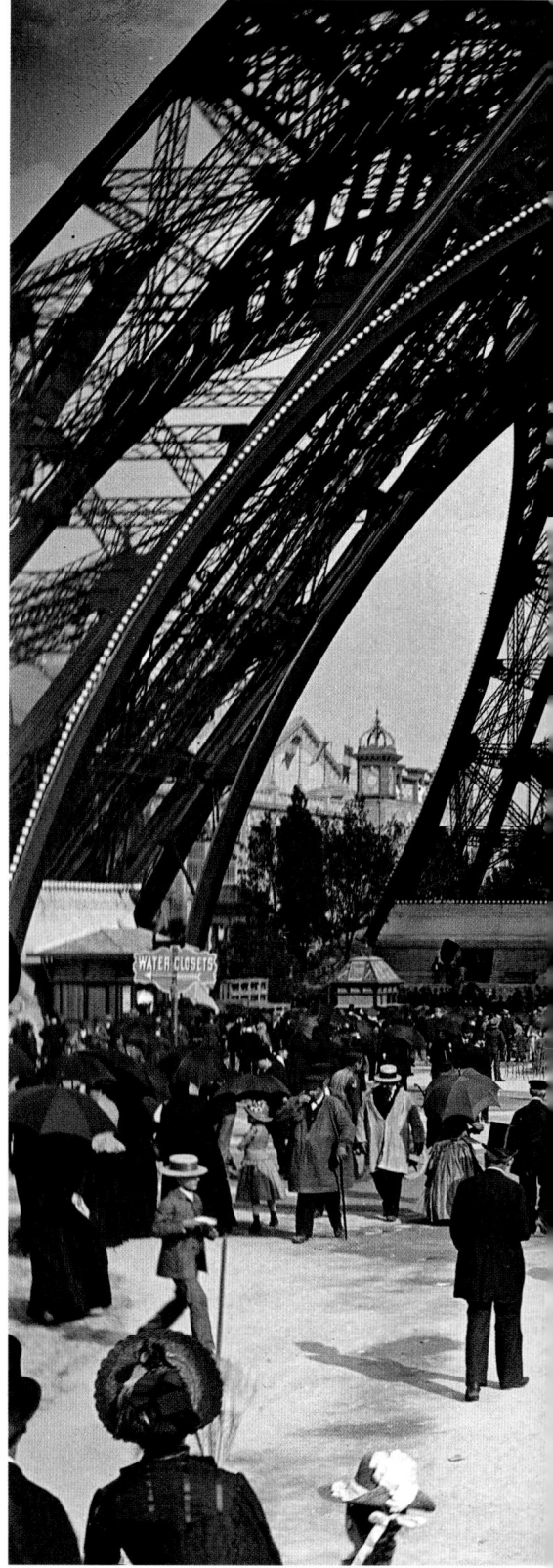

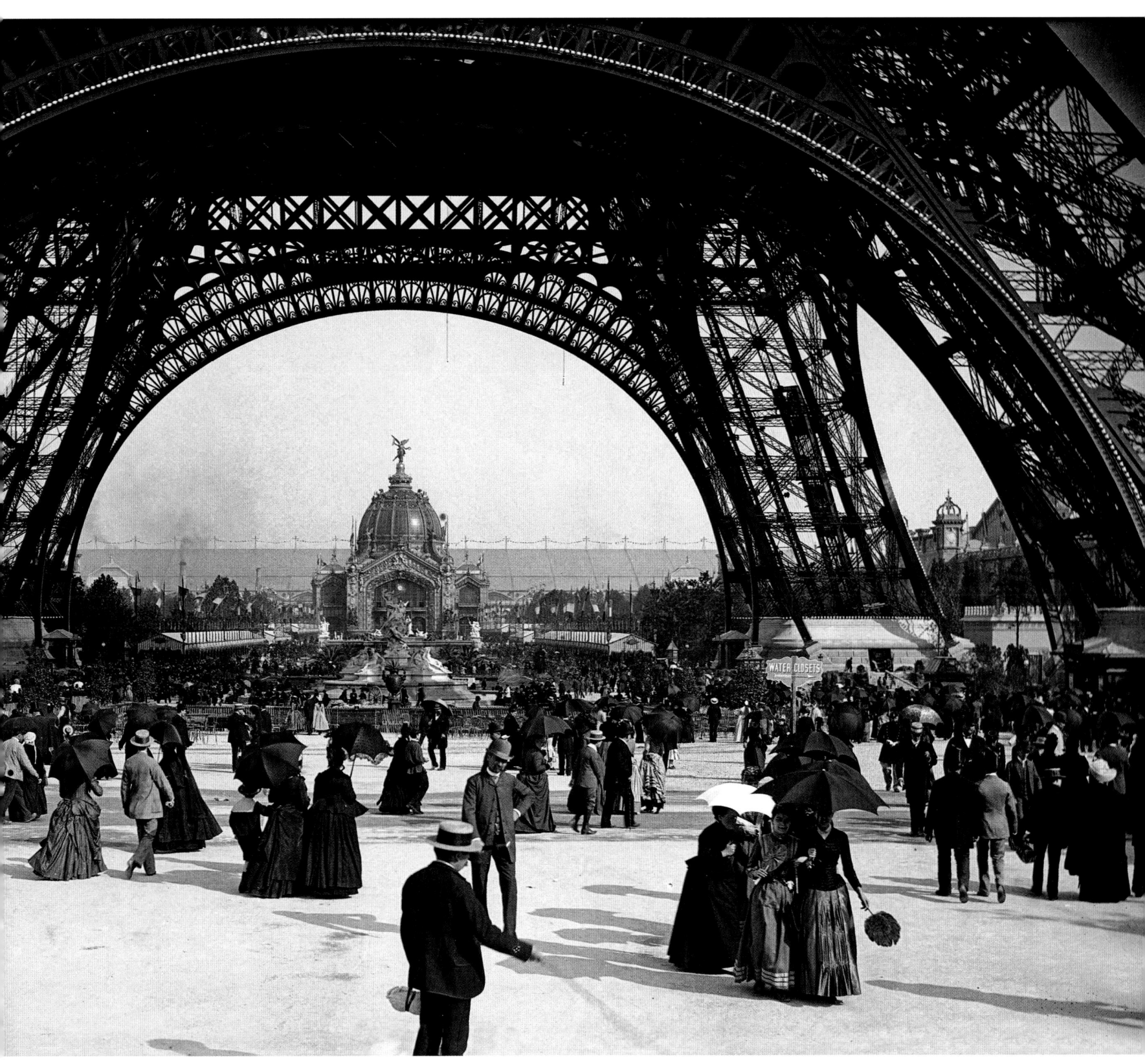

Photograph by Henri Roger-Viollet

The Arrival of a Train at La Ciotat Station

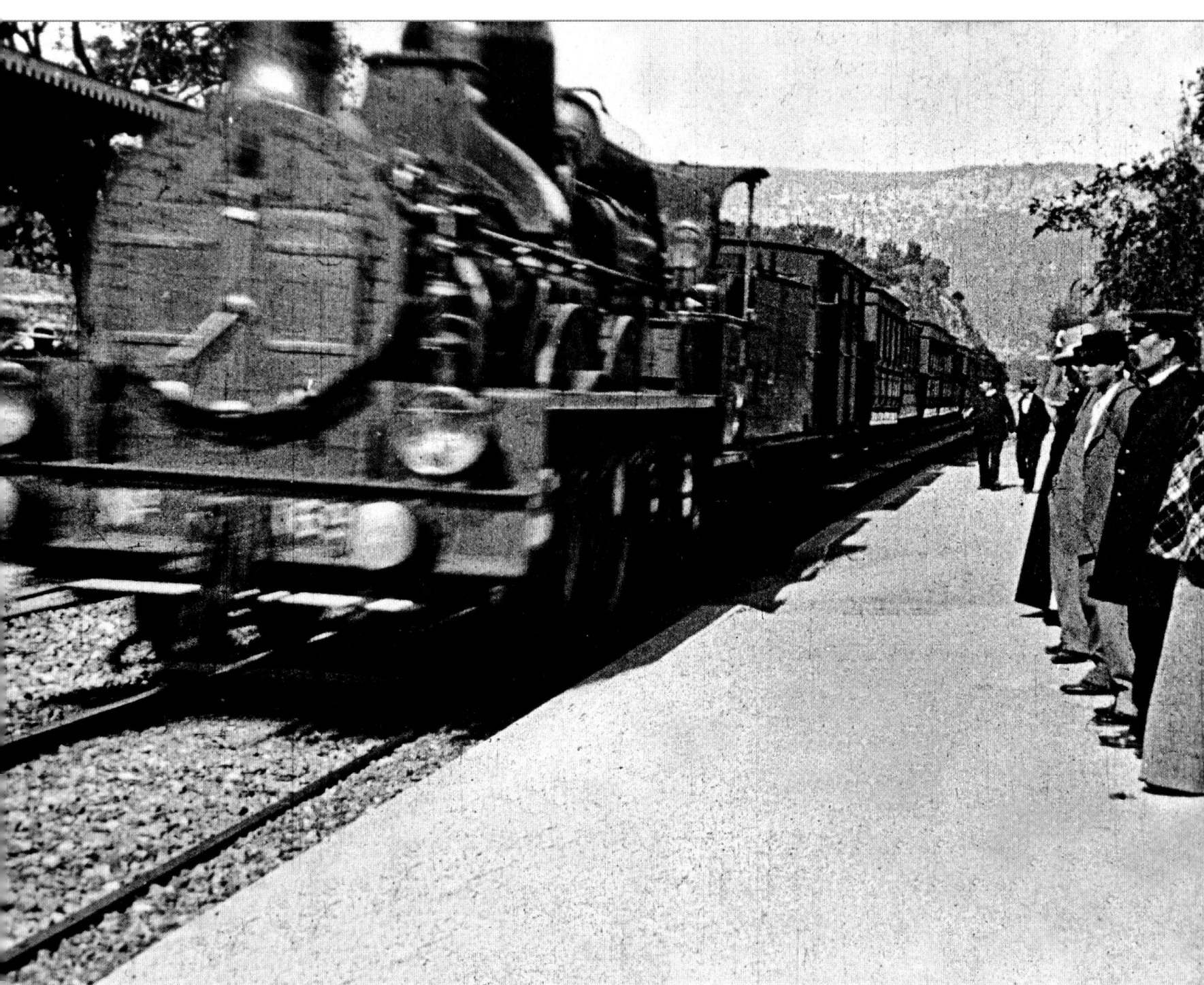

The Arrival of a Train at La Ciotat Station is one of the first short films of the so-called cinema of origins. This brief, fifty-second documentary about everyday life has greater historical than artistic value. Two French entrepreneurs who specialized in the field of photography made the film: the famous brothers, Auguste and Louis Lumière, patented in 1895 the projector they used for this work (and for many other contemporary works). Because of their invention, the Lumière brothers are known as the fathers of cinema.

This image is a frame from the film and it clearly shows many of its significant qualities: from the angle of the shot, which is not full-on but diagonal, to the depth of the visual field, and from the perfect focus of the people on the platform, to the strong dynamism of the moving train.

In spite of what is commonly believed, the film was not shown on the evening of December 28th in the Salon Indien du Grand Café, on the Boulevard des Capucines in Paris, which is often described as the place where cinema was born. Rather, the film was first shown a few days later, on January 6th. Legend has it that when the audience saw the projection of the approaching train, they were afraid of being run over and ran out of the room.

Apart from these curiosities, *The Arrival of a Train* offers an important link between photography, the art of the static image, and cinema, the art of the image in movement. The short film is also considered one of the key moments of the *Belle Époque*, the vibrant period in which the world experienced unprecedented technical progress. The concept of "free time" stems from that moment. That era of optimistic confidence will soon be ended by the trenches of the Great War.

Frame from the short film by Auguste and Louis Lumière

Wireless Telegraph Across the Atlantic

December 12, 1901 - Newfoundland, Canada

This historic black and white photo, like a classic medium shot from the movies, shows two men surrounded by equipment. They are closely examining what appears to be a strip of paper. It is December, 1901, and the formal style of the photograph – which, although established at the time, was not yet considered an artistic means of expression – gives no hint of the emotion the two protagonists are feeling. This photograph officially documents an experiment that marked a great step forward in scientific progress and opened the way to modern telecommunications.

The young man standing on the left is the Italian scientist and inventor Guglielmo Marconi, who at the time was barely 27 years old. The seated man is his British assistant George Kemp. The two are posing for the first wireless telegraph transmission across the Atlantic, an invention for which Marconi will be awarded the Nobel Prize for Physics in 1909.

To carry out this extraordinary experiment, Marconi had an enormous transmitter built at Poldhu, in Cornwall, with an antenna 425 feet high. Later, with his assistants George Kemp and Percy Paget, he left for the Canadian island of Newfoundland. He had ordered the station at Poldhu to transmit, every day at the same hour, the three dots of the Morse alphabet representing the letter S. He hoped to receive the message in Newfoundland. More than 1,800 miles of ocean separate Cornwall from Newfoundland. The message would have to bounce twice off the ionosphere and propel itself along the curvature of the Earth, which the scientific community of the time considered impossible. Then, against all odds, this happened: the three dots of the Morse code traveled from one continent to the other. The young scientist Guglielmo Marconi succeeded in astounding the world with his discovery.

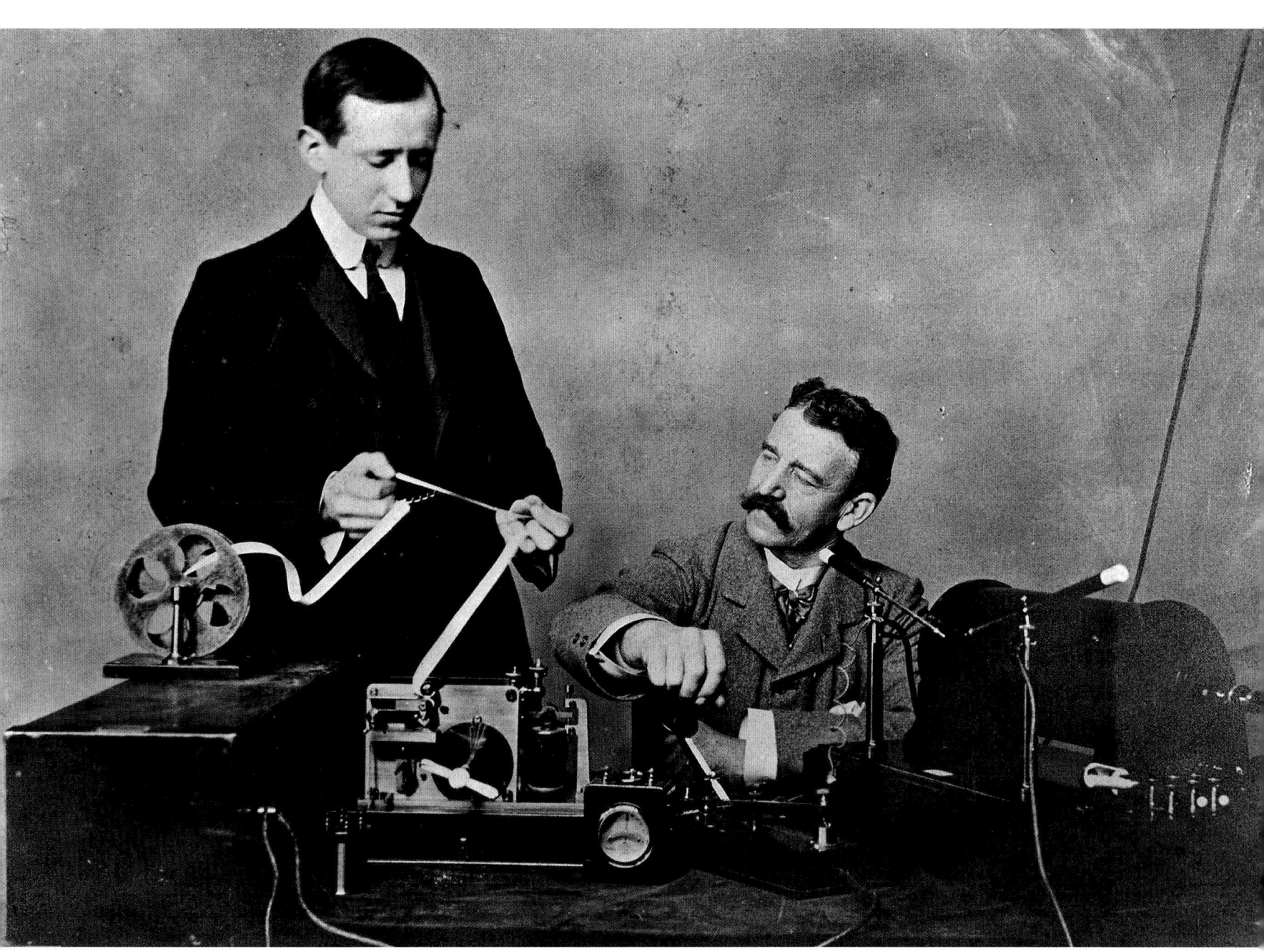

December 17, 1903 - Kitty Hawk, North Carolina, United States

On December 17th, 1903, the Wright brothers, two bicycle dealers from Dayton, Ohio, flew from a beach in North Carolina into the history books. Their experiment was to launch into the air the first piloted, motorized plane.

This photograph, which today is preserved in the National Air and Space Museum of the Smithsonian Institution, is precious testimony to the event. John T. Daniels took it. He was one of the men of the US Lifesaving Station at Kill Devil Hills called upon to give first aid in case of accidents. Daniels had never used a camera before that morning. But it was Orville Wright who skillfully decided the composition of the photo. Before lying down at the controls of the Flyer, Wright placed the camera so as to capture the biplane from the rear on the right, and also the path of the launch. Above all, he left enough room in the shot to take the plane when it was flying. The aircraft was placed on rails and held down by an anchor. Then the internal combustion engine was started and, once it was at high revolutions, the cable was released: the plane rose to a height of 10 feet and remained in the air for 12 seconds, covering about 120 feet before landing. The head wind was very strong. For this reason, Wilbur Wright, the man standing on the right, had no difficulty in following the flight. The Flyer took off three more times that day before it was damaged.

Since the end of the nineteenth century, scientists, technicians, and inventors had thrown themselves into research in aeronautics. They hoped to create a motorized flying machine. In a mood of euphoria, everyone sought the record. Yet it was two brothers who had not even attended university who achieved this, fulfilling one of man's most ancient dreams. It was the first step toward the sky.

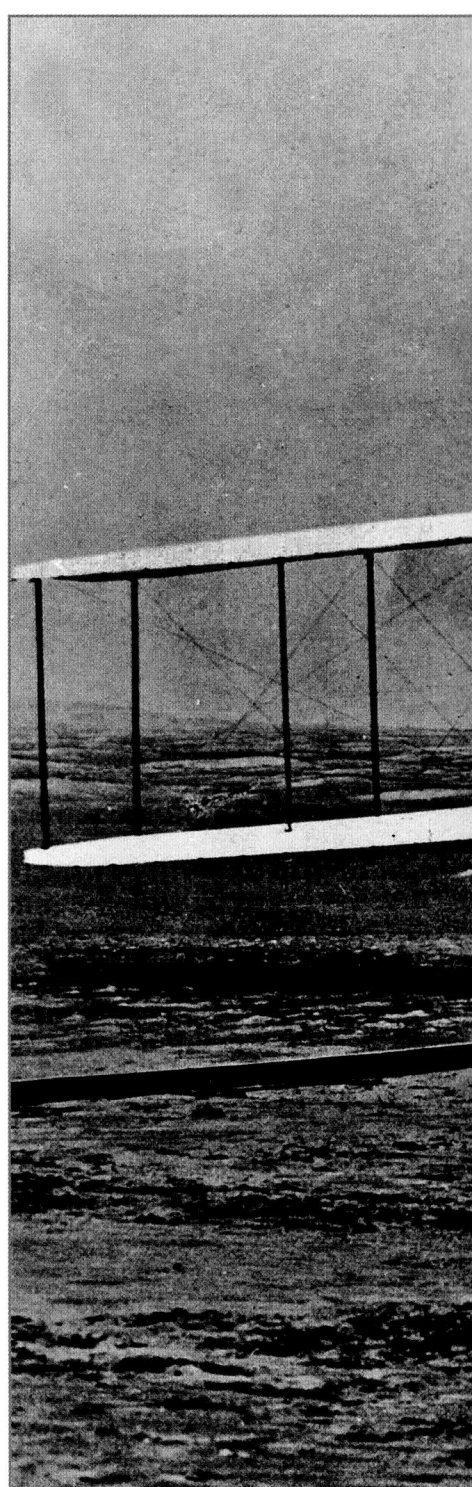

The First Flight

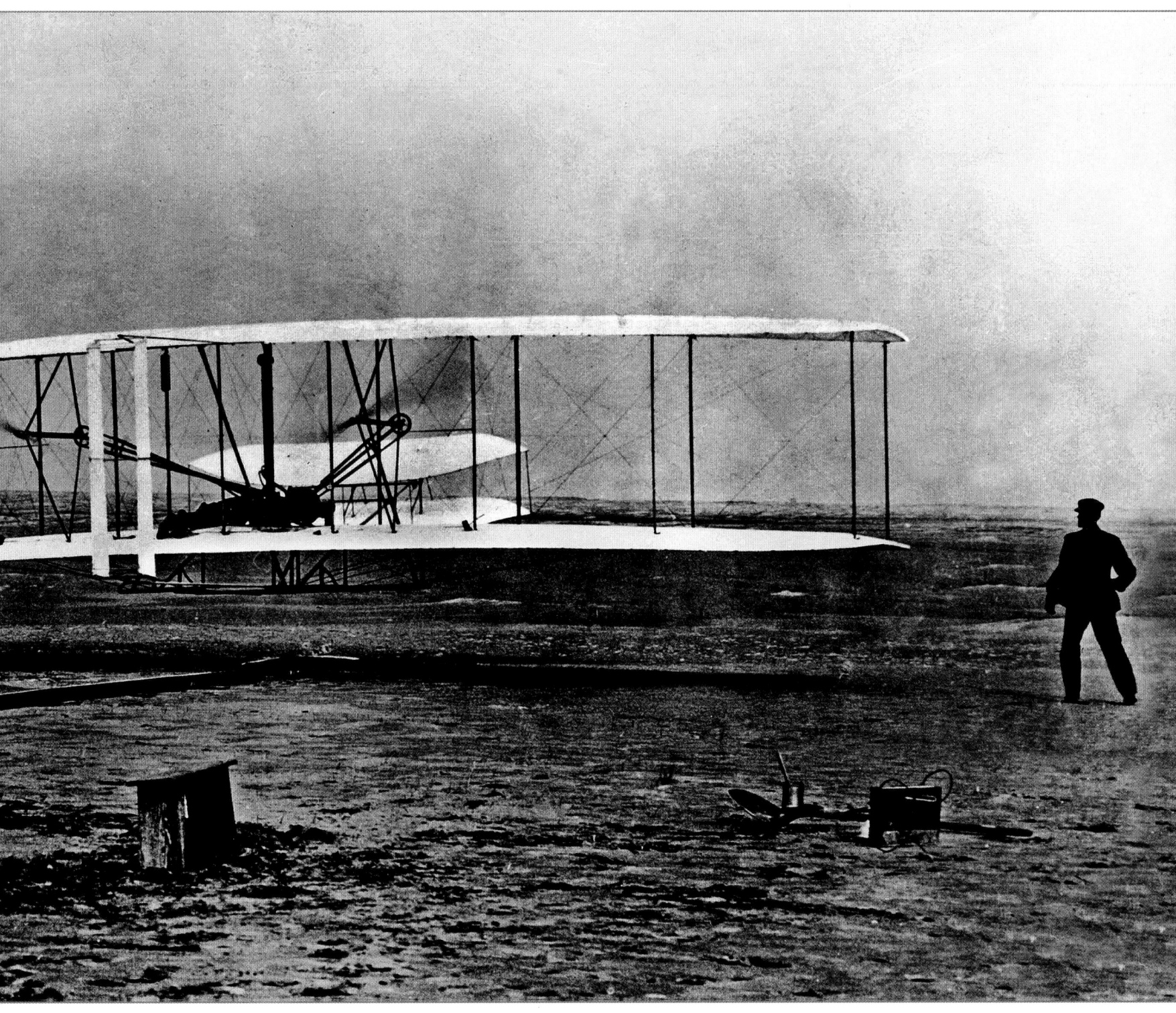

Photograph by John T. Daniels

The Struggle for Female Suffrage

February 13, 1908 - London, United Kingdom

Emmeline Pankhurst, the leader of the movement for female suffrage, advances with proud bearing and gaze, escorted by the police. She is arrested for the first time on February 13, 1908, while she is trying to present to the British Parliament one of her innumerable petitions.

In Britain, the movement for women's rights already had a long history, but it was only with the Women's Social and Political Union, founded by Emmeline in 1903, that the struggle became more organized. The first to join the movement were women of the middle-class, but soon the struggle spread to all social backgrounds. It involved associations of women workers in industry, where there was an ever-greater presence of women. The press referred to them disparagingly as "suffragettes." The militant women held meetings, planned ways of disrupting their opponents, distributed newspapers and pamphlets, made posters, and wrote on walls to draw public attention to discrimination against women. They resisted arrest with hunger strikes and daring escapes. In 1905, the arrest of two suffragettes resulted in an episode of intense conflict, with broken windows and fires in uninhabited homes, but fortunately nobody was hurt.

The First World War marked a pause in the activity of feminist groups, but in those years women performed many roles traditionally reserved for men, thus increasing awareness of their rights. Success occurred in stages: voting in local elections was recognized in the United Kingdom in 1894; in 1918, property-owning or married women over 30 years old were granted the right to vote in general elections. Ten years later, all women over the age of 21 were granted the right to vote.

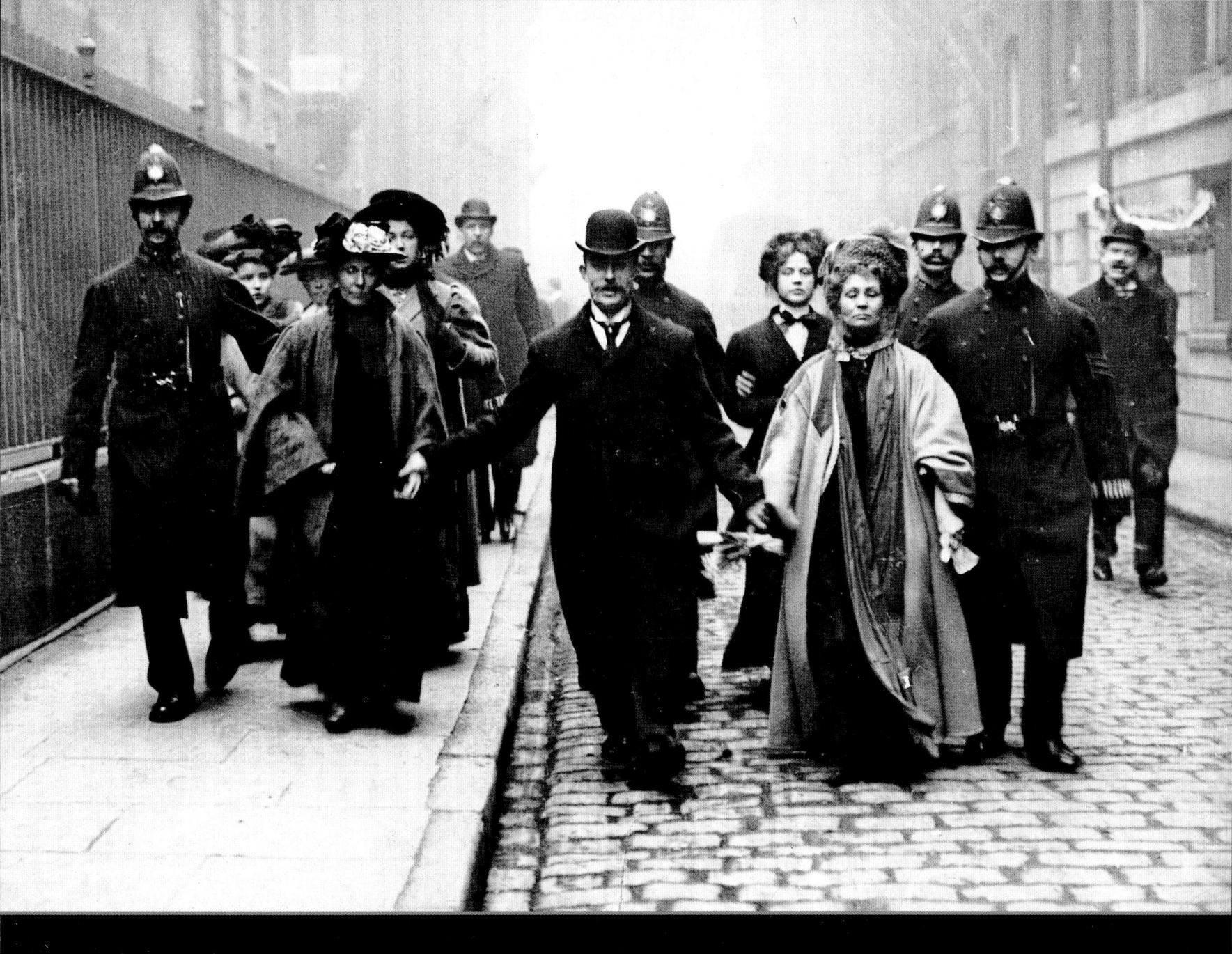

The First Flight
Over the Channel

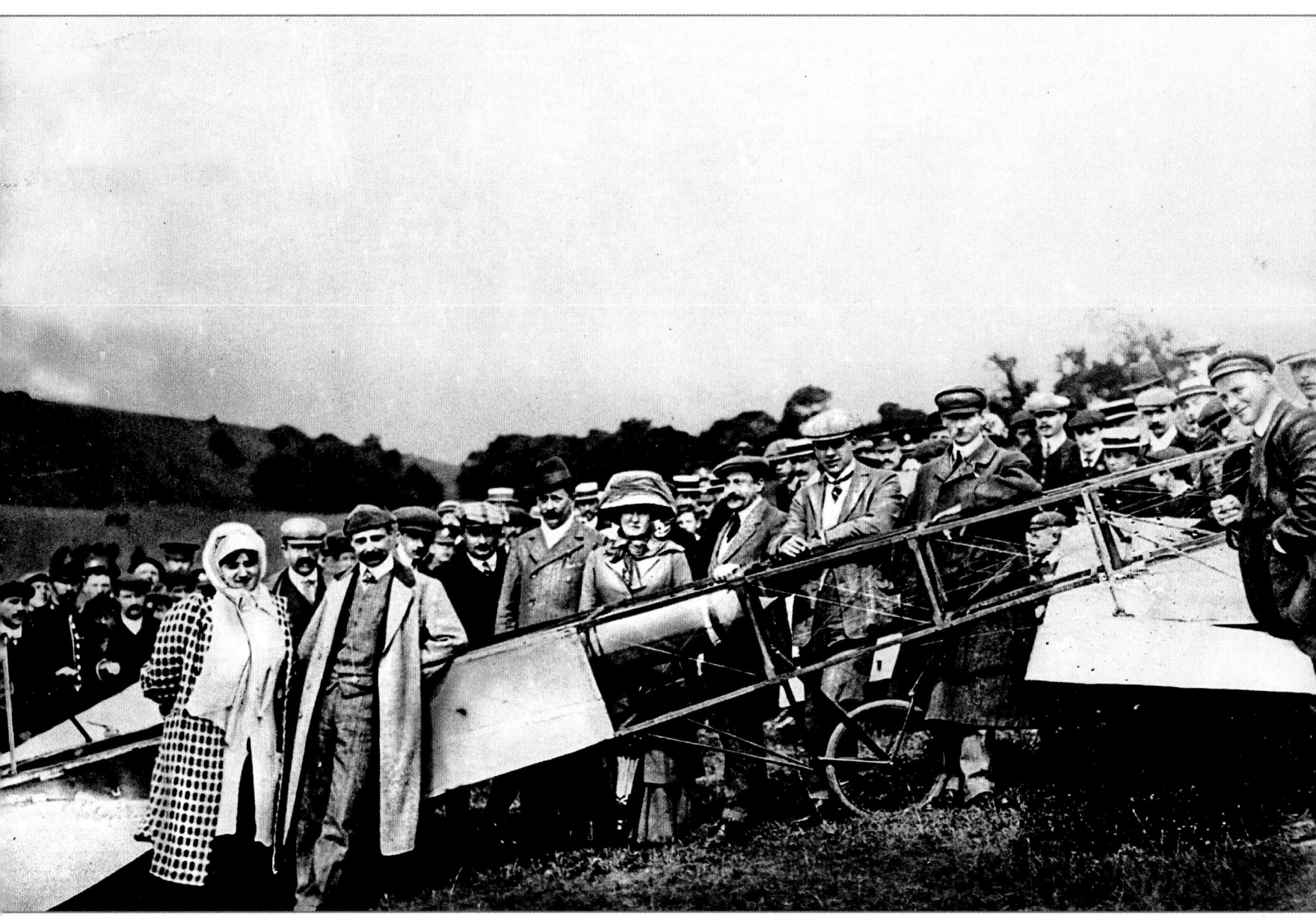

July 25, 1909 - Dover, United Kingdom

Nearly 25 miles separates Les Baraques (a little place near Calais) and Dover, in England. Between them is the Channel which, at the beginning of the twentieth century, was a considerable obstacle. To make such a crossing aboard a monoplane made of balsa wood and cloth, equipped only with a 25 horsepower engine, would be a heroic, and historic, enterprise. Several people had already flown for greater distances, but the "conquest of the Channel" had an enormous symbolic value: there had been several attempts, but all had failed.

Louis Blériot took off early in the morning on July 25th, 1909, to gain an advantage over another aviator, Hubert Latham, who was preparing to take off on the same day. Both pilots had already taken to the skies in previous days and both had had to make emergency landings, with various injuries. But a place of honor in the history of aviation was at stake . . . as well as the thousand pounds that the *Daily Mail* would give to the first flyer. Blériot's flight was brief, 36 minutes and 30 seconds, but not without its tense moments. Rain and wind almost brought the aircraft down. When he arrived, the propeller and the undercarriage proved to be damaged, but no other news counted: the French pilot had succeeded in his endeavor.

The fears were over, and after a night's rest July 26th was a day of celebrations. The photograph shows Blériot and his wife elegantly dressed, posing in front of the plane, a gentleman and his lady, with a crowd of admirers around them. There is little remarkable in the technique or composition of the image: we are confronted with one of those documentary shots which owe all their impact to the historic moment and to the subject depicted.

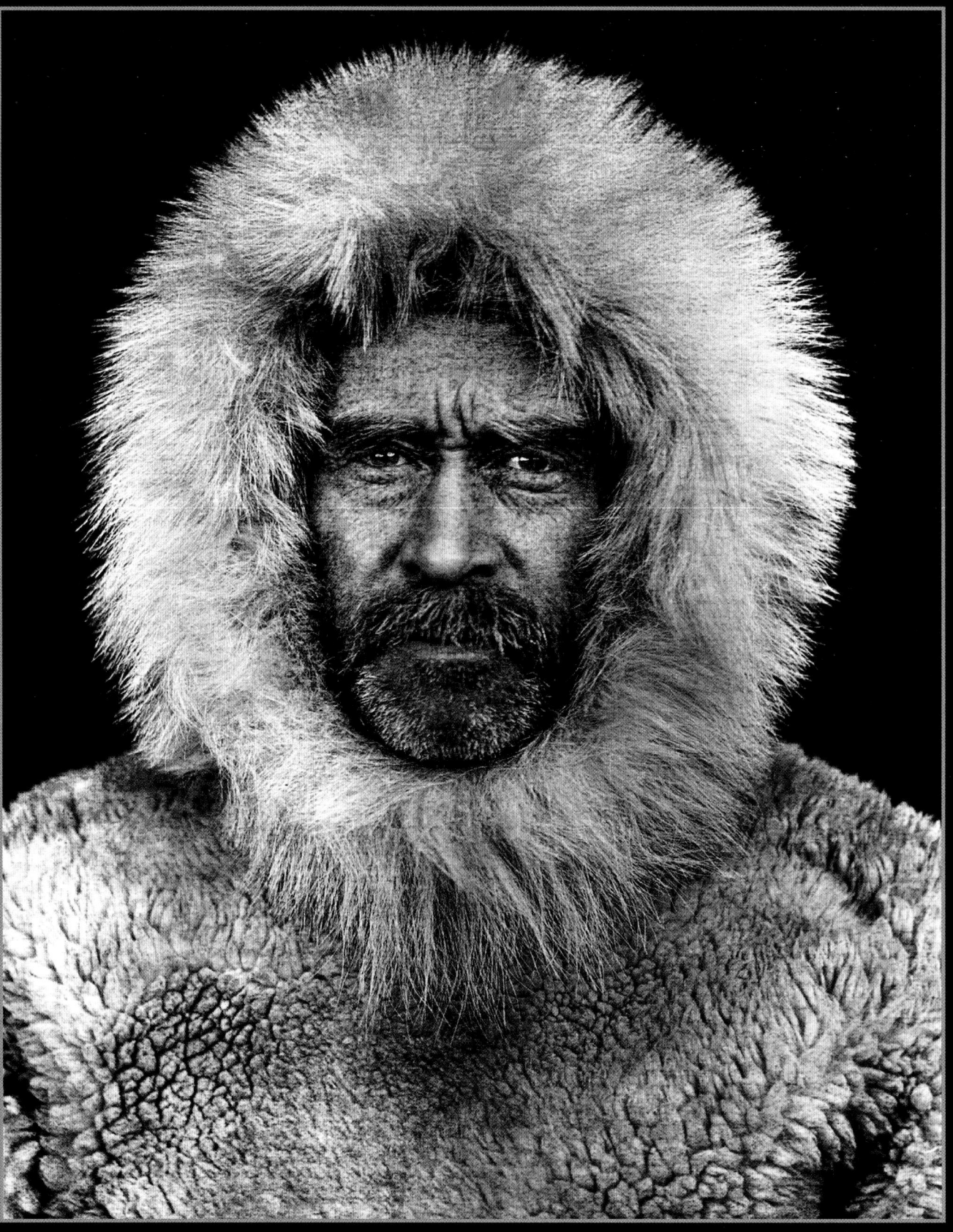

Robert Peary at the North Pole

1909 - Ellesmere Island, Canada

"The Pole at last!!! The prize of three centuries, my dream and ambition for 23 years, mine at last...." The date of this announcement, written on a loose sheet of paper tied to a log of the journey, was April 6th, 1909. They are the words of Robert Edwin Peary, US Navy engineer. The sentence, however, was probably written a few years later, when Peary published his memoirs. In the meantime, a fellow American, Frederick Cook (a doctor presumed to have reached the summit of Mount McKinley, the highest peak in North America), had returned from a harrowing Arctic exploration of more than one year, and declared in a telegram to the *New York Herald*: "We reached North Pole. April 21st, 1908."

Although the two explorers had collaborated on an important exploration in Greenland, they spent the following years arguing over who reached the Pole first. The epic of polar expeditions, from the legal point of view, was not at all heroic. The press and the National Geographic Society accepted Peary's claim; he was proclaimed a hero and appointed an Admiral in the Navy.

The photograph, taken in February, 1909, shows him on Ellesmere Island, the northern-most part of Canada, about to leave by sled with 22 Inuit and 130 dogs. But the shot is only of his face in a fur hood, and nothing else. Doubts about whether he actually reached the Pole remained until 1988, when research by the National Geographic Society ascertained that Peary had missed the North Pole by at least 30 miles due to calculation errors. His rival's records are today judged to be more reliable. It was belated rehabilitation for Cook who, after founding an oil company, was arrested for fraud and spent his last years in prison.

Conquest of the South Pole

December 14, 1911 - South Pole, Antarctica

The race to the Poles at the beginning of the twentieth century represented an authentic competition between explorers, hungry for adventure and fame, and between nations, which in these hopeless quests saw the last frontiers of colonialism. It was a race which thrilled the public through reports in books, magazines and newspapers. "Fresh" news was always arriving by telegraph. Photography was fundamental in informing readers and documenting events. For example, by examining the shadows in the photos taken by Robert Peary, in 1988 experts with the National Geographic Society concluded that the American explorer (accompanied only by Inuit guides) did not actually reach the North Pole.

However, there was never any doubt that Roald Amundsen and his companions (four fellow Norwegians: Oscar Wisting, Helmer Hanssen, Olav Bjaaland, Sverre Hassel) reached the South Pole. At the beginning of the expedition, in 1910, Amundsen was 38 years old and was perhaps the Arctic explorer with the most experience: he had spent a year trapped on a ship in the glaciers of the Antarctic Peninsula, and then had been the first to cross the Bering Strait to find the mythical North-West Passage. He was organizing an expedition to the North Pole, when news reached him that Frederik Cook (1908) and Peary (1909) had preceded him. Therefore, he directed his attention again to the Antarctic and to the South Pole, which were still uncharted. The expedition left Norway in August and only sixteen months after, on December 14th, 1911, was it able to plant the flag on the southernmost point of the planet.

The famous photograph, published in the book *The Year 1912 Illustrated*, shows Oscar Wisting, who was given the honor to plant the Norwegian flag on the Geographic South Pole, on skis near the sled, the Norwegian flag, with its cross, flies behind him. In the foreground we see a little team of dogs which are curled up at his feet.

With the attainment of the South Pole by Amundsen's expedition, the Norwegian explorer acquired mythical status. The legend would grow stronger 16 years later, when Amundsen and his seaplane disappeared during an attempt to help the crew of the airship Italia, which was lost in the Arctic.

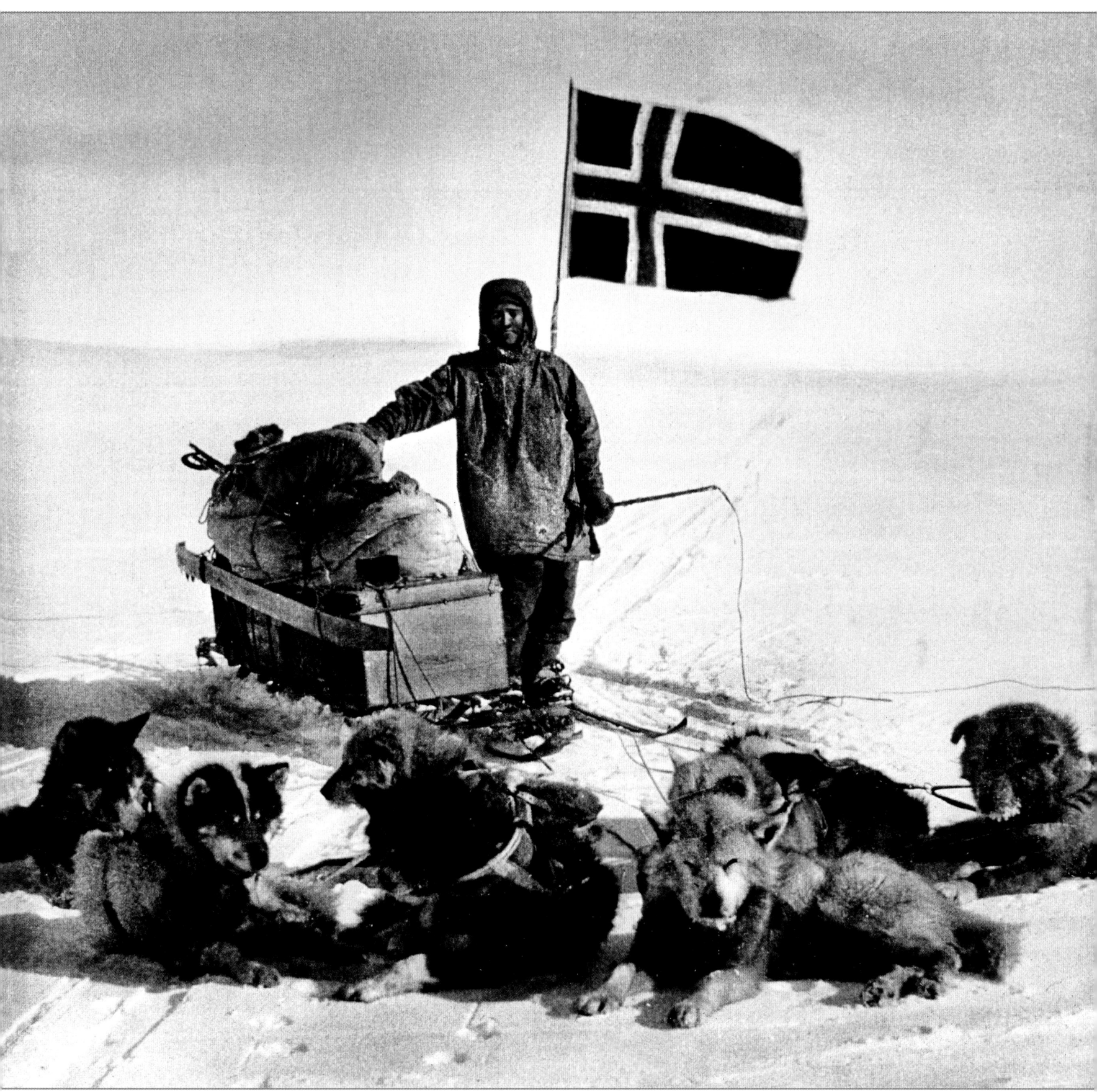

Great Loss of Life

April 14, 1912 - London, United Kingdom

"Great Loss of Life." On April 16th, 1912, in front of the offices of the White Star Line in London, a boy sells papers with the news of the sinking of the "most unsinkable" ship that ever sailed the oceans. Men read the news incredulously. The passengers' relations arrive to ask for information. Out of the about 2,220 who sailed, 1,518 people, passengers and crew, have died.

The Titanic left from Southampton on April 10th. The first class was full of important figures: everyone wanted to be present on the maiden voyage of the ship that was a legend before it was launched. But on the night of April 14th, the Titanic hit an iceberg. It was steaming at top speed to set the record for an Atlantic crossing, which would mean a prestigious Blue Riband. Various messages received from the other ships about the presence of icebergs never reached the bridge: they were considered superfluous. The lookouts did not have binoculars because they could not find the key to the cupboard containing them; and the ocean that night was so unusually calm that no spray from waves breaking on the iceberg was visible from far away. In the impossible attempt to avoid the impact, the officer on watch made the wrong maneuver: the iceberg literally ripped open 295 feet of the side of the steamer, as if it were huge can of sardines. There were half the number of lifeboats required on the liner. And while there was room for 1,176 people in the lifeboats, in the confusion only 705 took them. The greatest ship in the world sank in less than three hours and never reached New York. Its career lasted four days.

This photo became so famous that the boy, Ned Parfett, became known as the "Titanic paperboy." He was 16 years old at the time, and his future was no happier than the news he bore than day: six years later he died in France fighting at the front, only a few days before the end of the war.

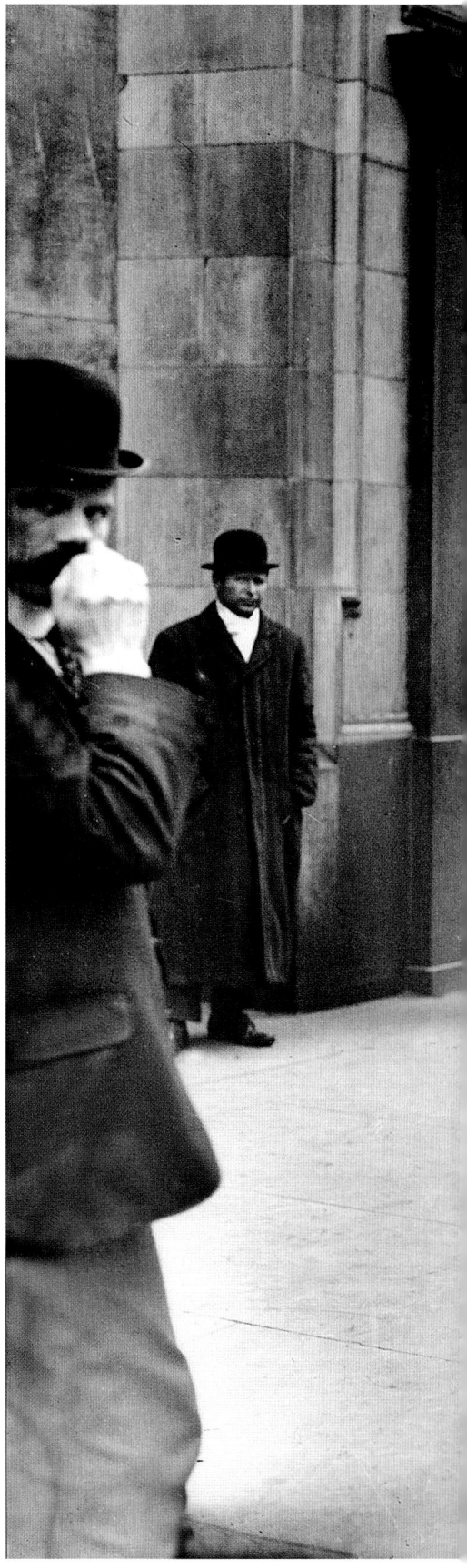

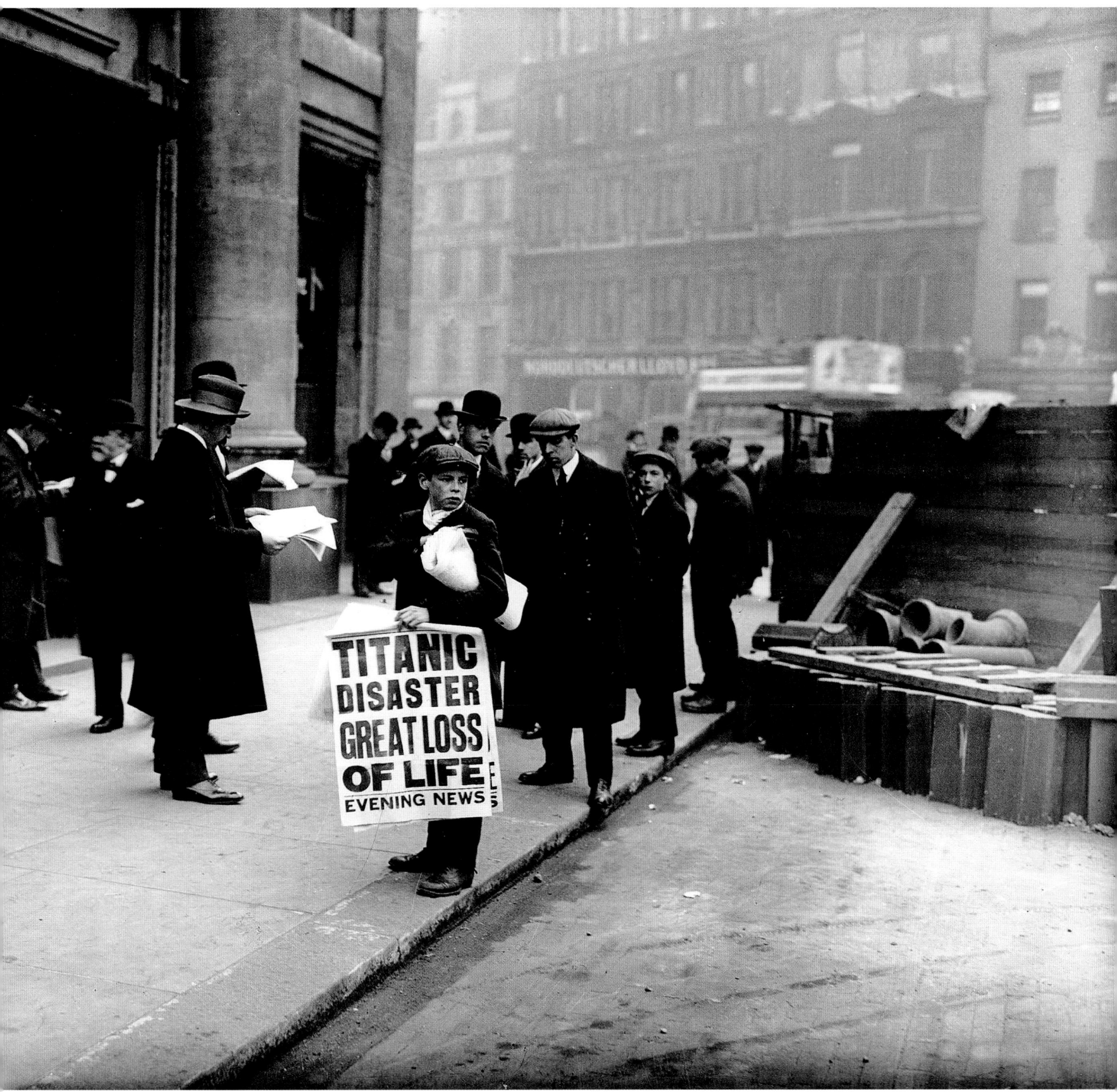

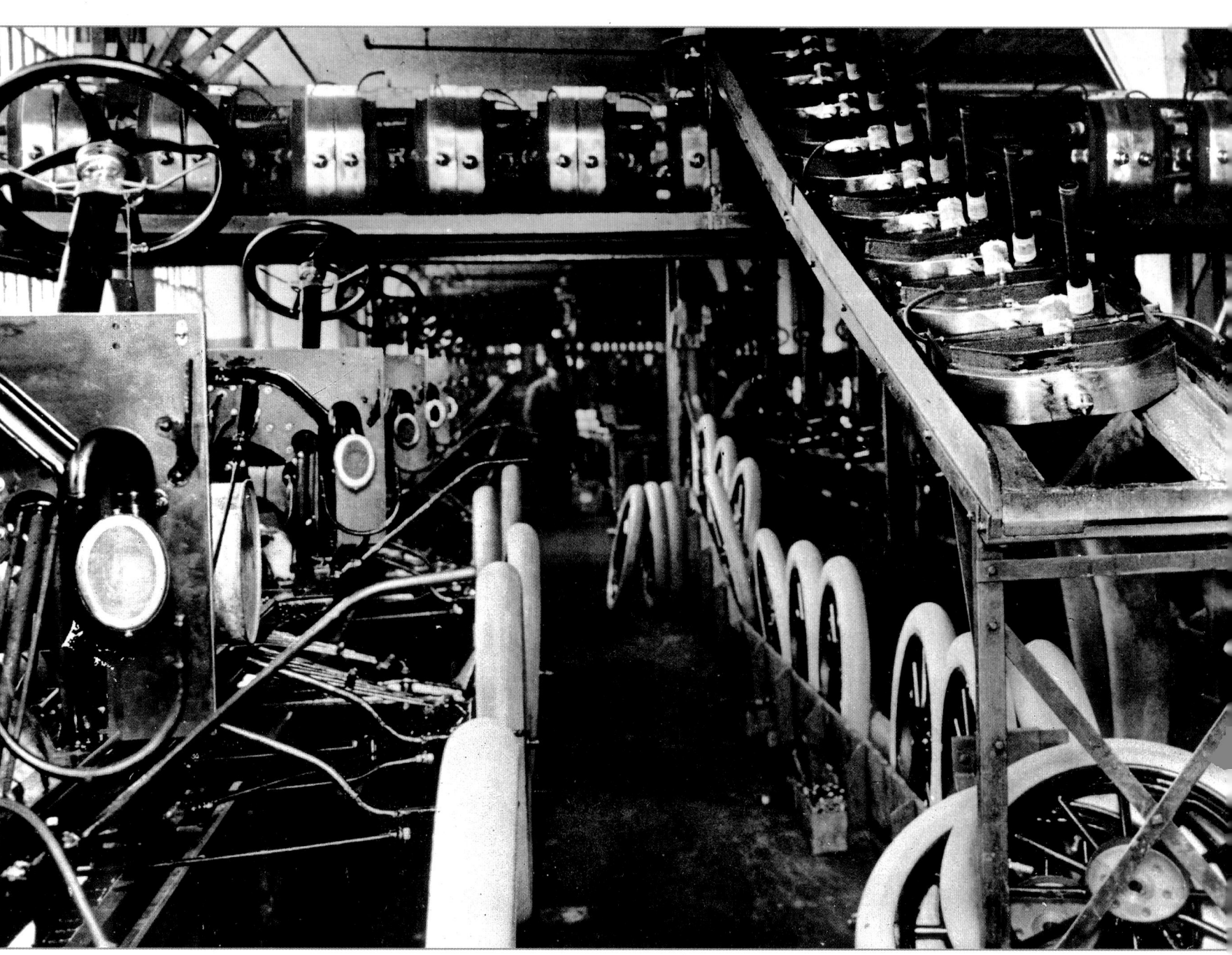

The First Moving Assembly Line

1913 - Detroit, Michigan, United States

Seriality, homogenization, and progress summed up in a single image that seems to anticipate two of the most striking and desecrating representations of these concepts: from out of the one-directional geometry of the factory could emerge, one after another, squads of workers, parading forth with the martial bearing in Fritz Lang's *Metropolis* (1927); while the same couple of bolts appear that obsess the frantic worker played by Charlie Chaplin in *Modern Times* (1936).

Apart from the references to the cinema, it is difficult to describe this photo from a purely aesthetic point of view. In fact, the shot, taken in a Ford factory in Detroit, does not have an artistic purpose. Rather, its intent is to clearly show the operations and advantages of the first assembly line in the world. If we need to speak of technique and art, knowhow, in this case, counts more than photographic beauty. That said, in the first part of the twentieth century, the Fordist philosophy of mass production did appear, to some, as a kind of art. This was especially the case when considering one of the first icons of modernity: the Model T Ford. In 1913, Henry Ford was able to produce a car every 93 minutes. Before then, the same factories produced only eleven cars per month. The time necessary to move from the bolt to the road – twelve hours – had not changed; Taylorist theories had simply optimized it. What *had* changed was society: the consumer was ready to welcome a future already neatly arranged on the conveyor belt of modern times.

Gas Attacks in the First World War

April 22, 1915 - Ypres, Belgium

"Drowning on dry land": this is the way soldiers describe the effects of asphyxiating chlorine-based gases. Taken by surprise, the soldier feels a burning sensation and unexpected suffocation. He feels the need to cough, but coughing is too painful. He begins to foam at the mouth and nostrils, and his skin becomes blue. He can no longer speak or move. If he's lucky, death comes quickly; otherwise, his agony can last hours, even days. Soldiers engaged on the Western Front in the First World War were the first to accurately describe the phases of the poisoning. They were the survivors, who bore forever in their souls the image of thousands of fellow soldiers killed by gas.

The photograph, which attempts to capture this horror, is not of a real event. It is still extremely effective. It was US Army Corps of Engineers Major Evarts Tracy who took it in 1918. Tracy was an expert in military camouflage. He did not immortalize what actually happened, but constructed a scene: the protagonist is the soldier in the foreground, who falls holding his hand to his throat. Photographs of this kind were used to impress on recruits what would happen to them if they did not obey the order, if it came, to put on gas masks, however uncomfortable they might be. The persuasive force of the image was greater than any officer's lecture: for obvious reasons, Tracy did not dwell on the horror of the death and took it for granted that the masks were always effective.

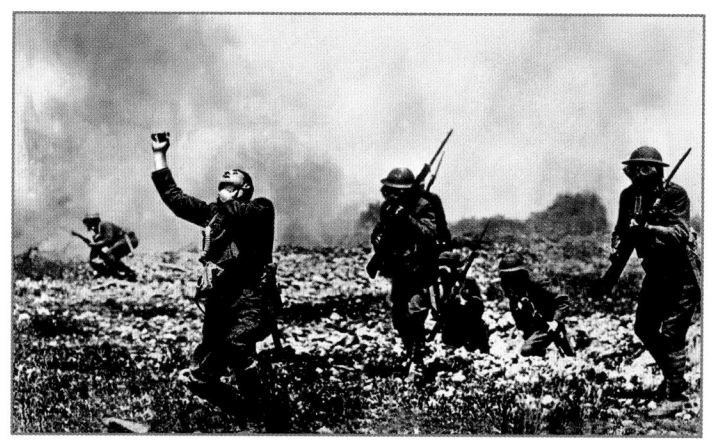

Photograph by Evarts Tracy

Asphyxiating gases had made their appearance in war three years before, on April 22nd, 1915: they were used on a large scale during the Second Battle of Ypres. At the beginning of the war, the Belgian town of Ypres, close to the French border, emerged as an important stronghold for the Allied forces. In fact, the German army later invaded Belgium, despite its neutrality. The Germans were the first to launch an offensive using chemical weapons. Taking advantage of the wind, which was in their favor, they released 168 tons of chlorine gas. The French and Algerian troops were decimated: 6,000 men died in less than 10 minutes, opening a breach of 4.5 miles. Not even the Germans foresaw such a result, and they didn't take advantage of the situation. It was a Canadian division that recaptured the frontline.

Although the practice was condemned by public opinion, soon every army included gases in its arsenal. Experiments followed to develop ever more toxic mixtures, until the advent of mustard gas, which was also used at Ypres, in 1917. While in 1915 the Canadian soldiers "only" had to urinate into handkerchiefs or rags and breathe through them (the ammonia in the urine neutralized the chlorine), with new chemical weapons came the appearance of the first gas masks. Their production, however, was always a step behind the development of new gas weapons.

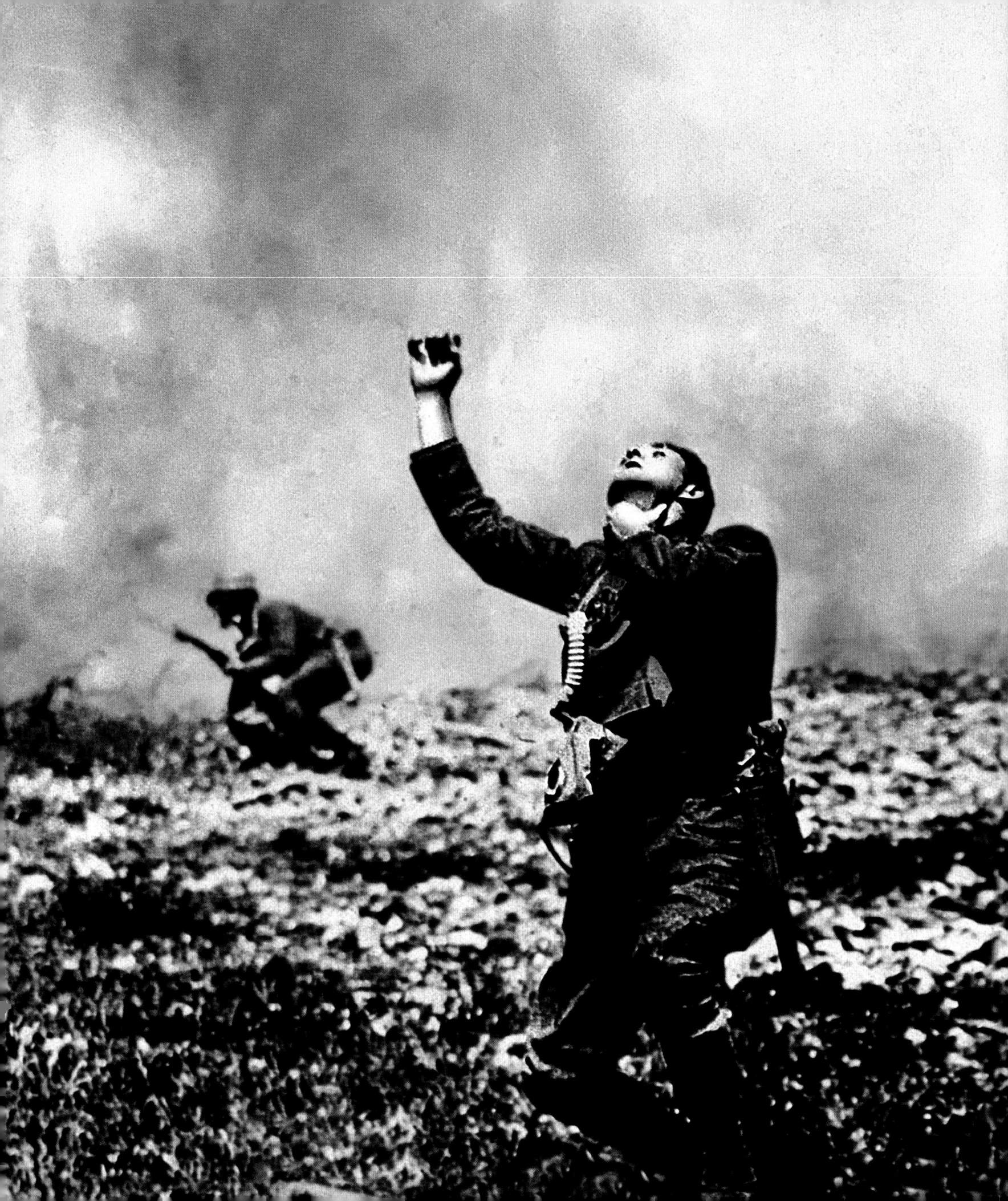

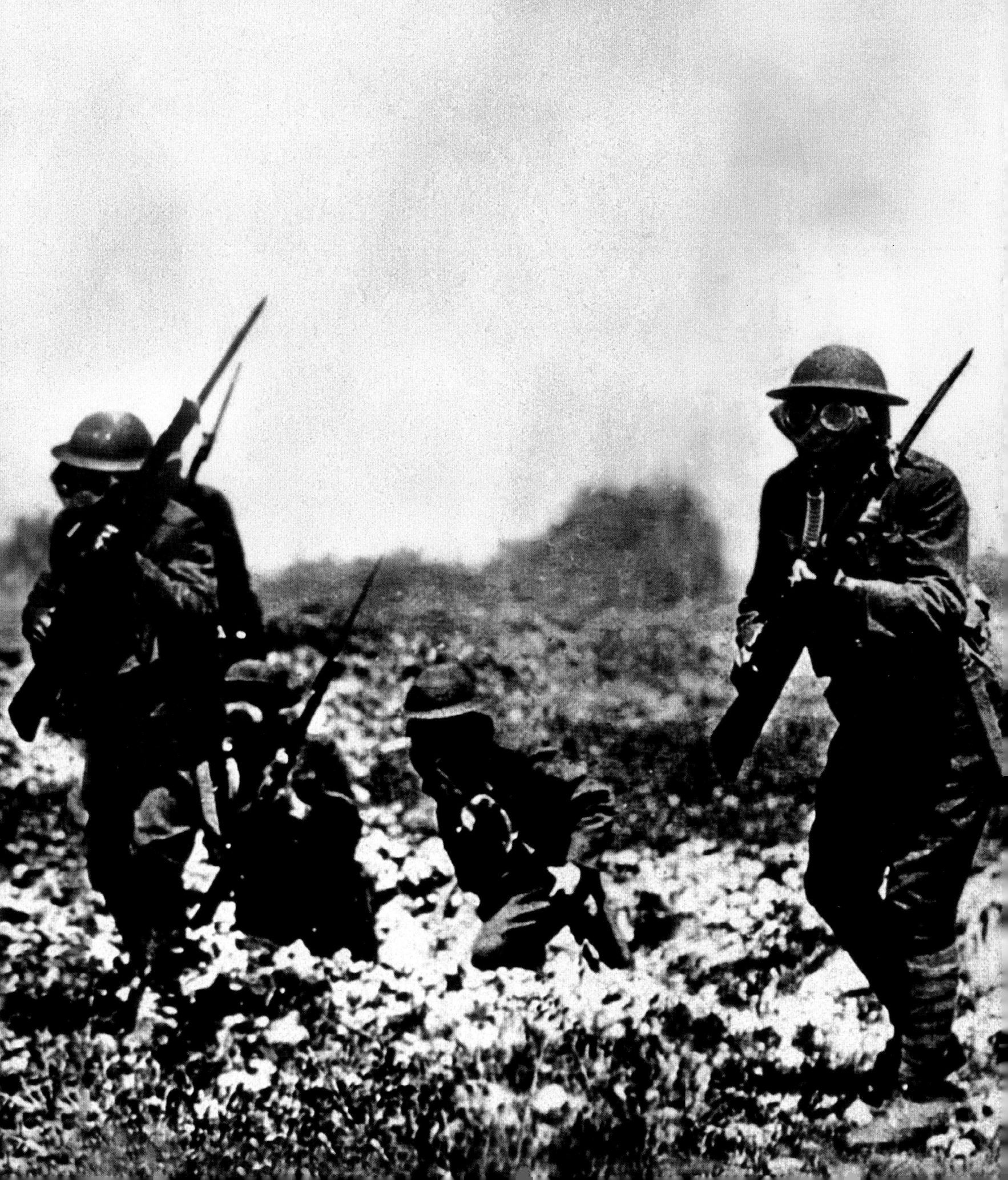

Assault on the Winter Palace

October 24-25, 1917 - Petrograd, Russian Empire

The guns of the cruiser Aurora echo in the air. It is a signal: a unit of committed and determined Red Guards advance on the Winter Palace in Petrograd to change the face of Russia. Inside the building, the ministers of what remains of Kerensky's Provisional Government await their fate.

It is the block of guards who dominate this scene in what is not a true photograph but a frame from Sergej Ejzenštejn's film *October* (1927), which celebrates the 1917 Revolution. It is a curious case of cinematic creation proposed and perceived as reality, authentic testimony: the film was first shown in January of 1928, in Leningrad – formerly Petrograd – and since then it has been the official portrayal of the taking of the Palace.

The scene has become rooted in the collective imagination partly because of its didactic effectiveness: the static quality of the building in the background contrasts with the dynamism of the people in the foreground. The guards seem to converge at a certain point, forming a kind of arrow. Overcoats and fur hats prevent us from identifying the people: individuals are not the real protagonists of the Revolution. Rather, it is the ideology that they carry forward that the scene emphasizes. The entire proletariat identifies with the avant garde that overthrows Kerensky's "bourgeois" government and takes possession of the historic residence of the Czars, who are guilty of having starved the people and dragged them into the First World War. The Bolsheviks promise the end of the war, the distribution of land to the people, and equality for all.

The future, however, is not so rosy. In 1917, the forced Russification of the country, the repression, and the gulags were far in the future. In 1928, under Stalin, not so far.

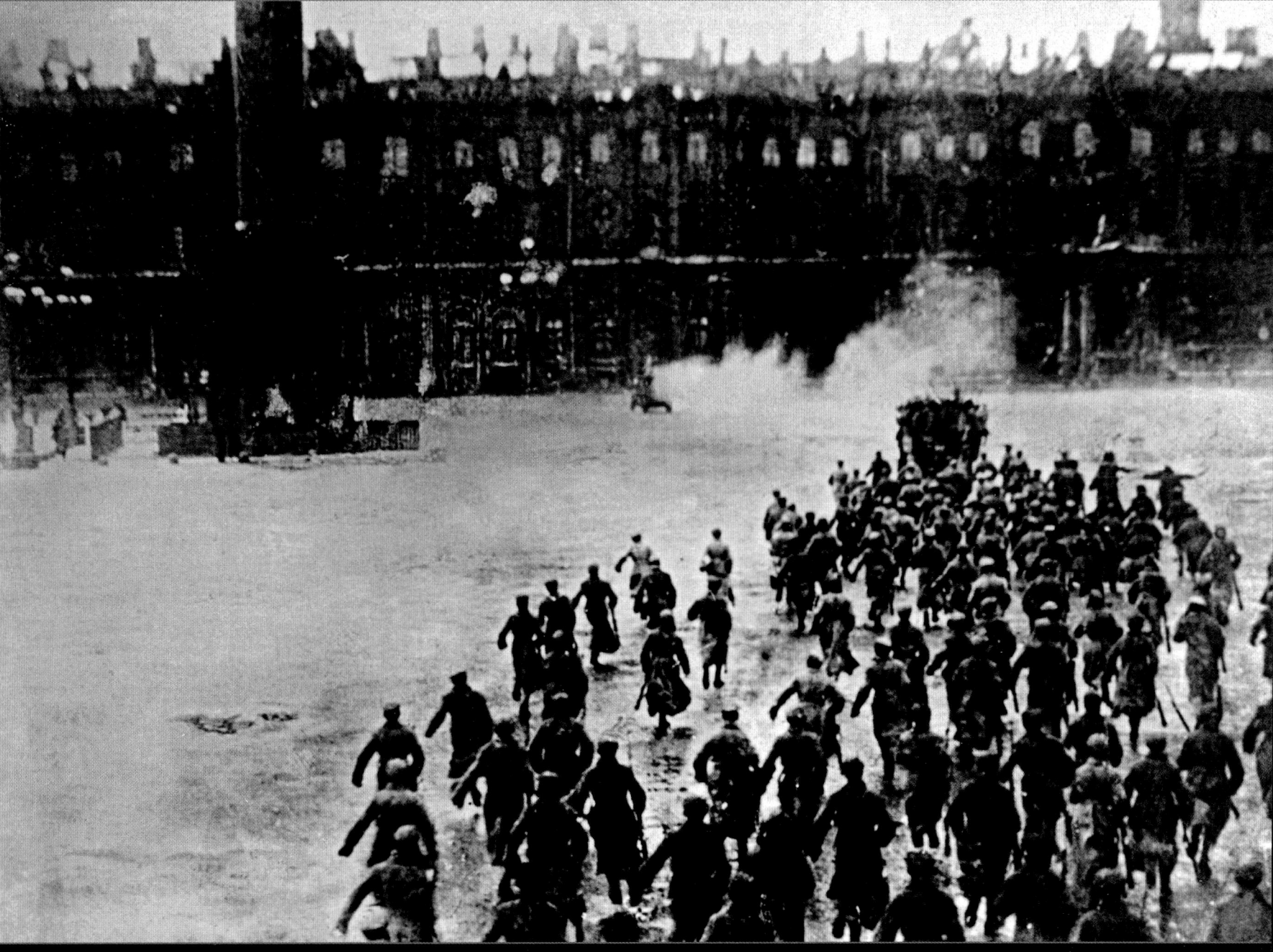

Frame from the film *October* by Ejzenštejn (1927)

Lenin's Speech to the Red Army

May 5, 1920 - Moscow, Soviet Russia

May 5th, 1920. Vladimir Il'ič Ul'janov Lenin addresses the Red Army in Teatralnaya Square, in the heart of Moscow. The stage is a makeshift wooden platform, the simplicity of which emphasizes the closeness of the October Revolution leader to the soldiers who are about to leave for the front. The war between Poland and the young Soviet Russia is well underway, and the army, at the same time, is also engaged in a civil war against the "Whites," the counter-revolutionaries supported by various foreign powers. The troops need the encouragement of their leader. In his speech, Lenin reiterates how the enemy is not the Polish people, but the capitalism that controls Polish institutions: "Show the Poles that you are the soldiers of a republic of workers and peasants, that you go there not as aggressors but as liberators. [...] Comrades, we have succeeded in defeating our landowners and capitalists, and we shall also defeat the Polish landowners and capitalists!"

Lenin is distinguished by his passion and by the civilian clothes he continues to wear even in wartime. There is a considerable difference between this leader and the official images that will soon immortalize Stalin, who is almost always in uniform and with more restrained poses. However, in a certain sense we owe the best-known version of this photo to Stalin: the dictator ordered the modification of Goldstein's photo, removing every trace of the presence of Lev Trotsky, the Commander of the Red Army. Originally Trotsky was recognizable beside the stage, as was Lev Kamenev, who could be glimpsed behind him. It wasn't enough to remove them from every position of power and then have them killed: they also had to be eliminated from the symbolic images of the Revolution.

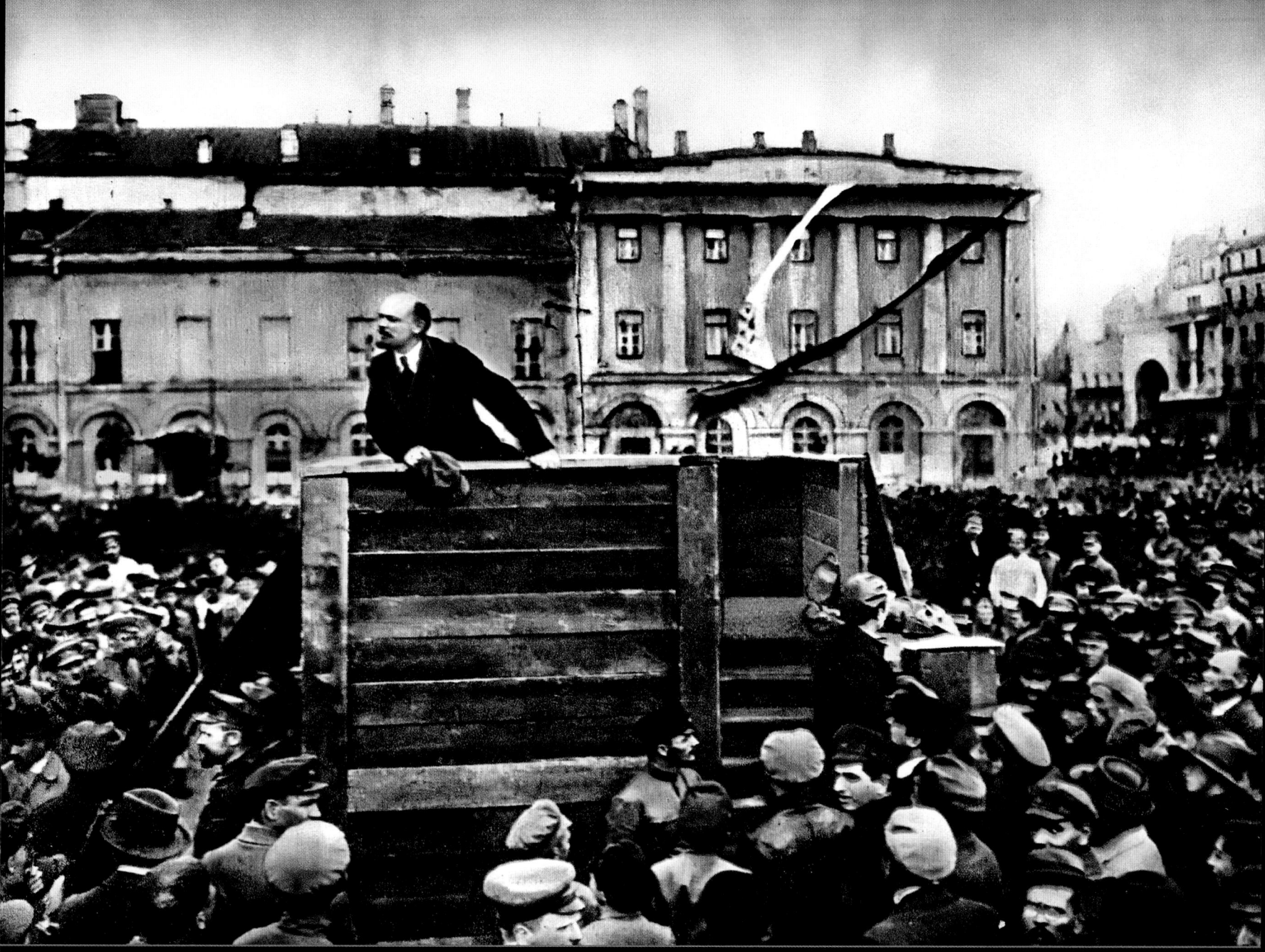

Photograph by Grigori Goldstein

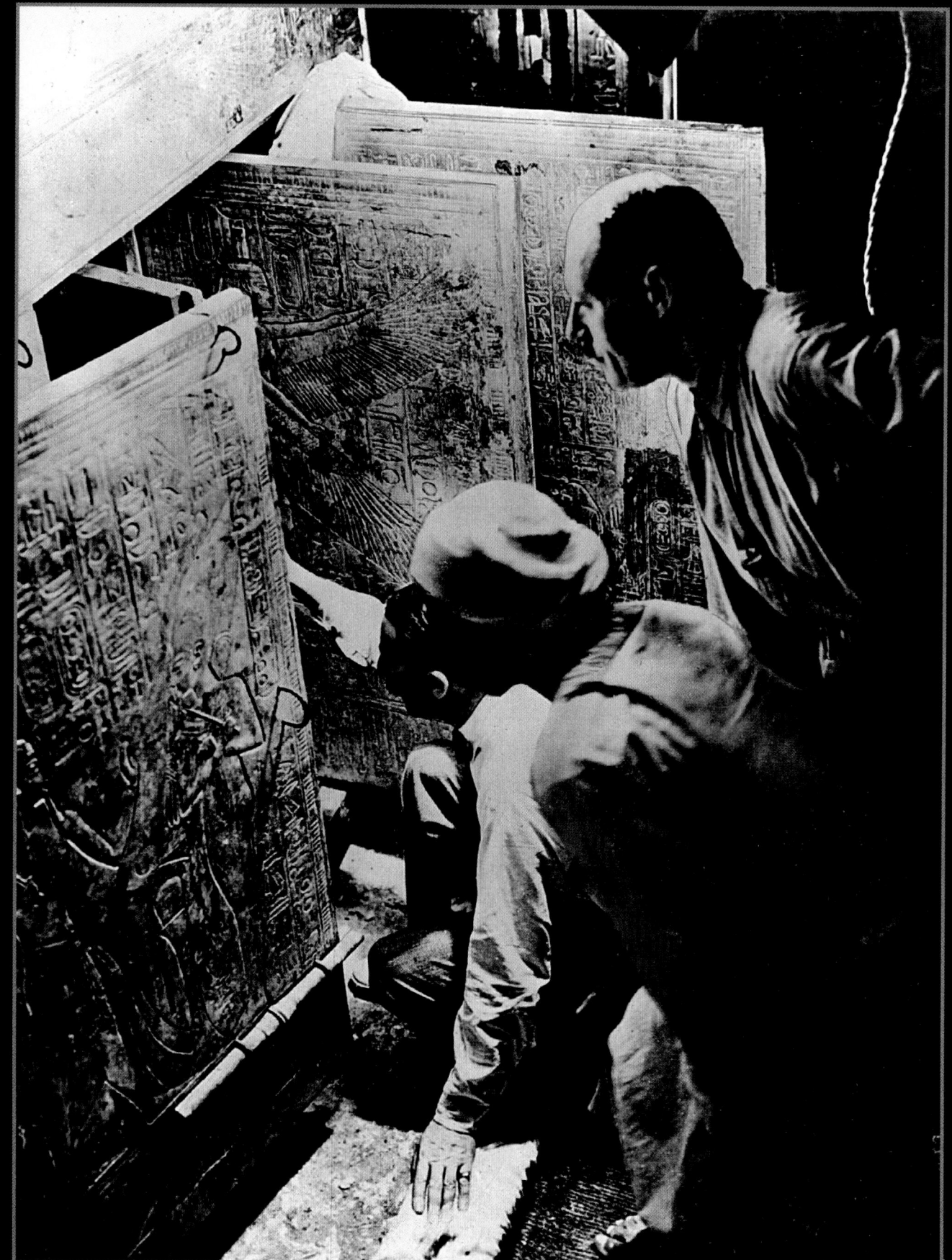

Opening of Tutankhamun's Tomb

November 25, 1922 - Valley of the Kings, Egypt

Every archaeologist hopes to make a sensational discovery, like the British Egyptologist Howard Carter (1874-1939) with one of the most famous discoveries in history: the tomb of the King Tutankhamun.

In 1907 Gaston Maspero, Director-General of the Egyptian Antiquities Service, introduced Carter to Lord Carnarvon, a lover of antiquity, and appointed Carter as the guide for Carnarvon's archaeological campaign in the Valley of the Kings. Carter's project, which began in 1917, aimed at unearthing the last two tombs of the Pharaohs of the Eighteenth Dynasty, Akhenaten and his son Tutankhamun, by means of the systematic excavation of the whole area. On November 4th, 1922, after years of failed attempts and unproductive leads, and after Lord Carnarvon had already declared an ultimatum for the operation, Carter's team discovered a flight of stairs leading to a sealed door: it was the tomb of Tutankhamun, the "boy Pharaoh," which had been preserved almost intact for more than three thousand years.

The photo was taken on November 25th, 1922 to mark the first internal inspection. It shows Carter kneeling, intent on touching the greatest object of his most arduous enterprise. Standing behind him is the engineer Arthur Callender, who had a crucial role in opening the precious sarcophagi containing the mummies. Beside Callender stands a local worker.

The Legend of the Curse of Tutankhamun spread quickly following the discovery: violation of his tomb would provoke the Pharaoh's divine punishment. And the presumed mysterious deaths of some of the people involved in the discovery only served to reinforce this superstition. In reality, however, the curse was a publicity gimmick designed to attract the attention of international papers. Only Lord Carnarvon died during the excavations, and it was due to the after-effects of a mosquito bite.

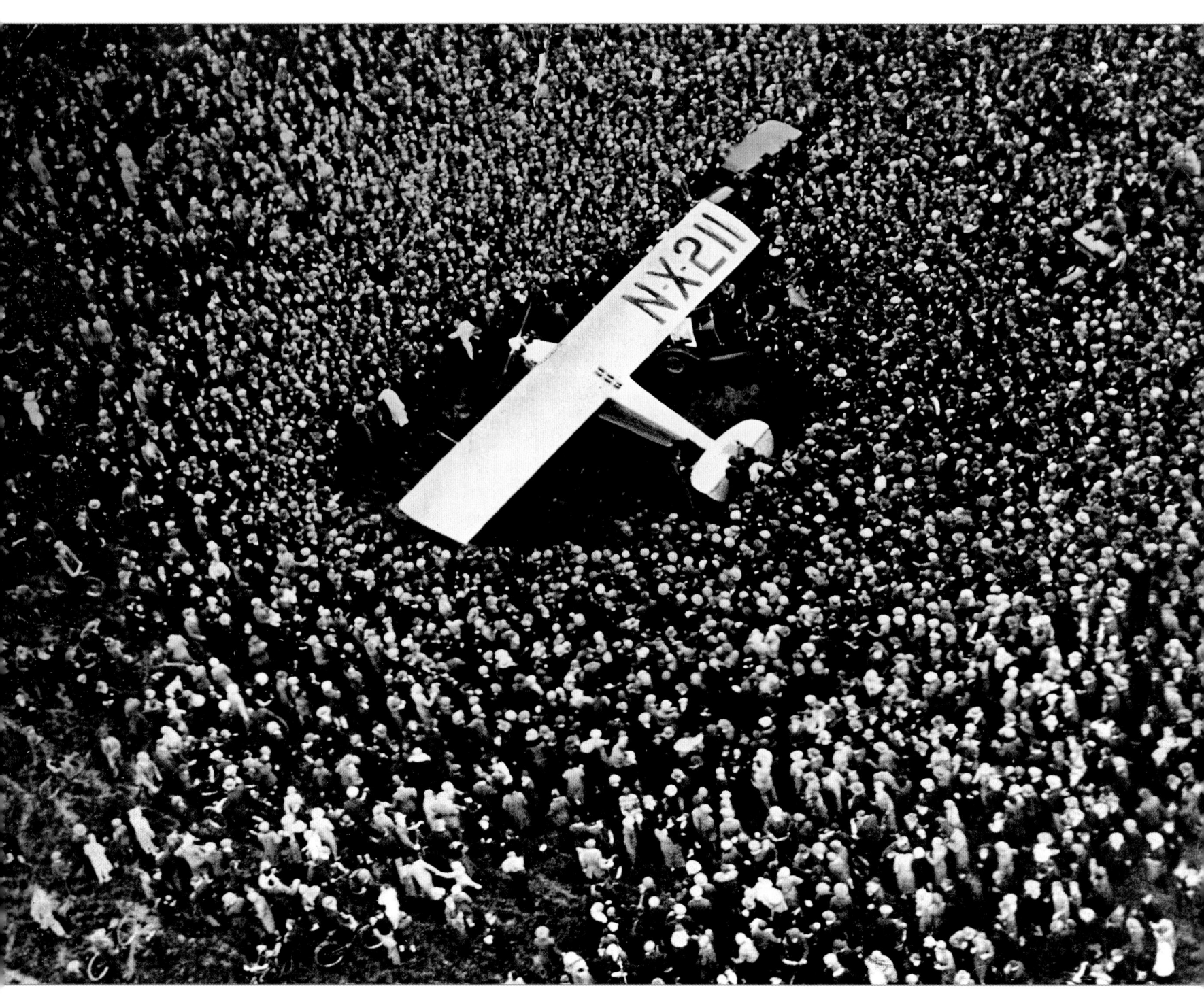

The First Solo Transatlantic Flight

May 21, 1927 - Paris, France

It was 7:52 in the morning on Long Island when Charles Lindbergh switched on the engine of the Spirit of St. Louis and, leaving behind him the muddy runway of Roosevelt Field, became a legend. Twenty-five years old at the time, and originally from Detroit, Lindbergh had always loved mechanics, and had been a professional pilot for several years. Raymond Orteig, a wealthy New York hotel owner, had persuaded Lindbergh that he could win the 25,000 dollar prize that he had announced in 1919 for the first man to fly non-stop across the Atlantic from New York to Paris. So the young aviator convinced a group of financiers in St. Louis to sponsor him and to order the Ryan Aeronautical Company in San Diego to build him a special plane.

Many pilots had failed in this endeavor, and some had died, but Lindbergh was destined to succeed and to awaken the enthusiasm of the world for civil aviation.

The flight lasted 33.5 hours. The equipment that Lindbergh took off with consisted of four sandwiches, two canteens of water, and 450 gallons of fuel. He had to overcome storm clouds and thick fog; and, en route, he tried (without success) to ask for information about the distance to the Irish coast by calling down to some fishing boats while he skimmed the water. But, after 3,600 miles of non-stop flight, he landed at Le Bourget Airport in Paris at 10:22 p.m. on May 21st, 1927. He found a crowd of almost 100,000 people waiting for him, so many people that he had to switch off the engine immediately to avoid accidents.

The photograph, giving us a bird's-eye view, graphically captures the spirit of this first transatlantic flight. The image went around the world and become an icon of courage and freedom, features of the pioneers of the air.

The Great Depression

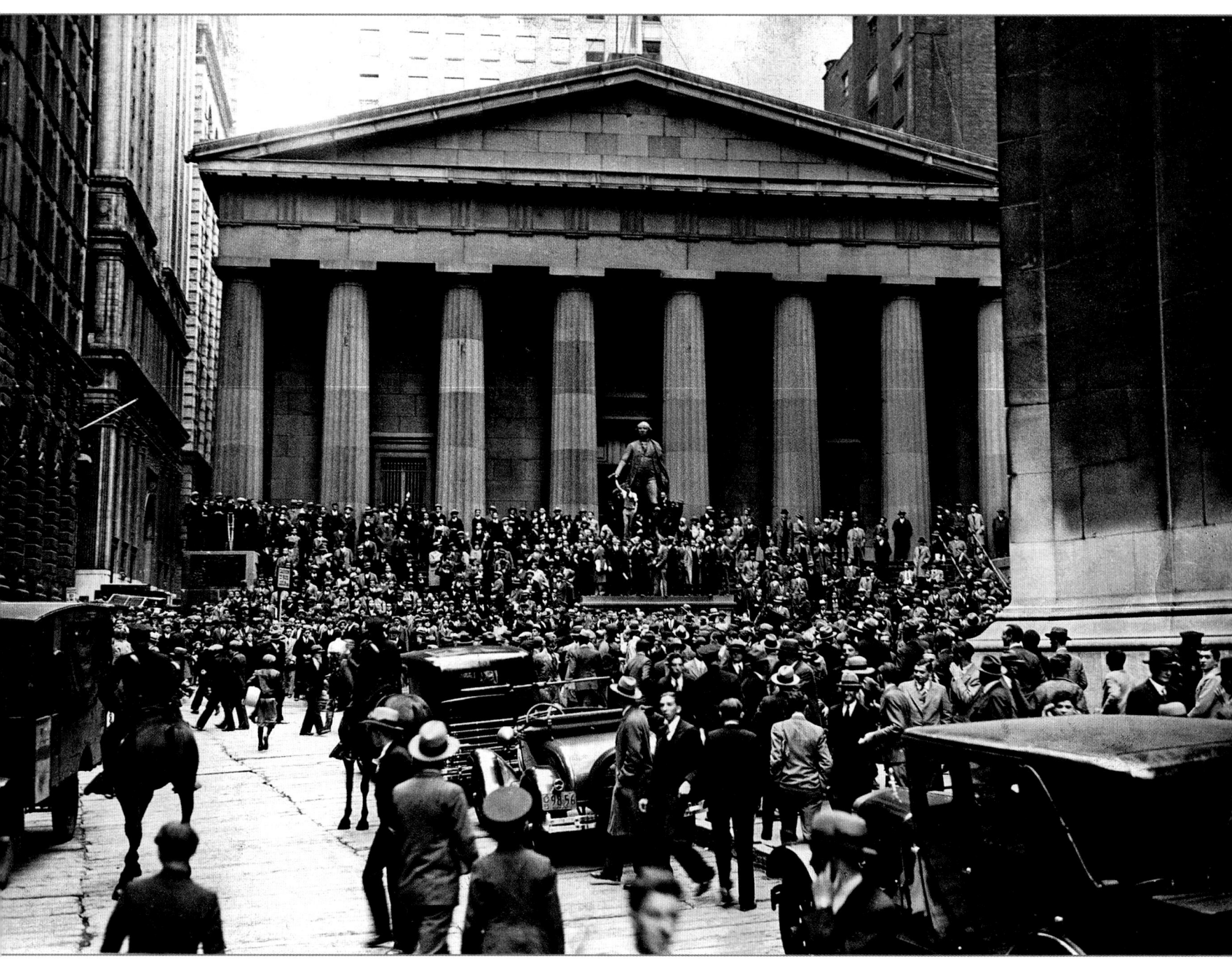

October 24, 1929 - New York City, United States

This anonymous photograph, taken on October 24th, 1929, appeared on the front page of the *London Herald* the next day: it announced the Wall Street stock market crash to Europe. A crowd, mainly of men, throngs the steps of the Sub-Treasury Building in New York City, surrounding a statue of George Washington. Inside of the building is the Department of the Treasury. (Today it's the Federal Hall National Memorial.) Opposite the building is the Stock Exchange, and all of these men are waiting for news. The crowd is anxious but still composed. Momentarily, the scene will explode into chaos.

After days of instability in the stock market, on October 24th, "Black Thursday," the most serious economic crisis in the history of the United States officially began. Panic spread in the morning, when in only a few hours about 13 million stocks were sold in a bear market. Investors continued to sell while thousands of incredulous and terrified savers thronged in front of the Stock Exchange or rushed to the banks to withdraw their savings. The police regained control of the streets, but could not prevent a long series of suicides of people who, in luxurious villas and small middle-class apartments, and in just a few hours, saw all their savings disappear. In the following days, the panic diminished slightly, due in part to reassurances from the media, but on October 29th, which has gone down in history as "Black Tuesday," the economic collapse was definitive: the financial disaster would have serious consequences for the economies of European countries. Thus the rich and carefree period of the "Roaring Twenties" ended, and a much sadder era, the Great Depression, began.

Gandhi and the Salt March

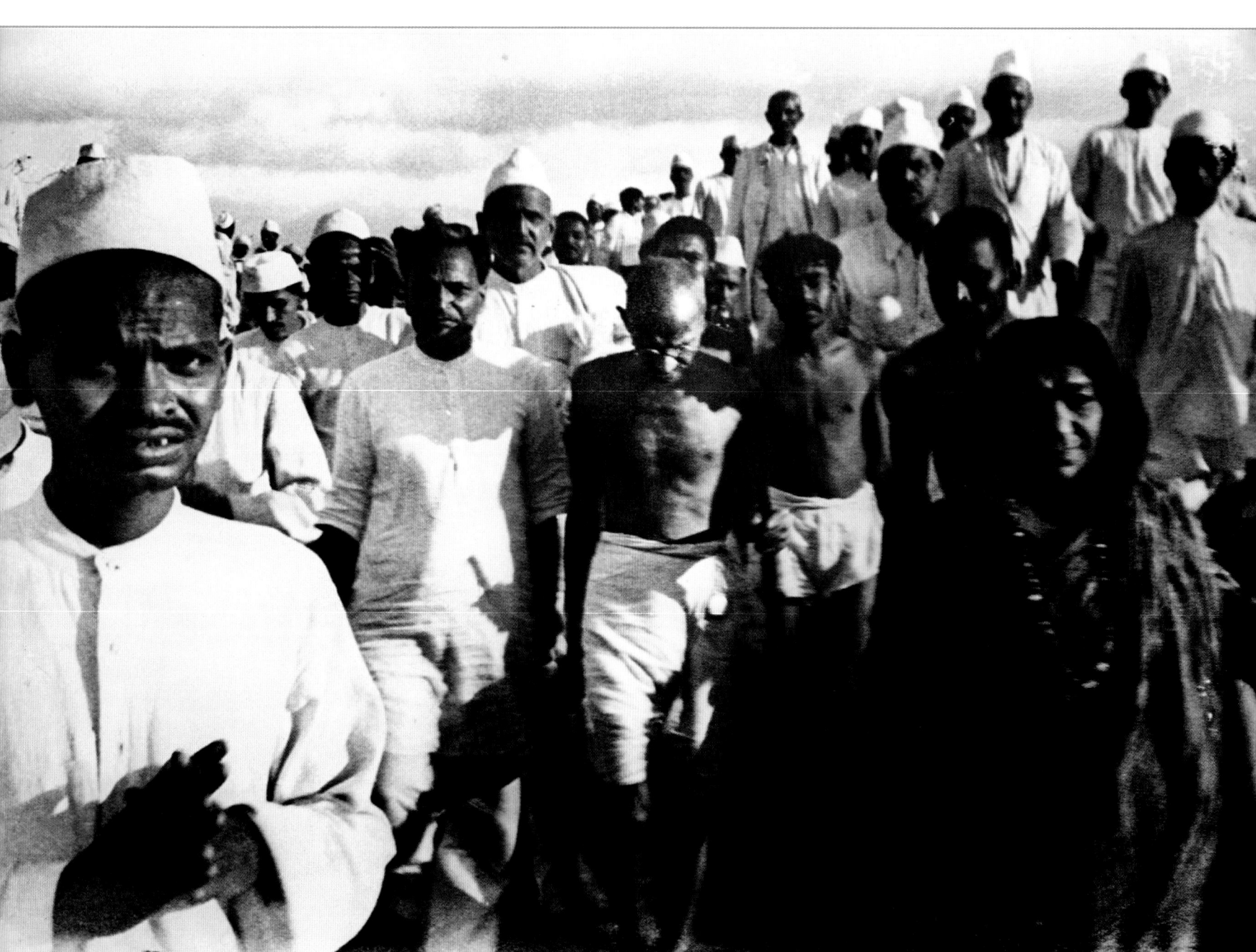

Photograph by Walter Bosshard

March-April, 1930 - India

It is easy to produce salt cheaply in India, a country that has thousands of miles of coasts, and for centuries this product was readily available. However, with British rule the low taxes that had always been the norm for salt were abolished, such that poor people could no longer afford it.

By January, 1930, the Indian National Congress had published a Declaration of Independence, and had already began organizing non-violent actions of civil disobedience to obtain full sovereignty. Gandhi, the leader of the anti-colonial movement, who had already been imprisoned by the British for "subversive activities," persuaded Congress that a battle against the salt tax would have a great impact, by uniting Hindus and Muslims.

On March 12th, he set out with 79 faithful followers from the *ashram* of Sabarmati. Together they marched about 250 miles to the village of Dandi, on the Indian Ocean coast, where, on April 6th, Gandhi symbolically grasped a handful of salt and asked his followers to break the law. During the walk, tens of thousands of people joined the "White River" (as the procession was called, since all wore a traditional white costume). The British reacted by savagely beating the demonstrators (who did not resist) and arresting thousands, among whom was Gandhi himself. The Swiss photographer Walter Bosshard recorded the protest. An attentive observer of South Asian culture and politics, in 1930 Bosshard published a report dedicated to the life of Mahatma Gandhi.

From a practical point of view, the Salt March was unsuccessful: the tax was only abolished in 1947. However, its symbolic value was enormous: it strengthened the struggle for independence and was an inspiration for non-violent movements that, in the following decades, would arise all over the world.

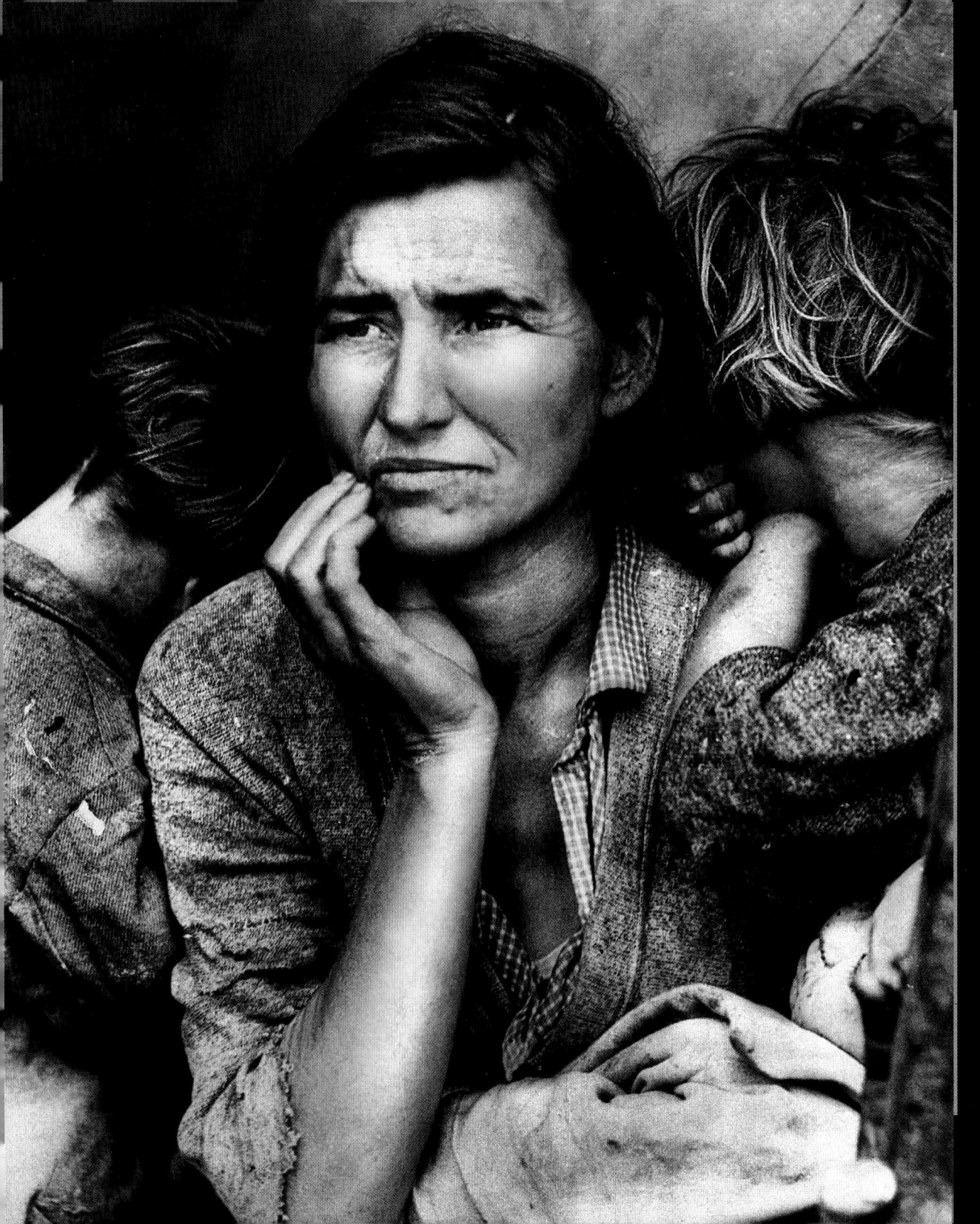

Migrant Mother

March, 1936 - Nipomo, California, United States

Migrant Mother was taken by Dorothea Lange in March, 1936, near Nipomo, California. It quickly became a symbol of the Great Depression. The photo sprang from a chance meeting between Lange and thirty-two-year-old Florence Owens Thompson, who was immortalized in the shot. Thompson was traveling, with her husband and seven children, in search of better fortune across an America hard hit by the economic crisis. After their car broke down, she pitched a makeshift tent near a field of peas while they waited to get back on the road. It was then that the photographer encountered Thompson, and Lange was immediately struck by the woman's face, marked by struggle but full of dignity, which showed all the difficulties of a country which, in spite of difficult times, would not give in and would continue to proudly fight.

Of the six photos Lange took of the Thompsons, *Migrant Mother* became the most famous. Its composition is perfect, with the woman surrounded symmetrically by her daughters Katherine and Ruby, and her baby daughter Norma in her arms. The faces of the two little girls, which the camera does not reveal, increase the emotion of the image, while their heads resting on their mother's shoulders emphasize her figure even more. The expressive strength of the photo resides in the simplicity of subject, which is underscored by the contrasting tones of black and white.

Dorothea Lange was interested in the social reality of the country and wanted to document, as directly and authentically as possible, such a vast dramatic phenomenon. Though she gathered photographic testimony from all over America, *Migrant Mother* has remained her best-loved photo. It is an icon of an era of social tribulations and human redemption.

Photograph by Dorothea Lange

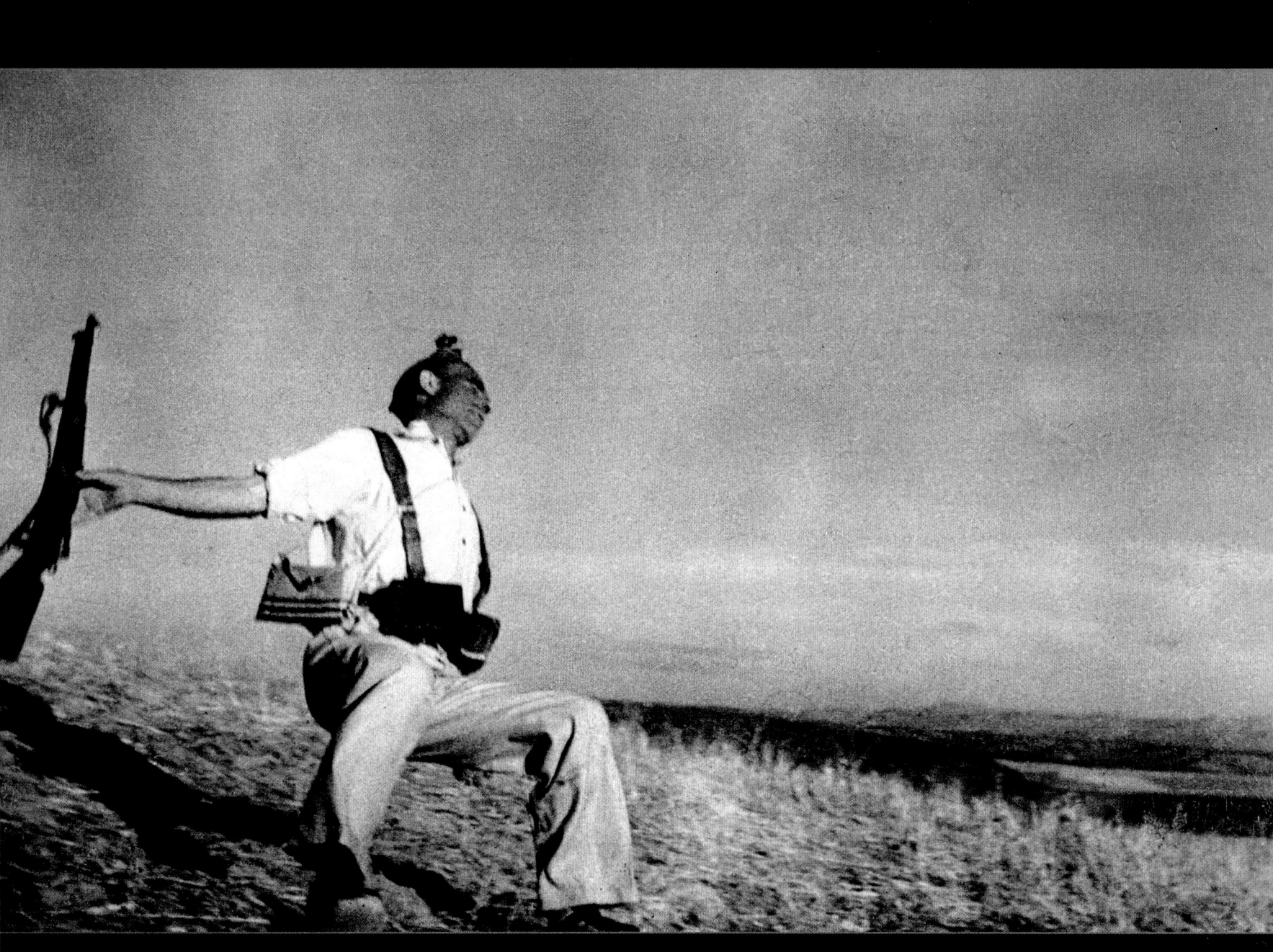

Photograph by Robert Capa

Falling Soldier

September, 1936 - Córdoba, Spain

A man dies, struck by a bullet fired by an invisible enemy. He isn't a soldier: he wears civilian clothes and not a uniform. He holds a rifle. He is a militiaman, fighting for the Republic of Spain against the Nationalist troops led by Francisco Franco. In a moment, his blood will bathe the soil of Andalusia, made arid by a burning sun, the sun of the tragic summer of 1936, the summer when the Spanish Civil War broke out. The image is absolutely clear. It captures the most dramatic instant without hesitation. So marvelous and ruthless, it is this image that comes to symbolize the war. The description could end here.

Yet few photos have aroused more doubts and among historians and scholars. The Hungarian photographer Robert Capa, whose original name was Endre Erno Friedmann, claimed that he took the photograph at the beginning of September, 1936, near Córdoba. It was published on the 23rd of that month in the French magazine *VU*, and then taken up by American magazines. To some people, the photo seemed too perfect to be authentic. People began to talk of a sham, suggesting Capa had acted more as a director than as a photographer. But the theory of the fake lost credibility in the eighties, when relatives of ex-combatants identified the protagonist: the anarchist "Taino" Federico Borrell Garcia was killed at Cerro Muriano, 12 miles north of Córdoba. The authenticity of the photo, however, has not been the only issue.

Another question concerns the photographer. Allegedly Gerda Taro (1910-37), Capa's girlfriend, took the photo, not Capa himself. Taro, who was killed in the conflict, was the first photojournalist in history to die in the field. A radio interview recorded by Capa in 1947, and rediscovered in 2013, would seem to refute this hypothesis. In fact, Capa related that he had taken the photo from a trench, raising the camera without looking. In short, he said that the icon of the Spanish Civil War was a chance result, a trick of fate. Is the mystery solved? Not really, because according to experts, characteristics of the image are not compatible with Capa's camera, a Leica, but suggest the use of a Rolleiflex, the type of camera used by Gerda Taro. . .

September 8-14, 1936 - Third Reich, Germany

Power, order, grandeur. The mystique of the fatherland. These were the principles communicated to the people and to the world during the military rallies held during the *Reichsparteitag des Deutschen Volkes*, the annual "national day" of the Nazi Party. Since 1933 the demonstration, held in Nuremberg, lasted on average eight days and covered an enormous area (4.2 square miles), its staging constructed by the architect Albert Speer. The city had a fundamental role in the building of German national identity through its imperial past, and the Nazis gave it strong symbolic value. It was no accident that in Nuremberg, in 1935, the Nazis first promulgated race laws. And here, too, at the end of the war, the Allies brought to court the German war criminals.

But in 1936, the year of the photo, the Second World War hasn't yet begun. Hitler sends conflicting signals to the world. In March, he remilitarizes the Rhineland, violating the Treaty of Versailles. In August, the Berlin Olympic Games offers a softened image of Germany. In September, for the *Reichsparteitage*, he resumes his bellicose attitude: the theme of the event is "German honor," an honor that the Führer claims he has restored by rebelling against the impositions of the international community.

The photograph perfectly expresses the spirit of the event. The viewer sees the army as an ascetic war machine, in which the individual soldier is faceless and only a disciplined cog, like all the others. The perspective of the columns of metal helmets converges toward the three great flags with the swastika, arranged vertically and fixed like standards. Not even the wind disturbs the geometric, inhuman perfection of the staging.

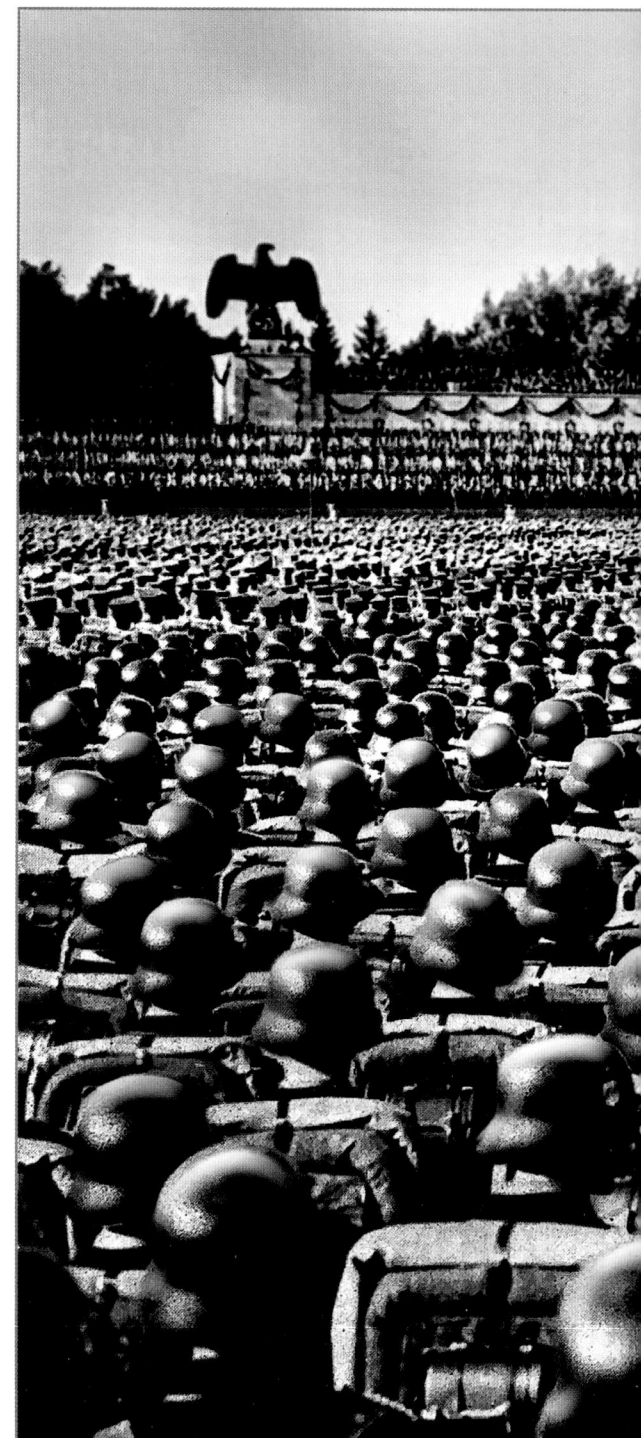

Nazi Party Rally

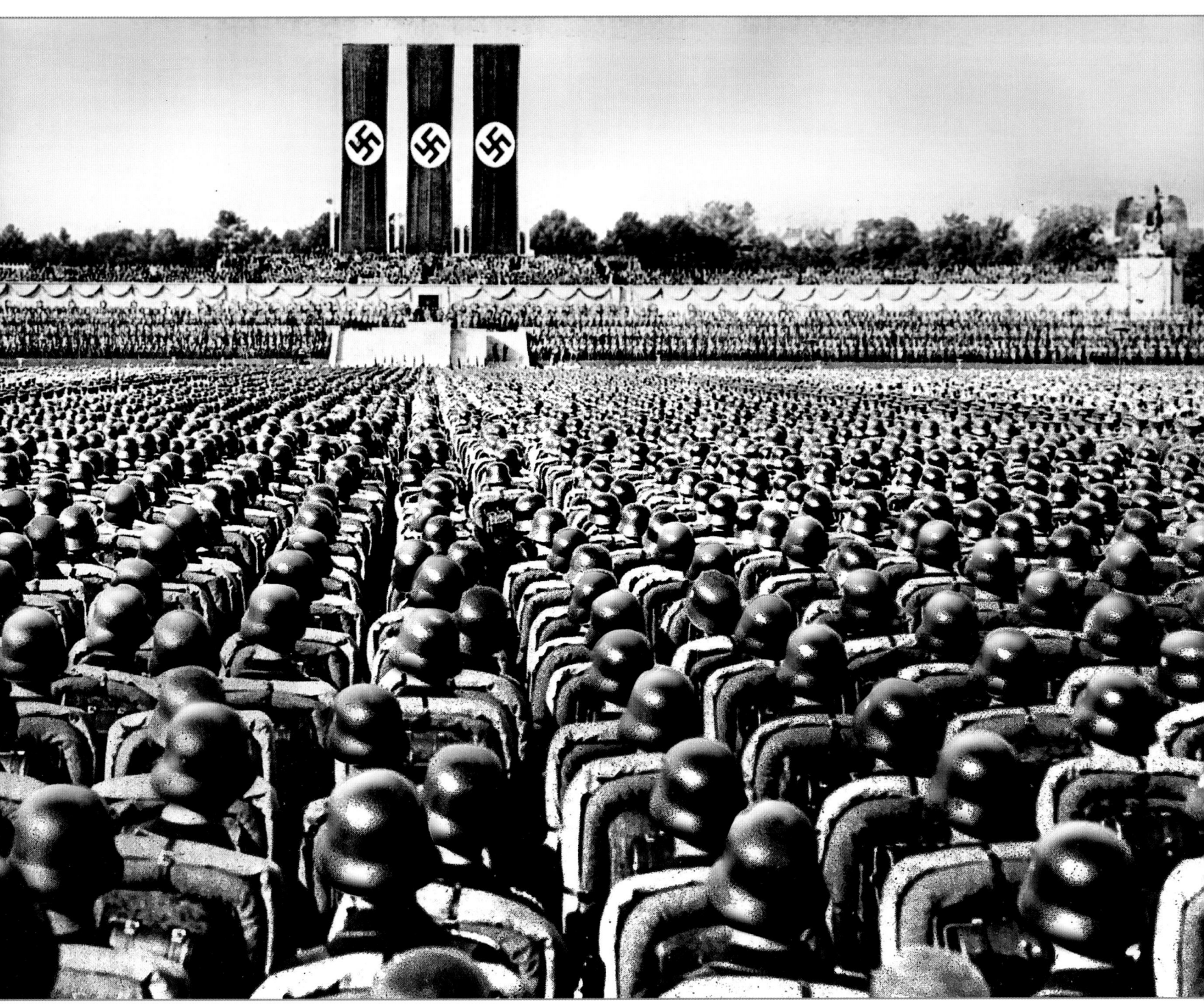

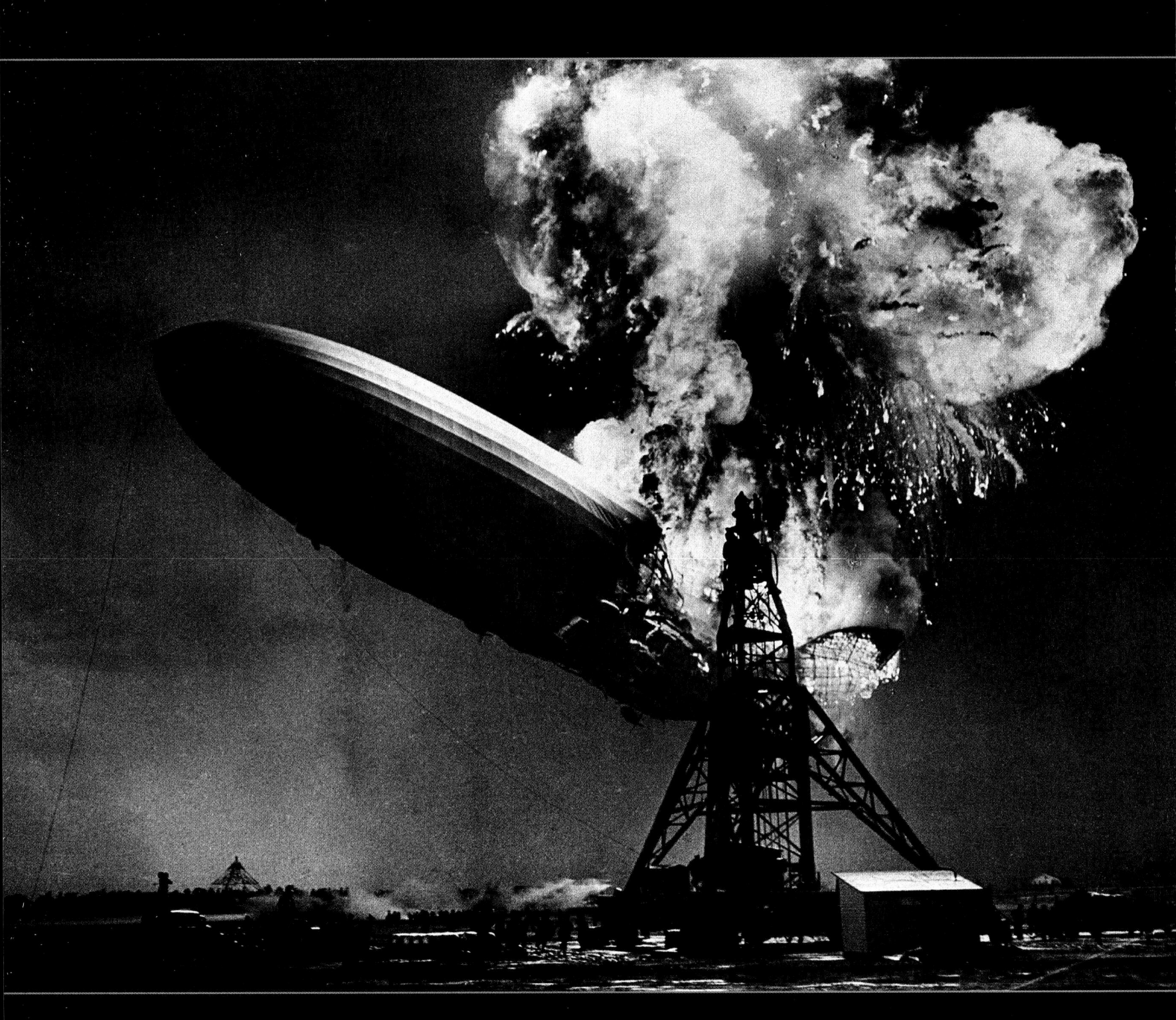

The Explosion of the Airship Hindenburg

May 6, 1937 - Lakehurst, New Jersey, United States

What the image shows so dramatically is the first catastrophe documented live on film and simultaneously reported on the radio. The photographer has captured the moment this enormous German airship exploded: it contained nearly 53 million gallons of highly flammable hydrogen. (The production of helium, which is non-flammable, was an American monopoly). It was built to be safe, but it was vulnerable to chance events, as always. The cause of the accident was the static electricity with which the outer-shell of the ship had become charged while passing through a thunderstorm. A mooring cable contributed to the explosion: it was connected to the ground, and provoked the spark. In less than 30 seconds, the airship sank to the ground and burned like an enormous torch.

It is 7:25 in the evening, May 6th, 1937. The place is the Airship Station at Lakehurst, New Jersey. The ship is the LZ 129 Hindenburg, the largest of its kind ever built: 800 feet in length, 155 feet in diameter, and with 16 tanks of hydrogen. The ship is propelled by four 1,200 horse-power steam engines, and can reach speeds up to 85 m.p.h.

The initials of the name, LZ, stand for Luftschiffbau Zeppelin, a brand that has become synonymous with "airship." Zeppelins have flown millions of miles, crossed the Atlantic 500 times, and never had an accident. Never. They are the pride of Nazi Germany's technology. The Hindenburg itself crossed the Atlantic shortly after its launch, in 1936: it did it in only six days. In the end, out of 97 on board, 62 people survived. But the collective trauma was so great that the accident changed the history of aviation forever. Photographs like this one, which were published immediately around the world, definitively ended the competition between airplanes and airships.

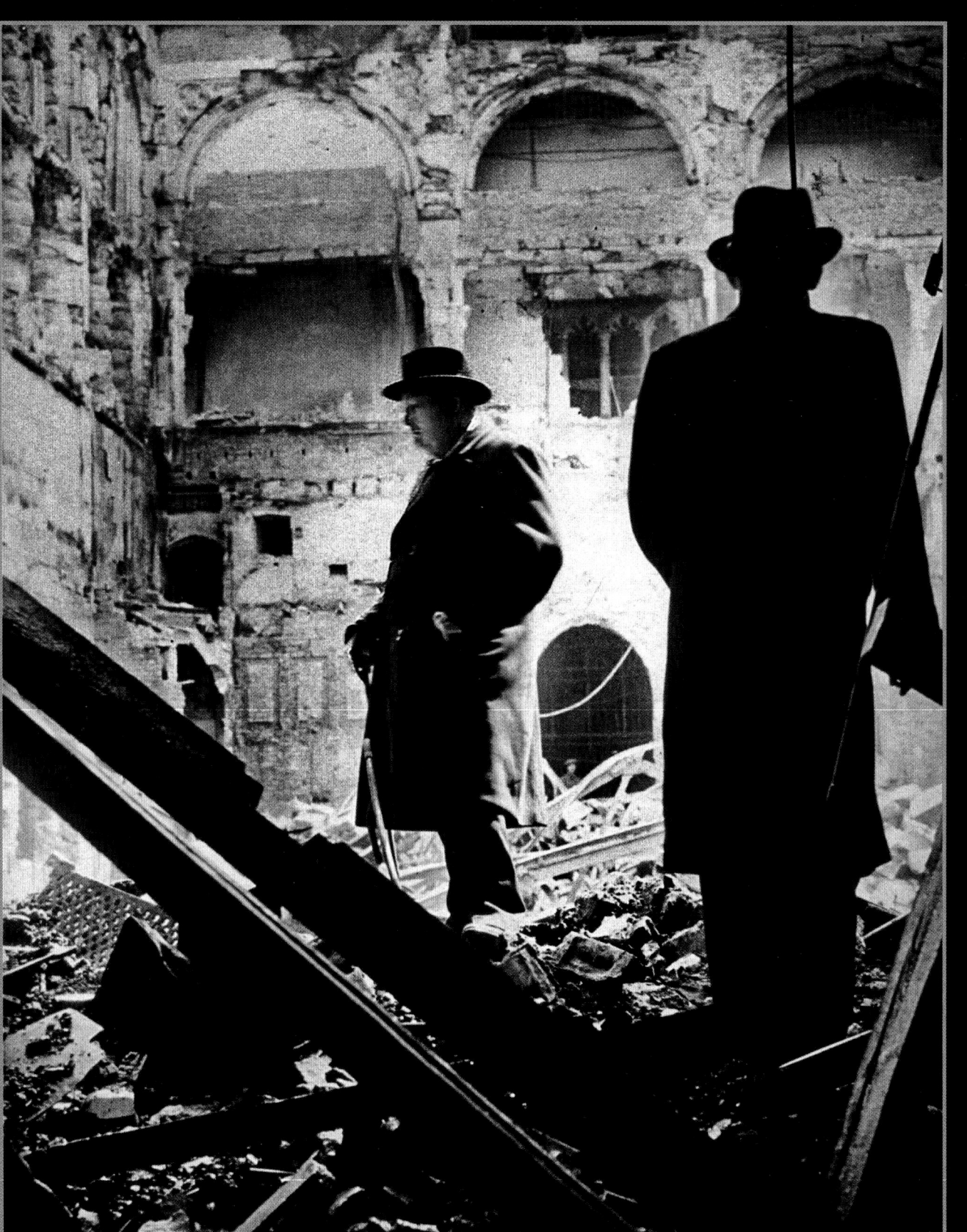

Churchill Among the Ruins of Parliament

May 11, 1941 - London, United Kingdom

"I would say to the House, as I said to those who have joined this government: I have nothing to offer but blood, toil, tears and sweat. We have before us an ordeal of the most grievous kind. We have before us many, many long months of struggle and of suffering." These are the words of Winston Churchill, spoken in May, 1940, in his address to the House of Commons.

A year later, on May 11th, 1941, Churchill found himself walking in the ruins of the very chamber he had made his terse, all too prophetic, speech. The night before Parliament had been hit by a German bombing raid. The incendiary bombs spared parts of the House of Lords but not the House of Commons.

Accompanying the Prime Minister is the businessman Brendan Bracken, his advisor and secretary for relations with Members of Parliament. Bracken will soon become the Minister of Information: he has always been one of the fiercest opponents of Hitler. In the image, they are two solitary men, alone among the ruins, their forms pronounced by dramatic *chiaroscuro*. And yet they stand calm, immaculately dressed. The United Kingdom doesn't yield or lose its aplomb. What is Churchill thinking about? Above all, of resistance and reconstruction. It is no accident that the arch leading to the rebuilt House of Commons is known as "Churchill Arch": it is guarded by two bronze statues, one of Sir Winston, standing proudly, hands on his hips, with the other of David Lloyd George, Prime Minister during the First World War.

Perhaps, while he surveys the ruins, Churchill is already thinking about how to avenge the blow that Hitler has inflicted on the symbolic heart of British democracy. It is an intolerable outrage. He will be ruthless when it comes to bombing Berlin, and still more when he orders the Royal Air Force to raze Dresden, in February 1945. But that's another story.

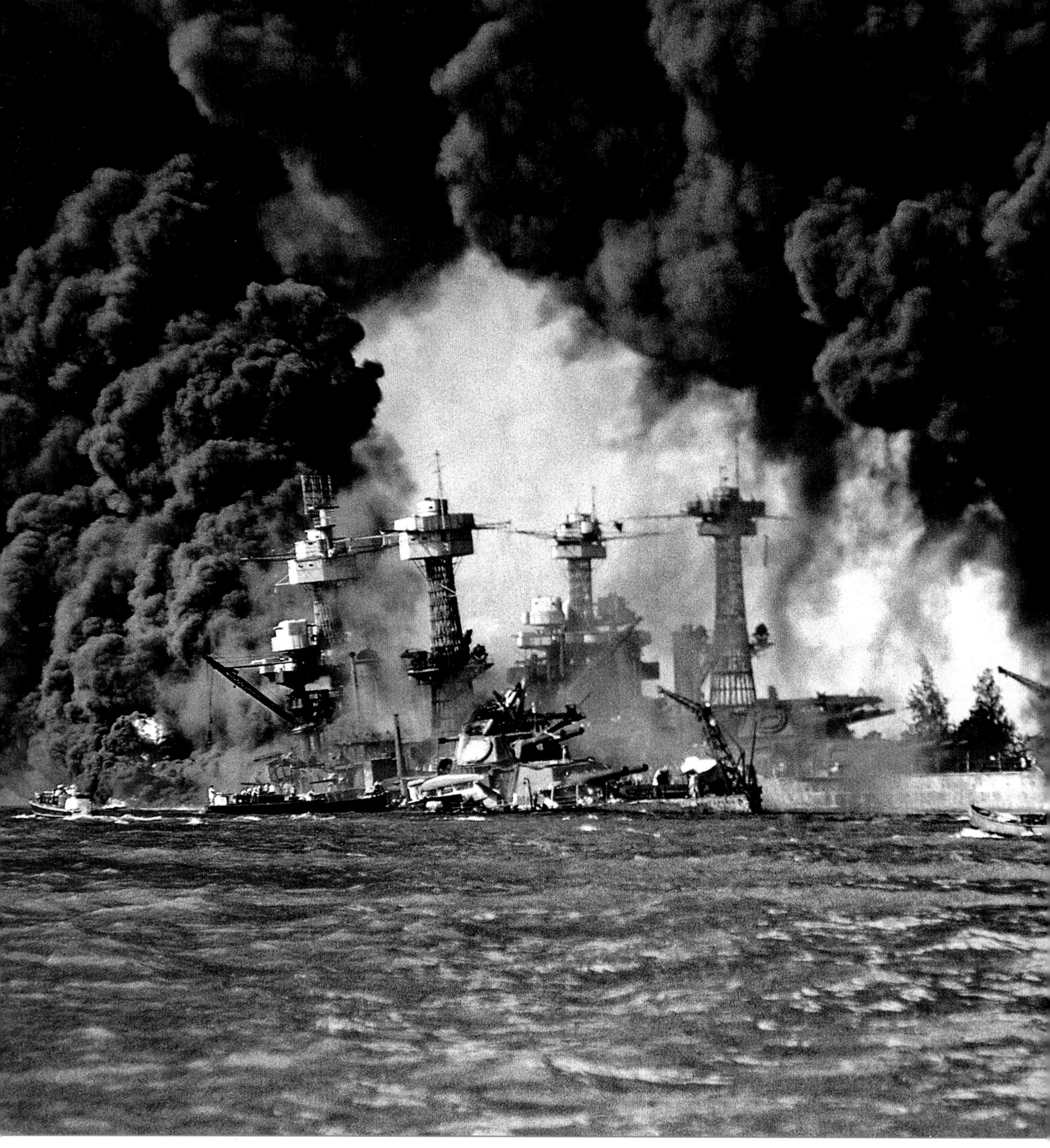

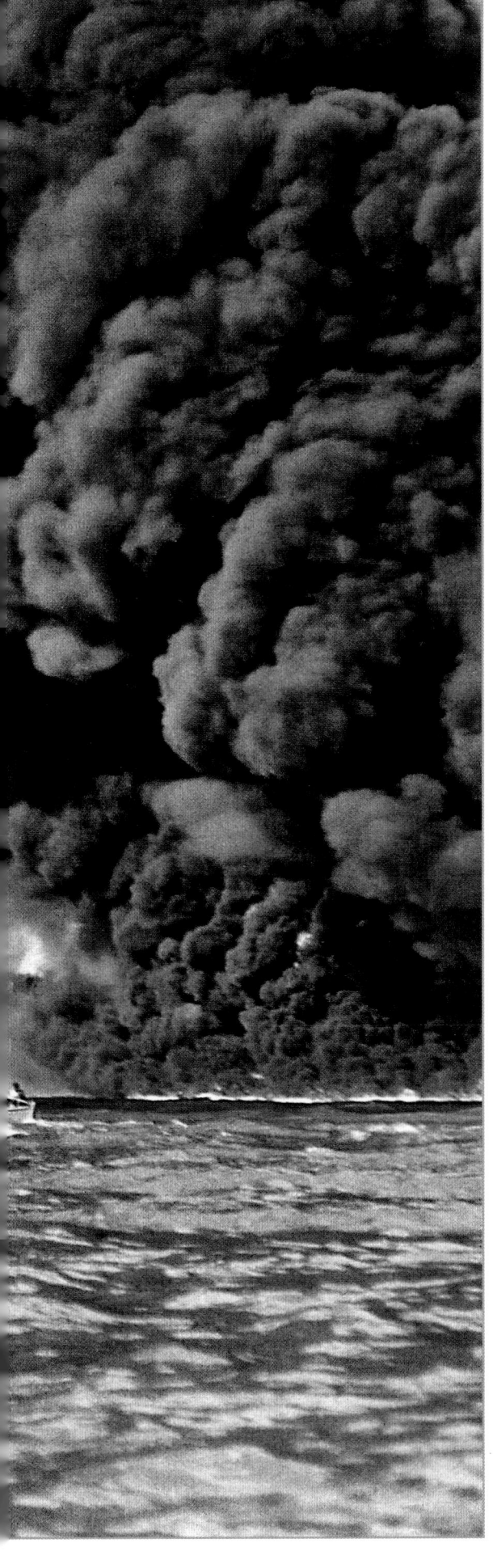

Attack on Pearl Harbor

December 7, 1941 - Hawaii, United States

At 7:55 on the morning of December 7th, 1941, 353 Japanese airplanes, which had taken off from six aircraft carriers of the Imperial Japanese Navy in the Pacific, launched a surprise attack on the American naval base at Pearl Harbor, in the Hawaiian islands. It was a disaster of unimaginable dimensions. In a few minutes, a dense black blanket of smoke covered the island of Oahu. To the whistling sound of missiles and nosediving aircraft, flames caused by ignited fuel from ruptured tanks rose from the water of the bay. All of the American warships in the port at the time of the attack were sunk or seriously damaged, and 188 aircraft were destroyed on the ground. The attack resulted in 2,403 fatalities, with 1,178 wounded. Japan's declaration of war had not yet been delivered to Washington. For years, people assumed that this delay was due to bureaucratic errors, but towards the end of the nineties some documents emerged in Tokyo which suggested that the delay was strategic and designed to guarantee the greatest possible surprise in the first phases of the conflict.

The impact of images like this one, showing Pearl Harbor in flames, the amount of damage caused by the attack, and the conviction that they were the victims of a crime, had the effect of removing any doubts in the American public about entering the war. They say that, when he heard that the attack had been launched before the declaration of war, Admiral Yamamoto, who planned the military operation, commented: "Japan has awakened a giant that from today will live only for revenge."

April-May, 1943 - Warsaw, Poland

"What was the Jewish quarter of Warsaw no longer exists. The *Grosse Aktion* concluded at 8:15 p.m., with the blowing up of the Warsaw synagogue. The total number of Jews we dealt with is 56,065. This includes those captured and those duly executed." These words by Marshal Jürgen Stroop accompanied his report to the Commanding General of the SS, Heinrich Himmler, on the repression of the revolt by the Jews, which occurred between April 19th and May 16th, 1943. The month-long conflict ended with the complete destruction of the Warsaw Ghetto. The document of 75 pages included 49 photographs taken by a German army photographer. Three albums of the photographs were made: one for Stroop, one for Himmler, and one for Commander Friedrich Wilhelm Krüger. The photos and the report were used during the Nuremberg trial, at the end of which Stroop was condemned to death. (The other two committed suicide in 1945).

The images in the album show men jumping from the windows of burning homes (they were nicknamed "parachutists" by the Germans), Jewish fighters shot, mothers and children with their hands up under fire. Every photo has a precise caption. (For this one: prisoners "forced out of their holes.") The album provides invaluable historic testimony; the cruel evidence it offers meant hanging for Stroop, which, after a second trial before a Polish court, was carried out precisely where the Warsaw Ghetto had stood. In particular, this image speaks for itself: the buildings on fire, the soldiers in their shiny helmets, the compact group of civilians marching towards the extermination camp. Exactly in the center, a little girl, 3 or 4 years old, clutches what could be a teddy bear made of rags. It is one of the most terrible images of Nazi atrocities, in a composition that could be a painting by Goya.

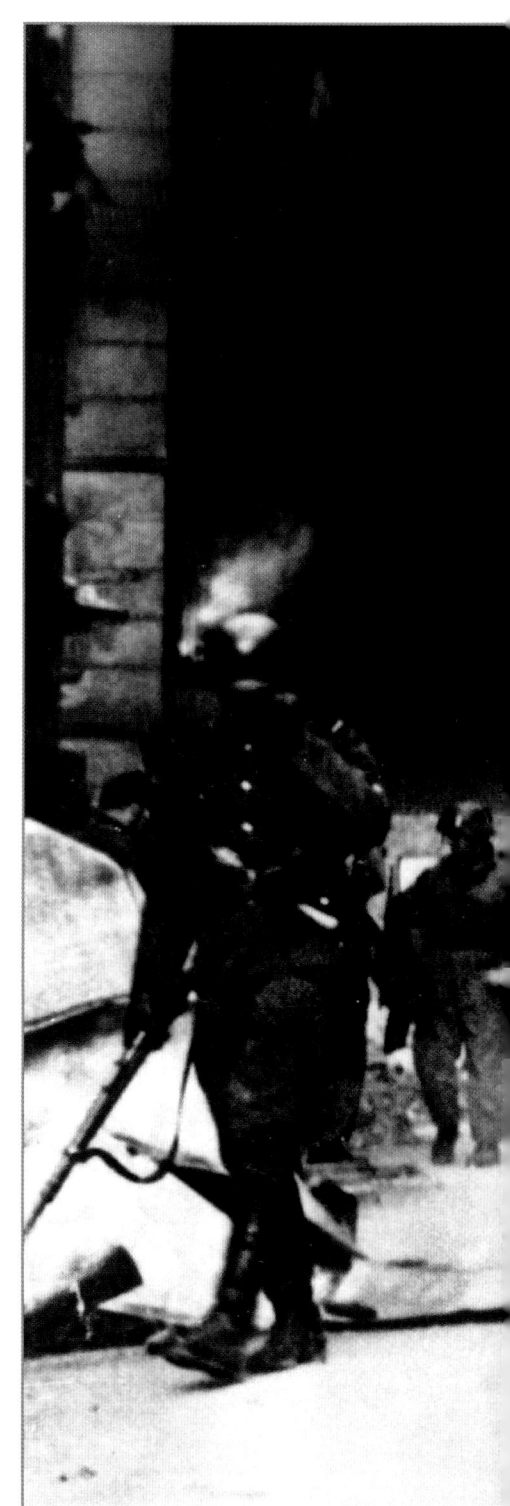

Destruction
of the Warsaw Ghetto

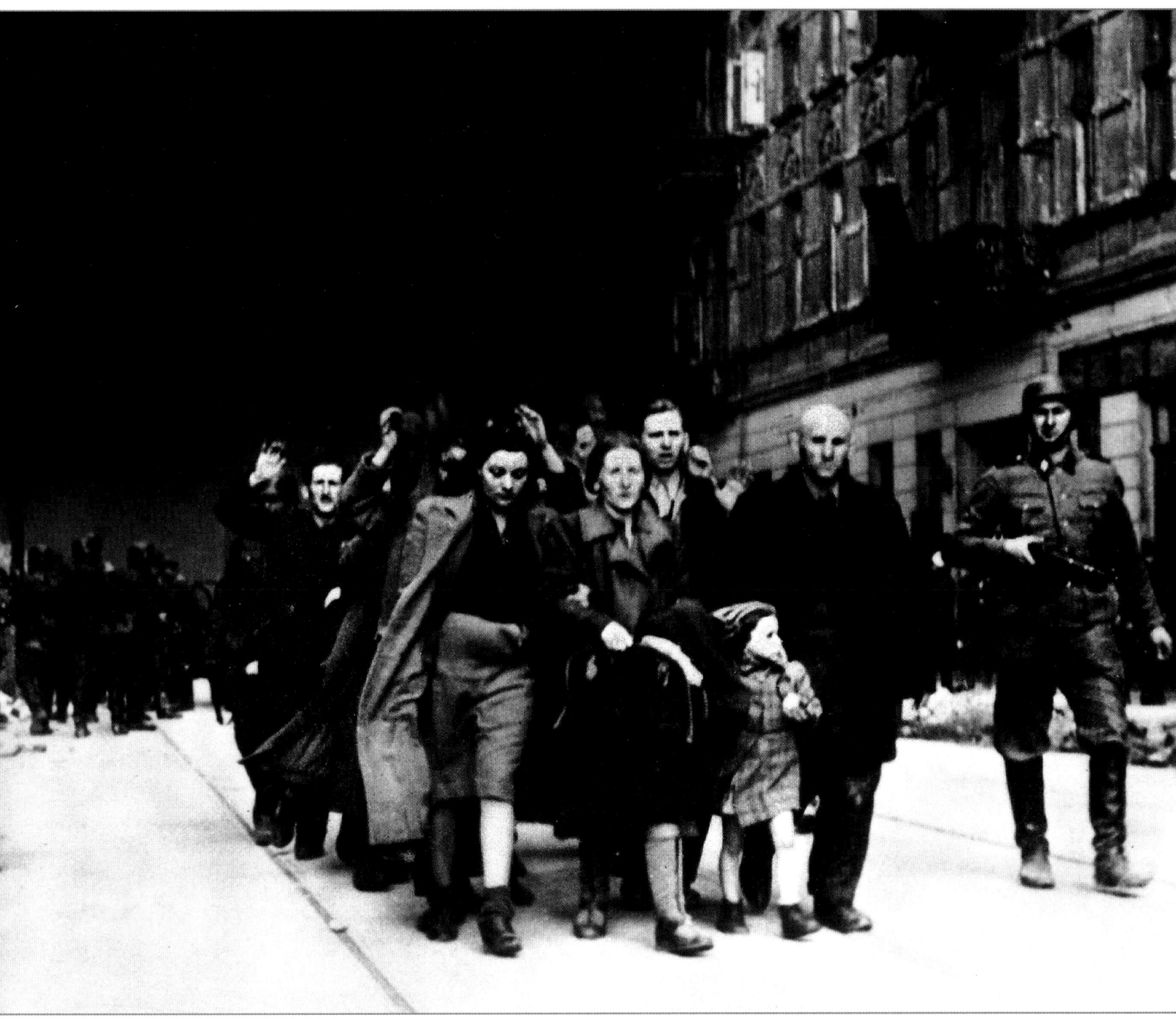

Allied Troops Land on Omaha Beach

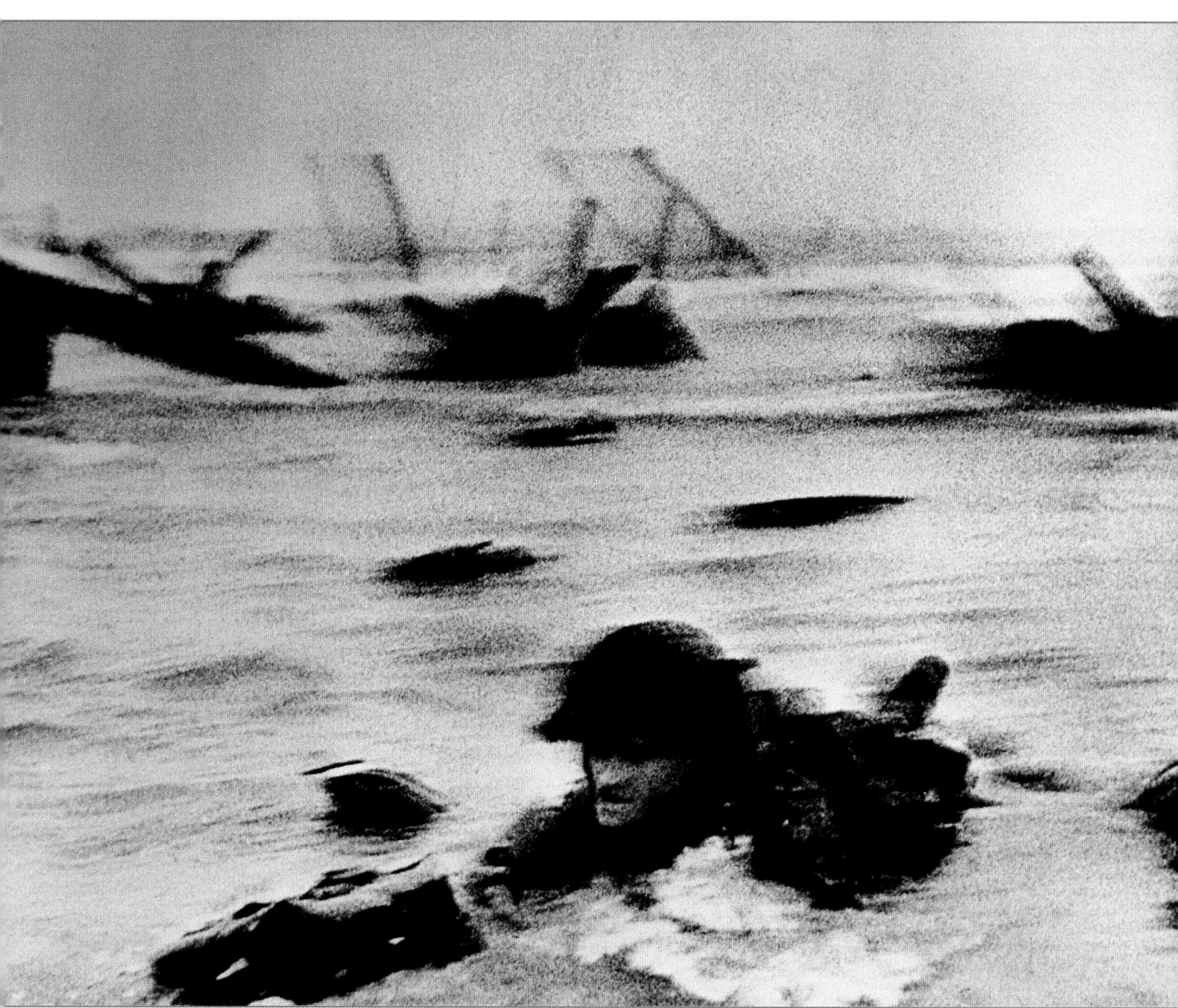

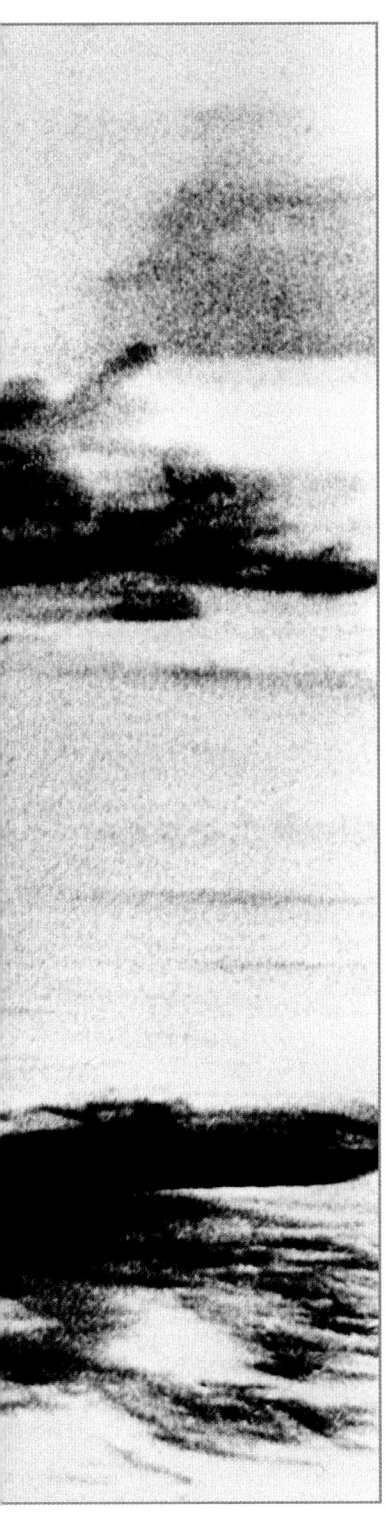

June 6, 1944 - Normandy, France

A tide of steel materializes on the horizon of the sea of Normandy. It is the morning of June 6th, 1944. The soldiers of the US First Infantry Division land on Omaha Beach under fire from German machine guns. Among the Americans that morning was a Hungarian refugee, Endre Erno Friedmann, sometimes called Bandi, who would later become the great Robert Capa. For him, he said, that was the longest day of his life: "If your photos aren't good, it means you weren't close enough" is his motto, and he wants to be close to the place where the winds of war suddenly blow. Around his neck he has two Contaxes and a Rolleiflex. There is dim, gray light. He manages to capture these famous moments between life and death, amid water, bullets, explosions, and the bodies of soldiers. Low shots, out of focus, taken between chaos and fear, excitement and terror. Capa moves out of danger. The moment he reaches the beach, he hands over his rolls of film to a motorcyclist, who gets them to offices in London. The rest is history. Still, the most phenomenal photographic reportage of the Second World War is almost completely ruined due to an accident in the darkroom. Only 11 of the 106 shots are saved. Yet by looking at the unfocused images of Private Houston S. Riley, flailing in the water among wreckage and bodies, published by LIFE on June 19th, 1944, the Americans immediately realized what was truly happening on the coasts of northern France.

In this image, which Capa described as "slightly out of focus," the black body of the soldier sinks into the silvery, gray sea of Normandy, a spray of bullets mixing with the whistling of the cold north wind on that long, interminable day. Instinctively, we lower our heads, like at the cinema during a battle scene, dodging bullets, and unconsciously we hope to be out of the line of fire of the enemy. In fact, these shots inspired the first images of the film *Saving Private Ryan*, by Steven Spielberg.

Photograph by Robert Capa

The Yalta Conference

February 4-11, 1945 - Yalta, Soviet Union

This photo is often referred to as *The Big Three*: the leaders Churchill, Roosevelt, and Stalin, the main protagonists in the struggle against Nazism. During the Second World War, the fate of nations was decided far from the battlefields, by means of a series of meetings in which the map of the world was redrawn. The conference, which took place in February, 1945, in Yalta, a small town in the Crimea, would become famous in public opinion. It was also the most symbolic meeting on a historical level, due to this photo of the three Allied leaders, seated next to each other. Surrounded by well-known figures in their respective delegations, the three men seem tired but satisfied.

Historians later questioned the importance of this conference, and attributed the most important decisions to other meetings before and after it. However, Yalta has retained its symbolic value due to the fact that it was the last time that the three leaders met. Roosevelt died the following April, when the war had practically ended; Churchill was defeated in the election in the summer of 1945, and replaced by the Labor leader, Atlee, as the leader of United Kingdom; Stalin remained in power until his death in 1953, but the Iron Curtain erected at the end of the war established an unsurpassable distance between the Soviet Union and the West. In this regard, the Yalta photo offers us precious testimony to one of the most important historical phases of the twentieth century.

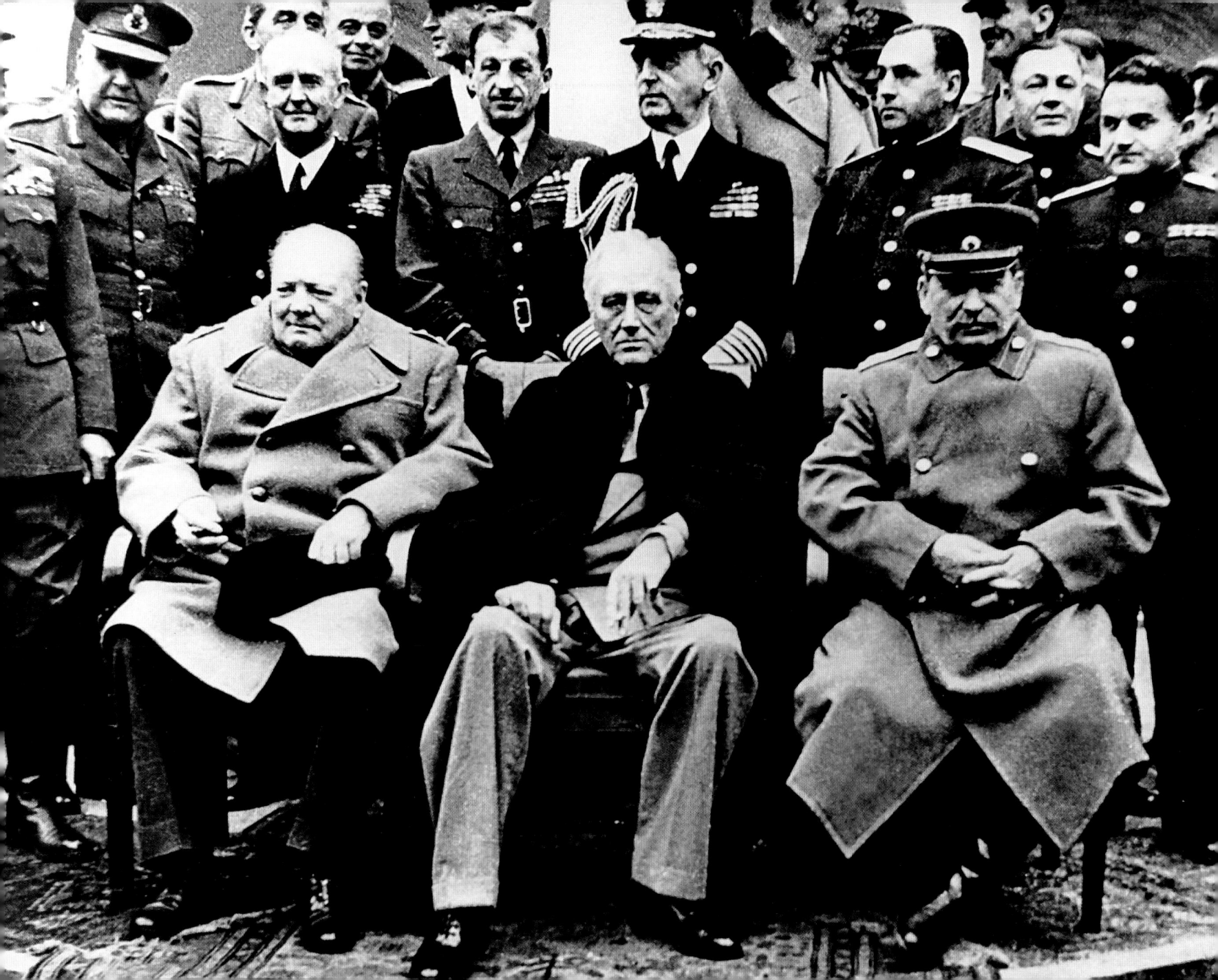

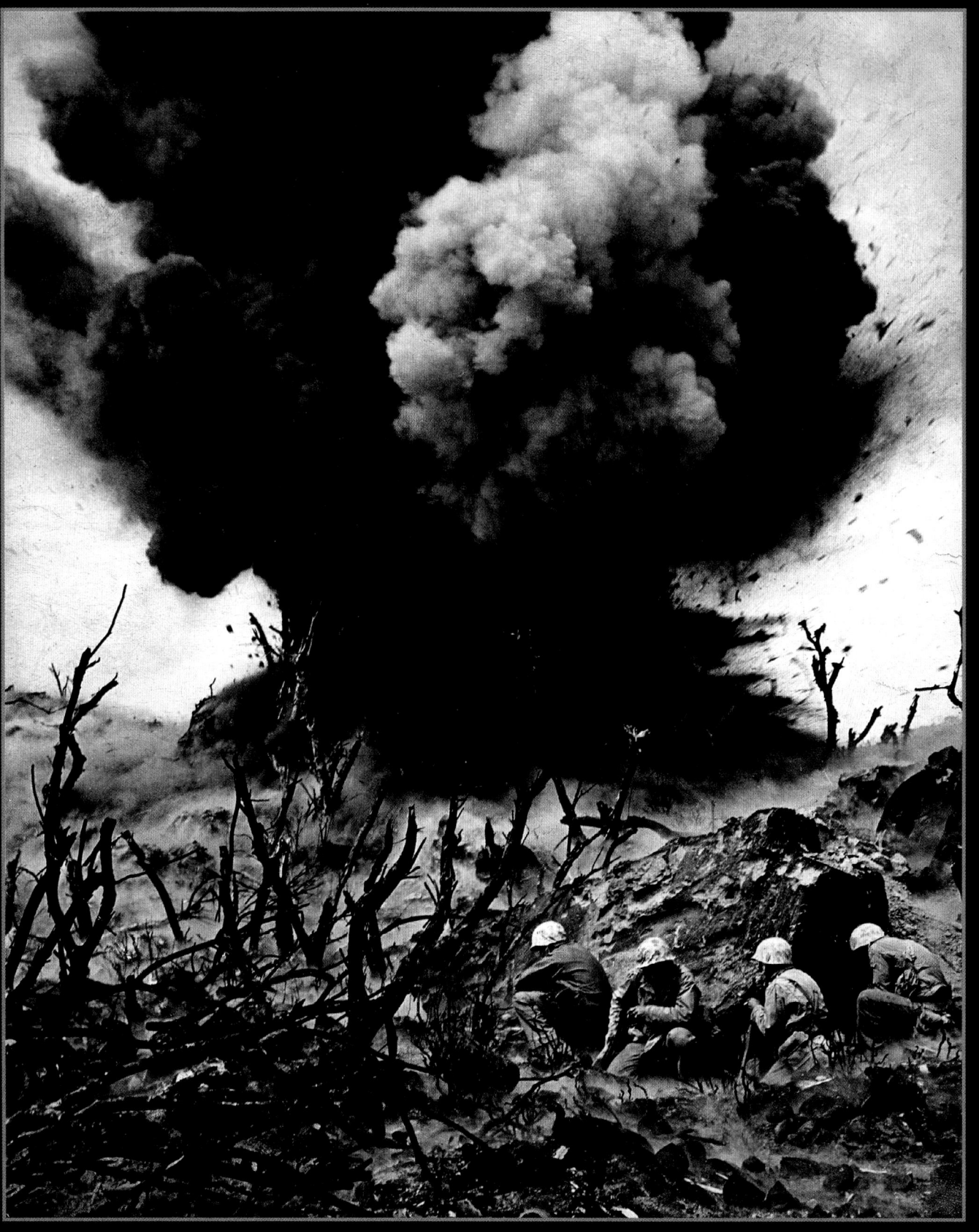

Photograph by W. Eugene Smith

The Battle of Iwo Jima

February-March, 1945 - Iwo Jima, Japan

For five weeks, between February and March, 1945, the Japanese island of Iwo Jima, in a strategic position about 620 miles south of Tokyo, was devastated by a frighteningly hard battle. About 18,000 Japanese soldiers and 7,000 Americans fell.

Various American reporters were active on the scene of this bloody chapter of the Second World War. Many of them believed in what propaganda described as the Allies' triumphal march toward victory. However, thanks to the work of photographers like W. Eugene Smith, we can "listen" to a much more realistic narrative and understand the price that was paid for the conquest of the island.

Smith describes the battle, pain, and death without sweetening the pill. His testimony is the most uncompromising of those days. In an attempt to crystallize the human condition, Smith succeeded in taking about fifty extraordinary photographs while on Iwo Jima. The protagonists of this image, in particular, are the devastated landscape and the huge cloud of smoke and dust created by an explosion: at first glance, one almost misses the soldiers ducking for cover. They are minute figures at the mercy of the destructive force of war. The black and white (which was then obligatory) drains the scene of color and hope.

Two months after filing this report, a mortar wounded Smith. This ended his career as war reporter (but not as photographer).

One can easily understand why Smith's shots were not chosen to symbolize the battle of Iwo Jima. This honor was received by the photograph in which Joe Rosenthal immortalizes the victorious Marines, as they raise the Stars and Stripes on a hilltop: the scene, in the opinion of some people, was arranged for the photographer.

Jewish Survivors in Buchenwald

April 16, 1945 - Buchenwald, Germany

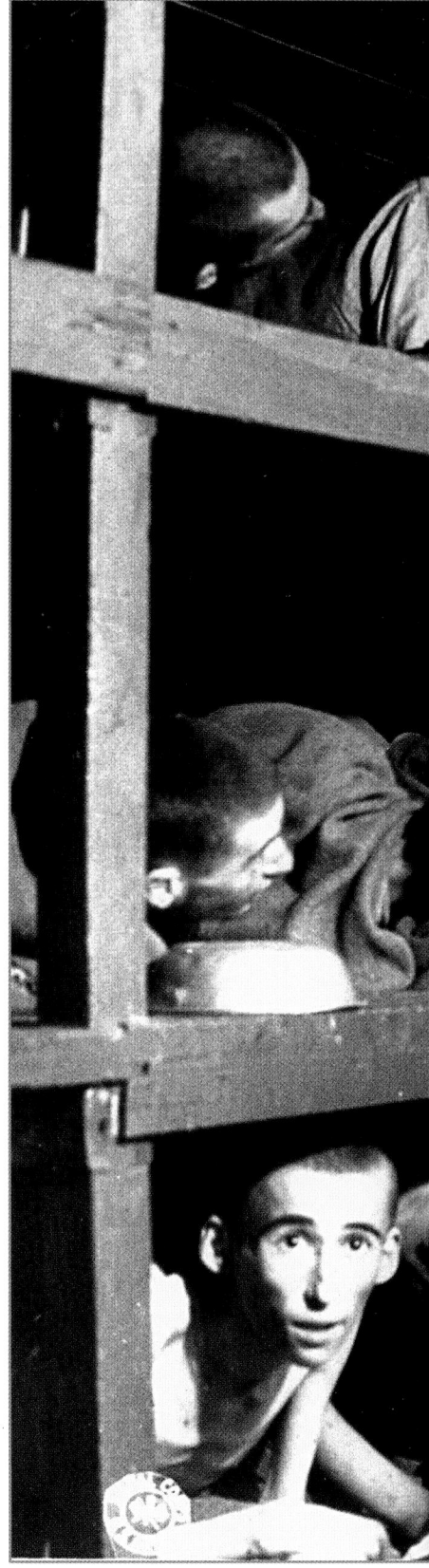

"Never shall I forget that night, the first night in the camp, which has turned my life into one long night, seven times cursed and seven times sealed." Thus wrote Elie Wiesel, the Nobel Peace Prize winner and author of the book *Night*, in which he recounts his tragic survival in a Nazi extermination camp.

Wiesel recognizes himself in this crude photograph, which was taken by Private Henry Miller on April 16th, 1945, five days after the Allies liberated the Buchenwald camp, in Germany. The writer states that he is the seventh man on the second level of bunks: we only glimpse his face in the darkness of the room. In the foreground, a young man, semi-naked and emaciated, looks incredulously into the camera. In the dim light his ribs stand out clearly in his pale chest. Other faces, amazed and gaunt, lean out from the bunk beds and stare into the camera. We can only imagine what these men felt when the Americans arrived, announcing the end of the war, and the end of their time as prisoners.

Early that April, 1945, the prisoners took advantage of the weakened SS, which was reduced in strength and nearing collapse because of the coming defeat. The prisoners attacked the guards and took control of the camp. A few hours later, American tanks broke down the gates of Buchenwald.

Private Miller's photo later raised some questions. The testimony of the other survivors did not agree with Wiesel's: they didn't recognize him among the men in the photo. Others have even insinuated that the Americans, choosing the weakest and sickest prisoners for an image of anti-German propaganda, carefully constructed the photograph.

Apart from the controversy, however, what remains in this photo is heartrending testimony to one of the darkest pages in history.

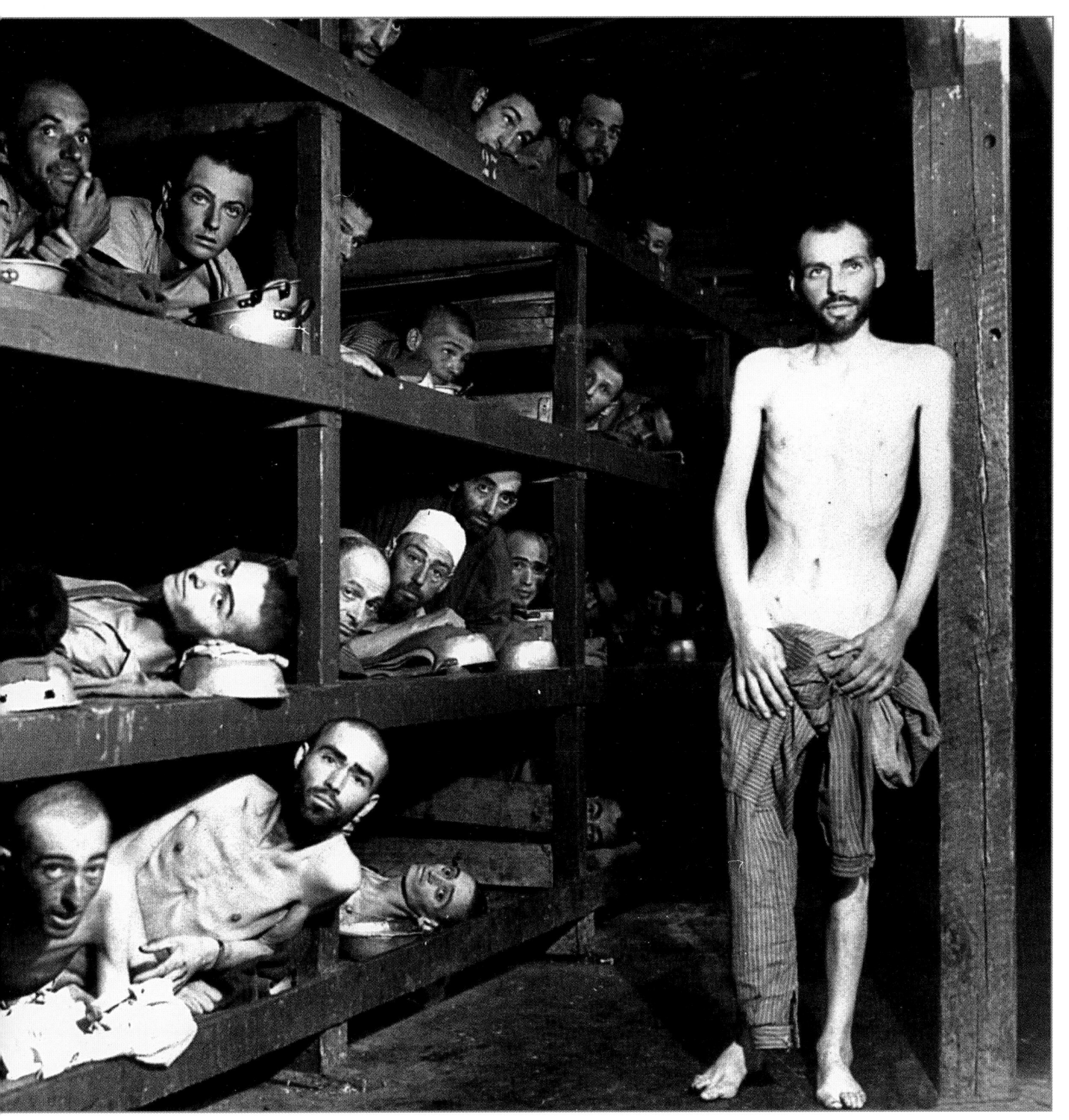

Photograph by Henry Miller

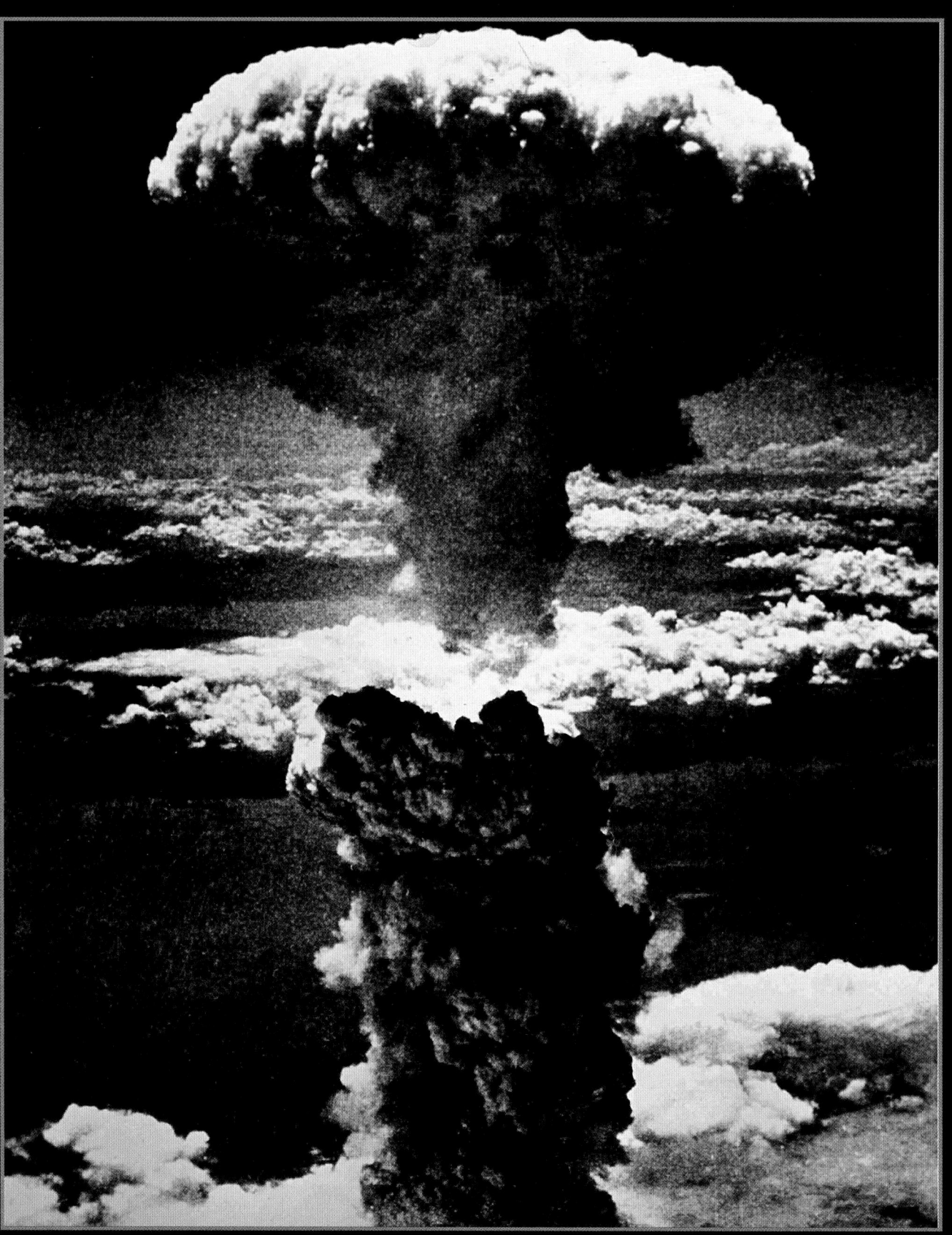

Photograph by Charles Levy

The Nagasaki Atomic Explosion

August 9, 1945 - Nagasaki, Japan

The Japanese city of Kokura was the target the United States intended to strike with "Fat Man," the second atomic bomb used in the Second World War. The squadron carrying the bomb was composed of six huge Flying Fortresses, as the B-29 bombers were called. Laggin' Dragon and Enola Gay, the plane which three days before had dropped the first bomb on Hiroshima, flew an hour ahead to check the weather conditions. They discovered that Kokura, the target, was covered by clouds on that day: the squadron decided to fall back on Nagasaki.

It was 11:00 on the morning of August 9th, 1945. The bomb exploded about 1,600 feet above the ground, producing a mushroom cloud that rose as high as 12 miles. Temperatures in the blast zone reached 4,000 °C (about 7,100 °F), generating extremely powerful wind currents. Even if the wave of fire on the ground was inferior to that of Hiroshima, in Nagasaki about 30,000 people died in a matter of seconds.

On that day, some of the bombers had the task of monitoring, measuring, and photographing the explosion. The science writer William L. Laurence, of *The New York Times*, and a young officer, Charles Levy, who was behind the camera, were on board the Great Artiste. It was through them that the world came to know about the terrible atomic mushroom cloud. It is a widespread view that the horror communicated by such images accelerated the end of the war.

No one expected such a result. Not even the scientists involved in the Manhattan Project – who as early as 1939 had begun research on nuclear arms, anticipating an atomic threat from the Nazis – knew exactly what to expect in Hiroshima and Nagasaki.

V-J Day in Times Square

August 14, 1945 - New York City, United States

Tuesday, August 14th, 1945: the Second World War has practically ended. The Japanese have surrendered and at precisely 7 p.m., Washington time, President Truman will officially announce victory to the people of the United States.

This unforgettable day will be remembered in history as "Victory over Japan Day," or V-J Day. Times Square, the heart of Manhattan, like thousands of other city centers across America, is crammed with celebrating men and women.

Alfred Eisenstaedt goes down into the street with his Leica IIIa. He has been taking pictures for *LIFE* magazine for about ten years, and is a master of the candid photograph: he uses natural light and manages to intuit in seconds the best moments for the photograph, often taking pictures without announcing his presence to his subjects.

This is exactly what happens to the sailor and the nurse who at 5:51 that evening kiss each other joyfully in Times Square, in front of a lens they don't see. Eisenstaedt takes four consecutive shots, and as the contact sheet shows he captures the perfection of the woman's body inclined precisely along the diagonal, and the marvel of her leg raised in parallel to the sailor's arm encircling her waist. Then Eisenstaedt moves off in search of new subjects.

When the photo appears on a full page in *LIFE*, an entire generation of Americans identifies with the happiness and lightheartedness of the two young people, and not only metaphorically. By covering each other's faces, the sailor and the nurse encourage the process of identification, so much so that the editorial department of the magazine is flooded with messages from readers who claim to be the protagonists of the photo. In short, the photo becomes a folk icon: it is no accident that a giant, vaguely pop, sculpture, *Unconditional Surrender*, immortalized the kiss scene. Created by Seward Johnson, the installation has been exposed in Times Square several times.

Photograph by Alfred Eisenstaedt

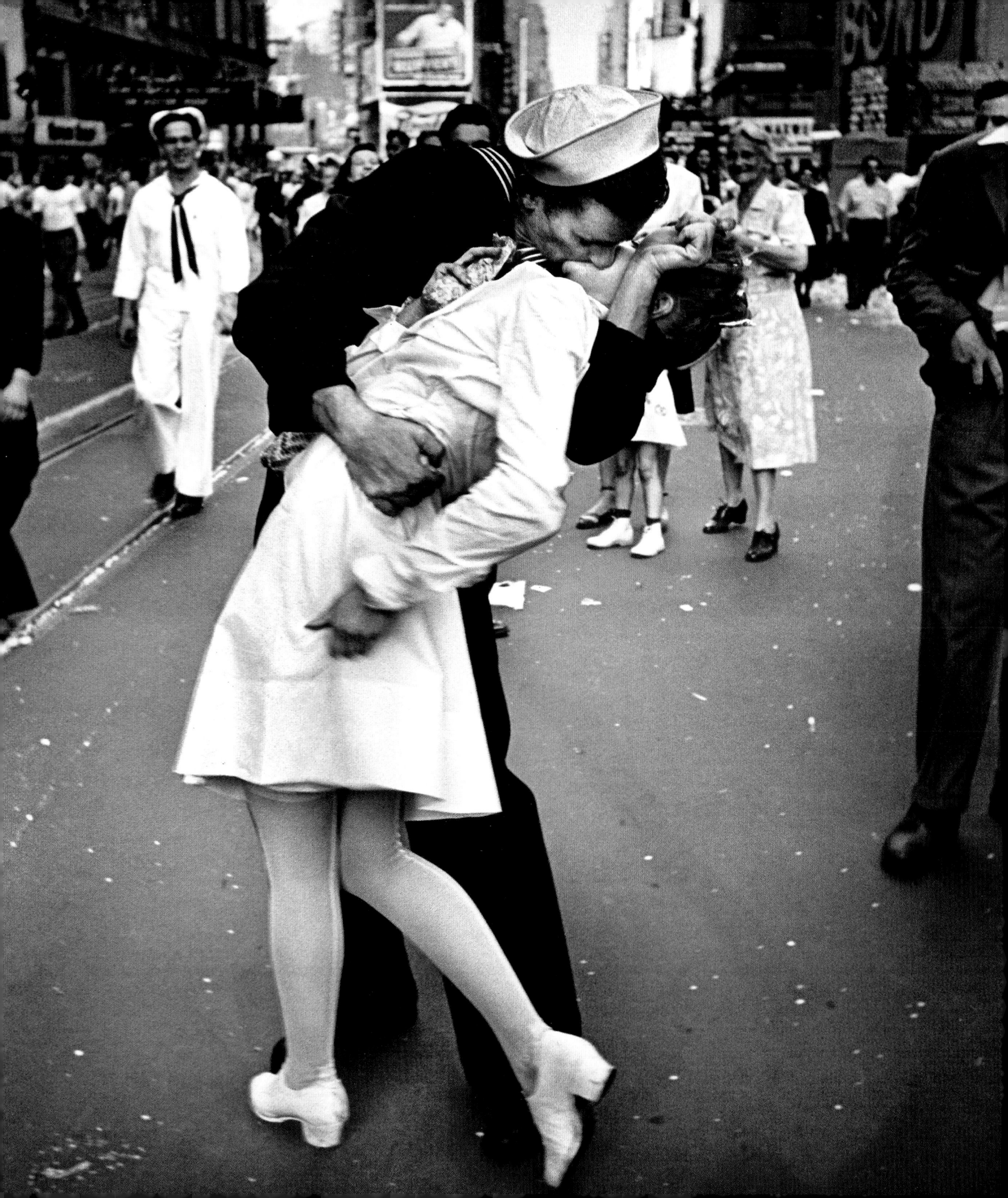

Mother and Child in Hiroshima

December, 1945 - Hiroshima, Japan

When the German-born American photojournalist Alfred Eisenstaedt arrived in Japan, immediately after the end of the Second World War, he faced a nightmare. It was December, 1945. In August the cities of Hiroshima and Nagasaki had been swept away by unprecedented violence, leaving the country on its knees and ready to surrender. Those who died in the explosions of the two bombs were perhaps more fortunate. Many of the survivors were to die slowly through radiation; they lost teeth and hair and vomited blood, wandering like ghosts among the radioactive ruins, waiting to die.

In the desolation of Hiroshima, Eisenstaedt took this photograph of extraordinary intensity. It is a portrait without rhetoric of a mother and child in traditional dress, who are seated against a background of burned trees. The subject and the composition recall the traditional iconography of Madonna and Child, and they show the same solemnity. The woman and her child are calmly seated, maintaining dignity in the midst of so much destruction. They look into the camera as if to ask for attention, and they force the observer to impress in their memory how far human cruelty can go.

When the photograph was taken, the Americans and the Japanese were no longer enemies, and war propaganda was no longer interesting. The Japanese were only a defeated people. Precisely for this reason, the image is still more disturbing. Even after decades, it is impossible to find an answer to the question in the eyes of this mother and child.

Photograph by Alfred Eisenstaedt

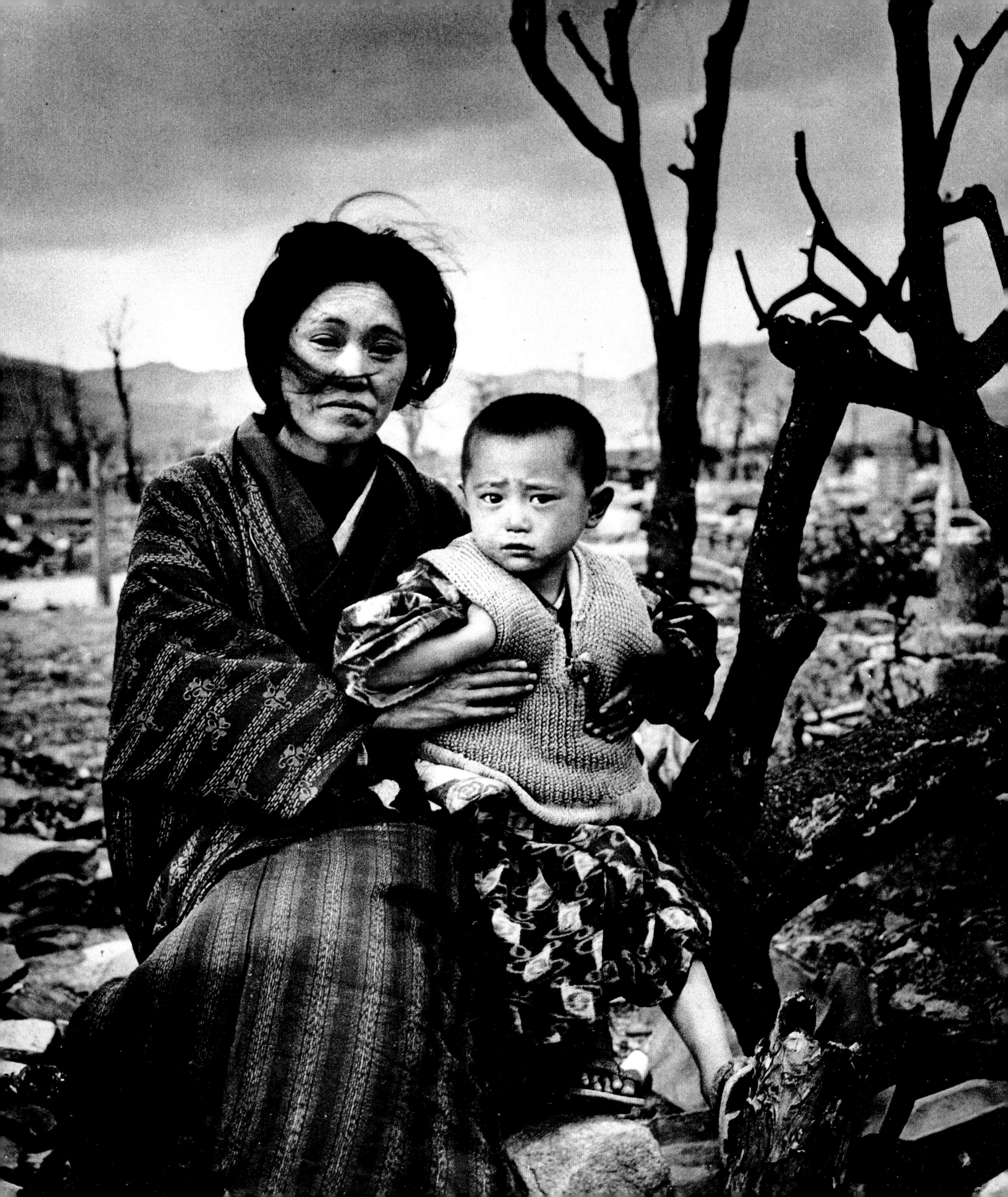

From Colonialism to Independence for India

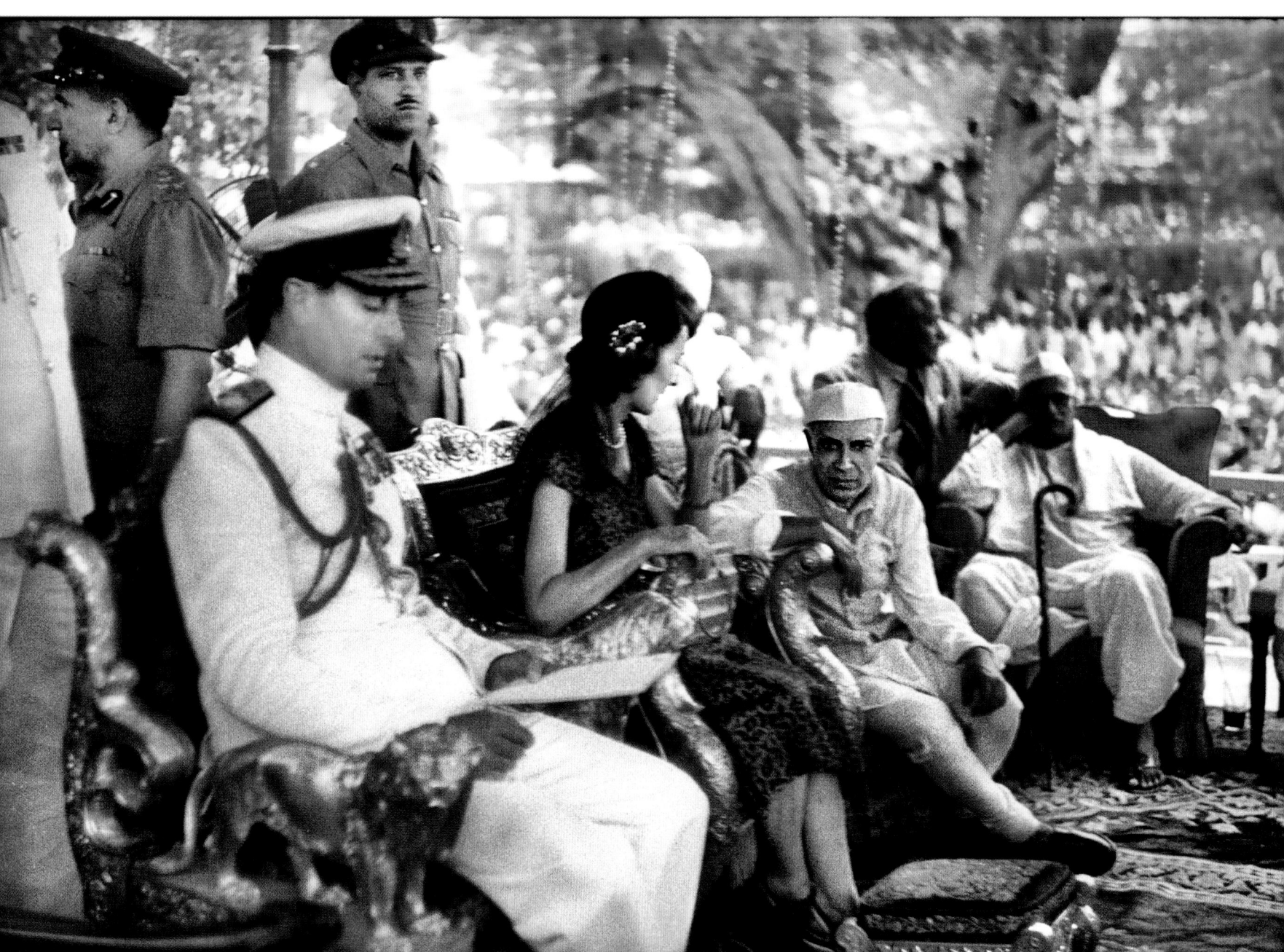

Photograph by Henri Cartier-Bresson

August 14-15, 1947 - Delhi, India

"At the stroke of the midnight hour, when the world sleeps, India will awake to life and freedom." With these words, Jawaharlal Nehru, the first Prime Minister of the country, announced the independence of India, which officially came into force on the night of August 14th, 1947. The separation of India and Pakistan, which was a Muslim country, was difficult and cost many lives: the successful outcome was the result of political commitment and a long campaign of non-violent protest led by Gandhi. But it was also due to the intervention of Lord Louis Mountbatten, the last British viceroy. The process, however, was not yet concluded: the Republic would be proclaimed only in 1950, and for ten months Lord Mountbatten remained in power in the office of Governor-General. He was responsible for leading the country in the first transition phase.

Henri Cartier-Bresson visited India between 1947 and 1948 to document this historic passage. Like many of his famous photos, this image, too, succeeds in distilling, in a moment, the essence of a story. Lord Mountbatten is in the foreground: his eyes are on a document, and he seems uninterested by what is happening around him. Nearby, his wife Edwina and Nehru, facing each other, are engaged in conversation and seem to show a certain veiled intimacy. Our gaze is led by the diagonal line from the Governor to Nehru, the new protagonist of Indian politics: the photographer focuses on him. Seated between the two men, Lady Mountbatten's profile is fleeting. The narrative thus moves from a public dimension to a private one, from the passage of institutional responsibilities to the personal relationships between the three figures. It is now known that there was an intense romantic bond between the Governor's wife and the Indian Prime Minister, which seems only to have been platonic, but lasted until her death.

The SS United Nations Lands in Palestine

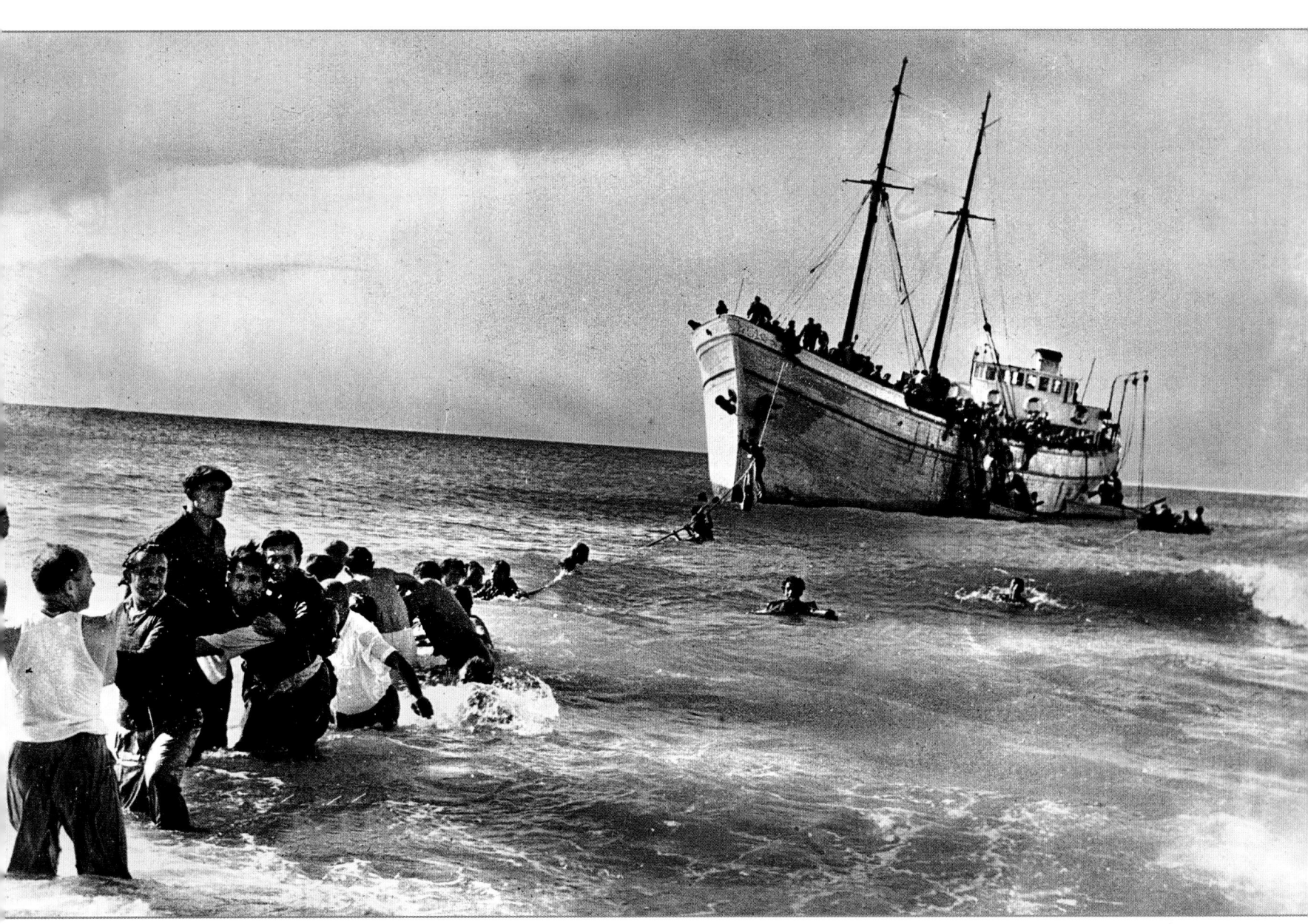

February 2, 1948 - Nahariya, Palestine

In 1948, three years after the end of the Second World War, many Jewish refugees who survived Nazi Germany still had no place to go. While discussions took place at the United Nations, many lived in refugee camps in central Europe. Others chose to emigrate to the United States. Still others wished to reach the numerous settlers already in Palestine, but restrictions imposed by the United Kingdom in the *White Paper* of 1939 limited the number of the immigrants to this territory. The refugees that we see in this photograph swimming to shore in the northern port of Nahariya, near Haifa, have arrived illegally on board the SS United Nations. The ship left Bari with 700 people on board and succeeded in breaching the blockade by British ships.

The anonymous photographer was on the staff of the Harris Agency Keystone, one of the first photography agencies to have an international presence.

The SS United Nations was not the only ship to attempt to cross despite all the bans. Between 1945 and 1948, Zionist organizations succeeded in launching dozens of ships full of refugees, mostly from the Italian coast, moving more than 69,000 people. However, British naval forces intercepted some ships and the passengers were interned in prison camps in Cyprus or sent back to their original countries. It was worldwide news when the SS Exodus, one of the largest of these ships, which left France on July 11th, 1947, was stopped a few days later by the British Navy and boarded. Fighting and resistance by the refugees resulted in three deaths and many wounded.

Everything changed in May, 1948, when the United Kingdom Mandate in Palestine concluded and the State of Israel, recognized by the United Nations, was founded.

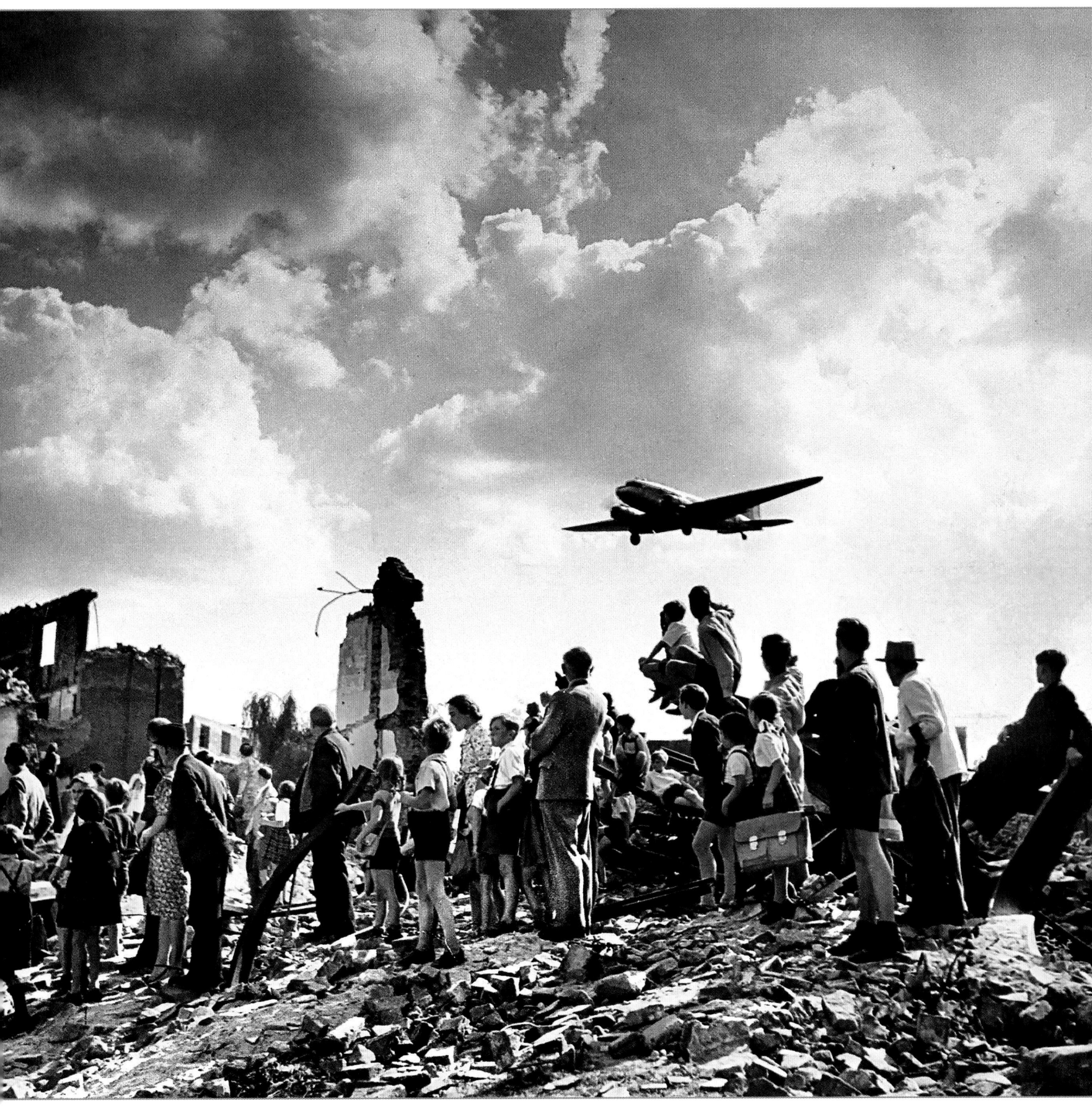

The Berlin Air Bridge

July, 1948 - Berlin, Federal Republic of Germany

Between June 25th, 1948, and September 30th, 1949, an entire city survived because of an air bridge, the largest humanitarian operation ever carried out: for 462 days, more than 278,000 flights took off from the United States, France, and Britain, bound for Tempelhof Airport in Berlin, where at the peak of the operation almost 1,400 planes landed per day. The air bridge guaranteed the supply of food, medicine, and coal to the population of the Western Sectors of the city. The Soviet army, by blocking roads and railroads, had isolated it from the rest of the world. It was the first event of the Cold War, and the dress rehearsal for the emerging geopolitical equilibrium that would last until the fall of the Berlin Wall.

At the time, Walter Sanders, one of the best photographers for the American magazine *LIFE*, recorded the air bridge in the divided capital. He was a photographer of German origin who emigrated to the United States in 1933, after the rise of Hitler. This black and white shot, with figures rendered sharp and dense because of the bright background, could be a frame from a John Ford film. The dramatic elements are all there, perfectly balanced: the rubble on the ground, the walls shattered by bombing, the crowd immobile with their eyes on the sky, and the form of a great airplane descending from the sun-bathed clouds. The plane was loaded not with bombs, but with candy: the C–47 cargo planes were in fact nicknamed *Rosinenbomber*, raisin bombers, because they used to drop packets of chocolate, chewing gum, and sugared almonds hanging from little parachutes, especially for the children. Thus, while Moscow attempted to starve Berlin, the United States launched candy diplomacy: an operation that had a strong emotive impact on German public opinion and contributed to defining the future relationship between the two countries.

Photograph by Walter Sanders

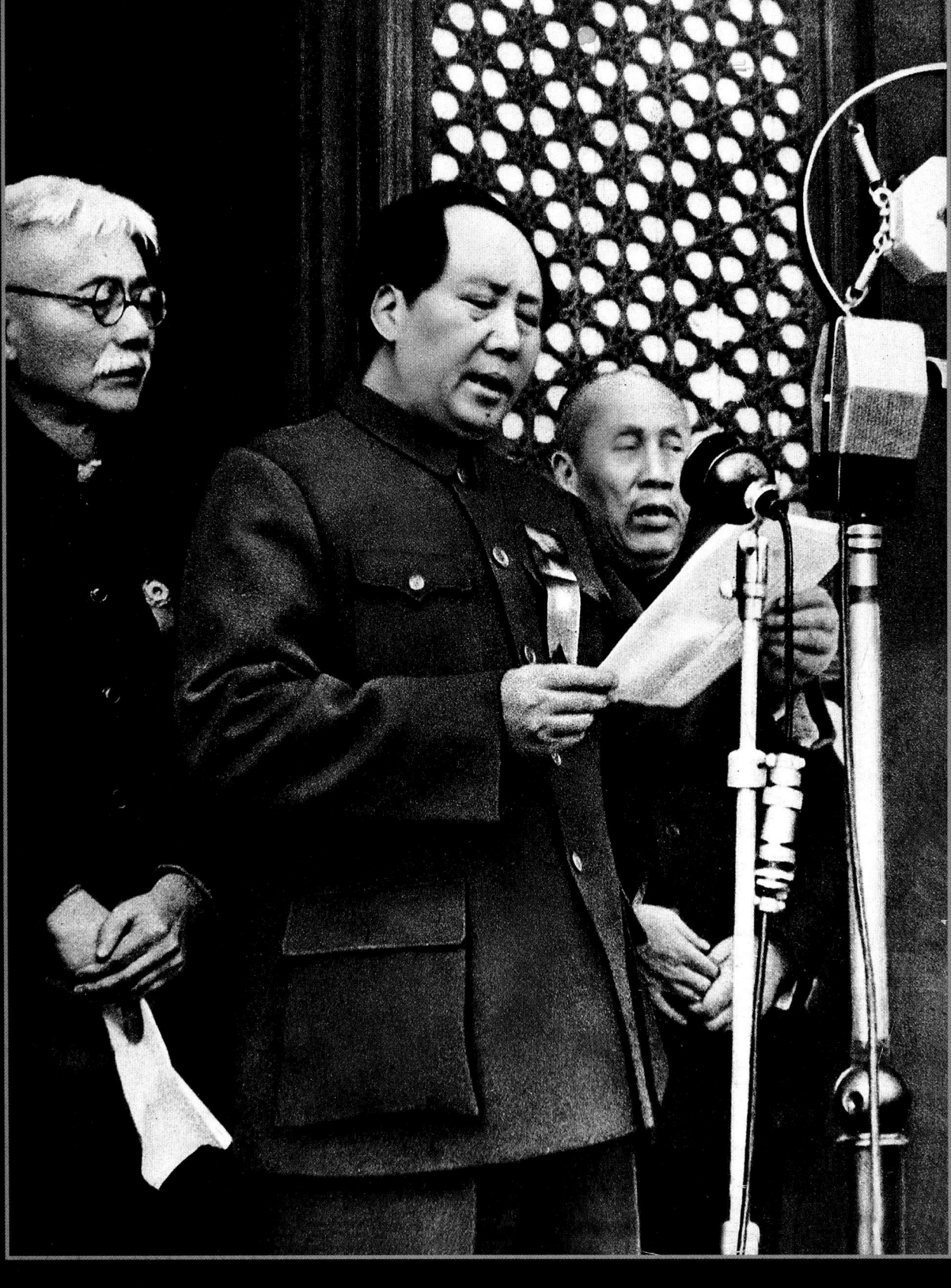

Photograph by Hou Bo

Mao Zedong Declares the Foundation of the PRC

October 1, 1949 - Beijing, People's Republic of China

The Long March of 1934-35 was only the beginning. Fifteen years after that epic retreat, the Chinese Red Army, which became the People's Liberation Army, achieved unimaginable success when it took full control of the immense country. This was due to the patient leadership of Mao Zedong, who succeeded in turning a dramatic series of events to his advantage: first was the Japanese invasion, which resulted in appalling atrocities; then there was the Second World War; and then a Civil War, against the Nationalists of the Kuomintang, who capitulated at Nanking in April, 1949. General Chiang Kai-shek, President of Nationalist China, was forced to take refuge on the island of Taiwan with what remained of his army.

On October 1st, 1949, Mao Zedong addresses an audience of 300,000 people at Tienanmen Square, colored red with flags, with the upraised handkerchiefs of the peasants, and with the gray-green of their uniforms. But the photographer, Hou Bo, a twenty-five-year old woman who, with her husband Xu Xiaobing, is Mao's official photographer, chooses to ignore the square. Instead, she concentrates on the leader's speech. Mao announces the foundation of the People's Republic "under the guidance of the Chinese Communist Party" and proclaims Beijing the new capital. He states that the assembly of the party delegates, along with the army, has appointed him President of People's Republic. A man named Zhou Enlai is to be the new premier. In fact, Mao, with his wife Jiang Qing, will be in power for almost 30 years. Jiang Qing, presently, does not entirely trust the young photographer, Bo, perhaps resenting how close she can get to Mao. Indeed, Jiang Qing, during the Cultural Revolution, will accuse Hou Bo of being a false communist, after which the photographer will fall into disfavor. But not even this will affect Hou Bo's total admiration for the Great Leader.

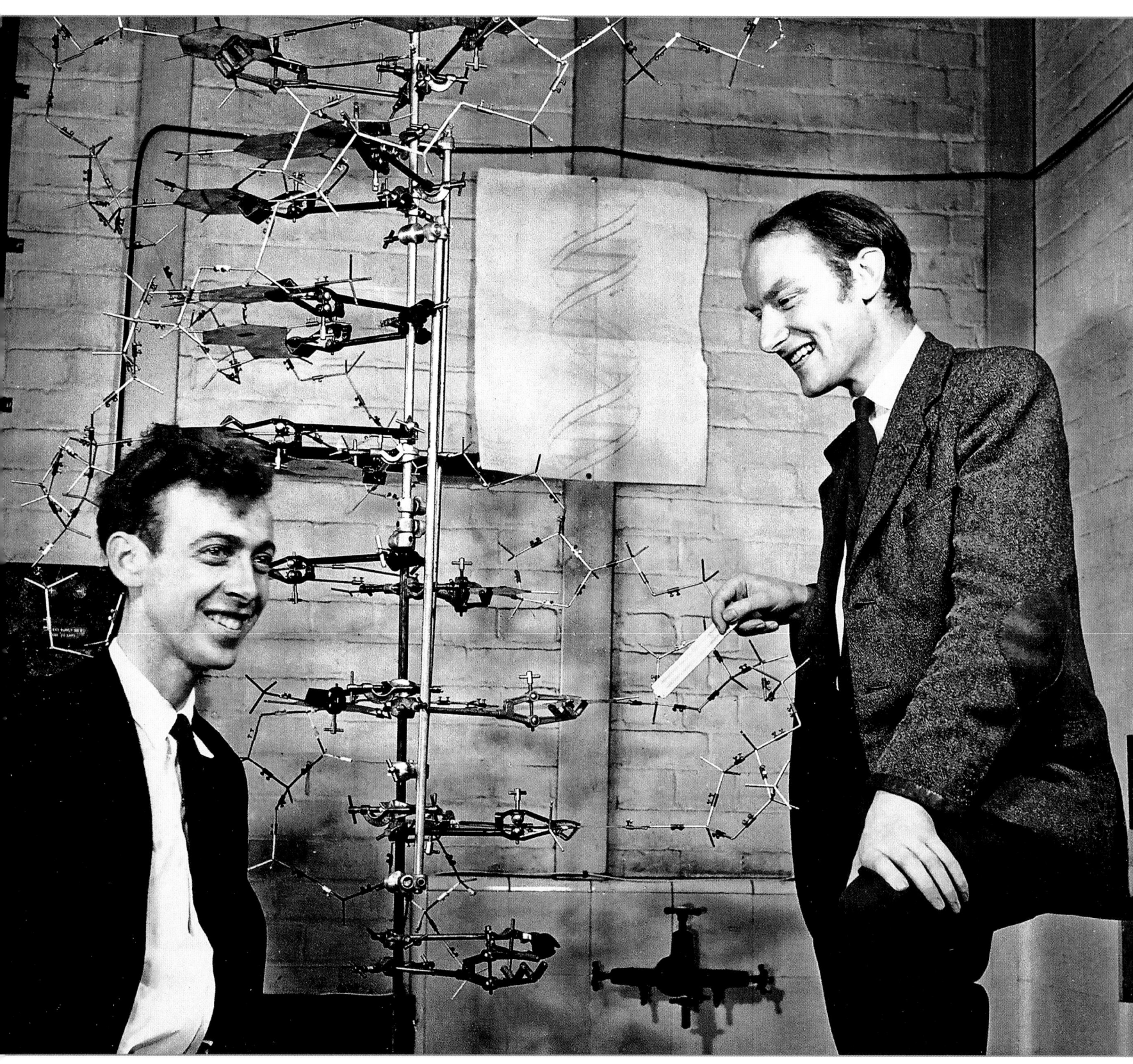

Photograph by Antony Barrington Brown

The Double Helix Model of DNA

April, 1953 - Cambridge, United Kingdom

When the scientists James Watson, an American, and Francis Crick, a Briton, began to analyze the structure of DNA, the hypothesis that it contained genetic information was not yet accepted by the scientific community. Yet, because experiments begun as early as 1944 had reached this conclusion, understanding the physical and chemical properties of deoxyribonucleic acid was becoming increasingly important. The fundamental contribution the two scientists made was the proposal of a model that demonstrated how the molecule contained not only genetic information, but also a "template" for its replication. The key came from studies of the diffraction of X-rays of DNA performed by Rosalind Franklin, a British scientist: the image she discovered suggested the now-famous double helix structure.

In the photograph, the two young men – Watson on the left, Crick on the right – stand beside their three-dimensional model of DNA, constructed in the Cavendish Laboratory at the University of Cambridge. It is one of a series of photos by the student Antony Barrington Brown, which dates from shortly after the publication of their research in the journal *Nature*, on April 25th, 1953. In the center of the wall behind them, there is a sketch of the helix drawn by the painter Odile Speed, Crick's wife. Their enthusiasm and satisfaction are palpable. The focus of the shot is one of the most important events in modern biology.

Brown's photos were rejected by *TIME* magazine. Not even in 1962, when the two scientists won the Nobel for Medicine, did any journal show interest in the photographs. Then, in 1968, one of them appeared in Watson's book *The Double Helix*, which quickly became a best seller, and since then they have been published widely.

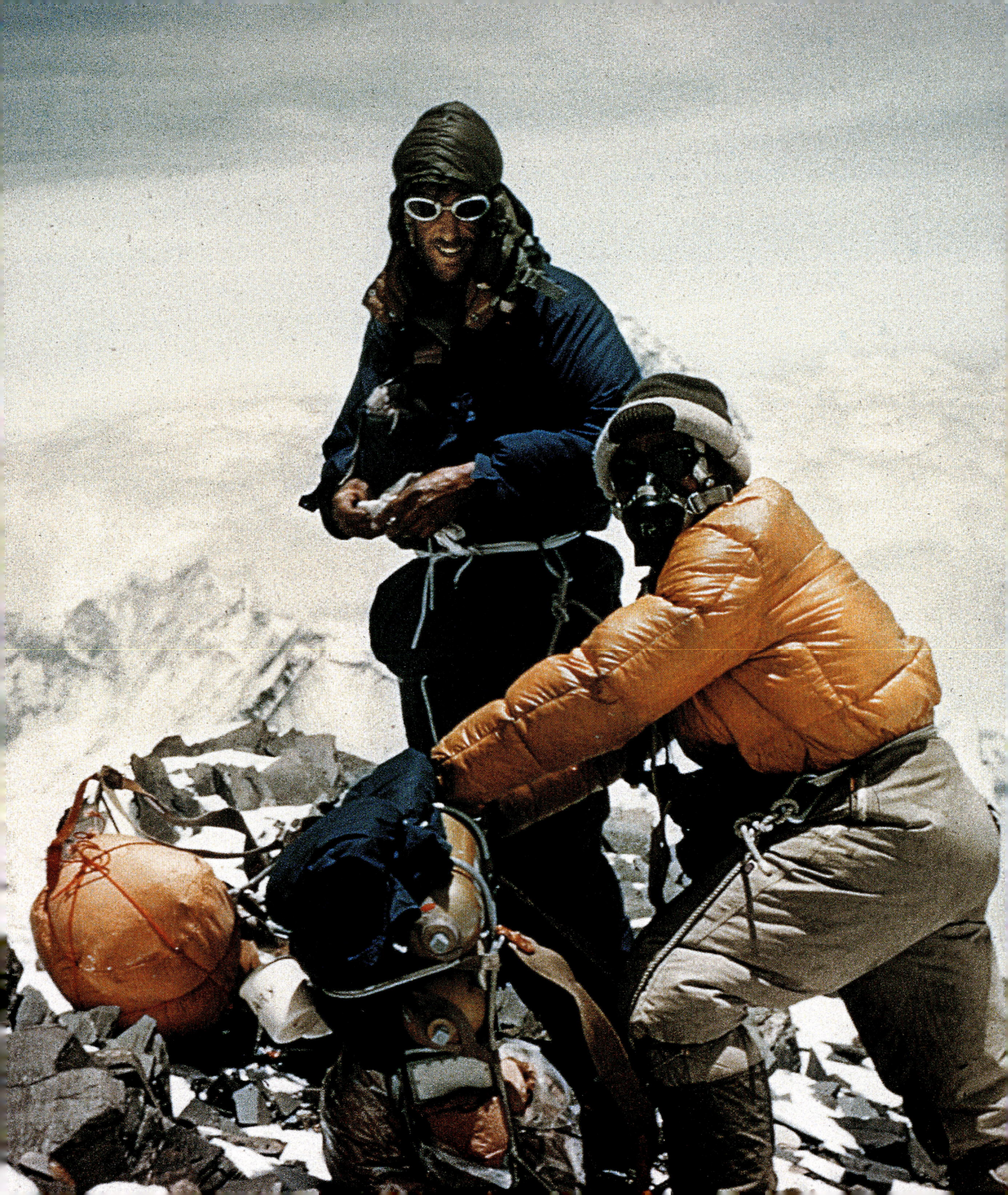

Hillary and Tenzing on the Summit of Everest

May 29, 1953 - Himalayas, Nepal

The conquest of Everest was an extraordinary feat which, for over 30 years, thrilled the world. The most determined participants in this effort, right from the first attempts in 1921, were the British; but only in 1953 did John Hunt, then a colonel in the British Army, manage to assemble an ideal team: strong climbers who were not "too young," because, as he said, the 8,000 meter ascent (26,000 feet) requires "gifts of discipline and extraordinary patience."

Edmund Hillary, 33 years old at the time, was part of the group. He was a beekeeper from Auckland. Although he had limited Himalayan experience, he was a man of exceptional strength and stamina. Another member of the group was a Sherpa named Tenzing Norgay, 38 years old, who boasted five attempts at summiting Everest, and who held the altitude record on the mountain, at 8,600 meters (28,000 feet), reached with a Swiss expedition in 1952. These two men, so different in culture and origin, proved to be the best-equipped party for the final assault: the photo, taken by fellow expedition member W. George Lowe, shows them at 8,500 meters (27,887 feet), the last camp before the summit. They left their tent at 6:30 on the morning of May 29th, and after five hours of struggle reached 8,848 meters (29,029 feet), the roof of the world: "We shook hands and then Tenzing threw his arms around my shoulders and we thumped each other on the back."

The victory was announced a few days later, on June 2nd, to accompany the coronation of Queen Elizabeth, and had an immediate worldwide impact: it was a day of glory for the Commonwealth, and for the two protagonists of the climb, who received the highest honors from their countries. After Everest, the two men also shared a common destiny: both dedicated themselves to supporting the Nepalese people by funding schools and hospitals, and even the airport of Lukla, which today bears their names.

Photograph by W. George Lowe

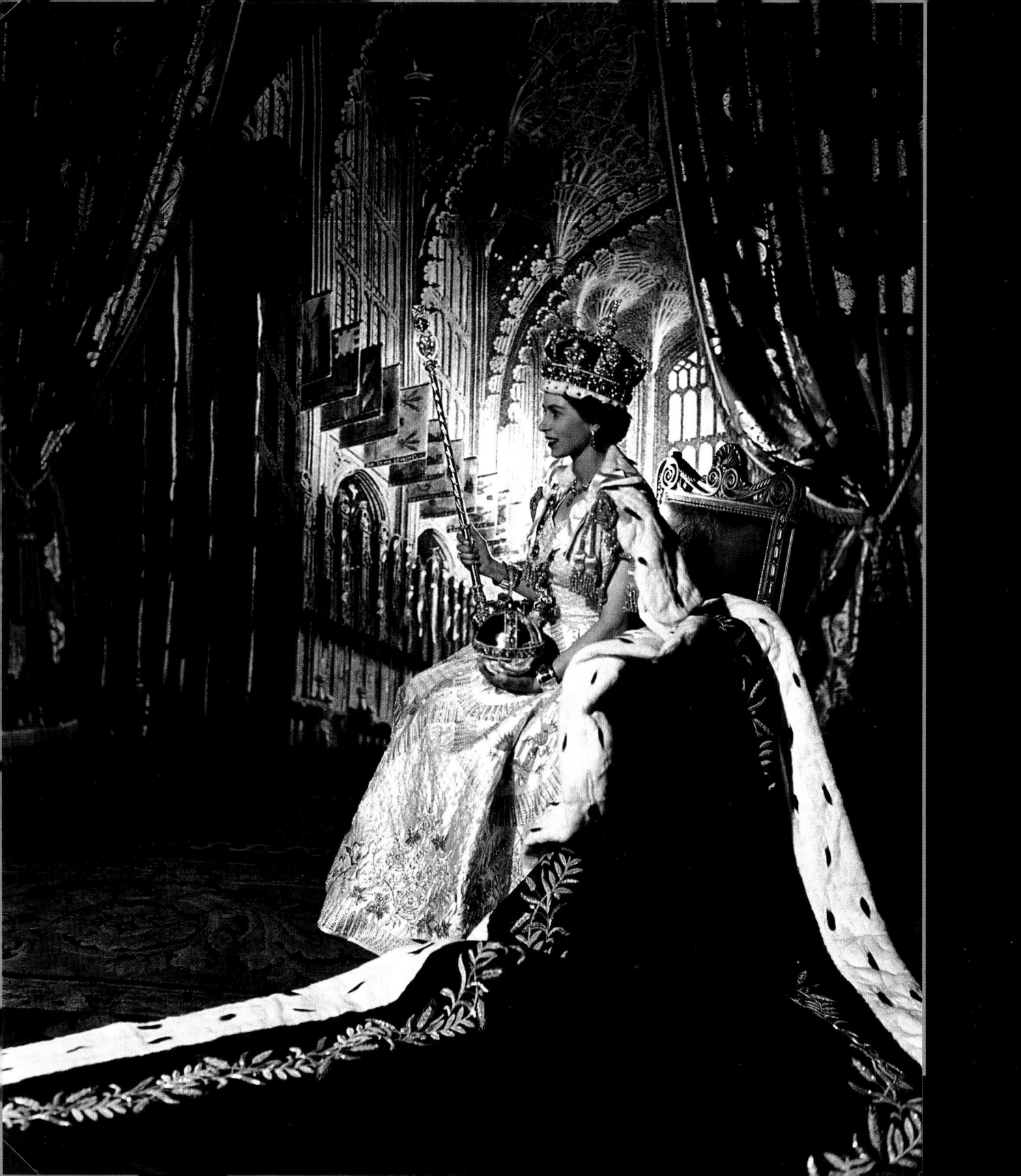

The Coronation of Elizabeth II

June 2, 1953 - London, United Kingdom

The young Queen is seated on the throne and looks toward the observer, dressed in the symbols of British royal power: the Crown of St Edward, the scepter, the globe, and the ermine robe, which is over sixteen feet long. In the background, one can see the Gothic vaulting and stained-glass windows of Westminster Abbey, in which the solemn ceremony of the coronation has just taken place. It is the most official of portraits: Cecil Beaton, who is also an extraordinary scenographer, takes the pose and the composition from pictures celebrating the great monarchs of the past. Yet we are in 1953, in modern times, and the decisive gaze of the twenty-seven-year-old who has ascended the throne is one that the world will come to know, over the sixty years of her reign, through the mass media.

Elizabeth II, in reality, had already become Queen of the United Kingdom, Canada, Australia, New Zealand, South Africa, Ceylon, and Pakistan in 1952, following the death of her father, George VI. The coronation took place only in the following year to observe the period of mourning for the previous monarch. The ceremony required more than 16 months of preparation, and the overall cost was 4 million dollars. According to rumors, Elizabeth had already spent days wearing the crown at home to get accustomed to its weight.

This was one of the first media events after the Second World War. For the first time, a ceremony of this kind was broadcast on live television, as ordered by the Queen herself. Elizabeth, in fact, chose to go against the opinion of Churchill and the government, who considered the presence of television cameras a risk for security. The ceremony was followed by millions of viewers, suggesting immediately how Elizabeth's reign would build a bridge between the ancient tradition of the monarchy and contemporary life.

Photograph by Cecil Beaton

Rosa Parks
and Civil Disobedience

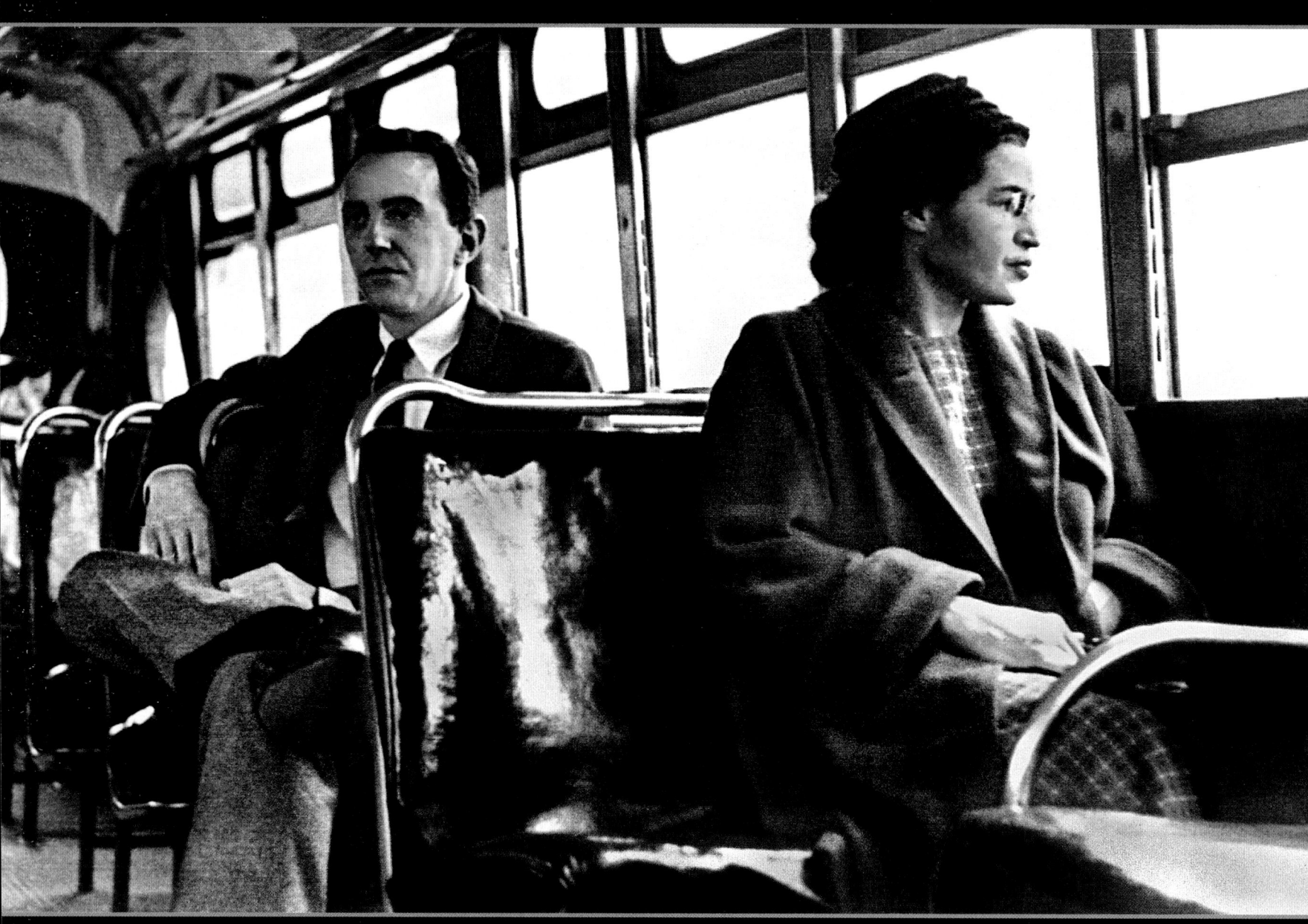

December 21, 1956 - Montgomery, Alabama, United States

Rosa Parks was coming back from a day's work like many others in a department store of Montgomery, Alabama, on the evening on December 1st, 1955. She was 42 years old and she was no more tired than usual. But she was tired of "surrendering," of enduring. She got on the bus for home and sat in the middle zone, between the seats reserved for whites and those reserved for blacks. During the journey, the bus filled up and some white passengers were left standing. So the driver ordered Rosa to give up her seat. She replied with a resolute and dignified "No," and was arrested.

It was not the first episode of the kind, but her case, a manifestation of an ever-more conscious mobilization for the rights of African Americans, produced a civil disobedience campaign that was to gain an historic victory. On December 5th, the black community of Montgomery organized a boycott of the buses, which went on for 381 days, until the Supreme Court of the United States declared segregation on public transport unconstitutional.

On December 21st, 1956, Rosa Parks was among the first African Americans to board a bus in the new era. The most famous photo of the day will always be this one: Rosa is seated in the first rows – the ones prohibited before – in front of a white man. The only people present look in opposite directions. They are near to each other, but belong to two different worlds. The image is constructed to celebrate the event; the subjects are posing, and Nicholas Chriss isn't a passenger, but a United Press International journalist. The photo doesn't lose its power and meaning for this reason, and more than showing successful integration, has become an icon of the protest of Rosa Parks, a woman who, simply by staying seated, stood up to defend the rights of blacks and was elected the "Mother of the Civil Rights Movement."

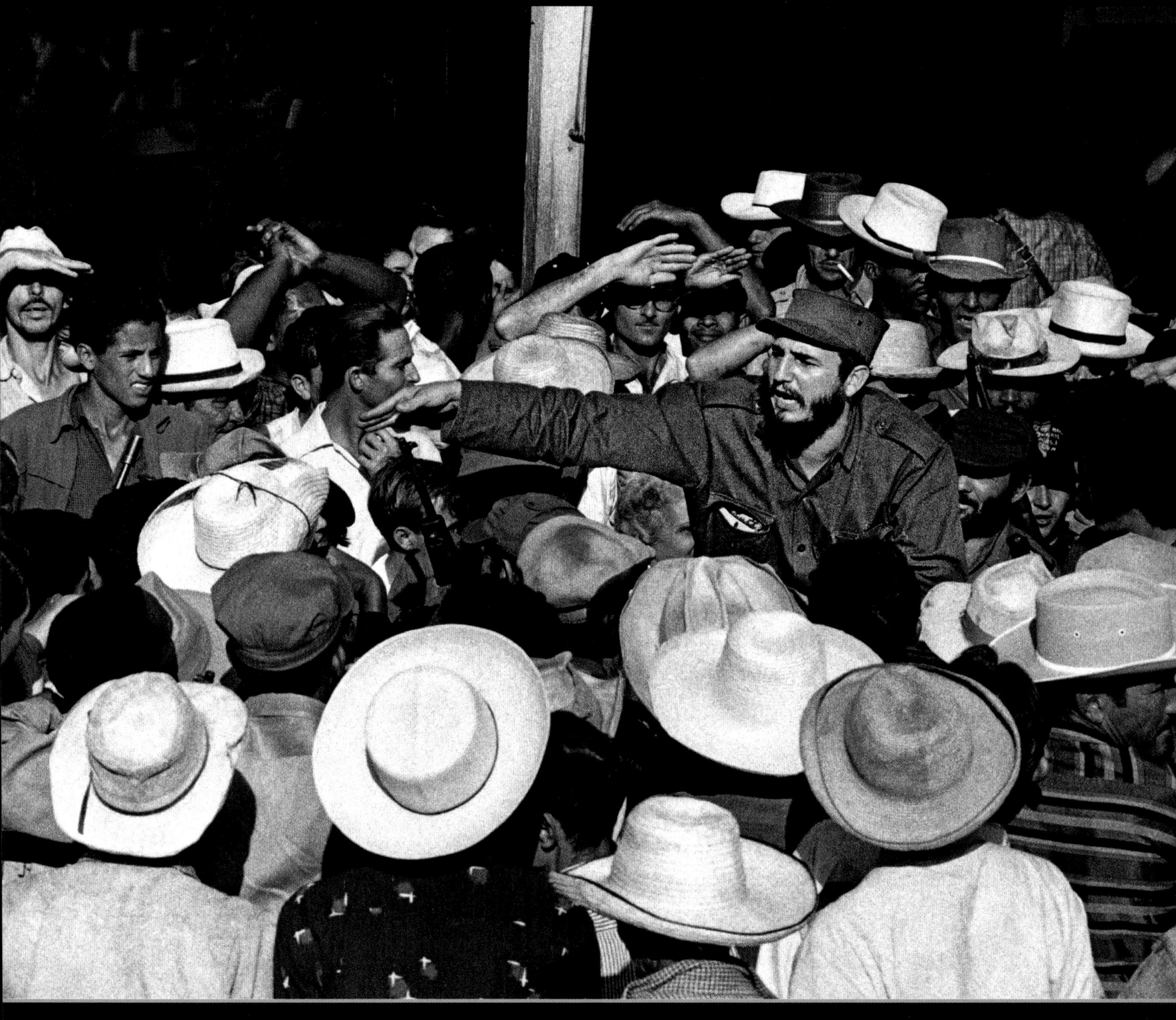

Photograph by Burt Glinn

Fidel Castro Entering Havana

January 8, 1959 - Havana, Cuba

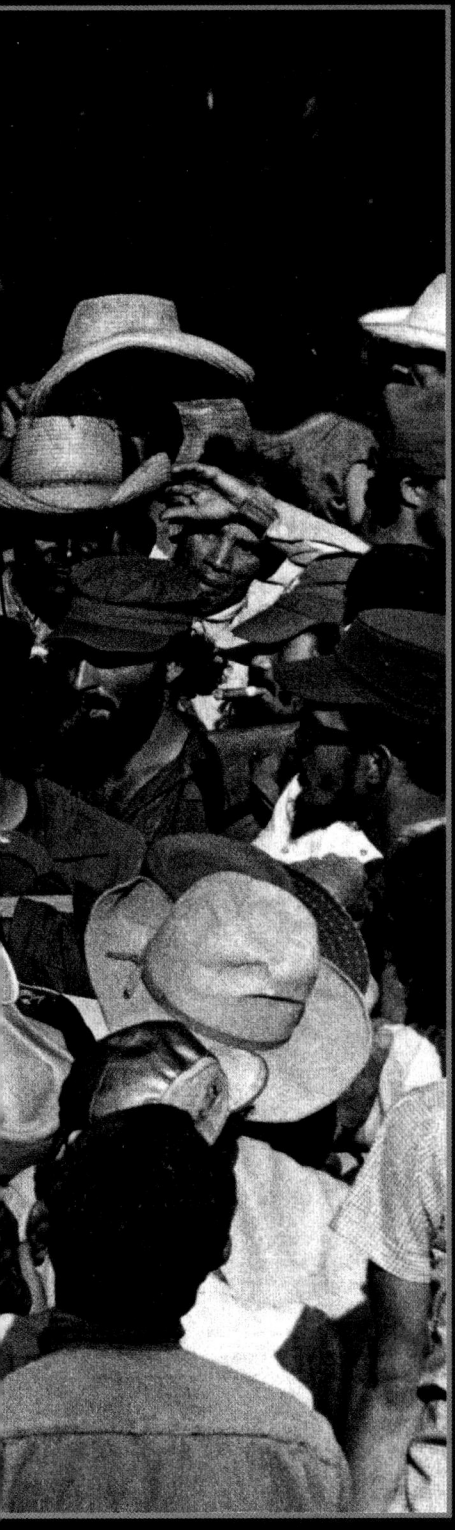

At the end of the fifties, post-war enthusiasm had given way to the Cold War between the United States and the Soviet Union. Early in 1959, Fidel Castro and his Movimiento 26 de Julio, which was clearly socialist, took power in Cuba.

On January 8th, 1959, Fidel Castro arrived in Havana where he and his guerillas were greeted by an enthusiastic crowd. News programs all over the world had been covering their feats for two years: Castro and his men were simply called the *barbudos*, "the bearded ones." Castro came from Santiago, in the east of the island, where the guerilla war began and developed. He was preceded by Che Guevara and Camilo Cienfuegos, who entered Havana on January 2nd and had already taken control of the capital.

On the night of New Year's Eve, the dictator Fulgencio Batista had fled by plane to Santo Domingo. By dawn, armed groups of students had occupied radio and television stations and institutions; the army didn't interfere. In short, the revolution began on January 1st, like an improbable screenplay.

In fact, after a long period of repression, corruption, and complicity with American economic lobbies and with the Cosa Nostra, the victorious revolt of the *barbudos* received great support from the people, from the poor but also from the middle-class. Castro's charisma, who in the photograph is surrounded by *campesinos* and workers, did the rest.

In those years, Burt Glinn, a great photojournalist from Magnum Photos, covered the Cuban Revolution. His relations with the *barbudos* allowed him to stay in the capital, even after Batista's flight, as the correspondent for American news magazines. He did an extraordinary job in terms of quality and historic importance, and his work earned him the Photographer of the Year award in 1959.

March, 1959 - Lhasa, Tibet, People's Republic of China

In the background, the sky and mountains of Tibet stand out. Beneath the sky rise the imposing white staircases and walls of the Potala Palace, the official residence of the Dalai Lama in Lhasa, an extraordinary complex built on a rock at an altitude of well over 11,000 feet. In the foreground, a long procession of men in traditional Tibetan dress line up behind a flag. Their dark clothes contrast with the plaster of the Palace and the snowy mountains. They are abandoning the palace forever.

The photo, by a journalist from the German agency Ullstein Bild, documents the surrender of Tibetan rebels after a short and bloody uprising that began on March 10th, 1959. The Tibetans hoped to free themselves from Chinese occupation. Since 1950, China had gradually invaded the country, imposing communism, the Chinese language and customs on Tibetans, and persecuting Buddhist monks all over the country.

The revolt was ruthlessly repressed: Tibetan estimates document about 80,000 victims. On March 17th, the fourteenth Dalai Lama, the supreme spiritual authority of the country, was forced to abandon the capital on foot to seek exile in India. He was followed by thousands of refugees.

The Tibetan diaspora continued in the following years, as China colonized the country. This failed revolt marks the end of Tibetan independence, and in many ways the extinction of an ancient civilization. Today, the Potala Palace, which was declared a UNESCO Heritage Site in 1994, is a tourist attraction, while the Dalai Lama and the Central Tibetan Administration (better known as the Tibetan government in exile) continue to take refuge in India.

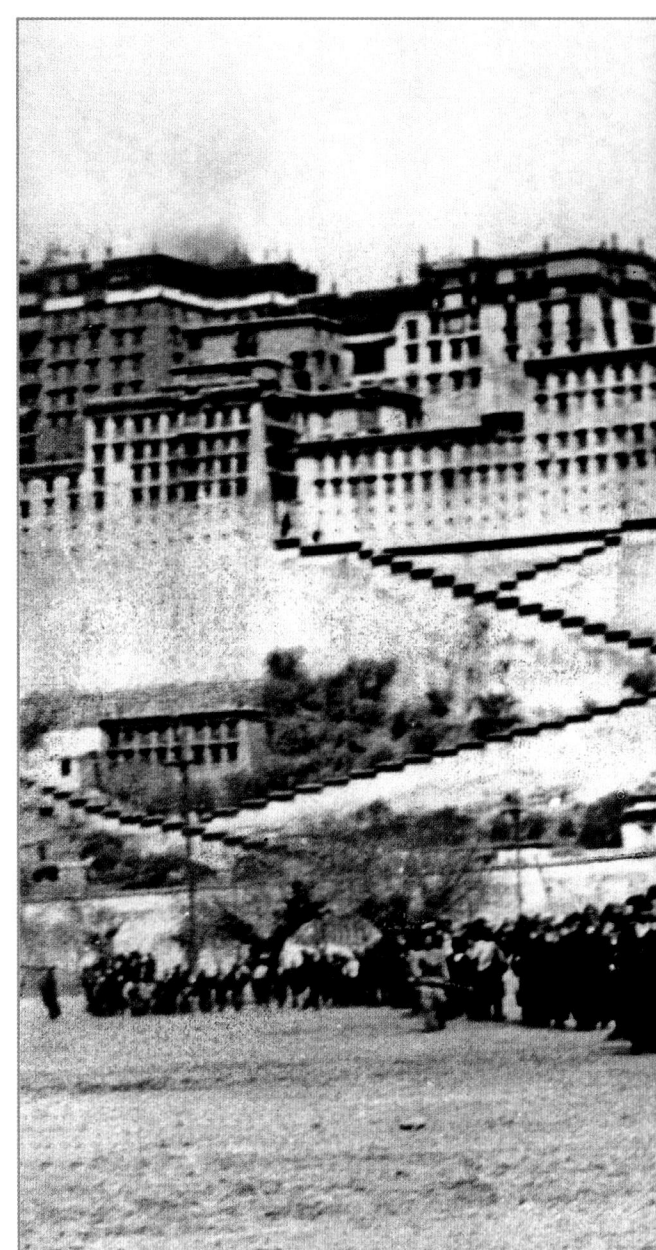

Tibetan Rebels Surrender to Chinese Troops

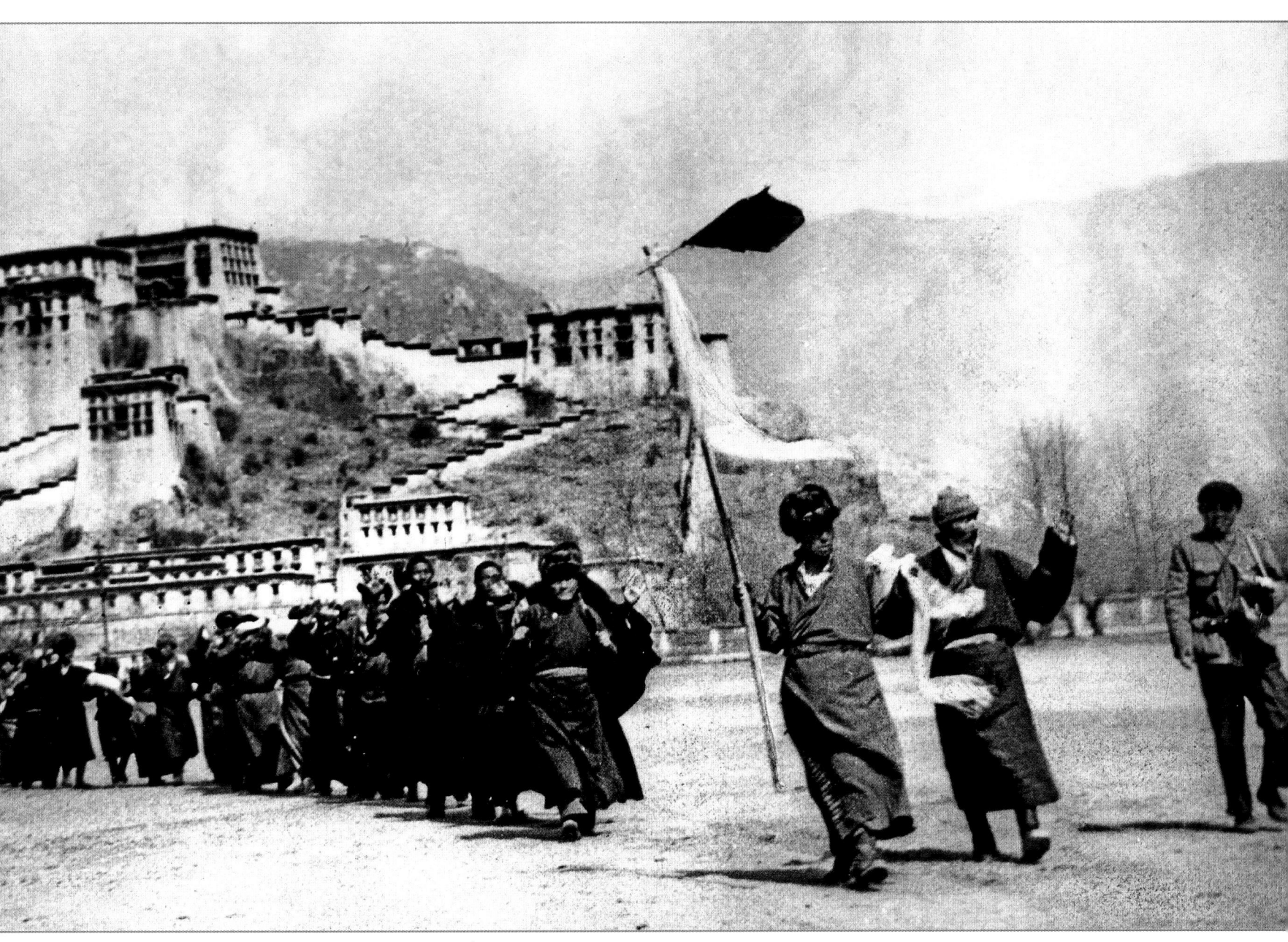

The First Man in Space

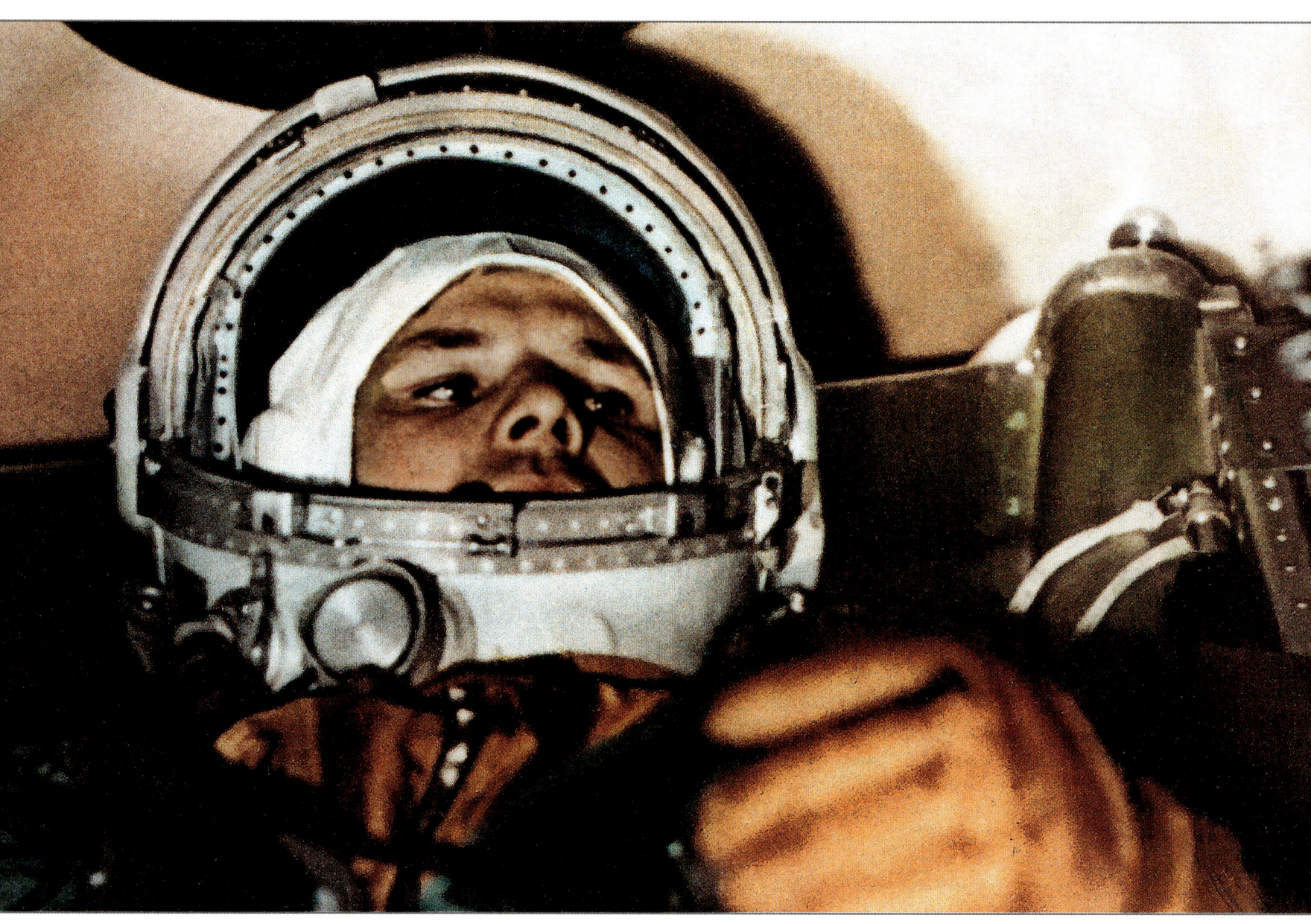

April 12, 1961 - Baikonur, Soviet Union

Minced meat, blackberry jam and, inevitably, coffee: not at all an astronaut's breakfast. Dawn, April 12th, 1961. It was still dark at the Baikonur Cosmodrome, a space base in Kazakhstan, which at the time was part of the Soviet Union.

This photo was taken a few hours later, inside Vostok 1, a thirteen-foot-tall metal box containing the cockpit, no bigger than an economy car, where the astronaut sat. The astronaut was Yuri Gagarin, who at 10:55 that morning would become the first man to return and walk on Earth after a trip to the end of the atmosphere. As he made his way toward the spaceship, he marked his progress with propitiatory gestures, like drinking a glass of champagne before leaving the accommodation on the base, signing the door of the room where he slept the previous night, and peeing behind the bus that took him to the launching pad. All the Russian astronauts after him without exception would repeat the same ritual. Gagarin must have forgotten something, however, on the day he died seven years later. He crashed in a fighter plane somewhere in the immense territory of Russia.

On his face, half hidden by his helmet, we see a look we can interpret in many ways: worried, concentrating, serious, thoughtful, attentive. Gagarin was 27 years old and, with an open face, there is something instinctively likeable about the expression: he never stopped smiling up to that moment. But that was *the* moment: shortly, he would close the outer hatch of the spaceship and switch on the rockets. And at last, at 9:07, he murmured into the radio: "We're off!" Then he began to smile again, because after *that* no second thoughts could separate him from his destiny, whatever it might be.

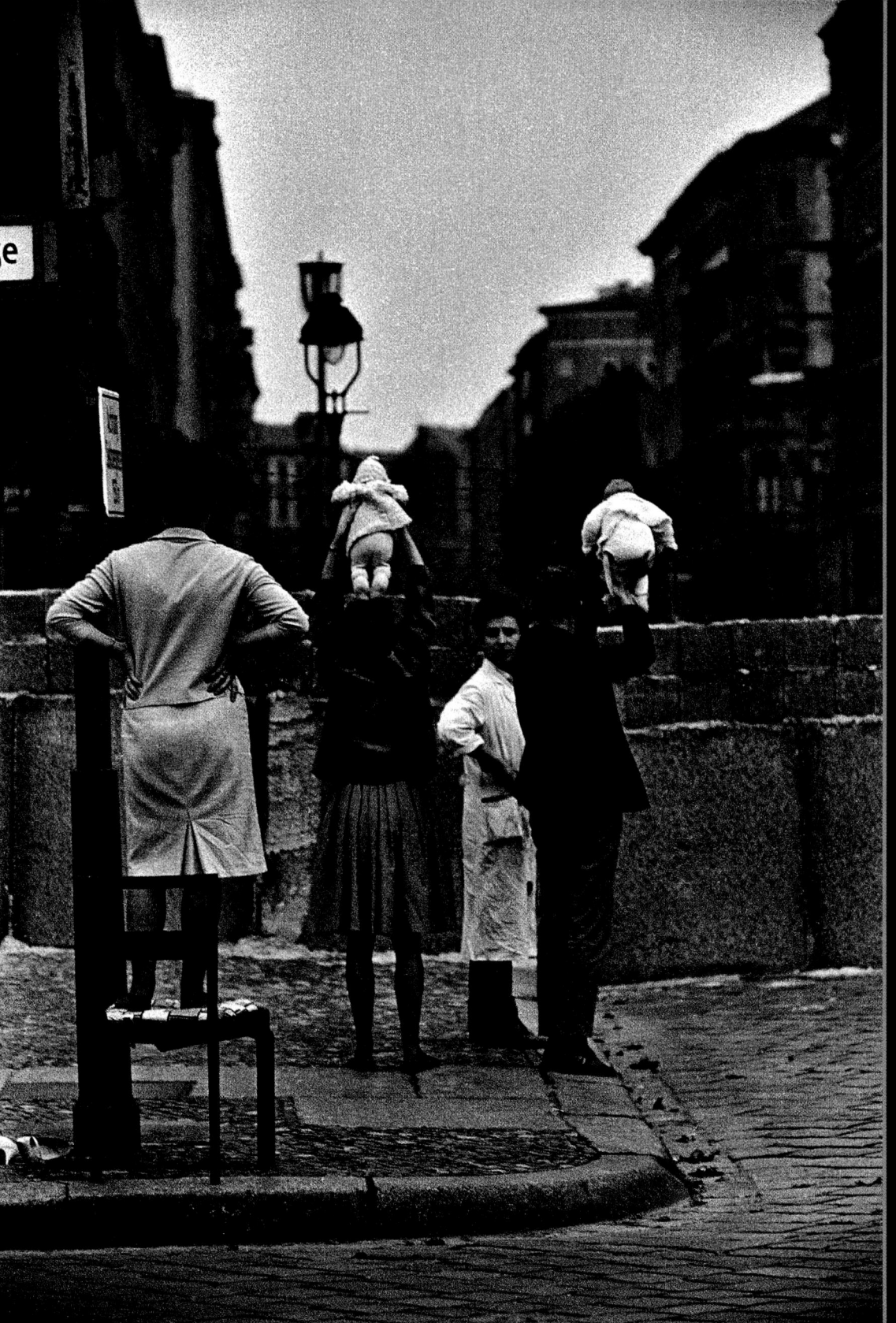

The Berlin Wall

September, 1961 - Berlin, Federal Republic of Germany

A family gathers in front of the Berlin Wall and lifts two little children above the barbed wire, to let their grandparents on the other side see them. Only a few days before, on August 13th, 1961, the people of Germany had woken up aghast to see the GDR army beginning to build a wall that would divide Berlin in two. We are on the western side, but this is not important: we can imagine a mirror image of the scene from the other side. Like this one, the wall separated thousands of families, forced them to be content with little gestures to preserve bonds threatened by international interests.

What was to be, according to the East German definition, an "Anti-Fascist Protection Wall," in reality worked to stop a massive flight of Germans to the Western Sector. It consisted of more than 96 miles of concrete, which the following year were reinforced in some sections by a second wall parallel to the first. Between them ran the "death strip," a corridor about 30 feet wide that was a no man's land fenced off with electrified barriers. It was scattered with land mines and watched over by guards authorized to shoot on sight. Despite the wall, many risked their lives to cross the border, inventing the most imaginative stratagems, from tunnels to hot-air balloons. There were about 5,000 successful escape attempts, but some hundreds of people died in the attempt: the youngest was only 18 years old.

The original print of this photograph, from 1961, is exhibited in the Ronald Reagan Presidential Library. Together with the Soviet leader, Mikhail Gorbachev, Reagan helped establish détente between the East and West, which led to the fall of the Berlin Wall in 1989 and to the end of the Cold War.

The Sacrifice of Thich Quang Duc

June 11, 1963 - Saigon, South Vietnam

"Before closing my eyes and moving towards the vision of the Buddha, I respectfully plead with President Ngo Dinh Diem to be compassionate towards the people of the nation, and to implement religious equality to maintain the strength of the homeland eternally."

The Buddhist monk, Thich Quang Duc, left this political testament on June 11th, 1963, moments before gasoline was poured over him and he set himself on fire as a sign of protest. Even if Buddhism expressly prohibits suicide, his immolation was not considered a sin, and after his death, his body was cremated again. The monk's heart, which remained intact among the ashes, was interpreted as confirmation of the purity of his gesture.

Beginning in 1955, the regime of Ngo Dinh Diem imposed the practice of Catholicism on the Vietnamese population, which was mainly Buddhist. Holy places were destroyed and many people lost their lives. The West displayed an obtuse blindness to conditions in Diem's catholic dictatorship, which was an exception in the heart of a Communist empire.

When on that day the procession of demonstrators stopped near the Cambodian Embassy, Malcom Browne, the American Associated Press correspondent in Saigon, guessed that something would mark this day in history. In the center of the road, Thich Quang Duc assumed the lotus position, began to meditate, and set fire to himself. In a series of photos, Browne's camera recorded one of the strongest and most shocking acts of protest in history.

The images shook the world: the veil of silence due to shortsighted political reasons of state was lifted. A few days later, John F. Kennedy withdrew American support from Diem and, on November 2nd, 1963, the dictator was overthrown and killed. In the same year, one of the photos won the World Press Photo of the Year award and in the following year Browne was honored with a Pulitzer. It is not surprising that the official media in communist countries passed the protest gesture off as an episode in the ongoing struggle against American imperialism. In a way, this, too, was unwittingly true.

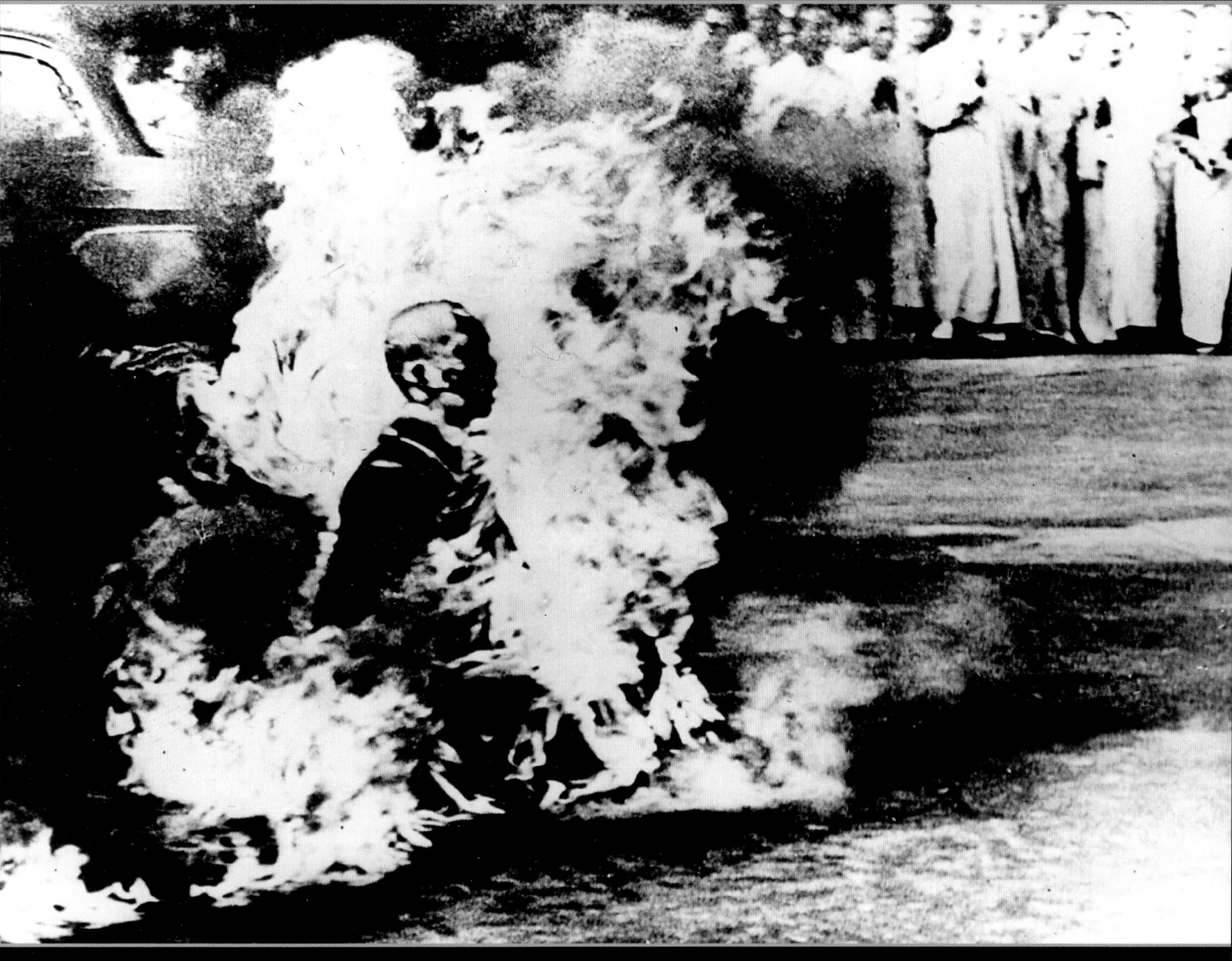

Photograph by Malcolm Browne

I Have a Dream

August 28, 1963 - Washington D.C., United States

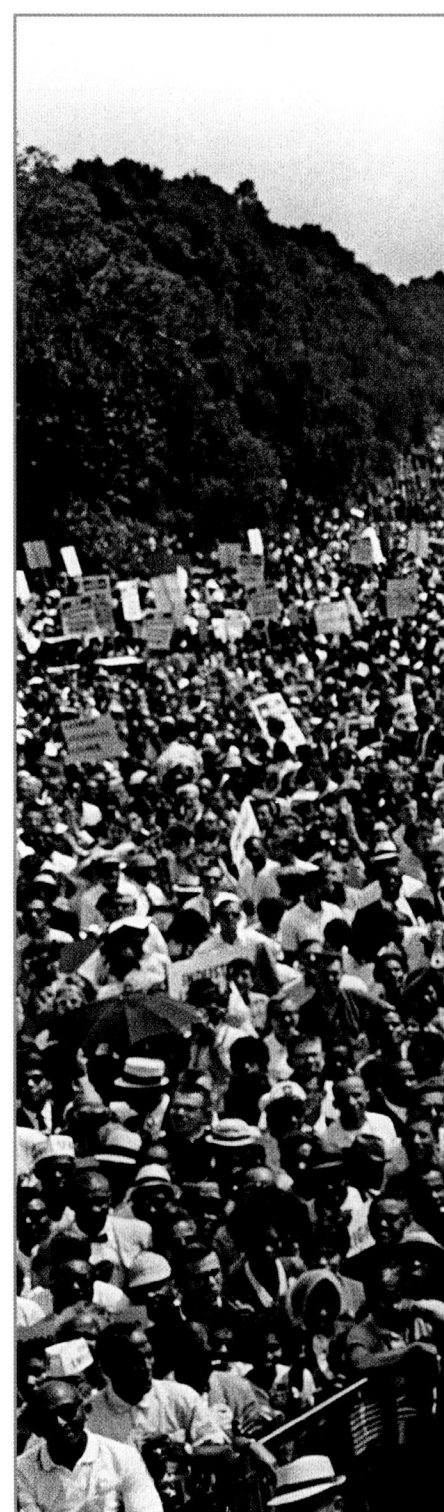

A few hours before, the Reverend Martin Luther King, a Protestant pastor from Alabama, didn't know exactly what he was going to say. The protest march on Washington promised to be one of the greatest demonstrations of the civil rights movement: on this day, August 28th, 1963, 250,000 people gathered in front of the Lincoln Memorial, and even President John F. Kennedy followed the event on television. The novelty was the massive presence of white Americans: only one fifth of those demonstrating against the racial segregation laws were African Americans. Thus, when Reverend King began to speak, he began to read a speech written quickly during the night before. His first words: "I am happy to join with you today in what will go down in history as the greatest demonstration for freedom in the history of our nation." The words immediately touched the hearts of the audience and of the speaker himself, who soon abandoned his notes. The result was possibly the most moving and quoted speech in the history of rhetoric. It was such a powerful speech that it opened the way to the approval, in July of 1964, of the Civil Rights Act, which marked the end of segregation, and won Reverend King the Nobel Peace Prize.

The speech takes its title, *I Have a Dream*, from the phrase, which is repeated nine times, with Biblical emphasis and cadence, in the concluding part: "I have a dream that my four little children will one day live in a nation where they will not be judged by the color of their skin but by the content of their character." In spite of the success of the demonstration and the new federal laws, King's dream remained only a dream for many years: Kennedy was assassinated a few months later, the climate of racial hatred would intensify for some time in the Southern States, and King himself would be assassinated in 1968.

The image of Martin Luther King in front of a vast crowd, with the scenographic background of the Washington Monument, remains, however, a moment of light and glory in the history of the United States. We still seem to hear in the image King's prophetic words: "Let freedom ring, let freedom ring, let freedom ring . . ."

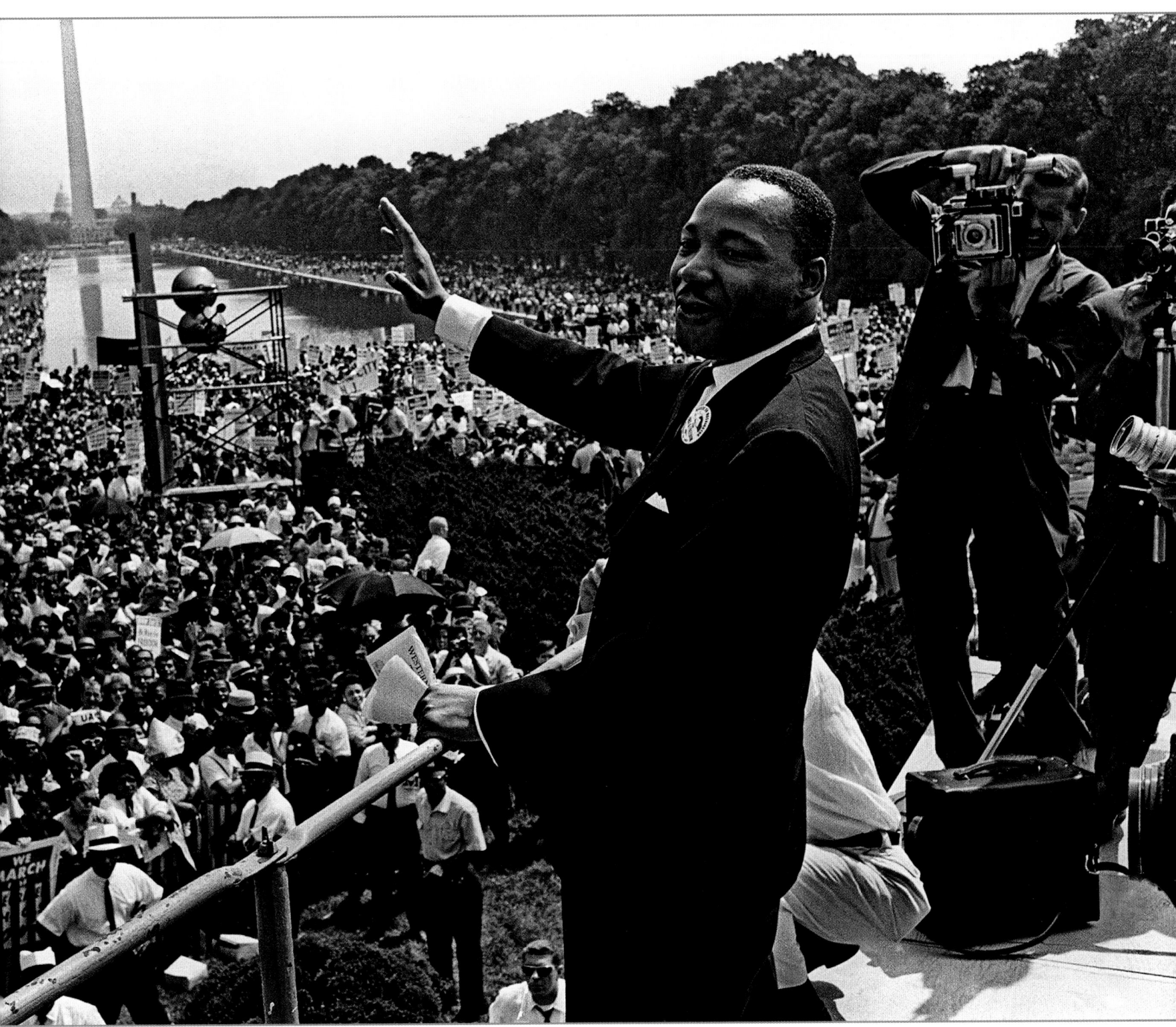

John F. Kennedy's Funeral

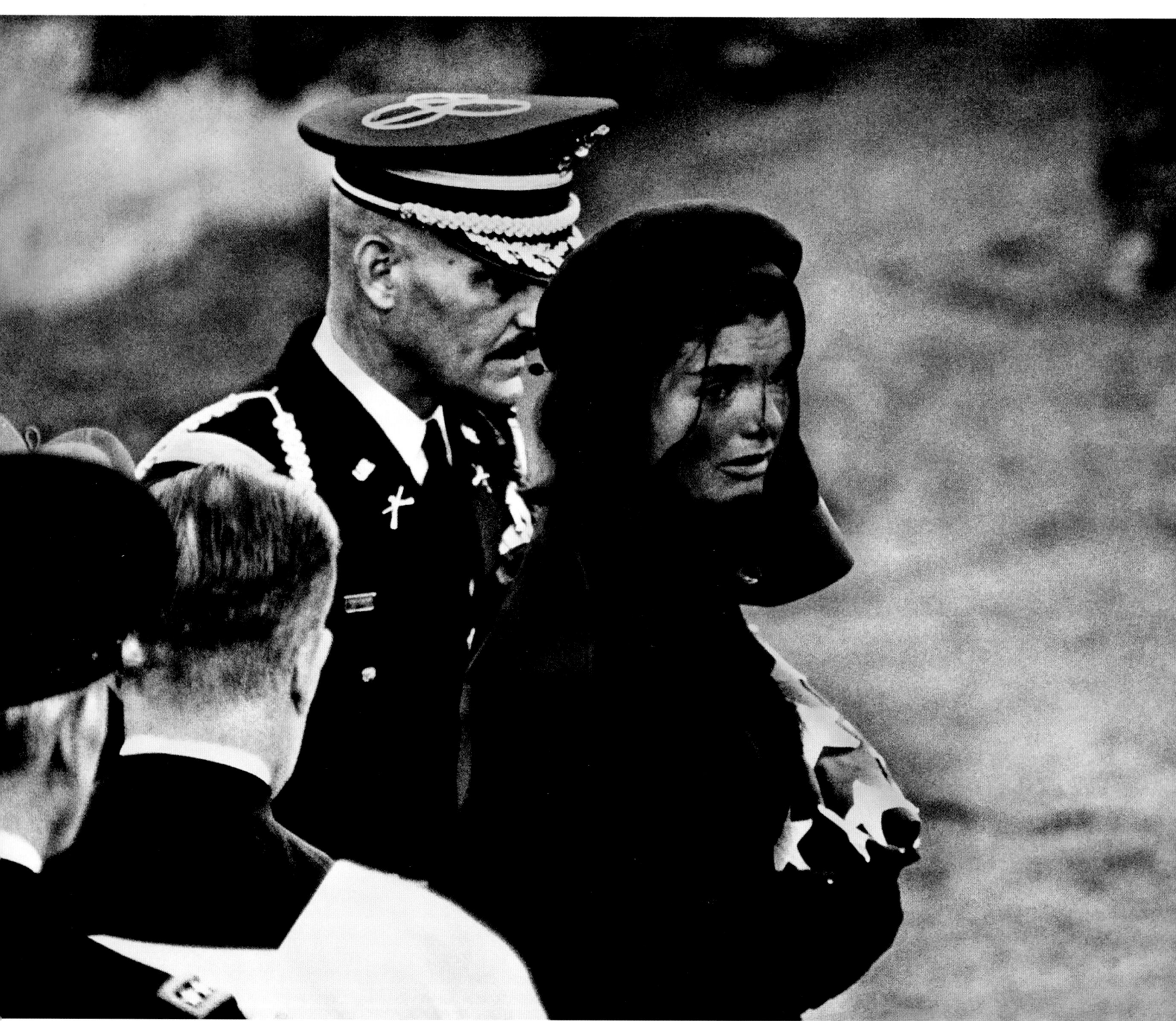

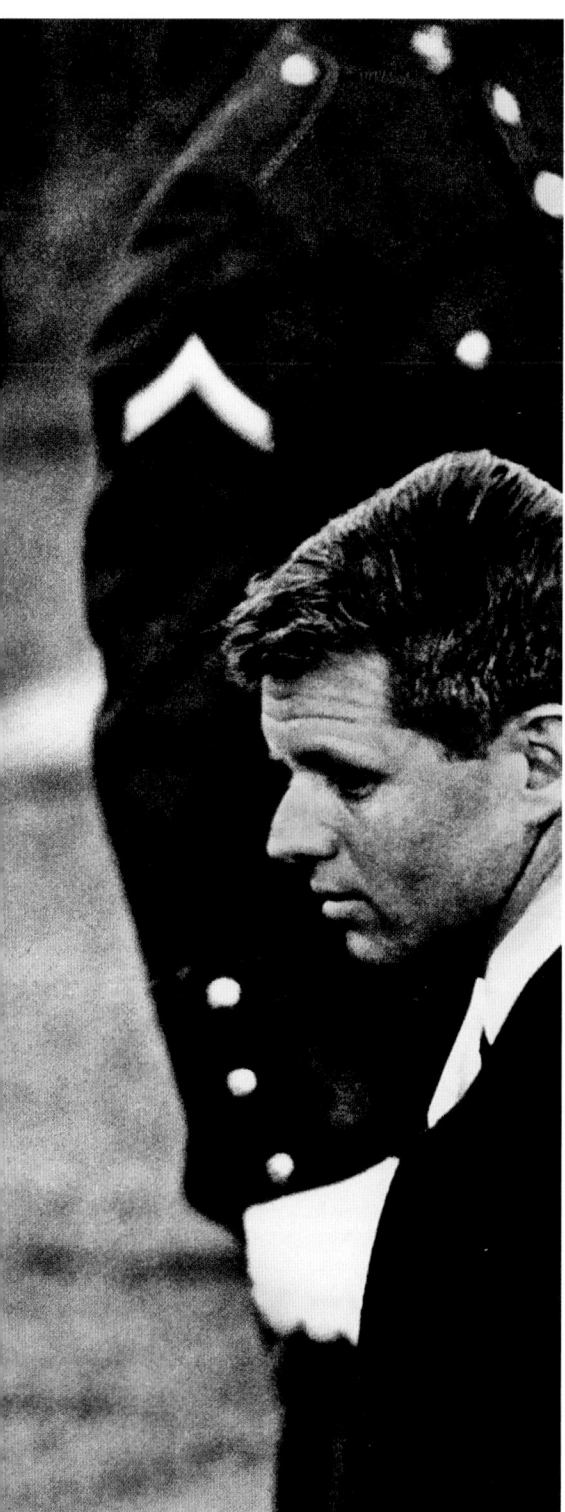

November 25, 1963 - Arlington, Virginia, United States

John F. Kennedy is dead. He was assassinated in Dallas on November 22nd, 1963. The United States is numb. Hundreds of thousands of Americans take part in the funeral on the 25th, in Washington, together with heads of state and delegations from many countries in the world. Those who have not been able to reach the capital follow the event on television.

The bewilderment and grief-struck face of his widow, Jacqueline, at the Arlington National Cemetery mirrors the feelings of an entire nation. Photographer Elliott Erwitt immortalizes the moment. Born Elio Romano Erwitz in Paris, Erwitt grew up in Italy, and took refuge in the United States in his teens to escape Mussolini's Anti-Semitic laws. He was inspired by Henri Cartier-Bresson and, like Cartier-Bresson, his work captures the moment in rigorous black and white.

This photograph becomes an icon, like the lovely Jacqueline and JFK himself, who were already icons. Kennedy was one of the most charismatic figures of the last century: he became president in 1960 at only 43 years old. He was a brilliant orator, inspired by progressive ideals, but he remained in power for only three years. Serious international crises made these years difficult: the Bay of Pigs landing, the Cuban missile crisis, and the first signs of the Vietnam conflict. Yet he succeeded in making the whole world dream, personifying hope in a more just future. His assassination is still controversial: it remains unclear if the man who fired, Lee Harvey Oswald, really acted alone.

Standing beside Jacqueline at the funeral is John's brother, Robert. He supports her, and strives to reassure her. He seems like a boy: he isn't even 40 years old, and he is already Attorney General of the United States. He will try to take up the political and moral legacy of his brother, but he too, in five years, will be assassinated.

Photograph by Elliott Erwitt

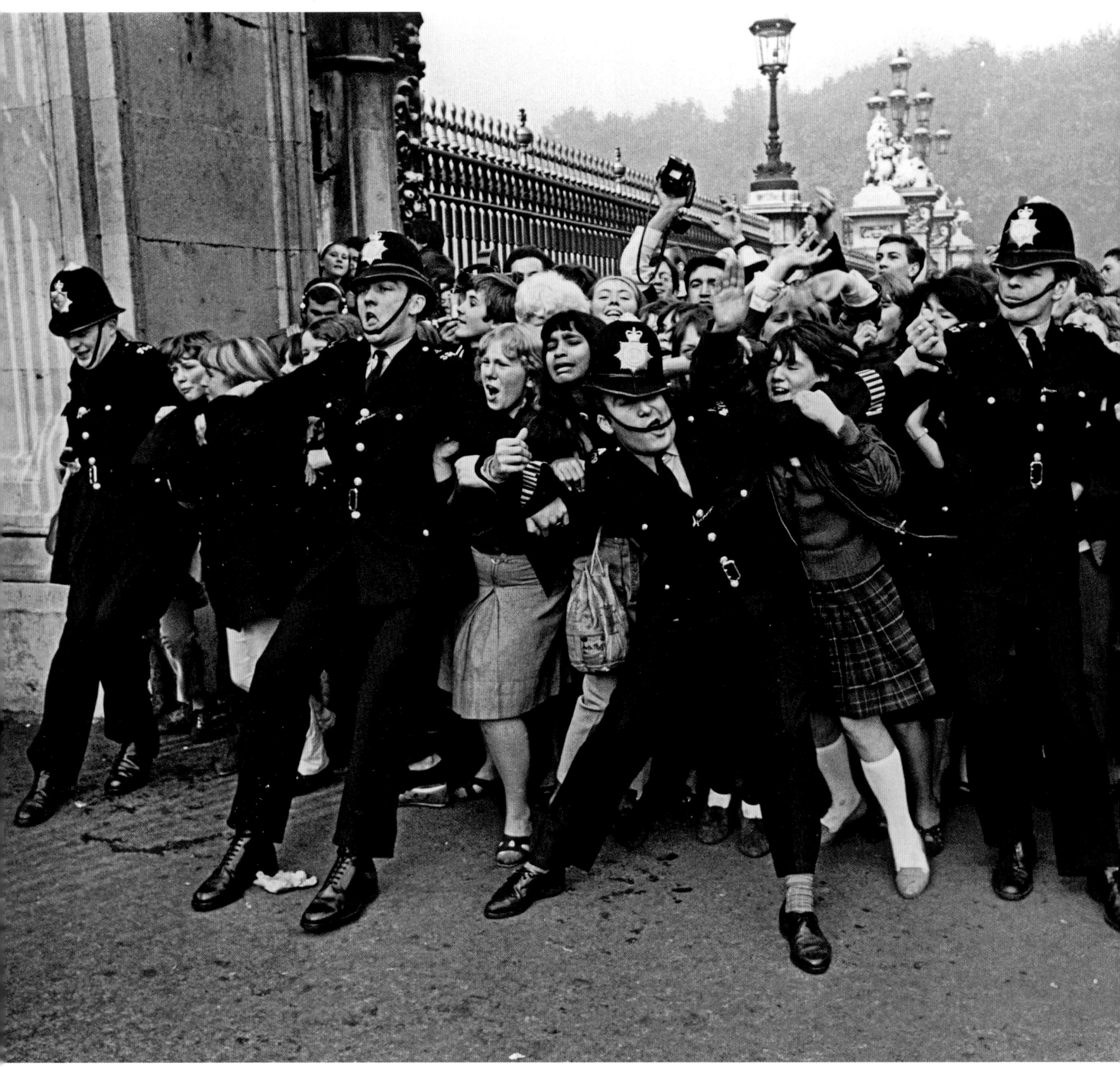

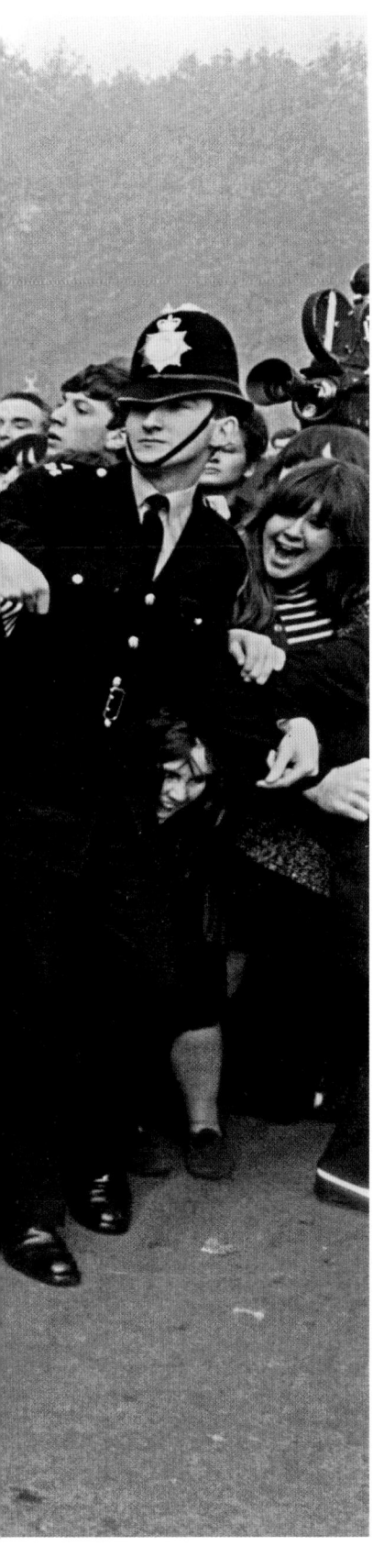

The Beatles at Buckingham Palace

October 26, 1965 - London, United Kingdom

In the spring of 1965, four envelopes from Downing Street mingled with the letters the Beatles received daily from fans. The Fab Four were thus taken by surprise when in May their manager Brian Epstein informed them that the Prime Minister and the Queen had decided to honor them with the Member of the Most Excellent Order of the British Empire (MBE) awards. None of the four knew of the existence of such an honor, a medal usually awarded for service to society. They received the news with amazement and amusement. There were contrasting reactions from the British people: most were in favor, but some were decidedly resentful, so much so that some holders of the honor returned the medal. "Lots of people who complained about us getting the MBE received theirs [...] for killing people," Lennon said. "We got ours for entertaining. I'd say we deserve ours more."

The ceremony was held on October 26th at Buckingham Palace. The Queen personally awarded the medal to each of the extremely nervous "beetles," who had received precise instructions on court etiquette. With 189 other nominees, they waited their turn patiently, signing autographs. Outside the Palace, an excited crowd of 4,000 fans had gathered.

In this shot, the photographer has caught a moment of great enthusiasm and tension: the teenage fans are going crazy, screaming, and trying to break through the precarious barrier formed by the arms of the police, who have comically distraught faces. The gates of the Palace have just opened to let in John Lennon's Rolls-Royce with the four Beatles. Moments later, the gates will close. The fans, left free, will press against the railings and grasp the bars. One girl will climb to the top of the gate, risking hurting herself on its sharp points. A policeman, in turn, will have to climb up to get her to come down.

Vietnam. October, 1966. In a perfect shot, the British photographer Larry Burrows transforms a scene from hell into a solemn painting full of emotions and humanity. The land torn apart by bombing is a hill just south of the so-called "demilitarized zone," a place where human lives are destroyed, and bodies mix with the water and the earth. The trees stripped of foliage frame the lost expressions of the young American soldiers, boys suffering under a leaden sky.

Reaching Out is the title of the photograph: outstretched arms reach for a comrade, support, the way back, but also to help a friend. The soldier wounded in the face, reaching out, is Sergeant Jeremiah Purdie: he wants to be close to a fellow soldier, a man wounded much more seriously than he is, in a gesture of instinctive solidarity.

LIFE magazine did not publish the photo immediately, perhaps because color, which at the time was rarely used in reportage, made Burrows' shot too realistic. His work showed the world a drama that the Government in Washington would refute in various ways, relegating such stories to the gray of partial information. Burrows, instead, chose to relate the brutality, the violence: he lets us become part of the action, lets us smell the blood. Yet even in the chaos of war, his best photos maintain an internal discipline: the shot is studied and becomes a picture, perhaps through an extreme form of respect for pain and death, which only art can in some way redeem.

Burrows himself will lose his life during the war, in an accident in 1971. Shortly before his death, Burrows said that "the war was his story, and he would see it through. His dream was to stay until he could photograph a Vietnam at peace." They are more the words of a man than those of a reporter.

Photograph by Larry Burrows

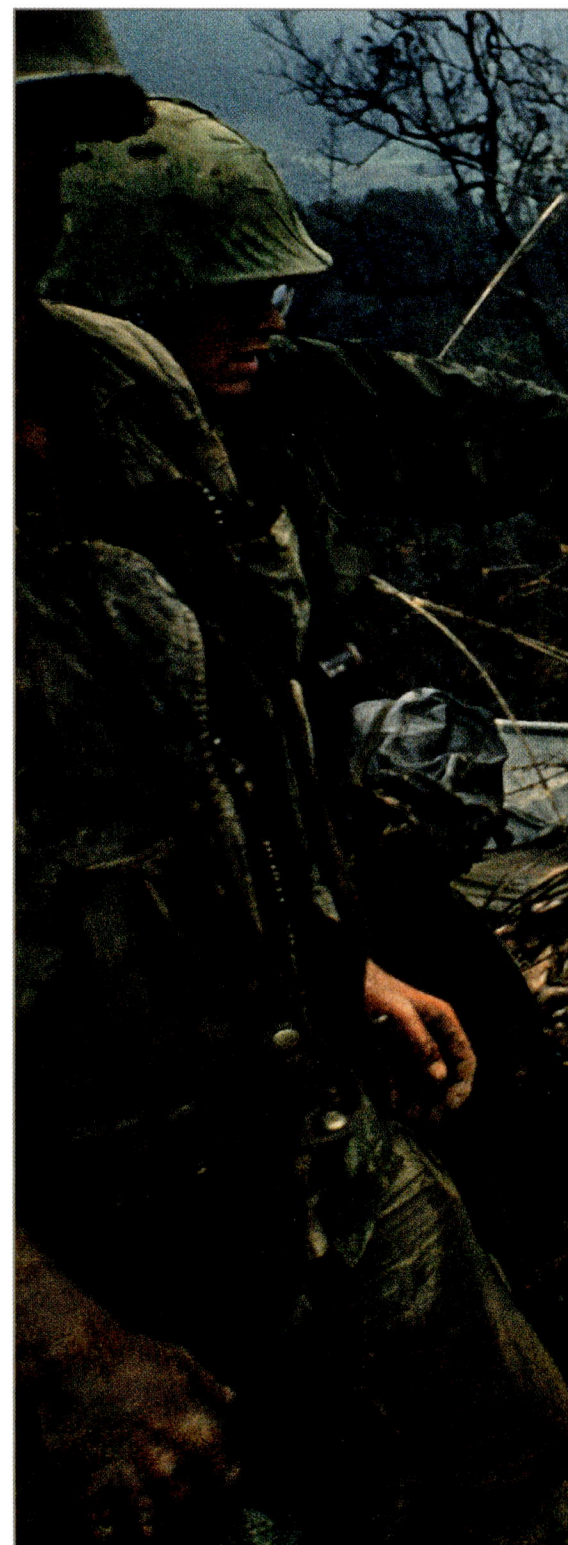

Reaching Out

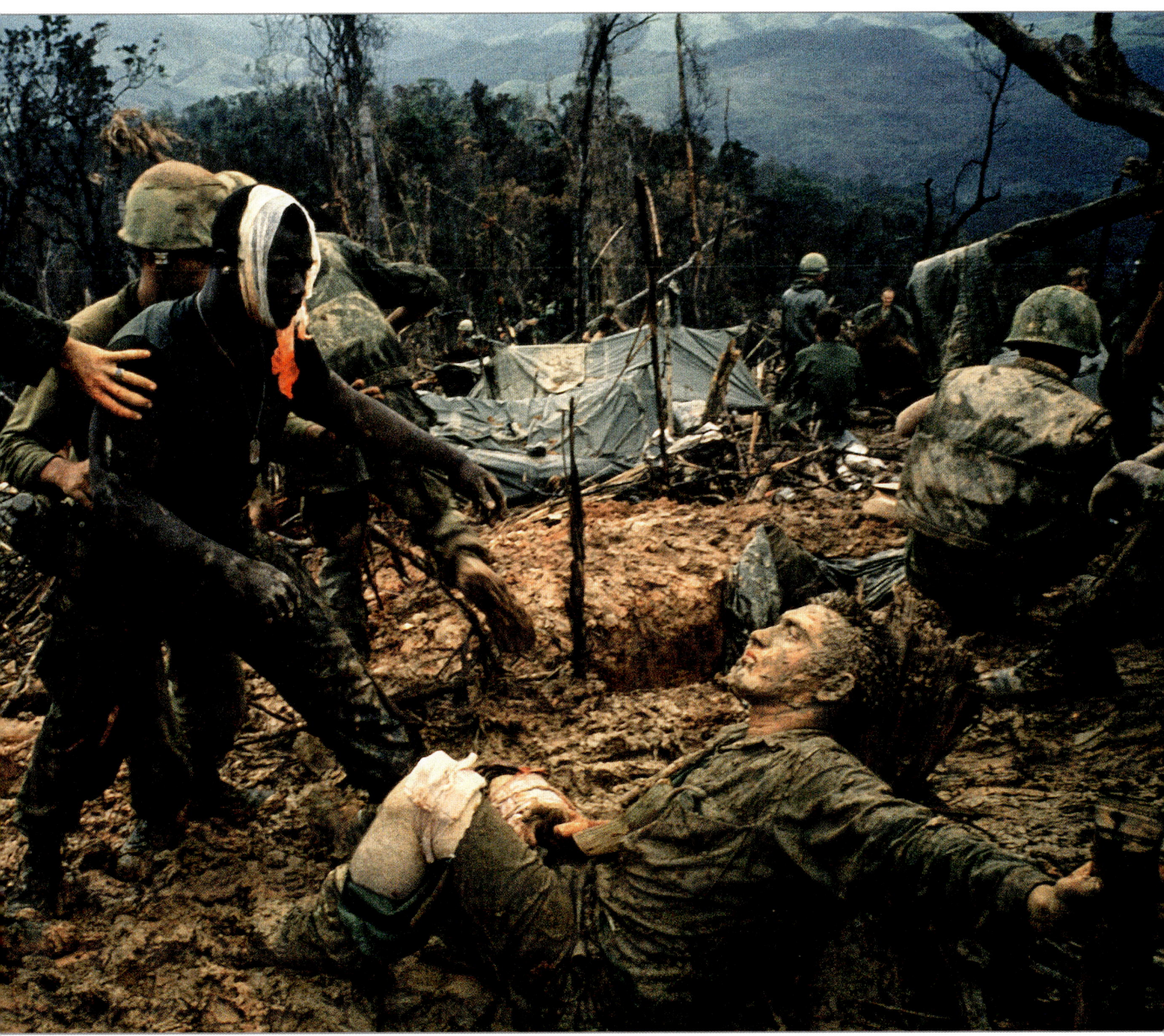

Six Day War

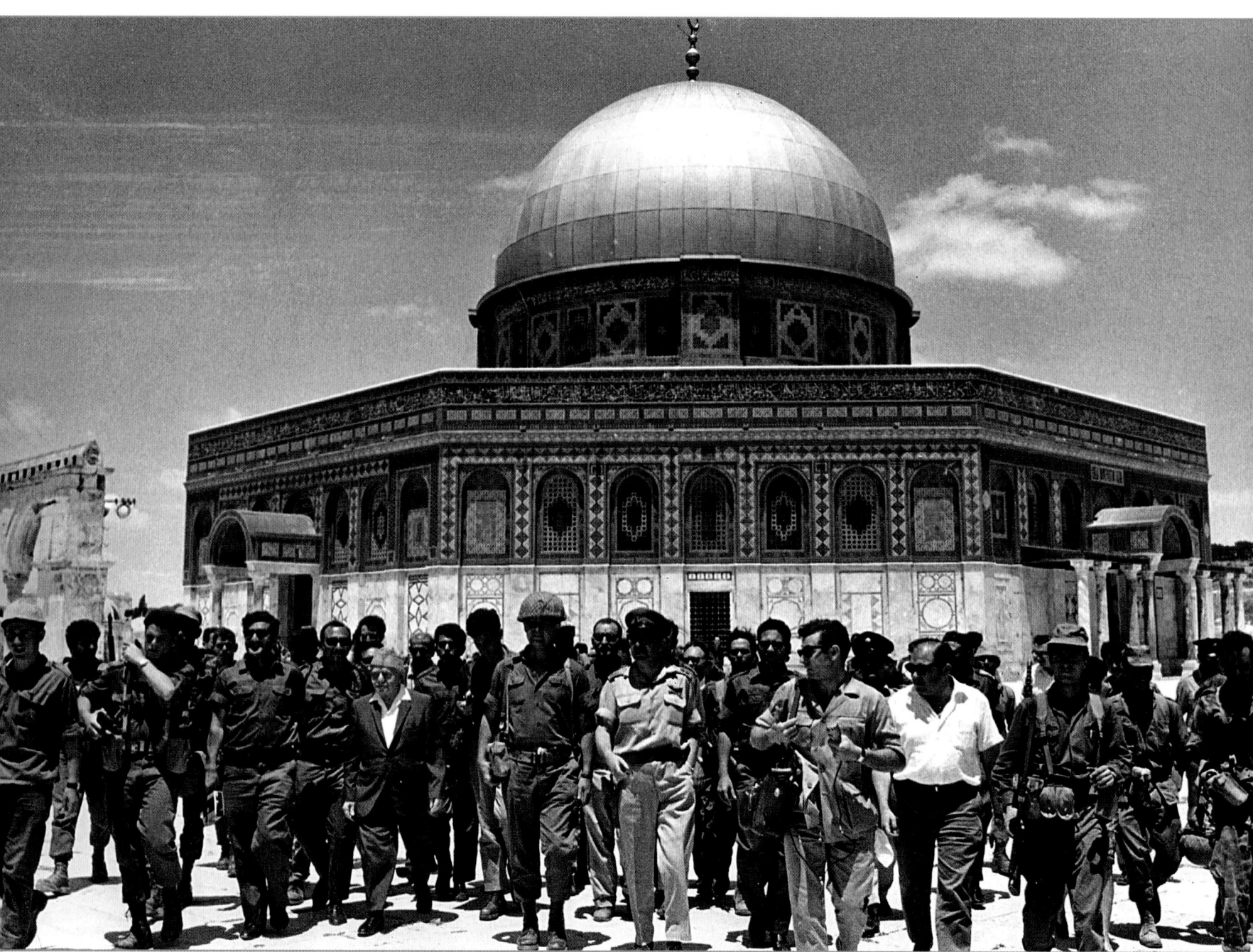

June 5-10, 1967 - Jerusalem, Israel

Between June 5th and June 10th, 1967, the frontiers of the Middle East were revolutionized by a short and cruel conflict, which led to a fourfold increase in Israeli territory. The Six Day War, of which this is one of the most significant images, broke out for various reasons. Historians remember the most contingent of them such as the threat by the Arab countries to divert the course of the Jordan, thus depriving the Israelis of their water supply; and the closing of the Straits of Tiran by Egypt, which isolated Israel's south. However, in the background of the conflict was the Cold War and the confrontation between the Soviet Union and the United States: the former supported the Syrians and the Egyptians, led by Nasser, while the latter were the international guarantors of Israel.

The conflict resulted in triumph for the Israelis. After destroying the air forces of their enemies with rapid and effective air raids, they occupied the West Bank, the Gaza Strip, the Golan Heights, and the Sinai Peninsula as far as the Suez Canal. But above all, they occupied West Jerusalem: on June 7th they took possession of the Temple Mount, known as the Esplanade of the Mosques to Muslims, and the Wailing Wall, a conquest worth more, symbolically and religiously, than any other.

The Dome of the Rock, one of Islam's holiest sites, rises emblematically in the background of this photograph. In the foreground, on the other side of an area that has just fallen to Israeli hands, Israel's founding father David Ben-Gurion and Chief of Staff Yitzhak Rabin advance confidently, accompanied by a group of soldiers. The prevalence of uniforms over civilian clothes is indicative of the situation: thanks to its army, Israel managed to significantly increase its geographical size in a veritable blitzkrieg. And the high-ranking officers who played a leading role in that undertaking, from Rabin himself to Ariel Sharon, would soon find themselves at the center of the country's political life.

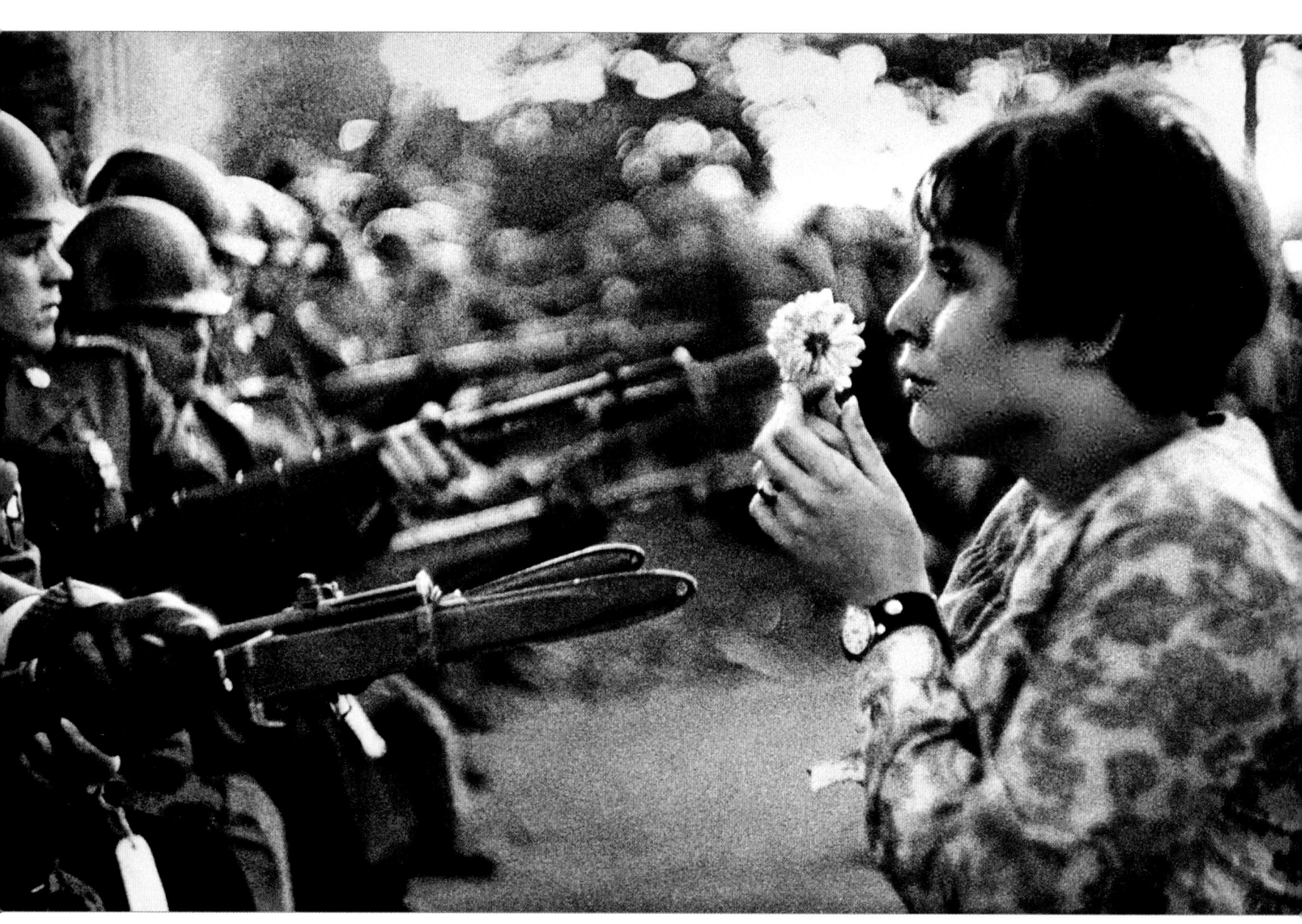

Photograph by Marc Riboud

Girl Holding a Flower

October 21, 1967 - Washington D.C., United States

In 1967, the United States had been living with the horrors of the Vietnam War for years. More and more young people opposed it. On Friday, October 21st, a large demonstration took place near the Lincoln Memorial in Washington D.C. After gathering at the feet of the president who had ended slavery, the procession headed for the Pentagon. Two thousand armed soldiers were there waiting for them, ready to repel the pacifist "offensive." The disheveled bob of the seventeen-year-old Jan Rose Kasmir in the crowd caught the eye of the French photographer Marc Riboud. The relaxed young woman, in a light-colored flowery dress, confronted the soldiers and offered them a chrysanthemum.

The photo sums up America's malaise. On the left, a rigid, indistinct line of bayonets, uniforms, and helmets. Faceless pawns, ready to stand against an enemy that takes the form of the young woman on the right. Kasmir's hands, pressed together, evoke a gesture of prayer in contrast to the strength of her gaze, which seems to respond to a moral obligation: she does not express scorn but conscious resolve. In the middle, there is an empty space, a couple inches that seem impossible to bridge. The distance is emphasized by the unfocused background, in which there seem to float the uncertainties and falsehoods proclaimed by politicians, while in Vietnam soldiers shoot and die. It is impossible to see the time on the young woman's wristwatch, giving the photo a sense of temporal suspension, which contributes to the unconditional value of her gesture.

On that day, nearly seven hundred demonstrators were arrested and many were charged, but Riboud's photo rose above such repression. It touched the conscience of a country divided by a conflict that was to continue until April 30th, 1975.

The Execution of a Vietcong

February 1, 1968 - Saigon, South Vietnam

Saigon, February 1st, 1968. It is the middle of the Têt offensive by the North Vietnamese army and the Vietcong against Saigon and the other cities of the south. Eddie Adams (35), an Associated Press photojournalist who already has many war stories to his credit, finds himself in the hotspot with an NBC cameraman. His camera captures the moment when General Nguyen Ngoc Loan, the national police chief, executes a prisoner in civilian clothes. Just one shot, and you can hear the impact on the temple, a moment before prisoner's death. The condemned man is a young Vietcong, Nguyen Van Lém, a member of the National Liberation Front. This image, one of the most dramatic of the Vietnam War, played a significant role in orienting American public opinion against the continuation of the conflict.

The photo won Adams the World Press Photo of the Year award in 1968 and the Pulitzer Prize the next year, but it was also a burden which obscured his subsequent work. He even once described it as "a bad photo" for its lighting and composition. Adams was a supporter of intervention in Vietnam, and did not anticipate the effect his photo would have on the American audience. It was published on the front pages of papers all over the world. Subsequently he was never willing to talk about it, even apologizing to the general for the damage it caused to the general's image. Indeed, although General Loan was never tried for his act, when Saigon fell he took refuge in the United States.

"Photographs are only half the truth," Adams wrote. "What this image doesn't say is: what would you have done if you had been the general at that moment?" But perhaps this is precisely the task of photography: to ask questions. For even today, this picture remains, in its fierce crudeness, a testimony against all wars.

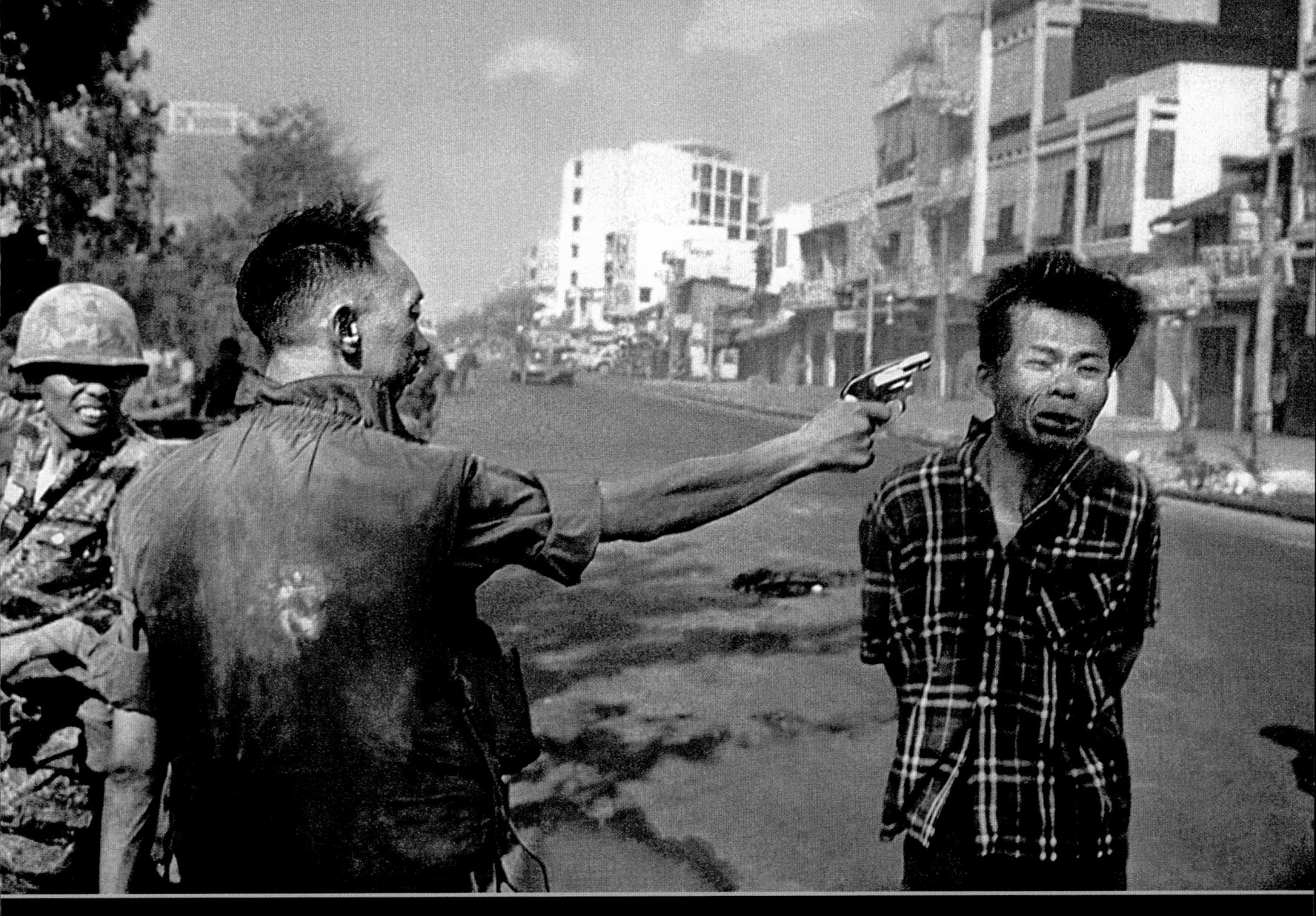

Photograph by Eddie Adams

The Funeral

April 9, 1968 - Atlanta, Georgia, United States

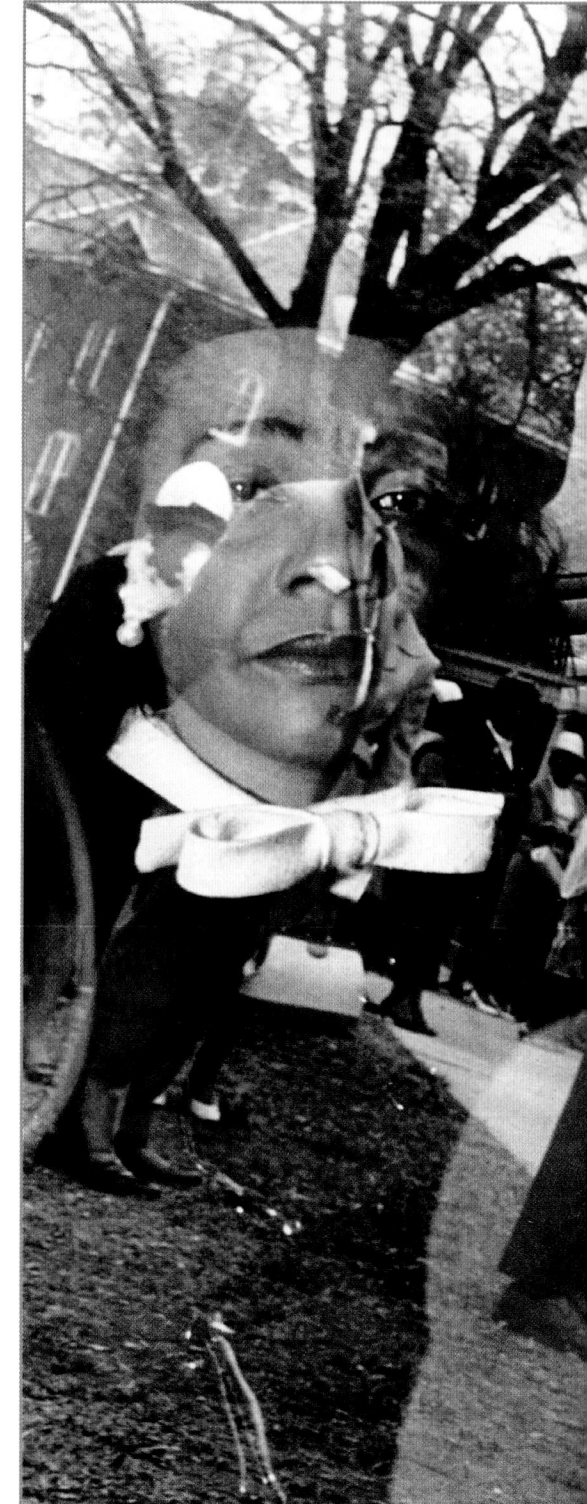

The first time that Santi Visalli, a young photographer from Messina, met Martin Luther King was in front of the United Nations building in New York City, in the early sixties. "When his eyes met my long lens, I immediately realized this man is going to be somebody," he said later. And so it was. Between 1963 and 1968, the Rev. Martin Luther King succeeded in starting the greatest peaceful revolution in American history and becoming an icon of the twentieth century, equal in significance to Gandhi and John F. Kennedy. And he was the last of the three to be assassinated. On April 3rd, 1968, one day before his murder, he preached in the Mason Temple in Memphis. His famous last sermon, *I've been to the Mountaintop*, ended in memorable and prophetic words: "Like anybody, I would like to live a long life. Longevity has its place. But I'm not concerned about that now. I just want to do God's will. And He's allowed me to go up to the mountain. And I've looked over. And I've seen the promised land. I may not get there with you. But I want you to know tonight, that we, as a people, will get to the promised land." The next day, Martin Luther King, standing on the terrace of the motel where he was staying, was assassinated.

On April 9th, his funeral was held and Santi Visalli, by now one of the most successful photojournalists in the United States, rushed to record it. The photos lack the protagonist, but the gaze, taken through a car window, of his daughter, Yolanda, who was then 12 years old, speaks of King's destiny. On her face you can read pain, dignity, and determination (Yolanda herself would become a great civil rights activist). Behind the girl, King's stone-faced wife, Coretta; in the reflections are Rev. King's followers, houses, bare trees, and an ashen, still wintry sky, the symbol of a season of violence that had yet to end.

# of Martin Luther King

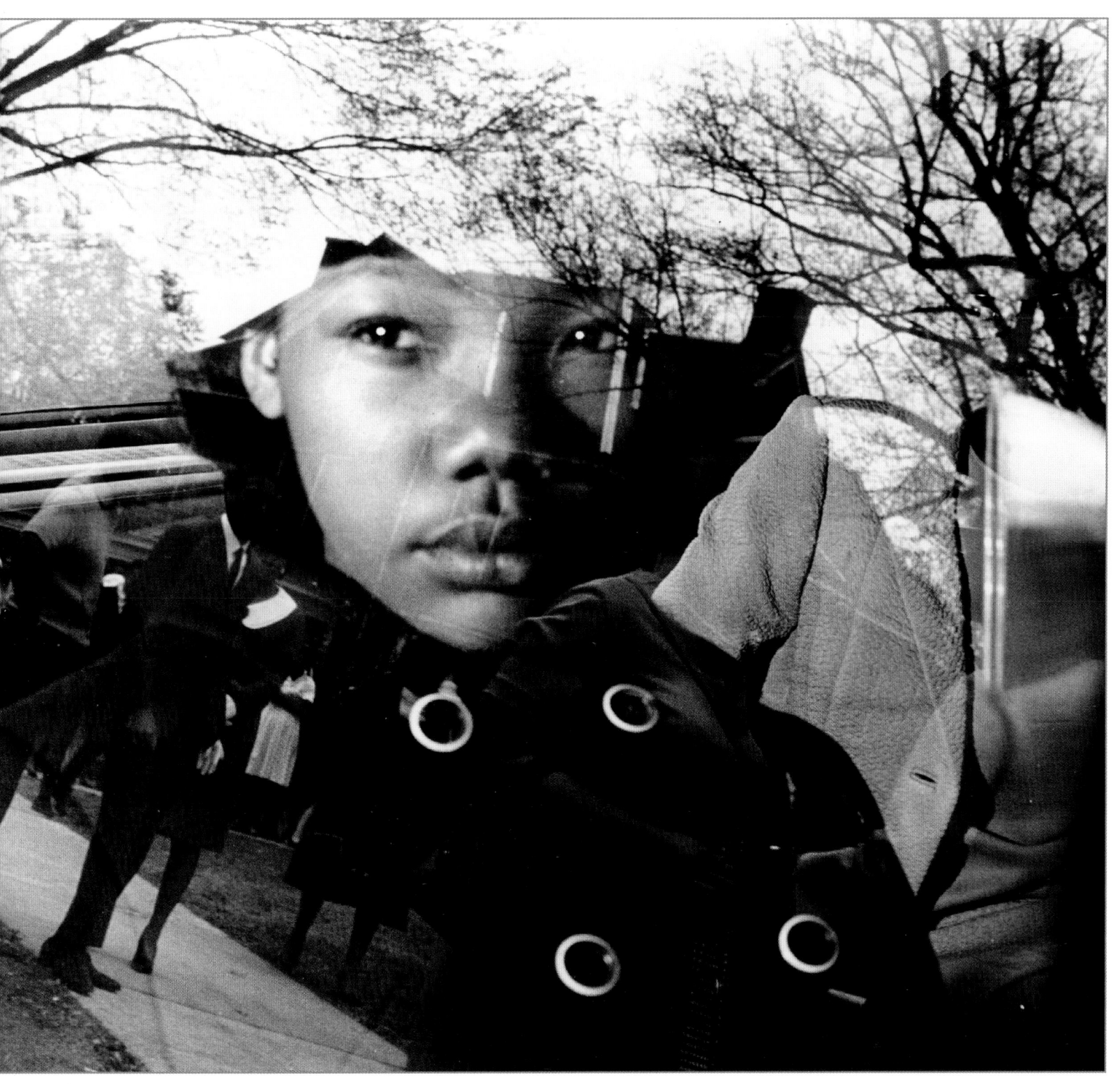

Photograph by Santi Visalli

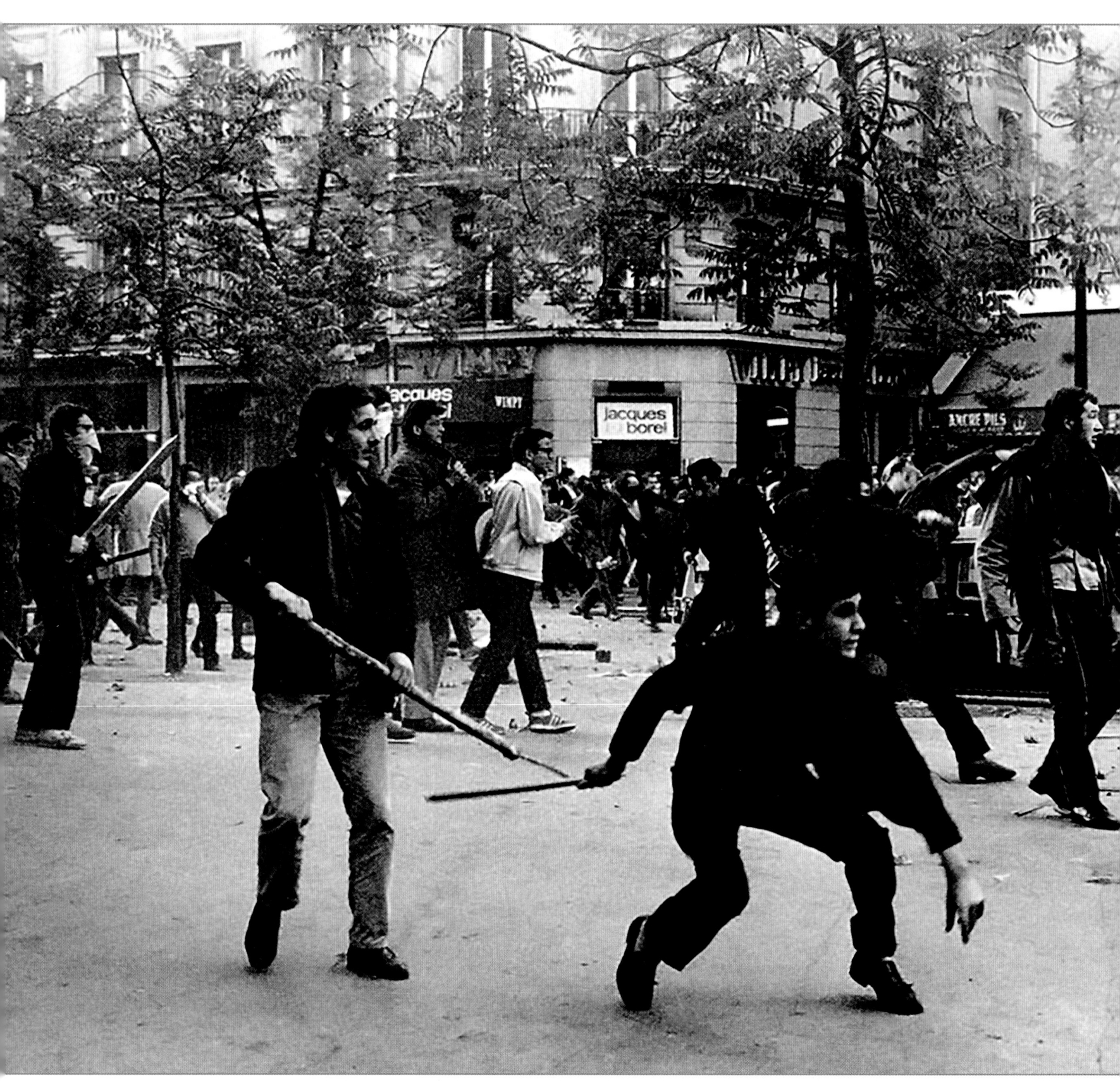

Photograph by Bruno Barbey

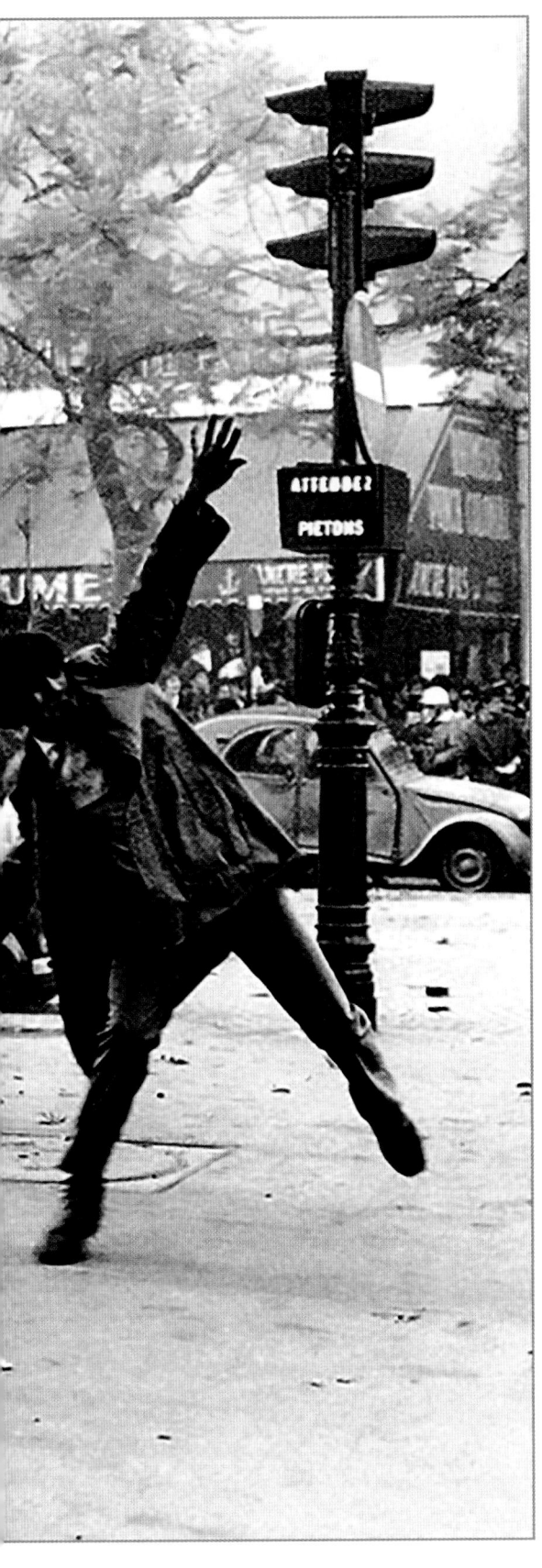

French May

May 6, 1968 - Paris, France

Encouraged by the culture of American hippy demonstrations and opposition to the war in Vietnam, for many Europeans 1968 was a year of protest that represented a social and generational turning point. Through rash and violent actions, protesters in many cities in Europe subverted the rigid *status quo* that had been imposed on culture for generations by politics, institutions, school, and religion. The year 1968 has become the year of protest par excellence. The protests pursued egalitarian values, fought against any form of authority, and shared a common aspiration for peace. Although no radical changes resulted, the different social backgrounds of millions of protesters in the world transformed collective awareness and moved society toward a fairer political and social system.

The young photographer Bruno Barbey, documented events in Paris during the so-called "French May," the peak of this period in Europe. The photo is from May 6th and shows students confronting police with sticks and stones, to the cry of *Il est interdit d'interdire*, "It's forbidden to forbid." The dynamism of the bodies frozen in movement seems to restore the energy and iconoclastic force inspiring the young demonstrators. The photographer mixes with the crowd, and with this deeper perspective shows the action; he puts himself on the level of his subjects, as if he were one of them. In a short time, the student demonstrations developed into the first general strike of workers, which immobilized the whole of France. Many intellectuals openly showed their support for the youth movements: among the most attentive observers was the philosopher Jean-Paul Sartre, who in those days made a famous speech to the students occupying the Sorbonne. The protest was both passionate and brief and fragmentary. It was a social explosion that the contested government of Charles de Gaulle finally managed to quell.

The Invasion of Prague

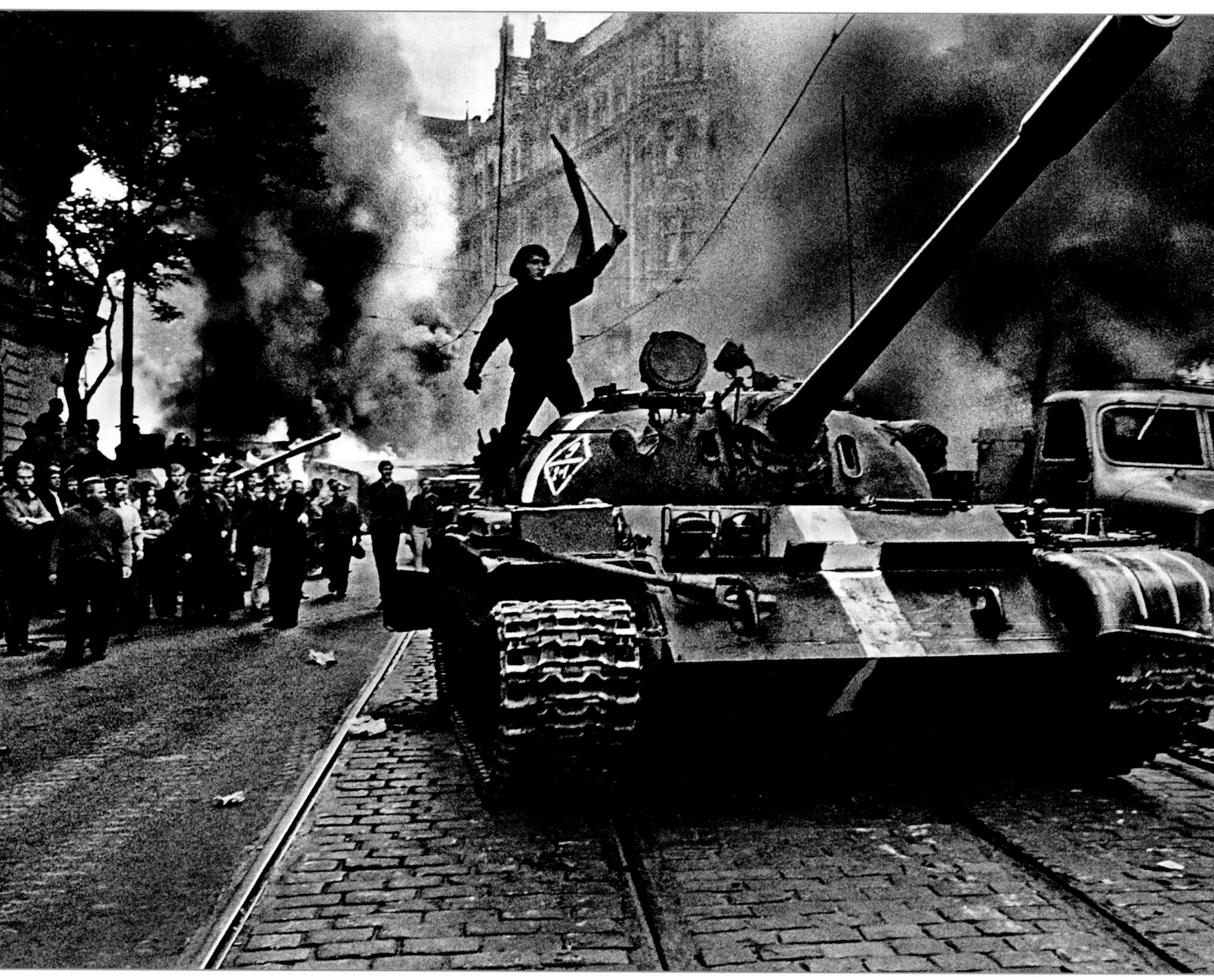

Photograph by Josef Koudelka

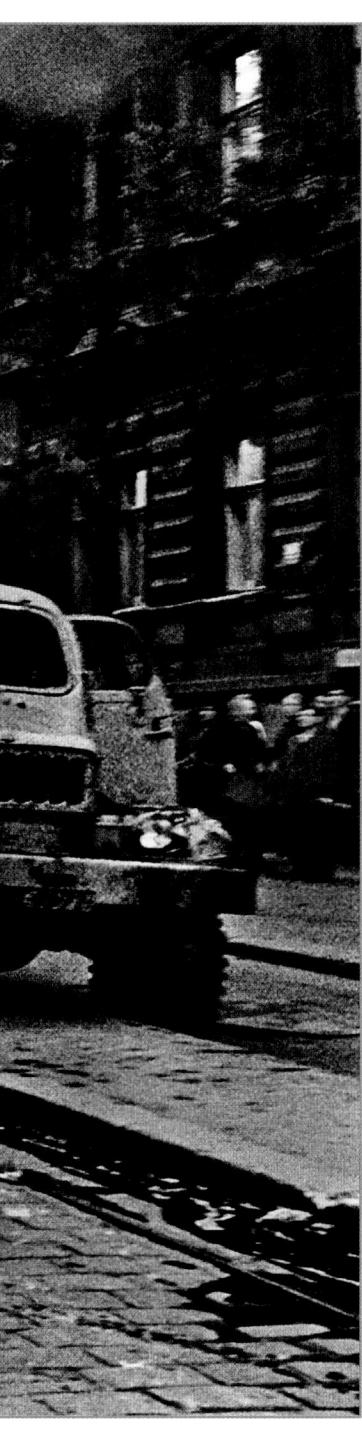

August 21, 1968 - Prague, Czechoslovakia

The young Czech, Josef Koudelka, earned his living as a still photographer in the theater. He had nothing to do with journalism until the night of August 20th, 1968, when Warsaw Pact tanks invaded Czechoslovakia, ending the period of reform and optimism known as the "Prague Spring." In those turbulent days, Koudelka took dramatic photos of the events he witnessed. The photos were smuggled abroad and ended up in the hands of the agency Magnum Photos, which began to distribute them a year later. The agency credited the photographs to a "Prague Photographer," to avoid reprisals against Koudelka and his family.

The photos, which had an extraordinary strength and documentary quality, were published for the first time in the United Kingdom in *The Sunday Times* and became one of the most powerful representations of the invasion of Prague. The following year, they earned the "Prague Photographer" the Robert Capa Gold Medal.

In the meantime, Magnum recommended Koudelka to the British authorities. He obtained a work permit and, in 1970, emigrated to the United Kingdom, where he obtained political asylum and stayed for more than a decade. Sixteen years went by before the Czech photographer could put his name to the famous photos. In 2008, after a travelling exhibition, the collection was published in the book *Invasion 68: Prague*.

Forty years after the Soviet invasion, this image, like many others in the hundreds captured by Koudelka in those days, still has the power to evoke the Prague Spring and make us relive its dramatic conclusion.

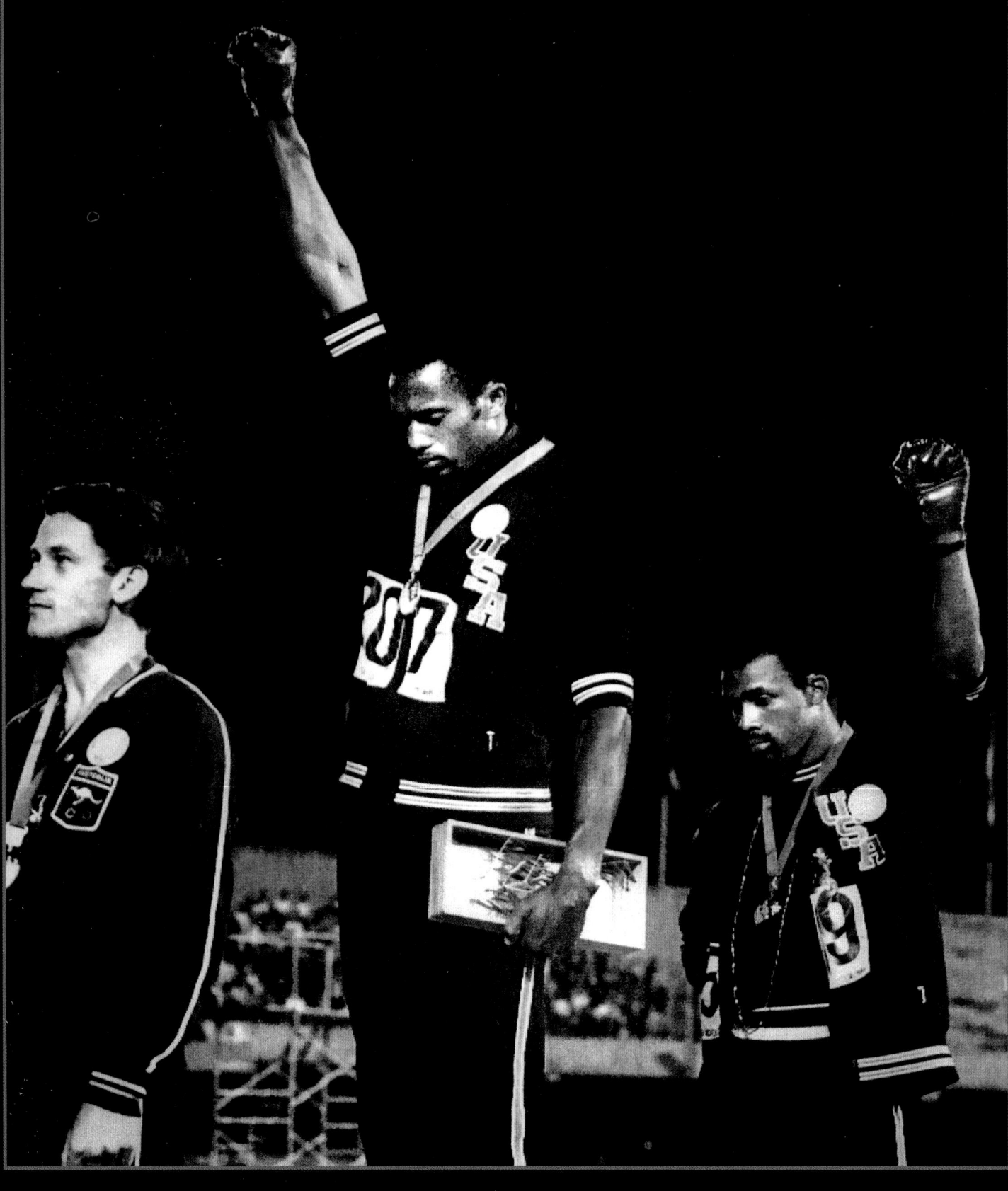

Photograph by John Dominis

Olympics Black Power Salute

October 16, 1968 - Mexico City, Mexico

October 16th, 1968. On the podium for the 200-meter dash of the Mexico City Olympic Games are not just three athletes but all of 1968, a year of protest around the world. Here we have Tommie Smith, 24 years old, son of a cotton picker, winner of the gold medal; and John Carlos, 23 years old, son of a Harlem cobbler, winner of the bronze. Each raises his black-gloved fist in an unforeseen, moving gesture of support for the Black Power movement, in protest against injustices suffered by blacks. Their silent cry rises with the highest notes of the national anthem. The next day people would talk about, not the color of the medals, but the color of the athletes' skin and the battles for civil rights in the United States, where Martin Luther King had been assassinated only a few months before.

The photo, taken by the well-known photojournalist John Dominis and seen all around the world, touches the unconscious more than any speech on equality. This is due to the universal context in which it was taken, the Olympic Games, but also to the symbolic effectiveness of its details. The shoeless feet of the two athletes, evocative of poverty, their bowed heads, Smith's black scarf, and the sweatshirt left open by Carlos, as by a manual laborer: underneath he wears a necklace, every bead representing a victim of lynching. They wear the cockade of the Olympic Project for Human Rights on their tracksuits. The Australian, Peter Norman, who won the silver medal, also wears one. He is white, and his moral support contributes to making the protest universal. Presently, like his Afro-American fellow athletes, he doesn't know that he will pay dearly for his gesture: he will be marginalized for life by his country's Sports Federation. But he never regrets this act of solidarity. Nor will he regret suggesting to Smith and Carlos, a few minutes before mounting the podium, that they share the only pair of black gloves they had. One took the right glove, the other took the left. It's an idea worthy of a scenographer.

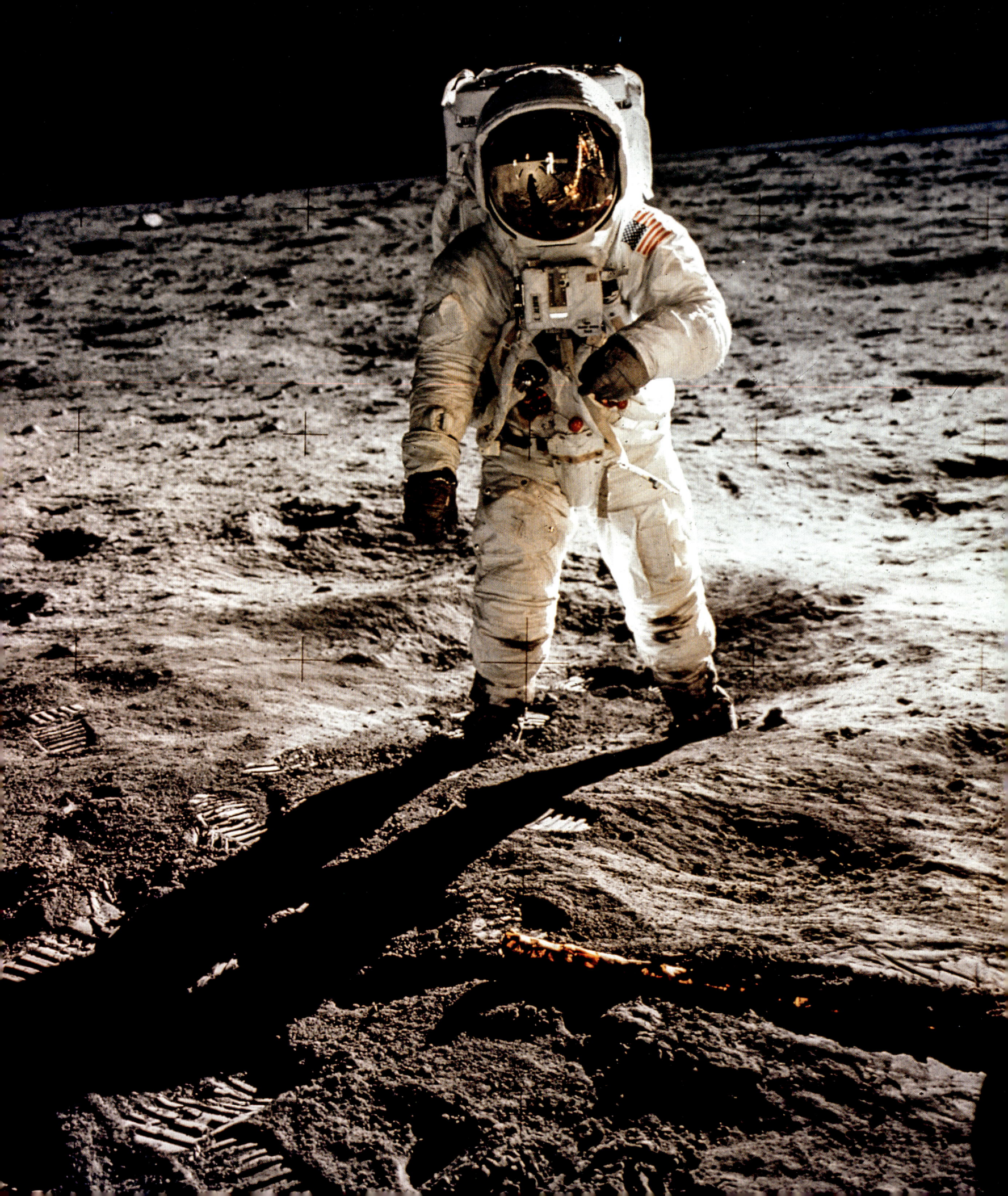

Man on the Moon

July 20, 1969 - Moon

Neil Armstrong was carefully exploring the surface of the moon – just twenty minutes before he had pronounced the historic words "that's one small step for [a] man, one giant leap for mankind" – when Edwin "Buzz" Aldrin left Apollo 11, descended the ladder, and became the second man to touch the surface of the most romantic object in the Solar System.

It was July 20th, 1969, and Neil Armstrong had the only external Hasselblad camera on the mission. But he didn't use this to photograph Aldrin setting foot on the moon: that was done by one of the television cameras on the LEM (lunar excursion module), the same one that had immortalized Armstrong himself twenty minutes before. However, it was Armstrong who captured on film Aldrin's first steps through the selenic dust. That Hasselblad was obviously a special camera. It was specifically equipped for the longest journey ever attempted, to the most alien place ever confronted: the moon would be cold, airless, and with an unknown quality of light. Then, while Aldrin made measurements and collected samples, Armstrong took pictures with a 500 EL 70 mm Hasselblad Electric Camera (HEC), soon to be known as a Lunar Surface Camera. Together, the two astronauts explored the Sea of Tranquility for more than an hour and a half. In total, the LEM, supported by metal legs that made it look like a giant spider, remained fixed to the moon's surface for two and a half hours before switching on the rockets to take off again. In the meantime, Michael Collins, the most experienced astronaut on the Apollo 11 mission, orbited the moon in the Columbia, the command module.

As often happens in life, also on that July 20th there could only be one "first" and Aldrin drew the short straw. In the same way that no one remembers Juan de la Cosa – who was Christopher Columbus' helmsman on his great voyage towards the unknown – Aldrin might also gradually fade away in the history books.

If it was, as some people suspect, all a set-up by the television cameras of Stanley Kubrick, we have to admit that we enjoyed it all the same.

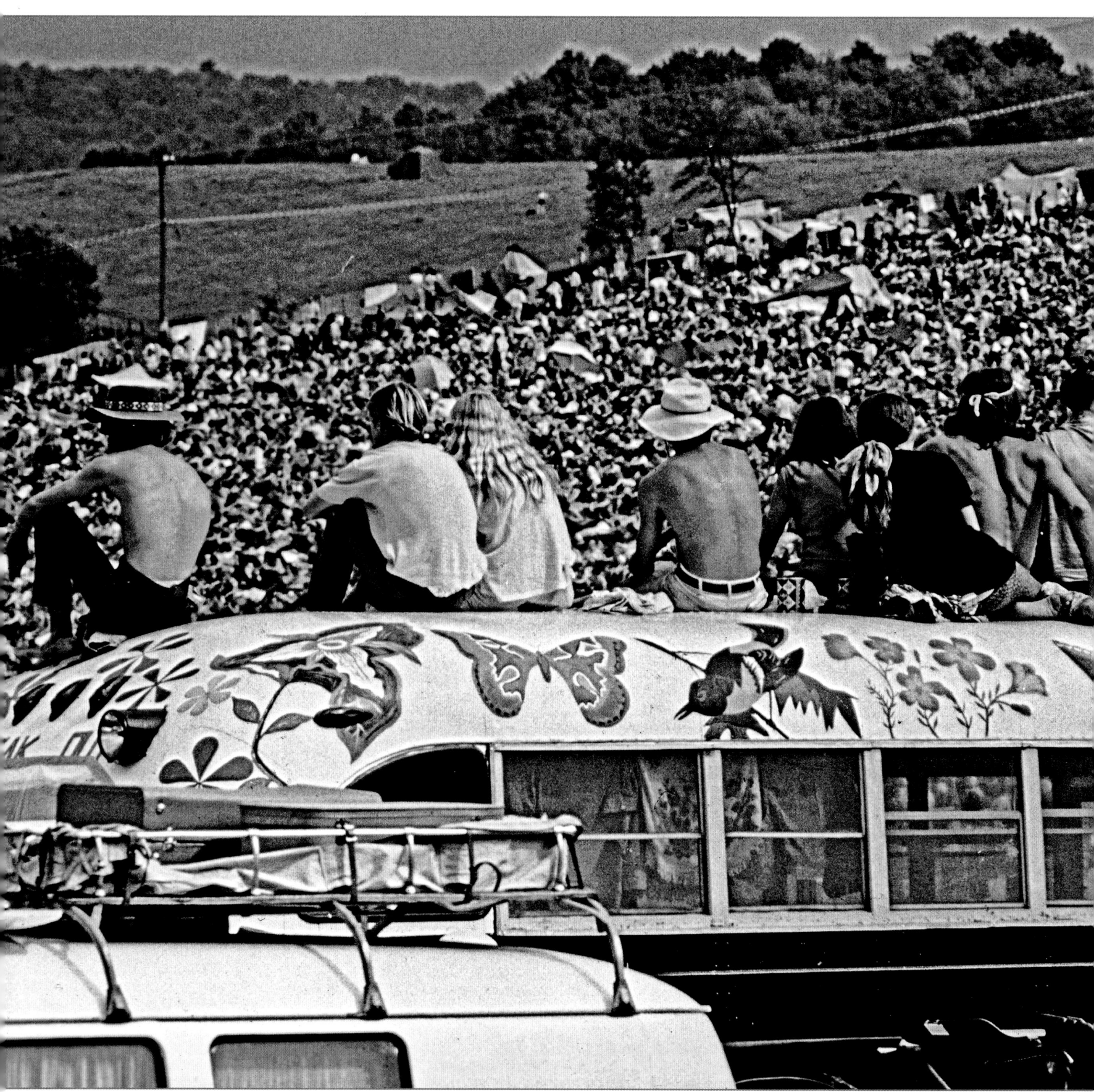

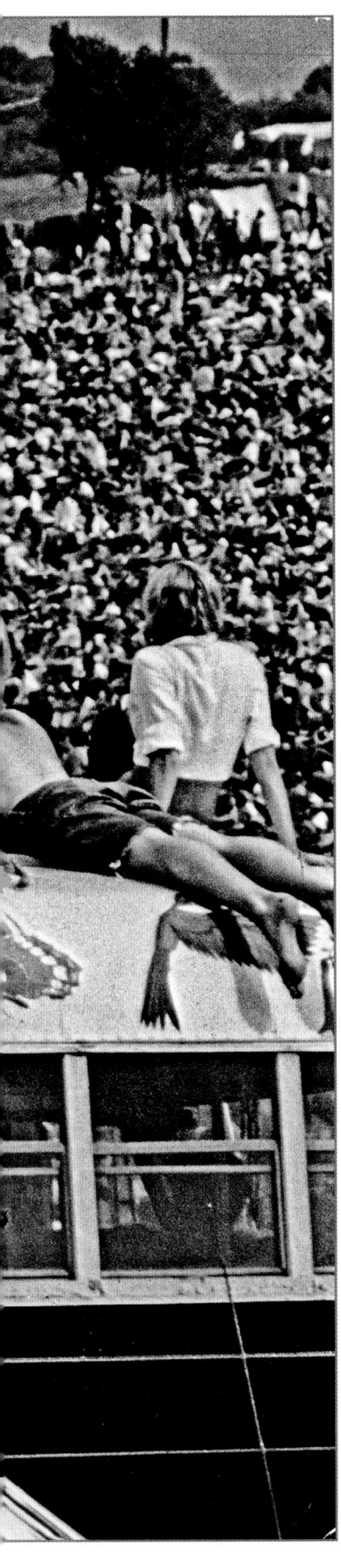

The Woodstock Festival

August 15-17, 1969 - Bethel, New York State, United States

Three days of peace and music: this is what the posters modestly promised when they announced the Woodstock Festival, which was to begin August 15th, 1969. And so it turned out, but the reality exceeded the most optimistic expectations. The promoters, Michael Lang, John Roberts, Joel Rosenman, and Artie Kornfeld were fascinated by the idea of organizing a musical event in the quiet little town in upstate New York. However, they had in mind a small-scale festival, with at most 50,000 people, and even with such limited expectations it was difficult to find a suitable venue. In the end they chose Bethel, a little town about 55 miles from Woodstock, where a farmer rented them 600 acres, which they extended by bargaining with nearby landowners. Soon it became clear that the event would be vastly larger than expected: the organizers sold about 186,000 tickets in advance. But then they had to let people in for free. The roads around Bethel were transformed into enormous parking lots, because the participants left their cars to walk to the event: a flood of almost half a million young people covered the countryside. For the whole of the festival, people camped in front of the stage and on the surrounding land. The best equipped people were in tents, though many simply had sleeping bags. There was free love, joyous nudity in the sun and the rain, lots of pot and acid, singing and dancing until early in the morning, baths in the pond, spontaneous cooperation to compensate for insufficient sanitary facilities, and not a single incidence of violence. There was also great music, which the less fortunate saw and heard from far off, perhaps perched on the roofs of cars and vans parked on the hillsides.

On the stage appeared a succession of 32 giants of the musical scene of the time, from Joan Baez to Janis Joplin, from the Grateful Dead to Jefferson Airplane. Finally, they heard the unforgettable closing with Jimi Hendrix and his legendary, scathing interpretation of the American national anthem: a sardonic provocation against the war in Vietnam, a performance that remains in the collective imagination the distinctive emblem of the greatest festival in the history of rock.

131

Bloody Sunday

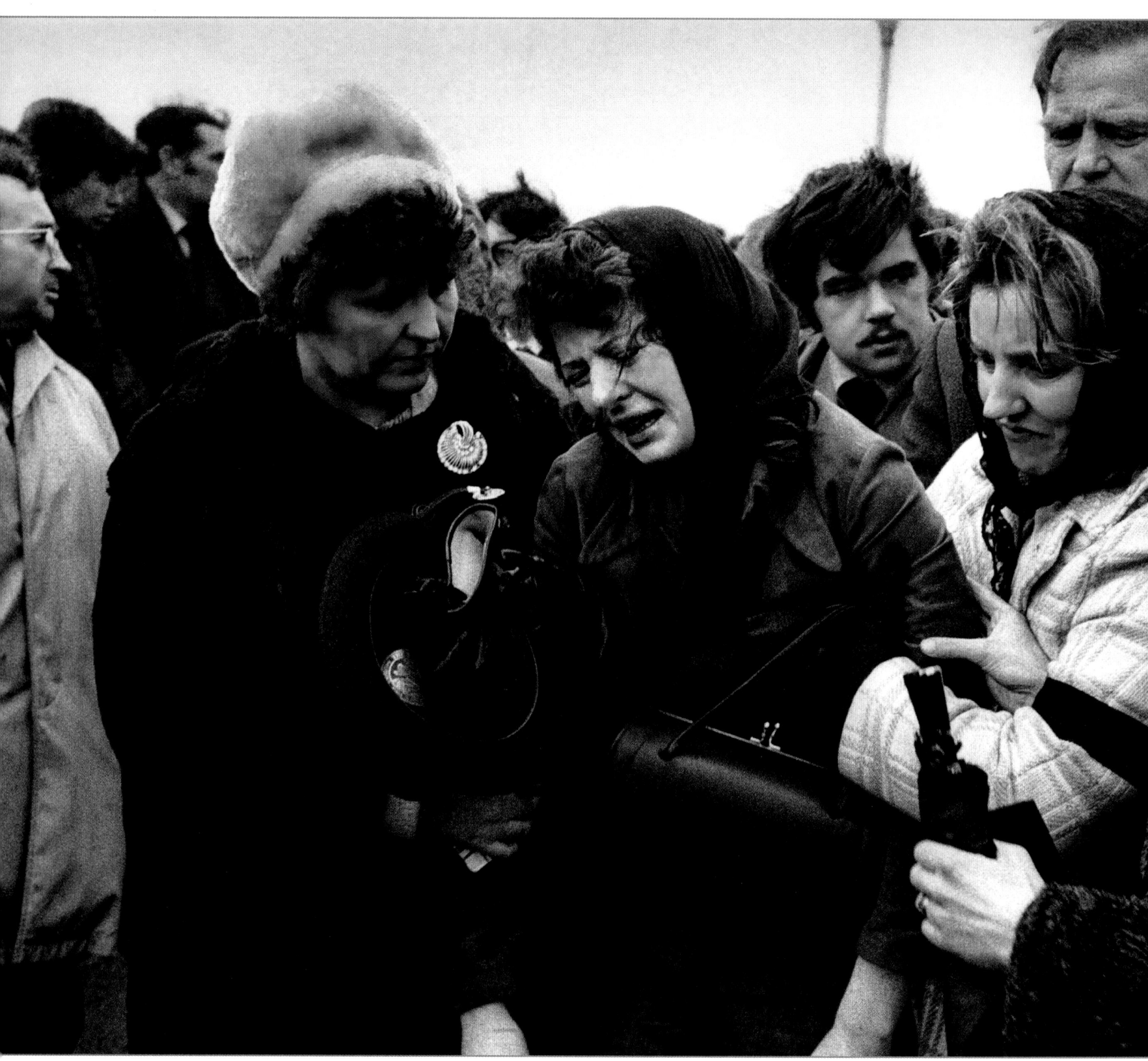

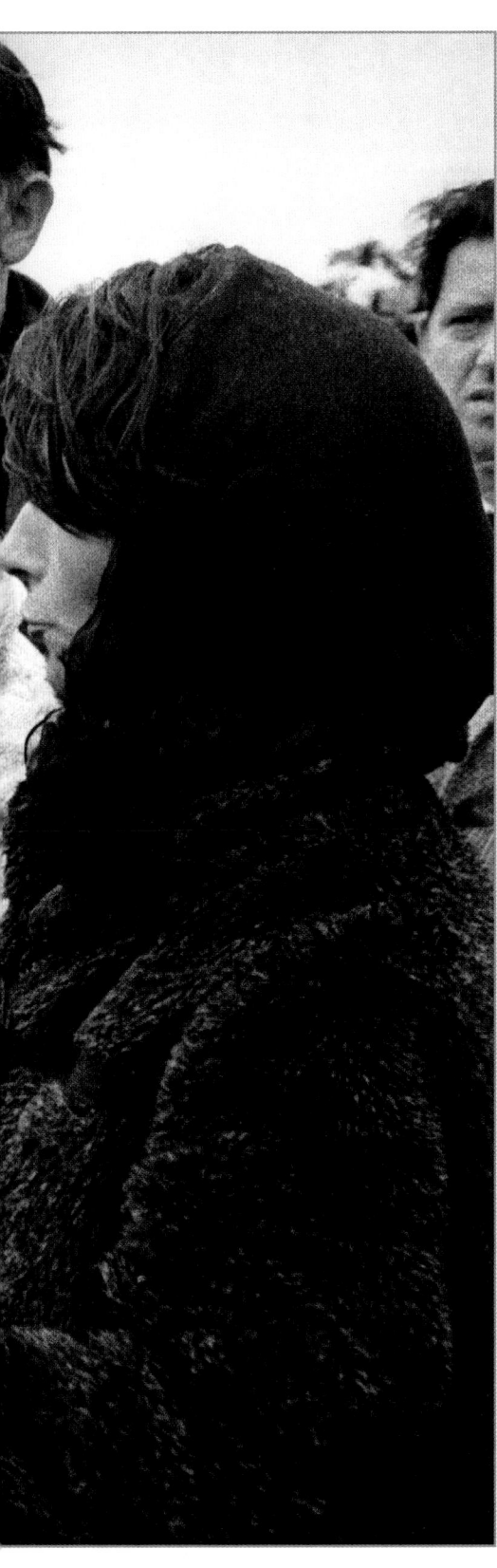

January 30, 1972 - Derry, Northern Ireland, United Kingdom

On January 30th, 1972 the French photographer Gilles Peress was present at the protest march in the town of Derry, Northern Ireland, against the repressive policy of the British government and the arbitrary powers it conferred on the police. Even though it was not authorized, the demonstration was peaceful and more than 10,000 people, many of them young, took part. A little more than an hour after the march began, the crowd was attacked by British soldiers, who fired on the demonstrators, killing 13. (Another died four months later as a result of wounds). Only in 2010 did the British acknowledge that the action was completely unjustified.

This photo, with the woman in the center wracked by grief and the others supporting and trying to comfort her, was taken at the funeral of the victims, which took place on February 2nd. The black and white film emphasizes the dramatic quality of the situation and the solidarity of the group gathered around the woman in tears, who is perhaps the mother of one of the young victims. At the time, Peress was beginning his career as a newspaper photographer. Employed by the Magnum Photos agency, he would go on to document the wars in Bosnia, Iran and Rwanda. But on that bloody Sunday, he was confronted for the first time with the killing of innocent people; he later recalled that while he was taking the photographs he was crying. Since then, in his reportage he has expressed his commitment to human rights, taking care in his work to record, not so much "beautiful photos," as testaments to history, so that such episodes are not forgotten. Following the massacre in Derry, the United Kingdom dissolved the Belfast Government and intervened directly in Northern Ireland. Consequently, there was an increase in membership in the IRA (the illegal Catholic army supporting independence and the reunification of Ireland), which further radicalized a conflict that would go on for over twenty years.

Photograph by Gilles Peress

The Terror of War

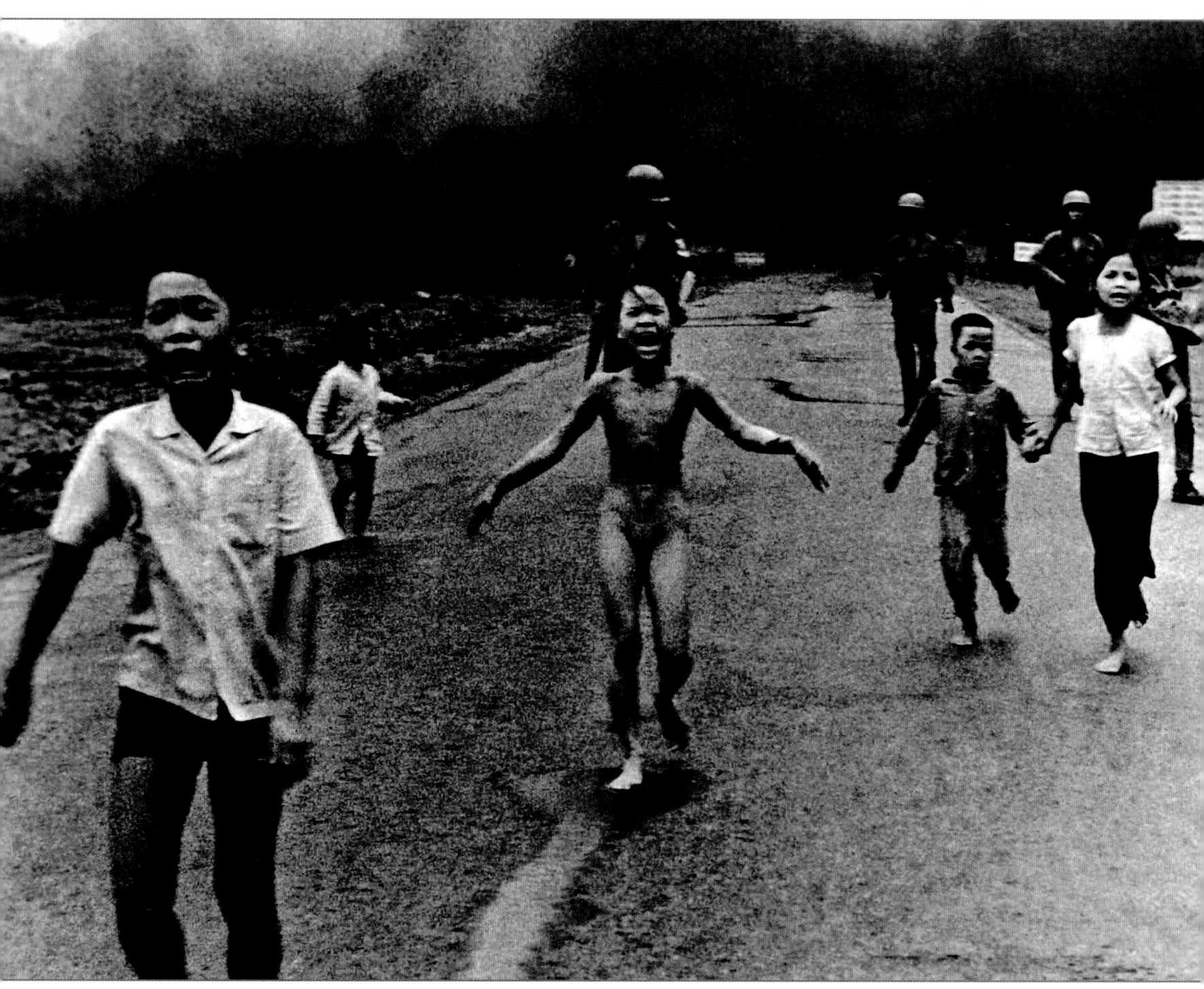

Photograph by Huynh Cong "Nick" Ut

The Terror of War

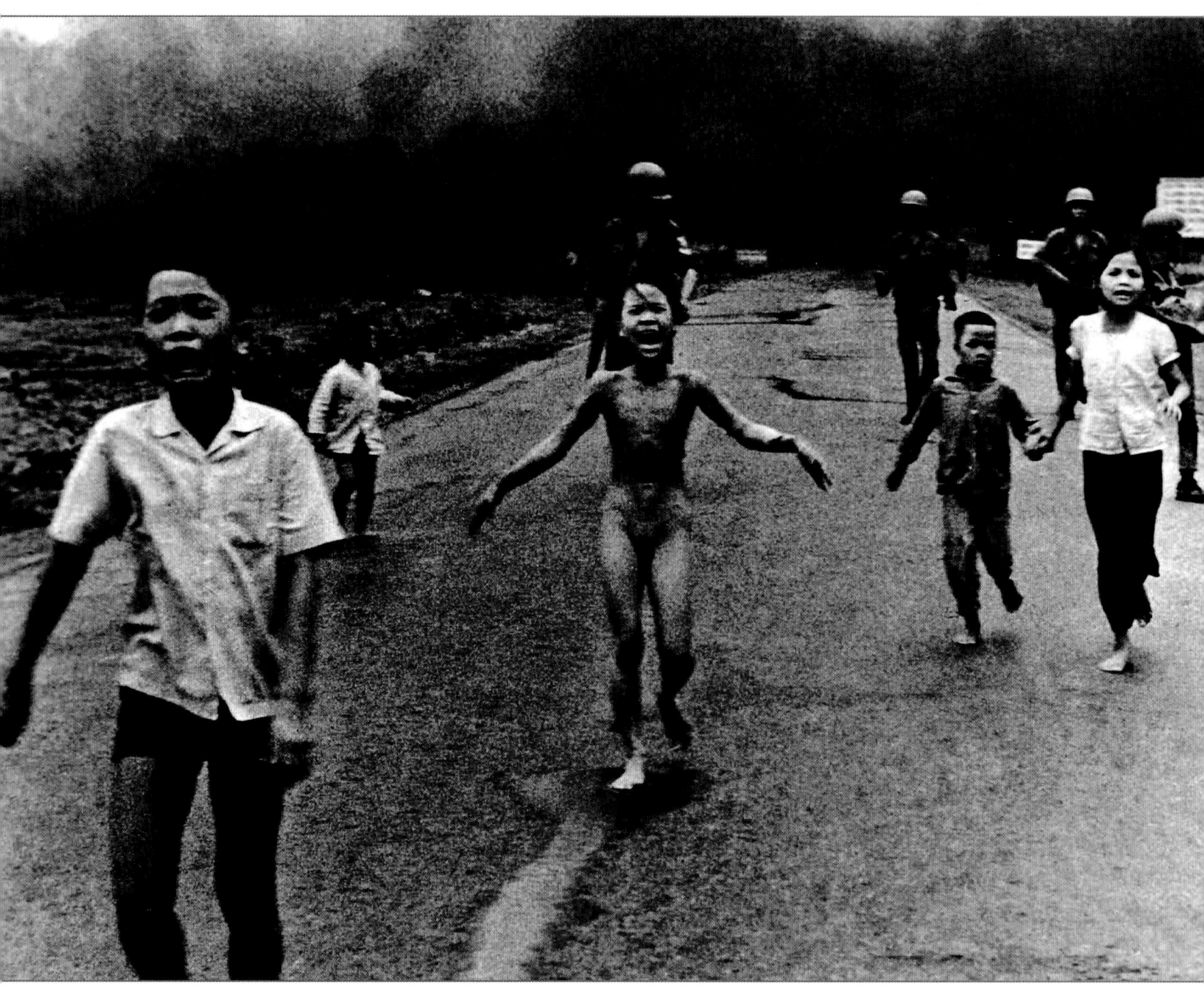

Photograph by Huynh Cong "Nick" Ut

June 8, 1972 - Trang Bang, South Vietnam

In a desolate landscape, children cry out and flee in terror from the dark smoke rising behind them. First we see, in the center of the photo, the naked little girl, and then we move to the boy in the foreground, to the three children following them, to the soldiers behind them, and finally to the background. A very young Vietnamese Associated Press photographer, Huynh Con "Nick" Ut, took the photo on June 8th, 1972, although this attribution has recently been questioned. It documents the napalm bombardments by the South Vietnamese Air Force of Trang Bang, a village about 25 miles from Saigon. Intending to strike a Vietcong refuge, it mistakenly destroyed a temple in which South Vietnamese civilians and soldiers had taken refuge, resulting in four deaths and the wounding of several others. The little girl in the center, Kim Phuc, who was seriously burnt, was assisted immediately afterward by the photographer himself and by the ITN journalist Christopher Wain, who had her taken to an American hospital where she was treated. Her brother, on the left, lost an eye; the other children are her younger brother and her two young cousins.

The newspaper photographer doesn't have time to study the composition: he takes several shots and only in the darkroom will he see the result. But this photo, chosen from a short sequence and published all over the world, could not be more effective. Yet, as often happens with the most famous photos, some speculated that it had been "constructed," doubting its authenticity. Nevertheless, it was named World Press Photo of the Year and awarded the Pulitzer Prize in 1973. The image had a strong effect on American public opinion, which was already mobilized to end the war in Vietnam.

The media followed the story of Kim Phuc, who had various operations, studied in Cuba, and then emigrated to Canada, where today she is a UNESCO ambassador and directs a foundation to help minors who are victims of wars. She has stayed in touch with Nich Ut, who still works for Associated Press.

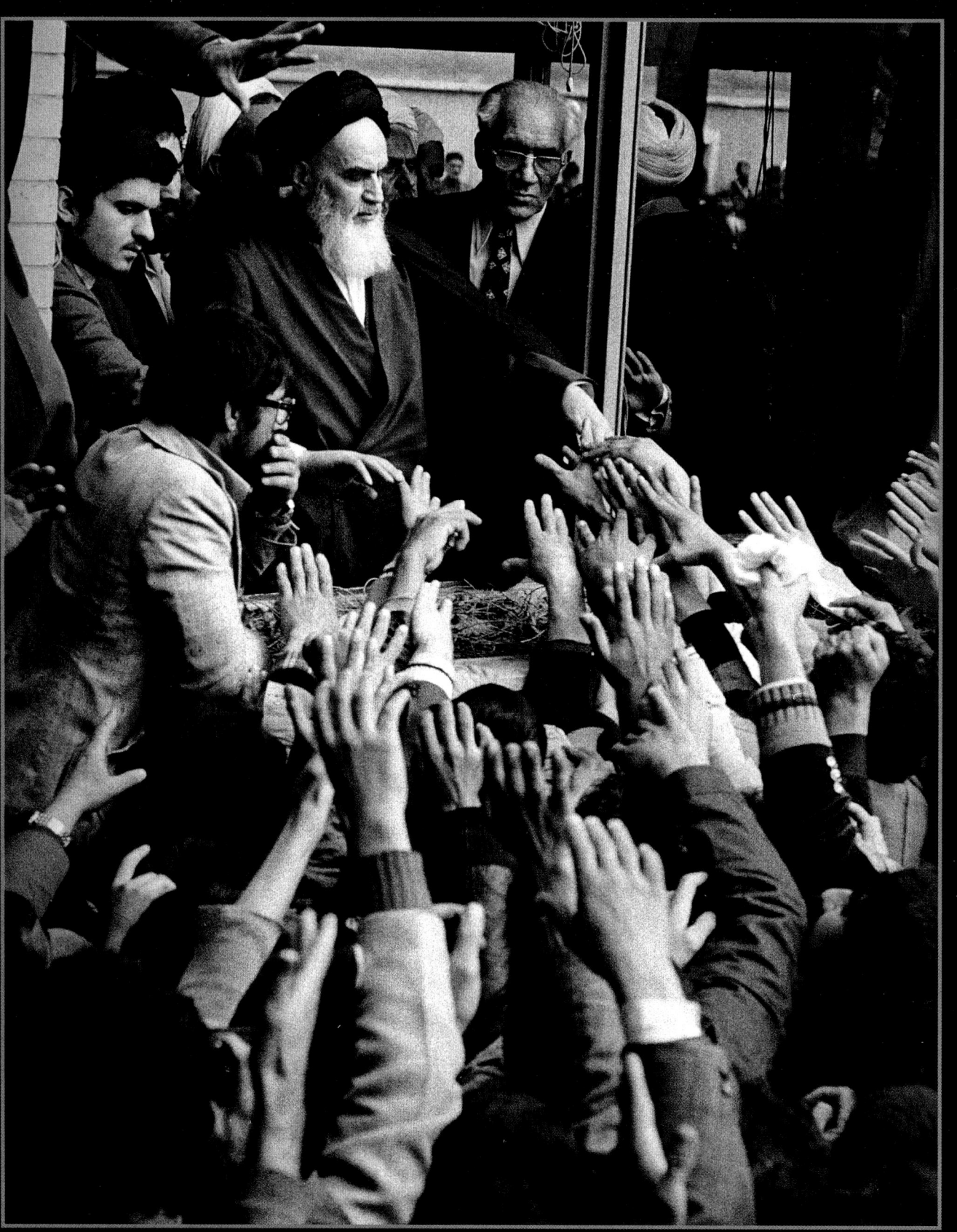

Photograph by Abbas Attar

Khomeini Returns to Iran

February 2, 1979 - Teheran, Iran

On February 1st, 1979, the Great Ayatollah Ruhollah Khomeini stepped down from an Air France flight, which had just landed at the Tehran Airport. The Shah had fled a couple of weeks before, under pressure from the Islamic Revolution, and so the Shi'ite leader, 77 years old, returned to assume leadership of the country. He had had an adventurous life: theological studies, military activity, plots against the Shahs Reza Pahlavi (father and son), and finally sixteen years in exile, in Turkey, Iraq, and then France. Before him lies, for his remaining ten years, the task of transforming Iran into the greatest theocracy in the world.

There is a talented photographer in the Iranian capital from the Gamma agency (the following year, it will become Magnum Photos), to document the revolution: Abbas Attar, an Iranian, though he resides in Paris, has worked in conflicts all over the world, from Vietnam to Ulster to the Middle East. He's the right man in the right place: as an Iranian, he deeply understands the reasons for the revolution; but as a journalist, he has a secular and disenchanted attitude regarding his country and, above all, religion.

In this image, taken on February 2nd, Khomeini is in triumph: on his right, in black turbans, are his son, Ahmed, and grandson, Hussein. The first is a hero of the revolution; the second is destined to become a dissident. In the foreground is a forest of the outstretched hands of his supporters, a historic foundation that almost seems to hold up the old Ayatollah. Khomeini needs all the popular support he can get: over the years, his power will have to deal with the American hostage crisis, a costly war against Iraq, international sanctions, and a protracted confrontation with the Great Satan, the United States.

The Killing Fields in Cambodia

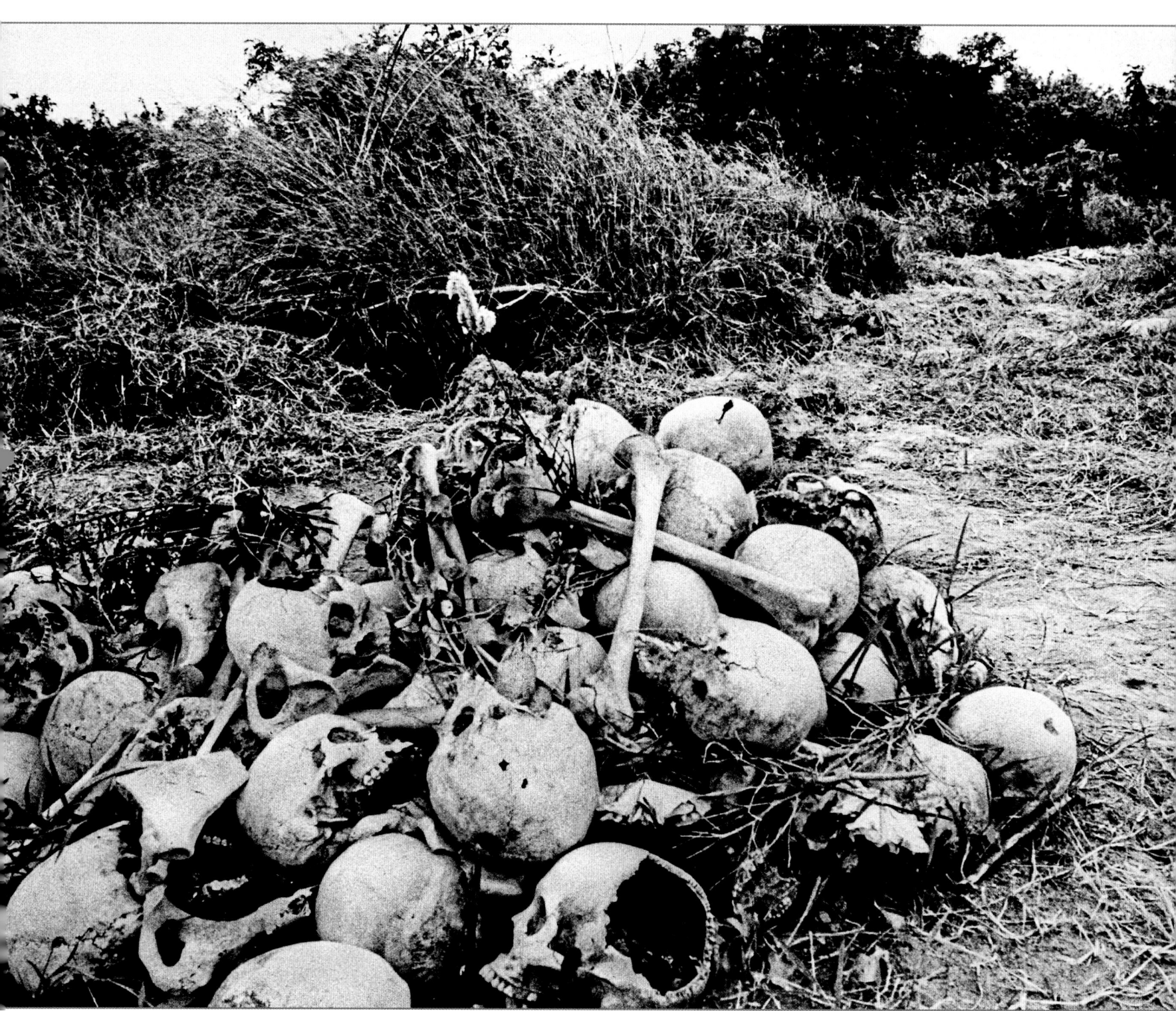

Photograph by Eric Piper

1979, September - Cambodia

No one knows exactly how many people were killed by the Khmer Rouge regime of Pol Pot, who was in power in Cambodia between 1975 and 1979. Amnesty International calculates almost a million and a half deaths, about 20% of the population. Most of them were due to the famine and extreme hardships Cambodians were forced to endure in labor camps. But many, between 50,000 and 100,000, according to CIA data, were the result of collective executions.

In January of 1979, Vietnam invaded Cambodia, occupied the capital Phnom Penh, and installed a new regime there. The Khmer Rouge retreated into the west of the country, which they would control for more than a decade. Only then, following reports and horrifying images by correspondents and freelance photographers, and with the discovery of mass graves, did the West come to realize the scale of the genocide that had transpired.

One of the most successful teams of journalists was that of John Pilger, a *Daily Mirror* correspondent and a human rights activist, and Eric Piper, who was among the winners of the World Press Photo prize for a 1981 photo of Cambodian refugees. This image is part of reportage shot in September, 1979, just two months after Pol Pot fled. Tibiae, jaw bones, and shattered skulls; white bones, as if picked clean by some bird of prey, in a heap just disinterred from a grave. It is a composition that has no need of a caption, and in its realistic crudeness it becomes the unconditional symbol of human ferocity and the criminal senselessness of all totalitarian regimes.

John Lennon's Murder

December 14, 1980 - New York, United States

For John Lennon and Yoko Ono, December 8th, 1980, a Monday, was a normal day, or even a day better than most. Lennon had just won the battle against the US Government, which wanted to reject his application for residence because he had supported the civil rights and anti-war movements; at last, it seemed he was finding peace in New York. He had stopped appearing in public five years earlier, and was trying to live an undisturbed life, like any other citizen, an unthinkable possibility in his years with the Beatles. However, a few months earlier, he had returned to work. Also on that Monday, he had had a long chat with a radio journalist, and then gone to the studio with Yoko to record a track. He didn't know that it would be his last interview and his last song. Mingling with fans, a crowd always present in front of the Dakota, the building looking onto Central Park where John and Yoko lived, a twenty-five-year-old, Mark David Chapman, awaited him. Chapman had seen Lennon go out, and had even approached him to have an album signed. But then, at 10:50 that night, as Lennon and Ono were going back inside the building, Chapman shot him five times in the back. The news of his death was a bolt from the blue for the whole world.

On December 14th, at the request of Yoko Ono, great commemorative demonstrations took place everywhere. In New York, 250,000 people gathered in Central Park to pay homage to John. The photo shows grief and consternation: "Why?" those who loved him ask. No one can answer. Lennon paid the price for being public and then recovering the life popularity had taken from him, arousing the mad homicidal indignation of a depressed admirer who felt betrayed. Chapman aspired to suicide and was disappointed above all by himself.

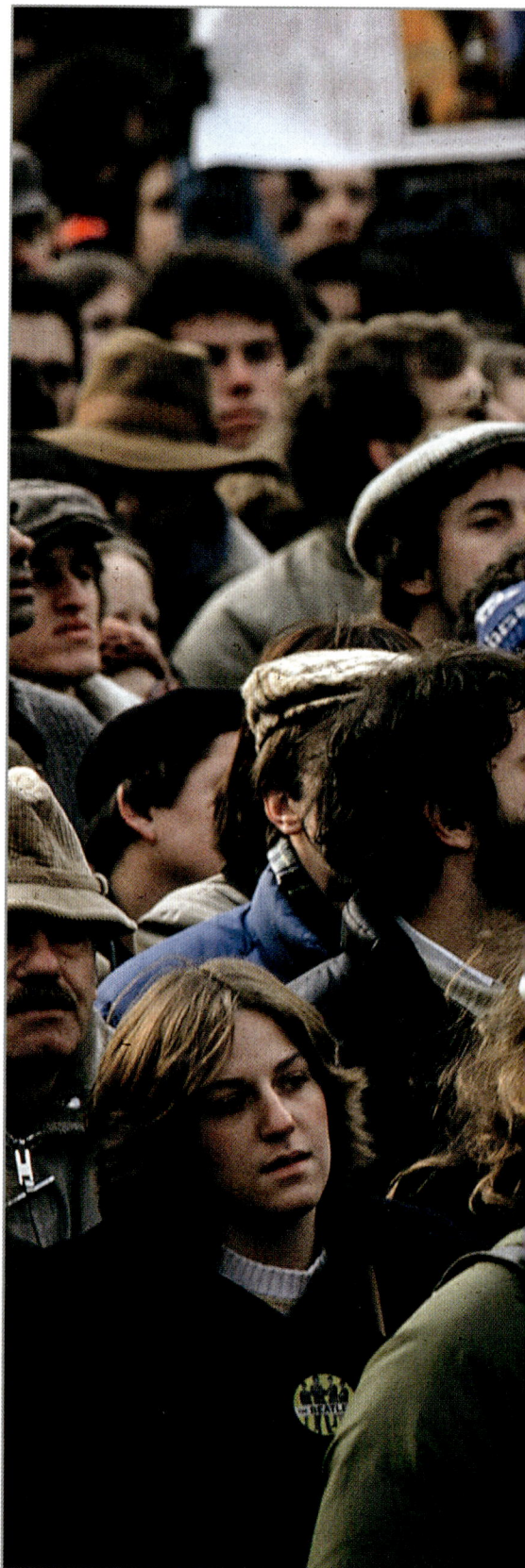

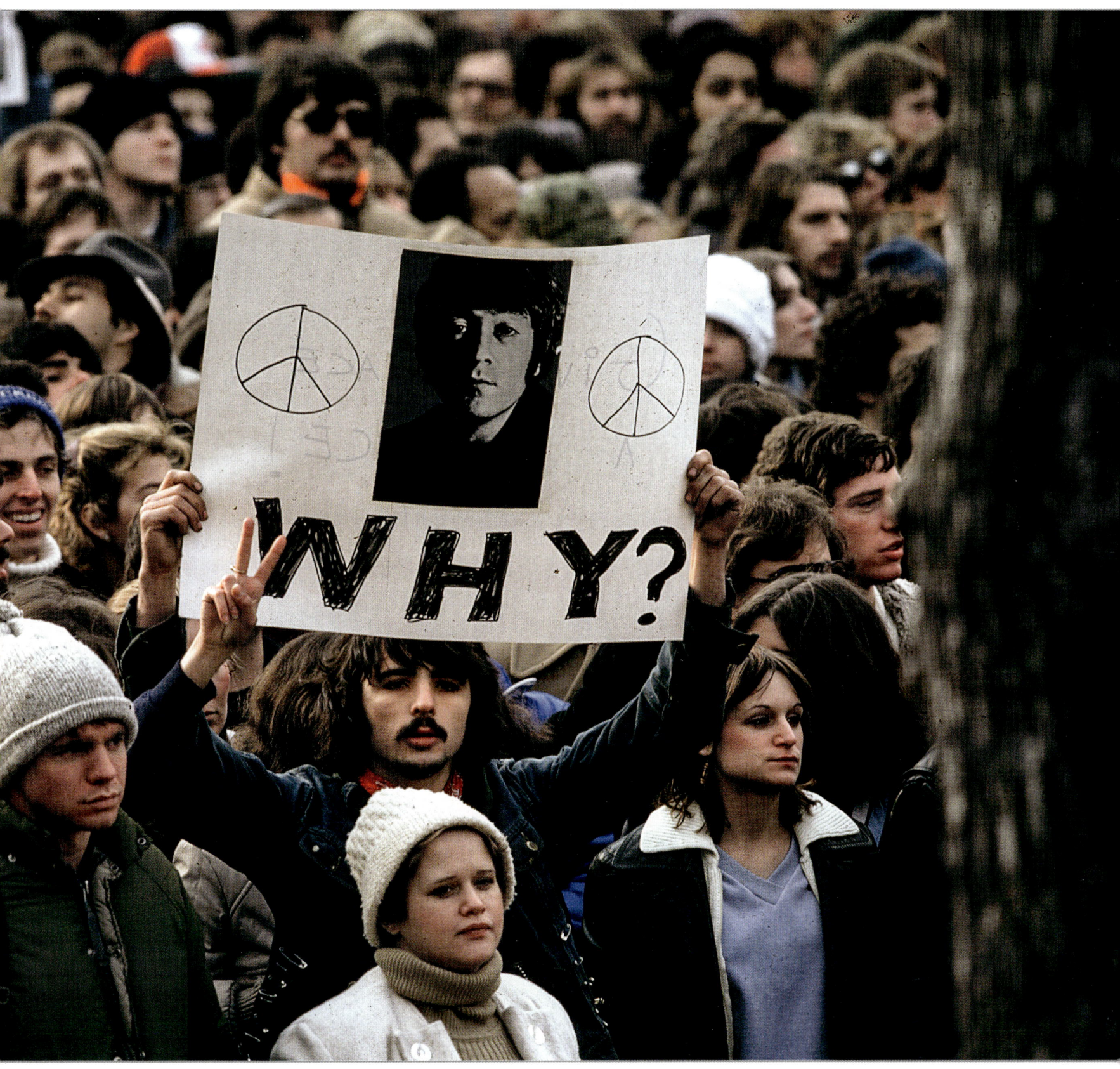

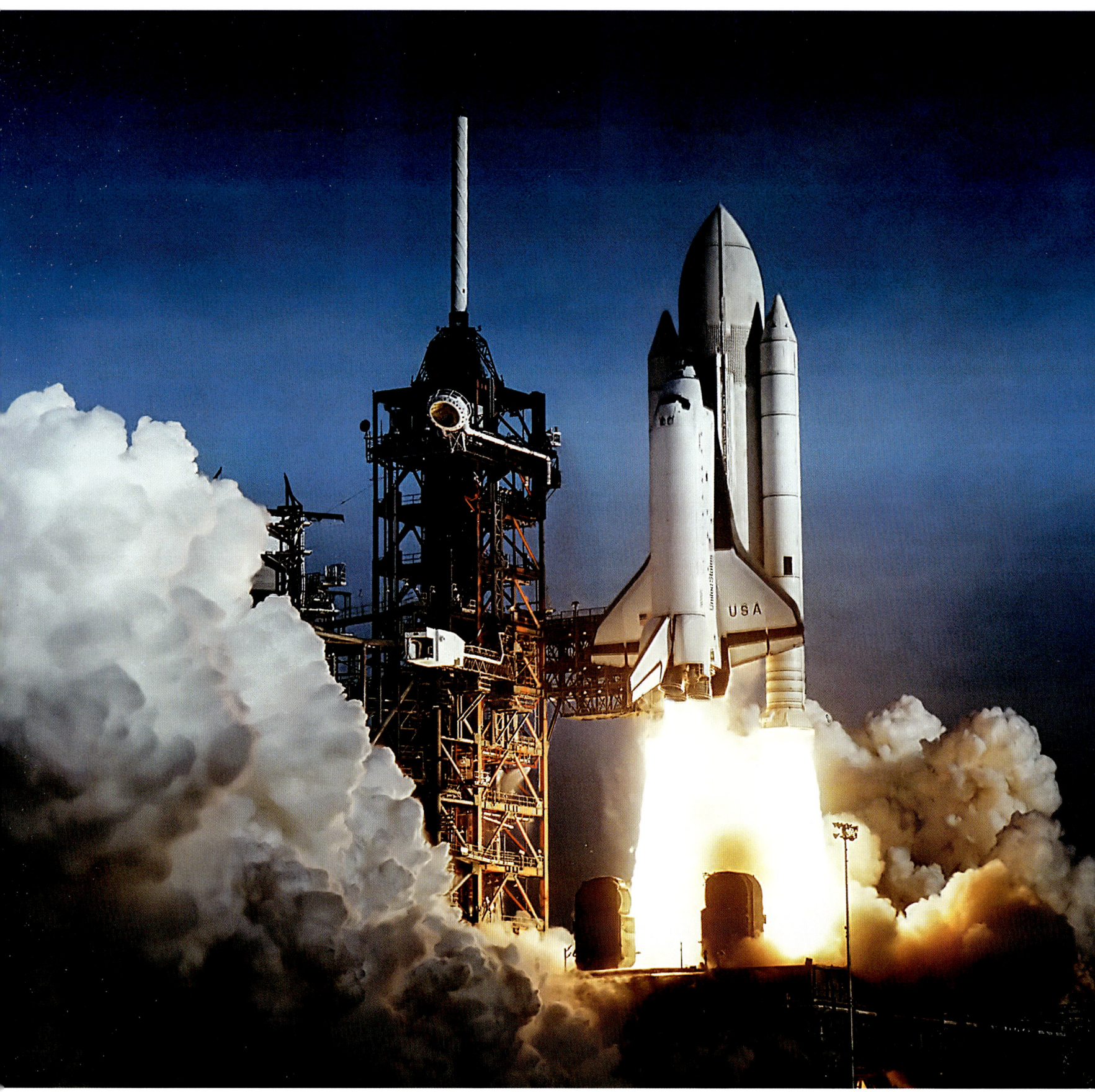

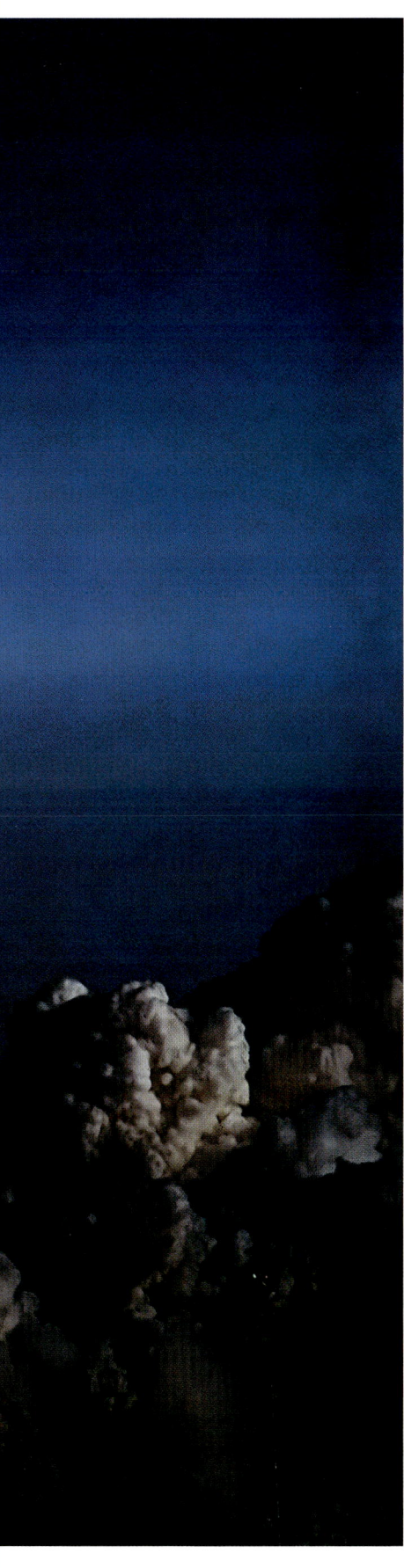

The Space Shuttle Columbia Launch

April 12, 1981 - Merritt Island, Florida, United States

Compared with many iconic photographs of the twentieth century, the image of the Columbia Shuttle, the first to complete an orbit in space around the Earth, owes much of its impact to the evolution of photographic equipment. First, color film helps convey the power and dynamism of the subject. And then there is the use of long, very powerful lenses which enable the photographer to capture the moment in a full frame, while remaining a safe distance away. The fire, the billowing plumes of smoke, the futuristic form of Columbia with its rocket, stimulate our imagination and make us think that the sky is, finally, within reach, like the moon and the universe. A spaceship that comes and goes from space revolutionizes the concept of a space mission, at least as this had been imagined until that April 12th, 1981.

Fundamentally, the name of the shuttle was also promising: Columbia had in fact been the first American spaceship to circumnavigate the earth, and it was the name of the command module of the Apollo 11 mission. Perhaps it was also intended to be an homage to Christopher Columbus and his desire to explore.

The photograph belongs to NASA and we don't know the name of the photographer. Certainly taking the picture must have been exciting. The image transcends its informative role and becomes the symbol of an era, the space era. In the case of the Columbia Space Shuttle, a tragic end is in store: on February 1st, 2003, on its return from mission STS-107, it disintegrates with all seven astronauts on board. In the collective imagination, however, the Columbia is reborn every time we look to the heavens.

The Assassination Attempt
on Pope John Paul II

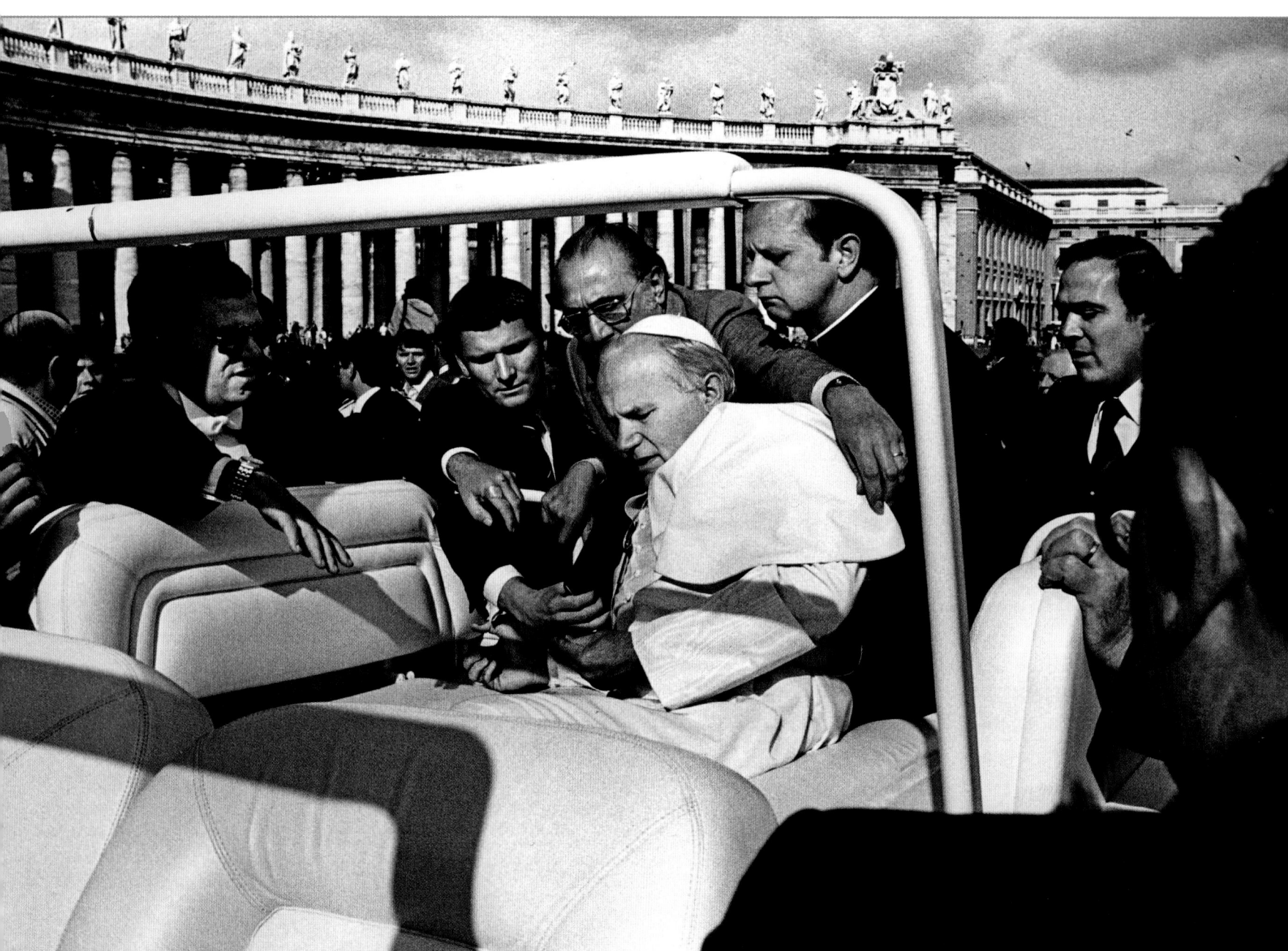

Photograph by Dölf Preisig

May 13, 1981 - Vatican City

John Paul II has collapsed after being shot twice. He looks at his bleeding hand: one of the bullets has wounded his hand and elbow, while the other has gone through his stomach and abdomen. The faces of the people around him – who include, behind him, his personal secretary, Father Stanislaw Dziwisz – are tense, darkened by the violence of the act. Mehmet Ali Agca, a Turkish terrorist, pulled the trigger.

It is a warm afternoon on May 13th, 1981. In the background of the photo, we see the colonnade of St Peter's Square, where the customary Wednesday audience with believers has just taken place. Attention is centered on the Holy Father: he is framed by the white profile of the car. It is as if he is already on a screen, before which the whole world awaits his fate in trepidation. The photo is abnormal, distorted, captured in a moment of panic for the photographer himself. Those in the crowd, who hoped for a handshake, are now in tears for the popular Polish Pope. This man, who in the middle of the Cold War courageously preaches the overcoming of economic and political divisions, is loved and respected by his followers. The Pope reaches the hospital after losing a lot of blood, but miraculously the bullets have not affected vital organs. An operation of more than five hours will remove him from danger.

It is never determined whether Agca's mission was personal or an international terrorist plan. In the several different and contradictory versions of the plan he gives while serving a life sentence, he admits, indiscriminately, links with the "Gray Wolves," a Turkish extreme right-wing movement, and suggests links with the Bulgarian military and secret service. In 1983, the Pope will meet him in Rebibbia Prison, a private meeting in which the Pope will forgive Agca. Before that conversation, Agca publicly stated that his only regret was not being able to kill the Pope. We can only wonder what would have happened if he had succeeded.

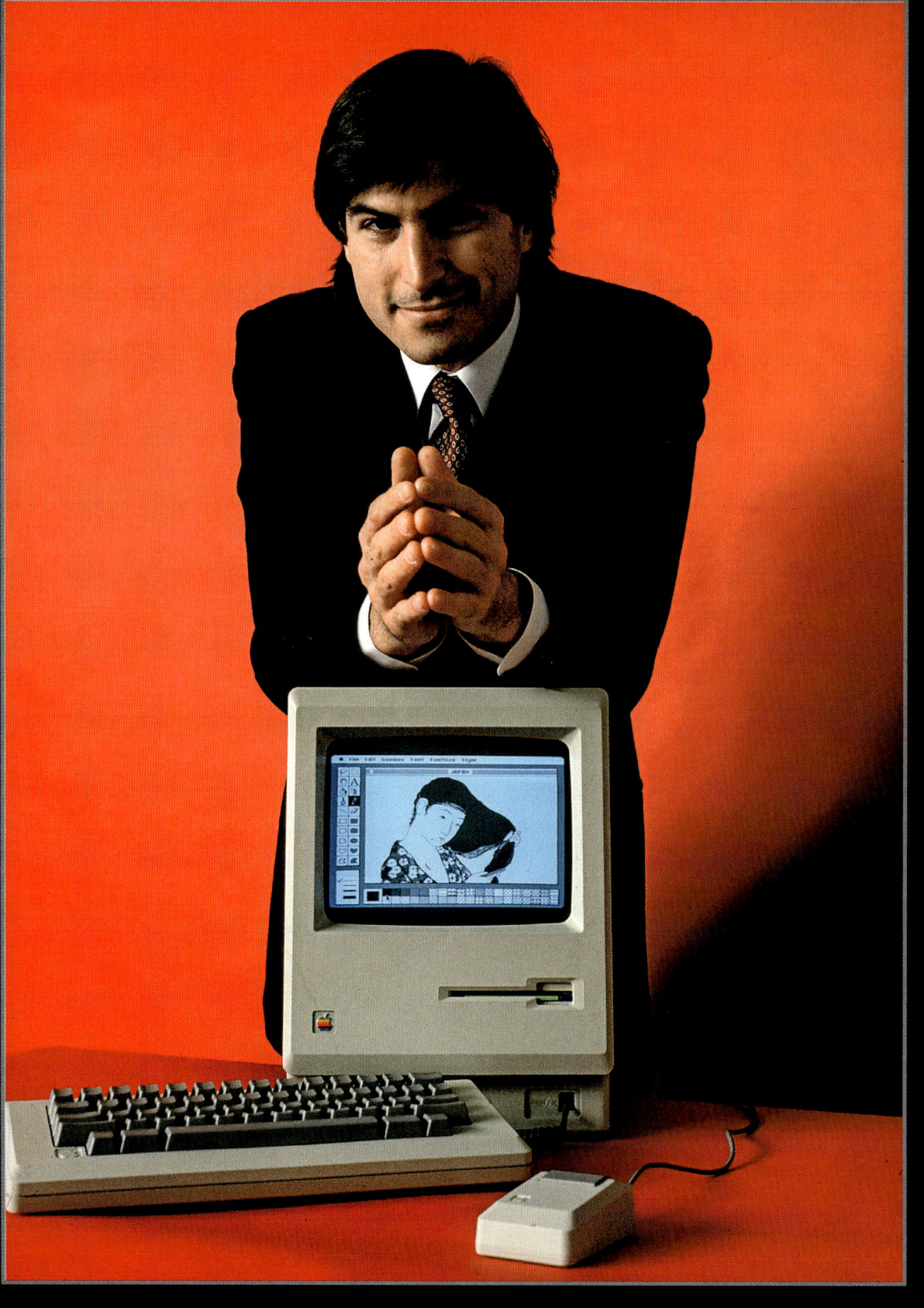

Photograph by Bernard Gotfryd

Steve Jobs and the Macintosh 128k

January 24, 1984 - United States

Confident gaze, satisfied smile, his pose exuding pride. It is 1984 and Steve Jobs presents his invention, the Macintosh 128k, the first Mac in history: the man and the machine that, aligned with his body, seems to hint at a playful expression; the man and machine that will change the habits of future generations. The creator of this shot is the Pole Bernard Gotfryd, a famous portraitist of figures in politics and show business. He certainly couldn't allow a promising young man like Jobs to escape his lens.

On January 24th, 1984, on the occasion of the presentation, the auditorium of the Flint Center in Cupertino, California, is alive with expectations. A commercial, directed by Ridley Scott, was televised only once, during the Super Bowl, but it detonated a hunger for novelty. Technology comes closer to humans, to their needs, to their creativity. The Mac 128k is a closed system, unassailable, with a combined screen and computer – it is already almost portable. The corners are rounded, the design is an integral part of the product. The real innovation is the graphic interface that simplifies its use. It makes using the computer intuitive even for a child, with a hand on the mouse. You only need a finger. The same principle will someday lead to multi-touch Technology, the iPhone, and the iPad. All the other manufacturers will have to adapt.

It will take a long time before Apple is among the largest and most influential companies in the world. Almost 20 years will pass, during which, at one point, Apple's unstoppable co-founder will be fired. By creating a new company, NeXT, he will save the "Think different" company from bankruptcy in 1998. But Steve Jobs is a visionary and understands the explosive power of his innovations. He is burning with desire to change the world. He's already "hungry and foolish."

Reagan and Gorbachev
at the Geneva Summit

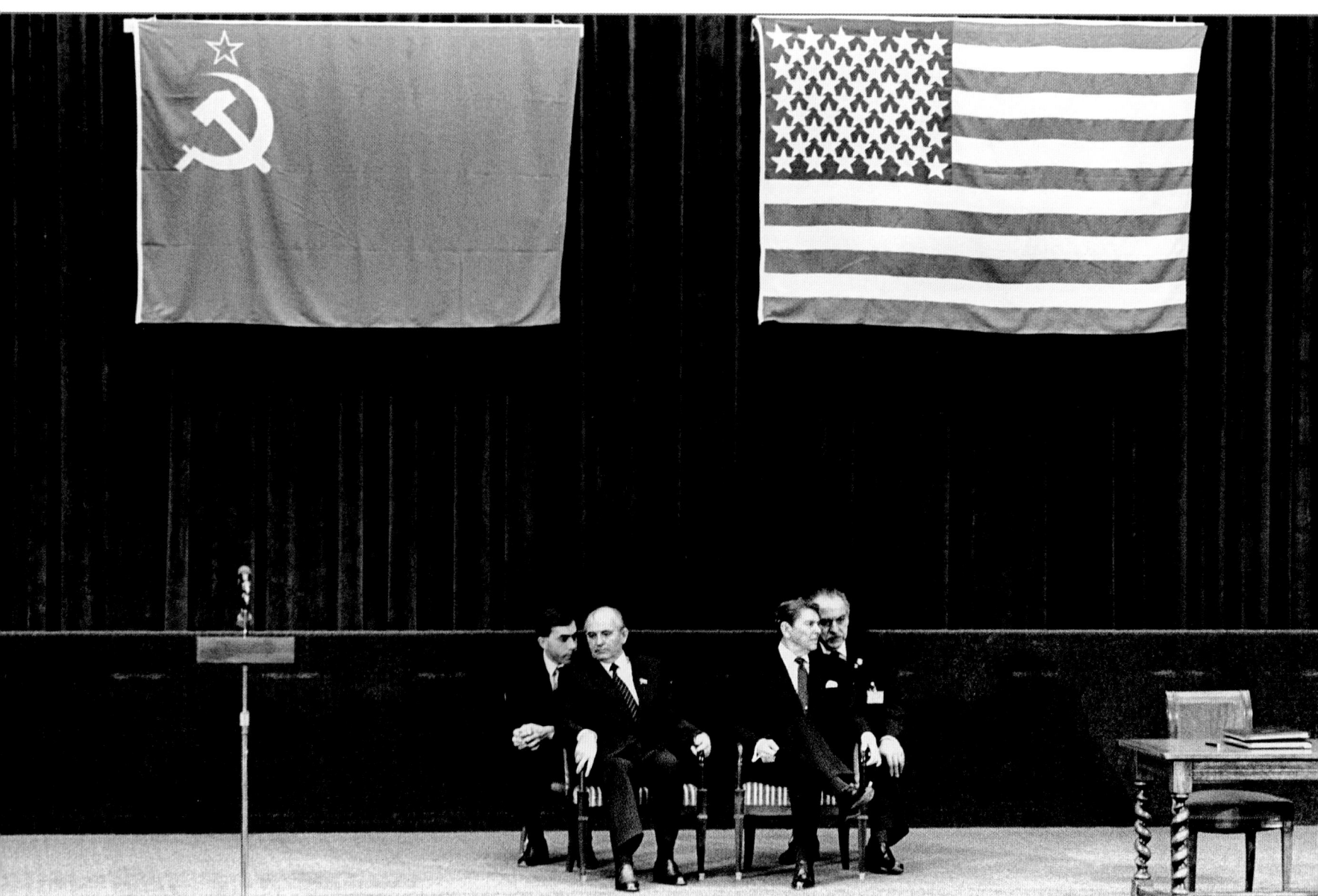

Photograph by Peter Marlow

November 19, 1985 - Geneva, Switzerland

On November 19th, 1985, a long awaited Russian-American summit opened in Geneva, in neutral Switzerland, to discuss the reduction of armaments. The protagonists of this meeting were Mikhail Gorbachev, elected a few months before as General Secretary of the Communist Party of the Soviet Union (CPSU), and the President of the United States, Ronald Reagan. The picture, by the British photographer Peter Marlow of Magnum agency, shows the two leaders at a press conference.

In the center of the shot, Gorbachev and Reagan seem small in comparison to the enormous flags of their countries: it is not two men we see here, but two superpowers, two opposing worlds in confrontation. The photographer captures the protagonists at a moment when they are not looking at each other but are addressing, symmetrically, the two interpreters behind them. There seems to be a certain coldness and mutual mistrust. In reality, the meeting took place in a relatively open climate, which was very different from the heated tones that had marked USA-USSR relations in previous years. It was the first time that Reagan and Gorbachev had met personally. In the course of several talks over three days, they dealt with difficult topics like human rights in the Soviet Union, and the Strategic Defense Initiative proposed by Reagan, thus giving the first signs of détente after nearly forty years of Cold War. On November 21st, Reagan and Gorbachev were able to announce on worldwide television that they had reached an agreement for the reduction of nuclear warheads. What the American President described as "his longest day" concluded a meeting invested with many expectations, and created good prospects for subsequent meetings between the two leaders. One took place the following year in Reykjavík, and the decisive one was in Washington, in 1987. These led to the end of the Cold War.

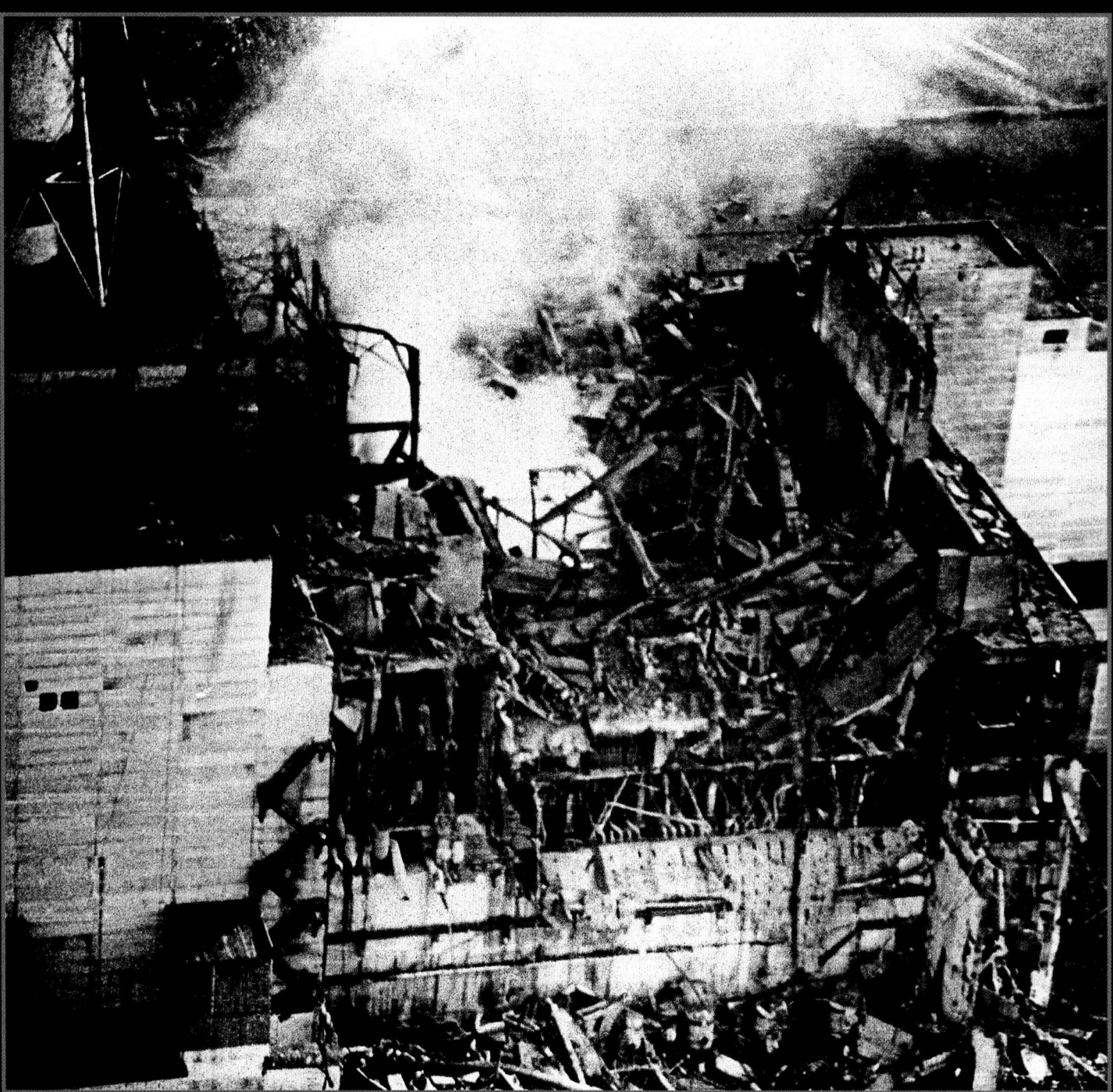

The Explosion of the Chernobyl Reactor

April 26, 1986 - Kiev Oblast, Soviet Union

From the ruins of an industrial building, a toxic cloud rises menacingly to the sky. The events of April 26th, 1986, have branded the name of Chernobyl, in the Ukraine, as one of the most tragic in the history of atomic energy. The accident, which was caused by a combination of personal errors of judgment and structural defects in the power station, provoked an explosion in a reactor. Initially, the Soviet authorities kept the accident secret: they were totally unprepared for such a disaster, and they did not even bother to evacuate the inhabitants of the nearby city of Pripyat. The evacuation was started only 36 hours after the accident, and about 100,000 people were forced to leave their homes.

Officials acted with the same indifference and disorganization in containing the contamination, which was due to a great fire that had developed in the power station following the explosion. Two weeks was needed to extinguish the radioactive plume, and the individuals involved in this difficult task – firefighters, soldiers, technicians, but also volunteers – were exposed to enormous quantities of radiation without adequate protection. Many of them would die in the following weeks and months.

The Chernobyl disaster was classified as a "catastrophic accident." It caused 65 deaths directly, but a much greater number of people, the estimate of which is still controversial, were involved indirectly. The consequences ranged from tumors to the birth of children with serious malformations. The contamination affected almost all of the European continent: the wind blowing in the following days in fact pushed toxic clouds first toward the north – toward nearby Belarus – then to the west, and finally south. Once the fire was put out, a concrete containment vessel was built to isolate the reactor from the surrounding environment. Despite this, part of the power station was in operation until 2000.

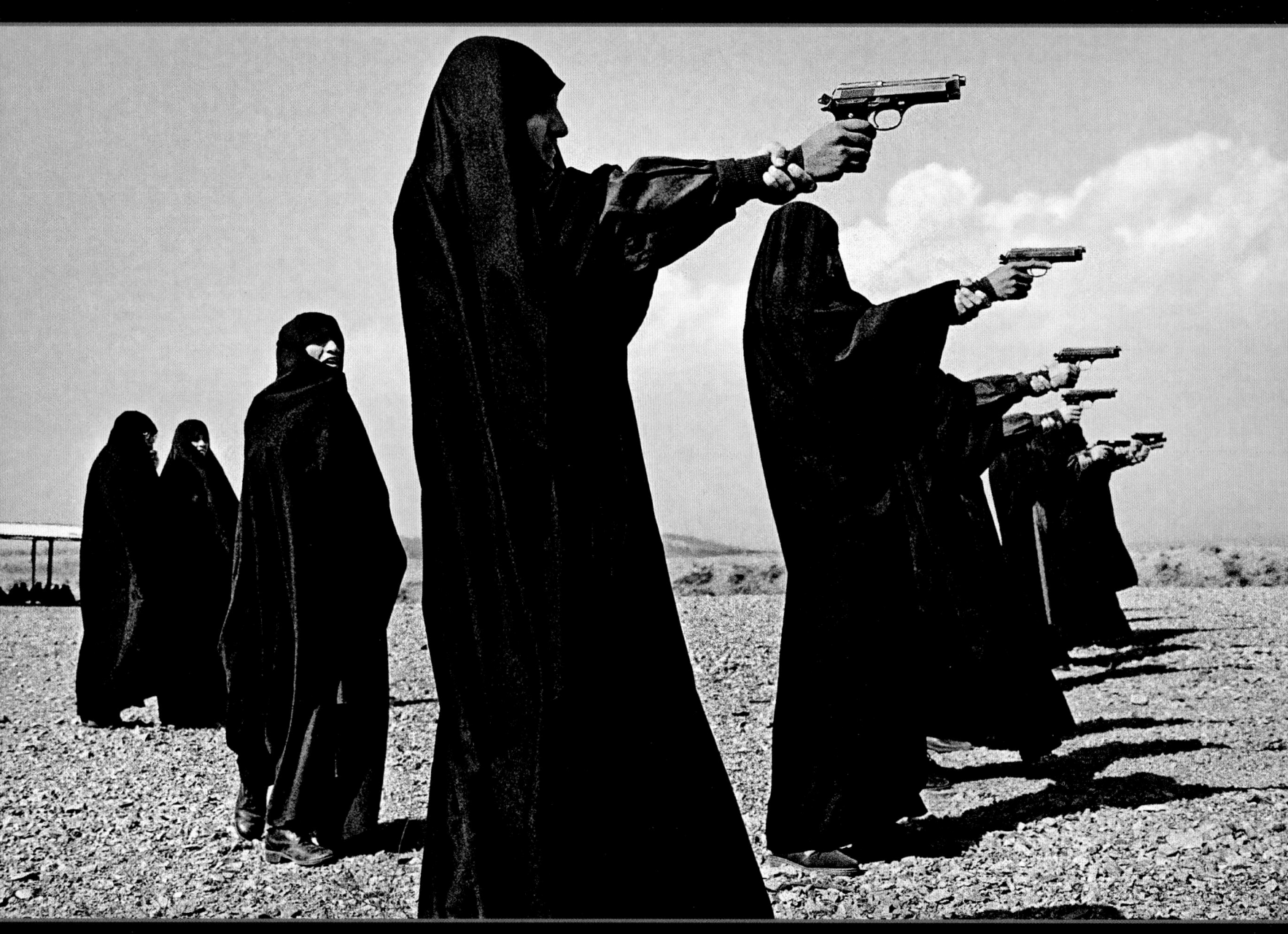

Photograph by Jean Gaumy

Veiled Women Practicing Shooting

1986 - Tehran, Iran

In the middle of the eighties, the French photographer and journalist Jean Gaumy left for Iran to record the radical changes following the Islamic revolution of 1979. His photographs gave evidence of a disturbing situation: the country, which had been at war with Iraq since 1980, was embracing radical religious fundamentalism.

This black and white image shows several women practicing shooting on the outskirts of Teheran. They all wear chadors, and they cast long shadows on the parched earth. They all look the same, and they stand in an orderly line: they hold pistols and point them at an invisible enemy. They seem to ignore the photographer, and yet they form two diagonal lines which converge precisely in front of his lens. It is impossible to know what they are thinking: are they firm followers of the ayatollahs leading the country, or are they only patriots who intend to support Iran against Iraq? Or perhaps they are still angry about the repression and executions which, in the seventies, were a feature of the rule of the Shah Reza Pahlavi, who was then overthrown by Khomeini.

Yet under the Pahlavi dynasty, women obtained many rights, starting with electoral rights. In contrast, Khomeini, even before the proclamation of the Islamic Republic, began to enforce literal obedience to the Koran and the Sharia, reversing reforms of the previous decades. Soon women lost civil rights and their personal freedom was strongly curtailed: they could not attend higher education or work without the consent of their husbands, who were to make all decisions within the family. The regime imposed the veil and introduced severe corporal punishment for violations of Islamic law. The right to enroll in the paramilitary forces was one of the few rights left for women.

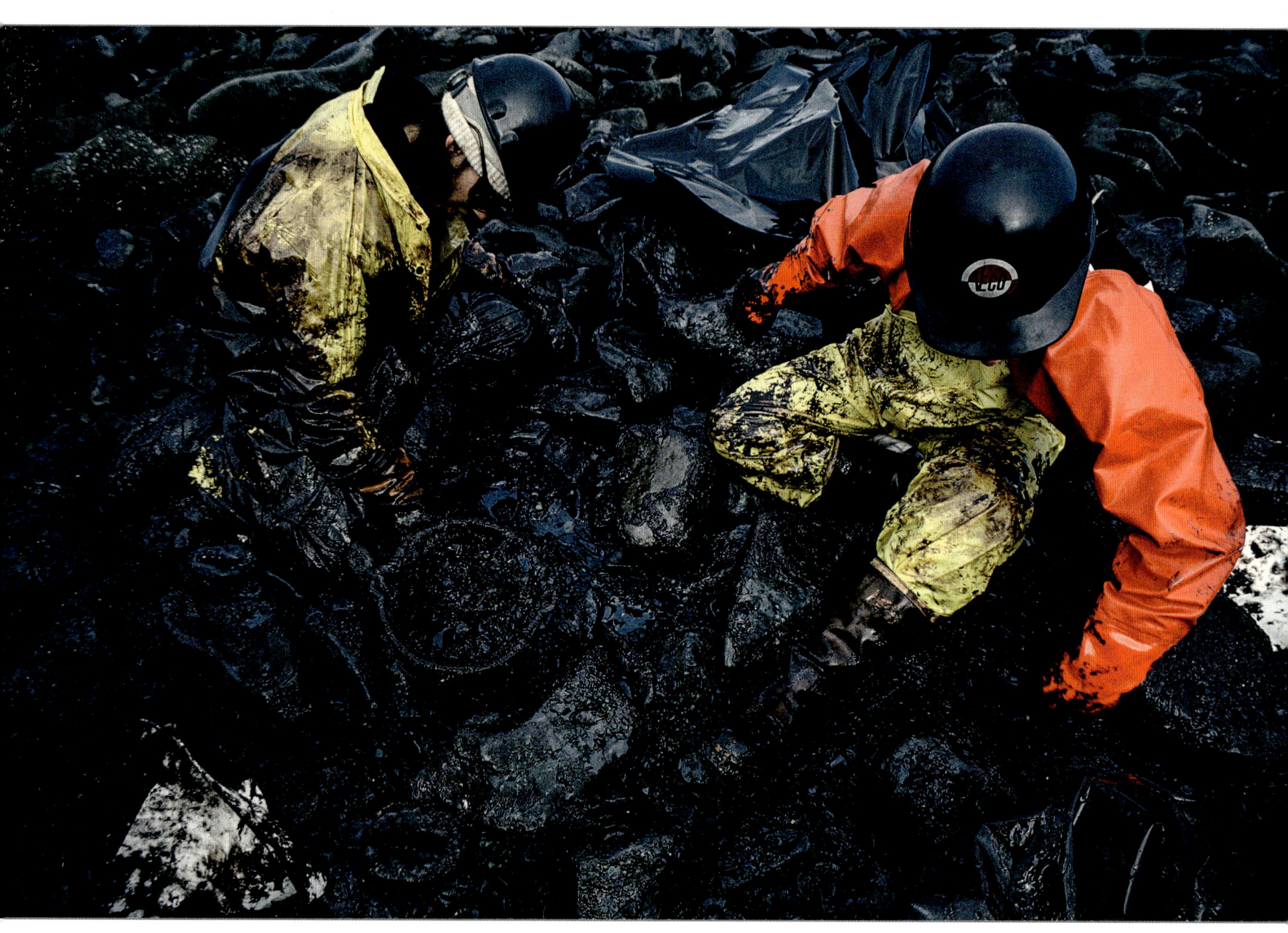

Photograph by Paul Fusco

The Exxon Valdez Environmental Disaster

March 24, 1989 - Alaska, United States

Besides spectacular glaciers, Prince William Sound, along the Pacific coast of Alaska, is home to the city of Valdez. Since July of 1977, Valdez has been the terminal of one of the greatest pipelines in the world: 807 miles of pipe move crude oil from the Prudhoe Bay, in the Arctic Ocean, to the Pacific. The pipeline covers a wild, wonderful region, populated by bears, deer, orcas, whales, and a superb variety of avifauna. Right in the middle of this paradise, on March 24th, 1989, the oil tanker Exxon Valdez ran aground, pouring out from its ripped hull 11 million gallons of crude. It was the greatest technological disaster in the history of the United States. The catastrophe wiped out the local fishing industry, inflicted a deadly blow on numerous species of animals in the area (many of which were already threatened by fur hunters), and upset the ecosystem of the entire region.

If today the signs of the tragedy are not obvious, this is due to the gradual action of time and the commitment of public safety professionals and the numerous volunteers who immediately got to work cleaning up the coasts and saving the many animals trapped by the crude. The catastrophe also attracted reporters and photojournalists: the Exxon Valdez was on the front pages of papers around the world. Photographs like this one, taken by the Magnum Photos agency photojournalist Paul Fusco, woke up that part of public opinion that was uninformed and insensitive to the dangers of the environmental disasters. Photographs like Fusco's forced oil companies to promise to adopt more rigorous safety measures.

The strong chromatic contrast gives this photo a distinct character: the two patches of color show the presence of human beings, who otherwise are lost in the darkness of the oil that covers everything in a funereal blanket. Taking the photograph from overhead captures how the subjects might feel crushed and overwhelmed by their hopeless struggle.

Tank Man

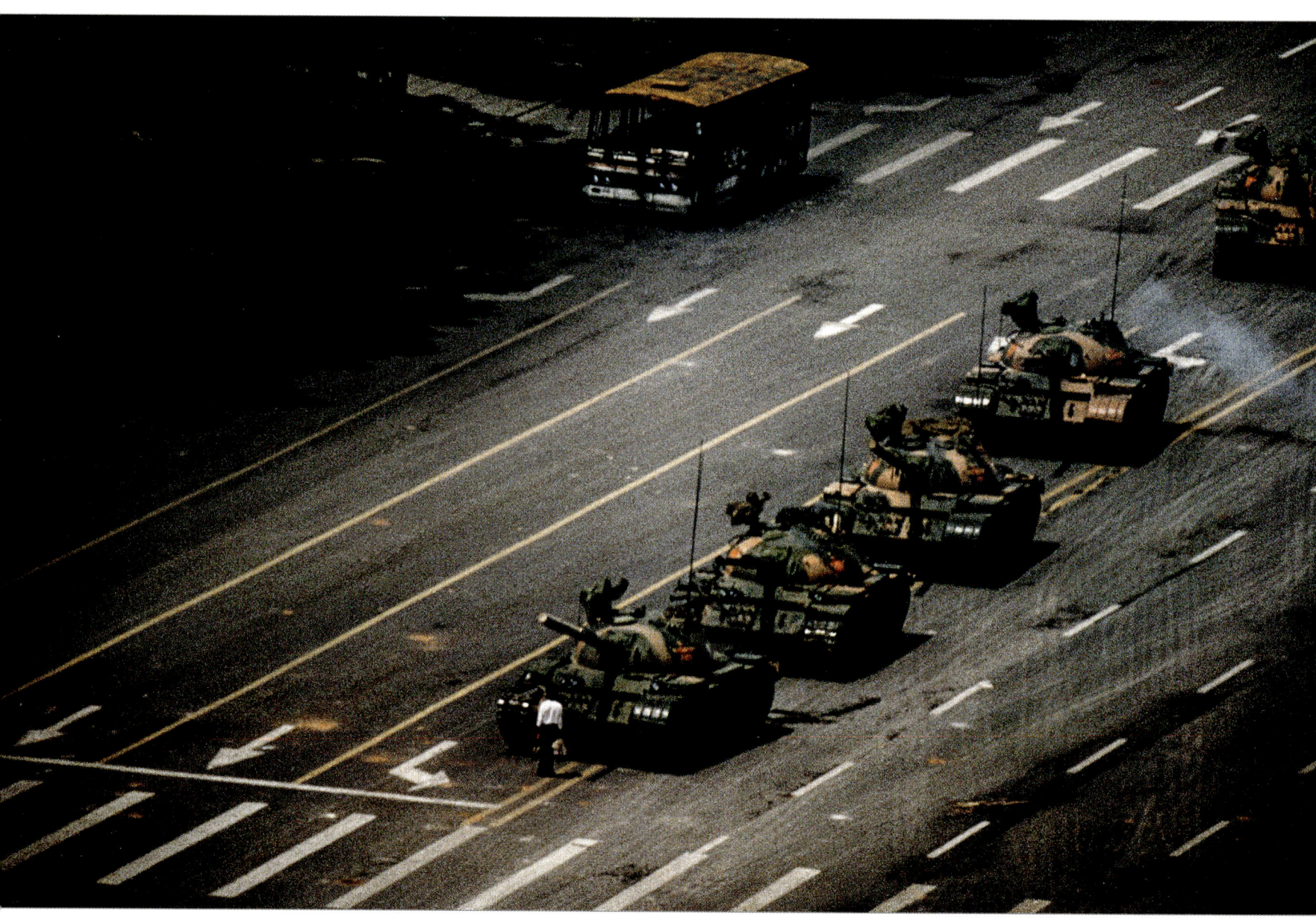

Photograph by Stuart Franklin

June 5, 1989 - Beijing, People's Republic of China

The year 1989 marked a turning point in the second half of the twentieth century, and the protest in Tiananmen Square was one of the main events in the year. It exploded in the middle of April, following the death of the Chinese Communist Party Secretary Hu Yaobang, and involved an ever greater number of students, intellectuals, and workers taking to the streets and demanding the so-called "Fifth Modernization": a reform which would open China to democracy, following Soviet *glasnost* and the collapse of the regimes in Eastern Europe.

The protest lasted until the beginning of June, when the leaders of the government, advised by the old leader Deng Xiaoping, ordered the army to intervene and occupy the capital. On the second day of the repression, some Western journalists following the evolution of events from the Beijing Hotel noticed a strange scene along Chang'an Avenue, the great road leading to Tienanmen Square. About half a mile away, a mysterious white-shirted boy, completely disarmed, had blocked a line of tanks.

There are two famous photographs of this event, which became a worldwide symbol of the protest. One, by Jeff Widener, offers a small field of view: the young man and the four tanks take up the entire scene. The second photograph, by Stuart Franklin, included here, provides a much wider field of view, and allows us to see other tanks and the remains of a bus, testament to earlier violence, in the top part of the photo. The protest and student movement will soon be put down, and the repressive government will emerge triumphant. The identity of the young rebel shown here, and the fate reserved for him by the Chinese regime, remain unknown.

The Fall of the Berlin Wall

November 9, 1989 - Berlin, Germany

November 9th, 1989. 6:53 p.m. During a press conference, Riccardo Ehrman, ANSA correspondent, asks Günter Schabowski, the DDR Minister of Propaganda, when permits will be issued for transit from East Germany to West Germany. On hearing the Minister's surprising response ("immediately, without delay"), thousands of East Berliners pour into the streets and gather along the Wall.

The border guards are unprepared. They have not received orders and fear the crowd's intention. So they decide to open the checkpoints. In a moment, a river of people pass through the Wall, West Berlin inhabitants joyously welcome their East Berlin fellow citizens, and all through the night songs and shouts of joy resound from one side to the other of what had been the "strip of death."

Groups of people armed with hammers and pickaxes take out their anger on the Wall and on what the barrier has meant to them since 1961: they are remembered as the *Mauerspechte* (literally, "pickaxes of the Wall").

In the photo by the young American newspaper photographer Alexandra Avakian, the *LIFE* correspondent in West Berlin, a man seems to be engaged in a personal battle with the reinforced concrete. All his body is involved in the movement, starting from his gaze. On the other side, the DDR soldiers don't dare to use their arms against him: they try to discourage him with a hydrant, directing jets of water into the breech in the Wall. In the background, his companions encourage him not to stop. Their cries of encouragement go beyond the limits of the image and resound as an invitation to break down every kind of wall, to overcome conflicts and divisions.

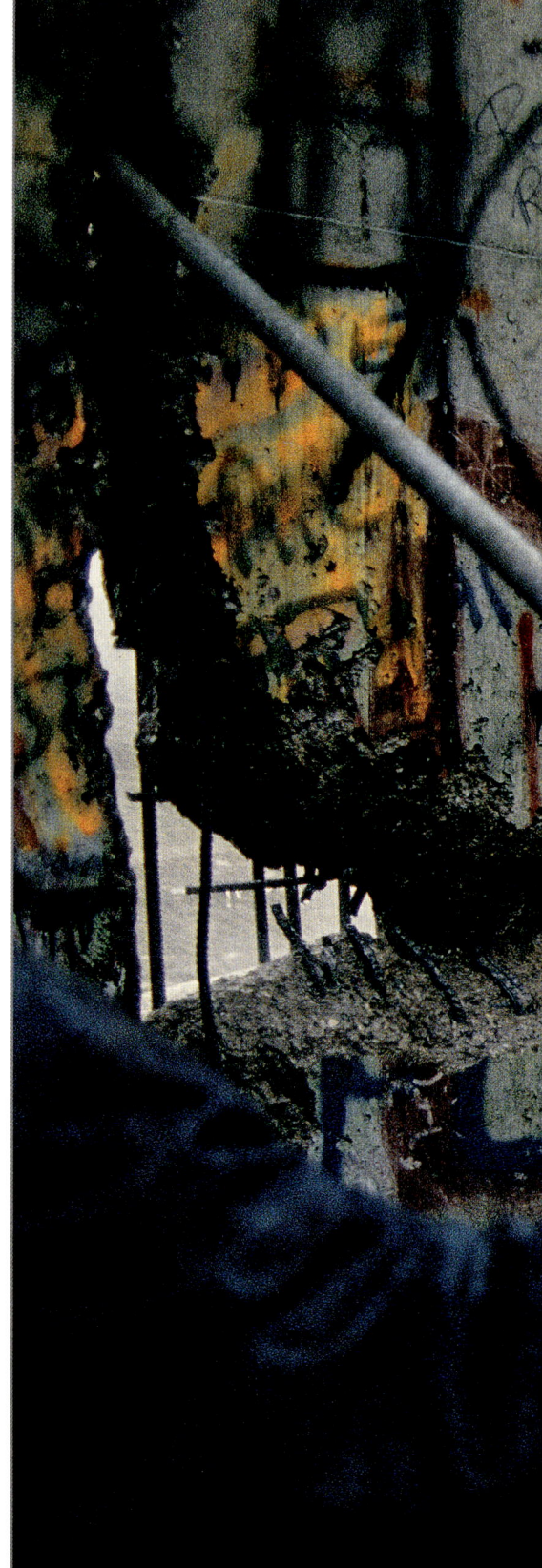

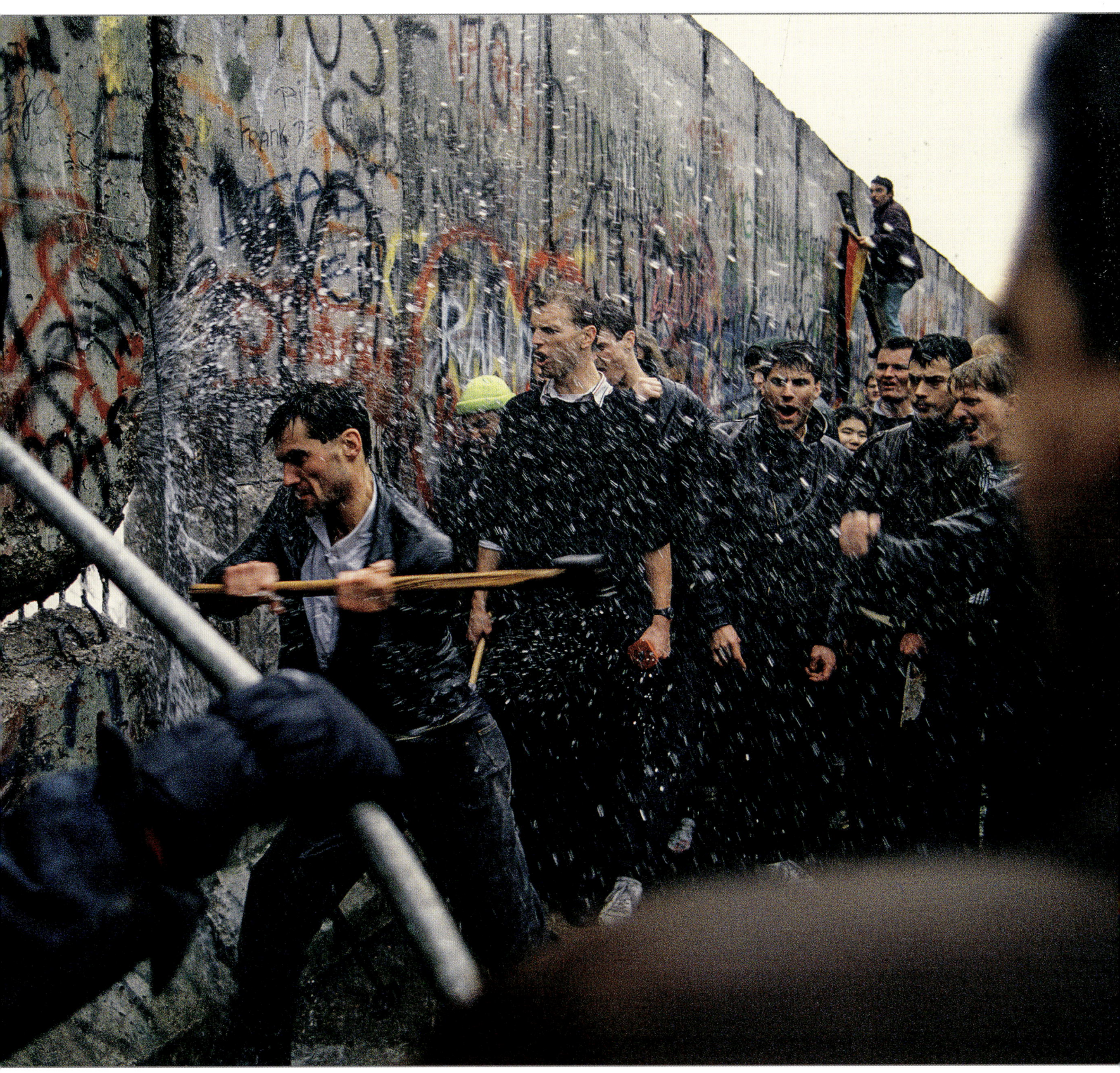

Photograph by Alexandra Avakian

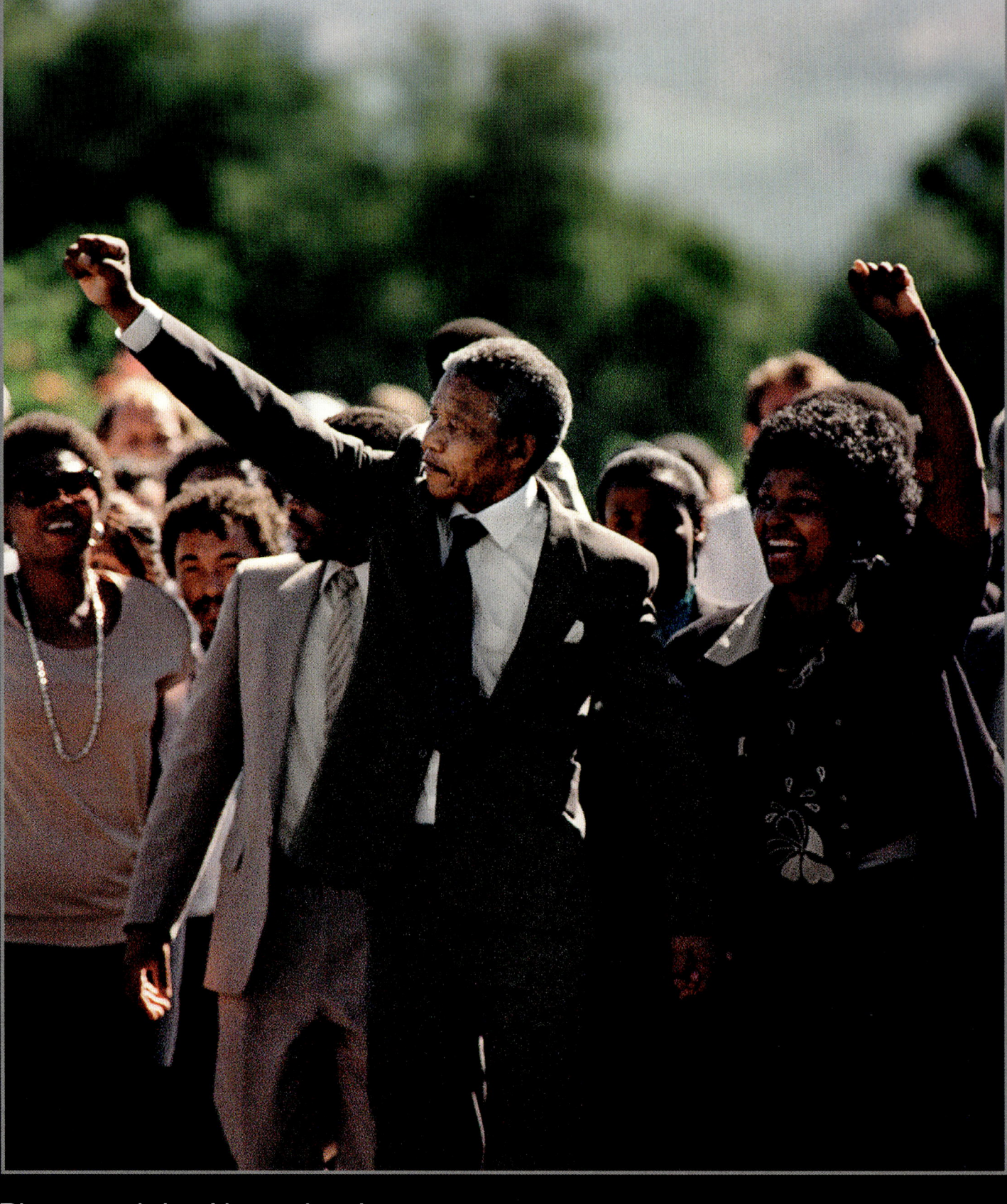

Photograph by Alexander Joe

The Liberation of Nelson Mandela

February 11, 1990 - Cape Town, Republic of South Africa

The protagonist of this image doesn't appear to be a man who's been in prison for 27 years. Quite the opposite. Judging by his clothes, the elegant single-breasted jacket worn casually over a light blue shirt, with a necktie and a handkerchief in the top pocket, you might think he was businessman at the height of his success. And his gestures, his fist raised towards the crowd, the other arm accompanying a smiling woman, could be those of a politician who has just won an election. Yet he is a man who was sentenced to prison for life: Nelson Mandela, photographed here with his wife Winnie and his supporters, on the day as his liberation, February 11th, 1990.

The leader of the anti-apartheid movement, Mandela was arrested in August 1962. This did not prevent him, as a representative of the ANC (African National Congress), from carrying on the political struggle, or from becoming the very symbol of the protest movement in South Africa and in the rest of the continent. Mandela was awarded the Sakharov Prize in 1988, and the Nobel Peace Prize in 1993, together with Frederik de Klerk, the white President of South Africa who had ordered his release. The end of apartheid and national reconciliation were ratified in the following year, when Mandela won the election and became President in his turn. He nominated de Klerk as his Vice President.

Mandela can be considered a world icon more than an African politician, and this is precisely what the image conveys. It was taken by Alexander Joe, a Zimbabwe-born photographer, one of the best photographers of the AFP. In a deliberately informal setting, which is underscored by the low, late afternoon light, Alexander manages to communicate Mandela's intimate and human side, along with the triumph of justice and freedom.

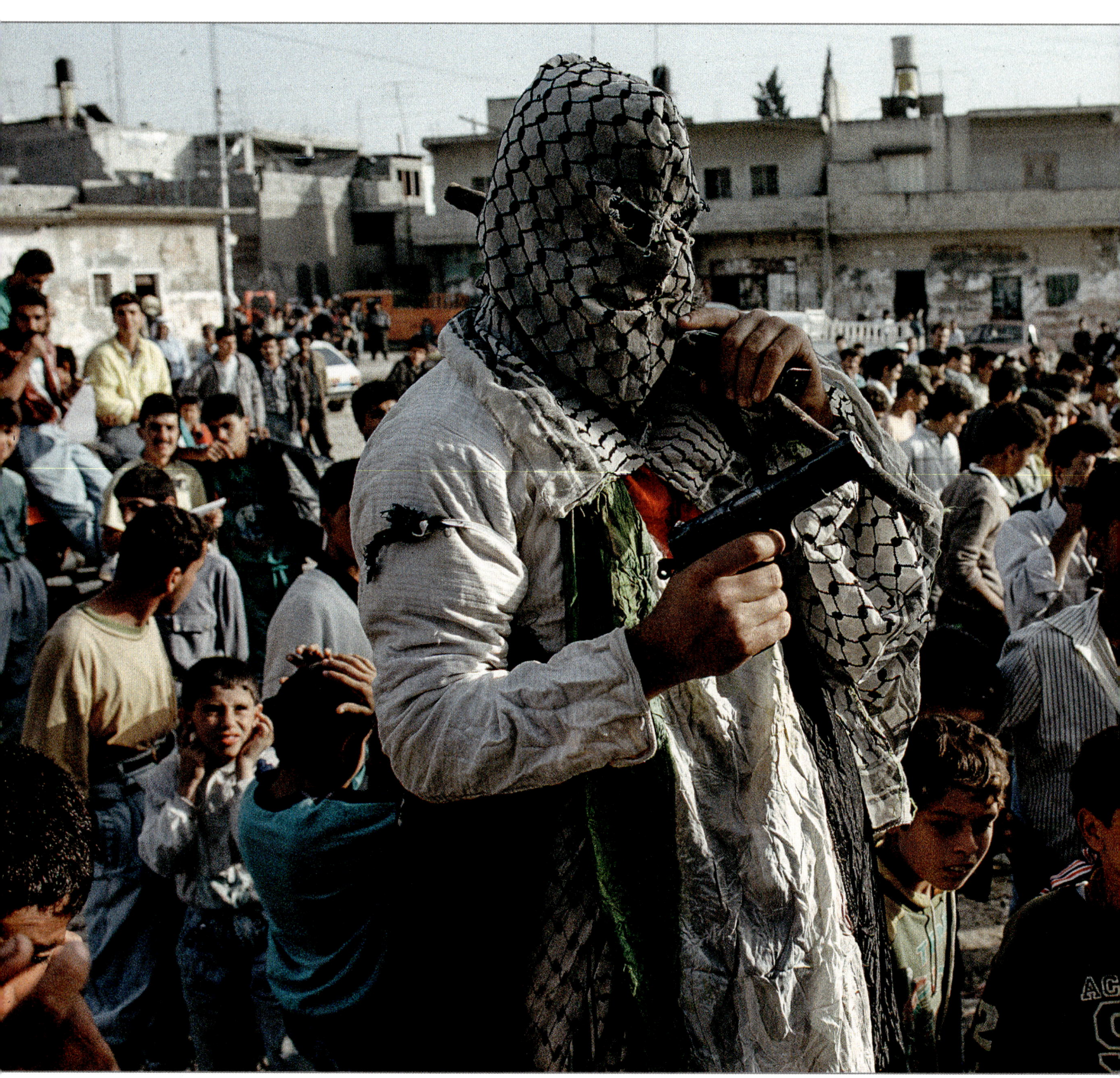

Photograph by Abbas Attar

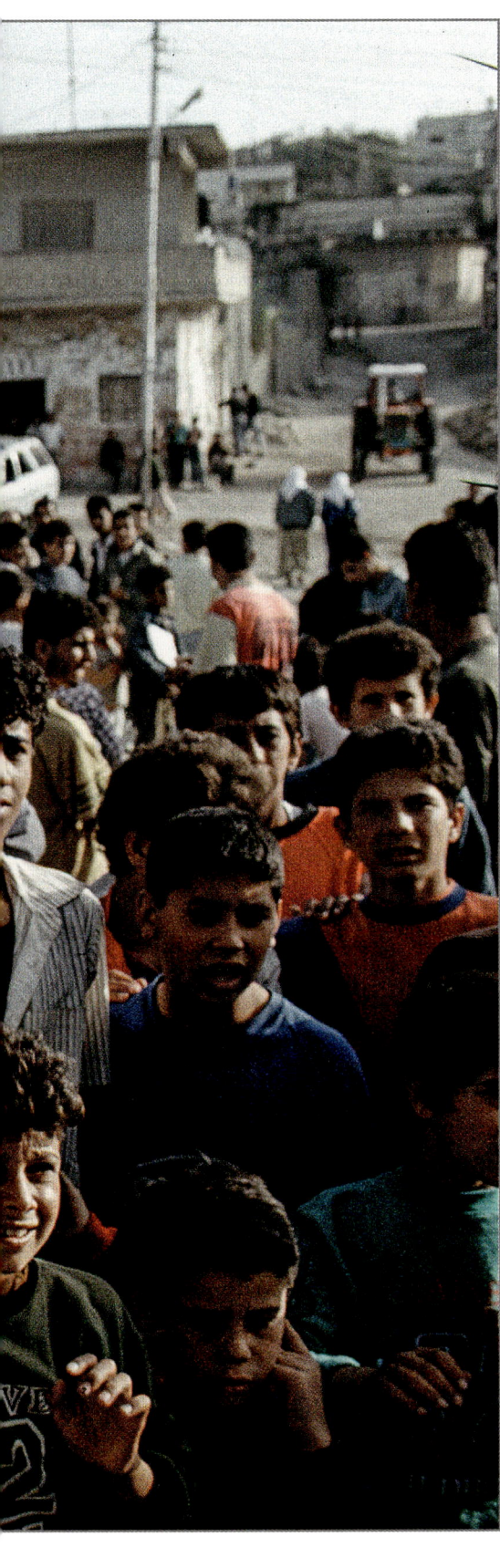

The First Intifada

1991 - Jenin, Israel

He has a *kefiah* over his face, like a balaclava; on his left shoulder he has what could be truncheon, while, more frighteningly, in his right hand he has a pistol, his index finger on the trigger. He is a Palestinian, perhaps awaiting an attack by the Israeli army, perhaps defending the crowd of children and teenagers around him. Abbas Attar, of Magnum Photos, took the photo near the city of Jenin in the northern West Bank in 1991: we are in the middle of the Intifada and not a day goes by without violence and clashes occurring in the Palestinian-occupied territories. On one side, the Israeli soldiers with tanks and bulldozers; on the other, the young people of the West Bank and Gaza, armed above all with stones and Molotovs. They consider each other terrorists and oppressors. The revolt, which will be called the First Intifada or Intifada of Stones, began in December, 1987: the contingent cause was an army lorry which collided with two vans full of Palestinian workers, killing four, at Jabalya, Gaza. The real causes were the frustration and sense of abandonment (abandonment by Arab nations, especially) felt by the Palestinians who lived in the territories, the poverty, and the crowded conditions of the refugee camps. The clashes continued for six years, causing the death of 160 Israelis, soldiers and civilians, and more than 1,000 Palestinians (to which one should add 1,000 deaths through vendettas and settling of scores within the Intifada). The Oslo agreements of 1993, between the Palestine Liberation Organization and Israel, temporarily ended the violence, and laid the foundations for a true Palestinian State. But the West Bank and Gaza continued to exist without international status. The children in Abbas' photo would probably be the protagonists, or the victims, of the new revolts: the Second Intifada (that of Al-Aqsa, 2000-2005) and the Third (that of the knives, since 2015).

Burning Oil Wells

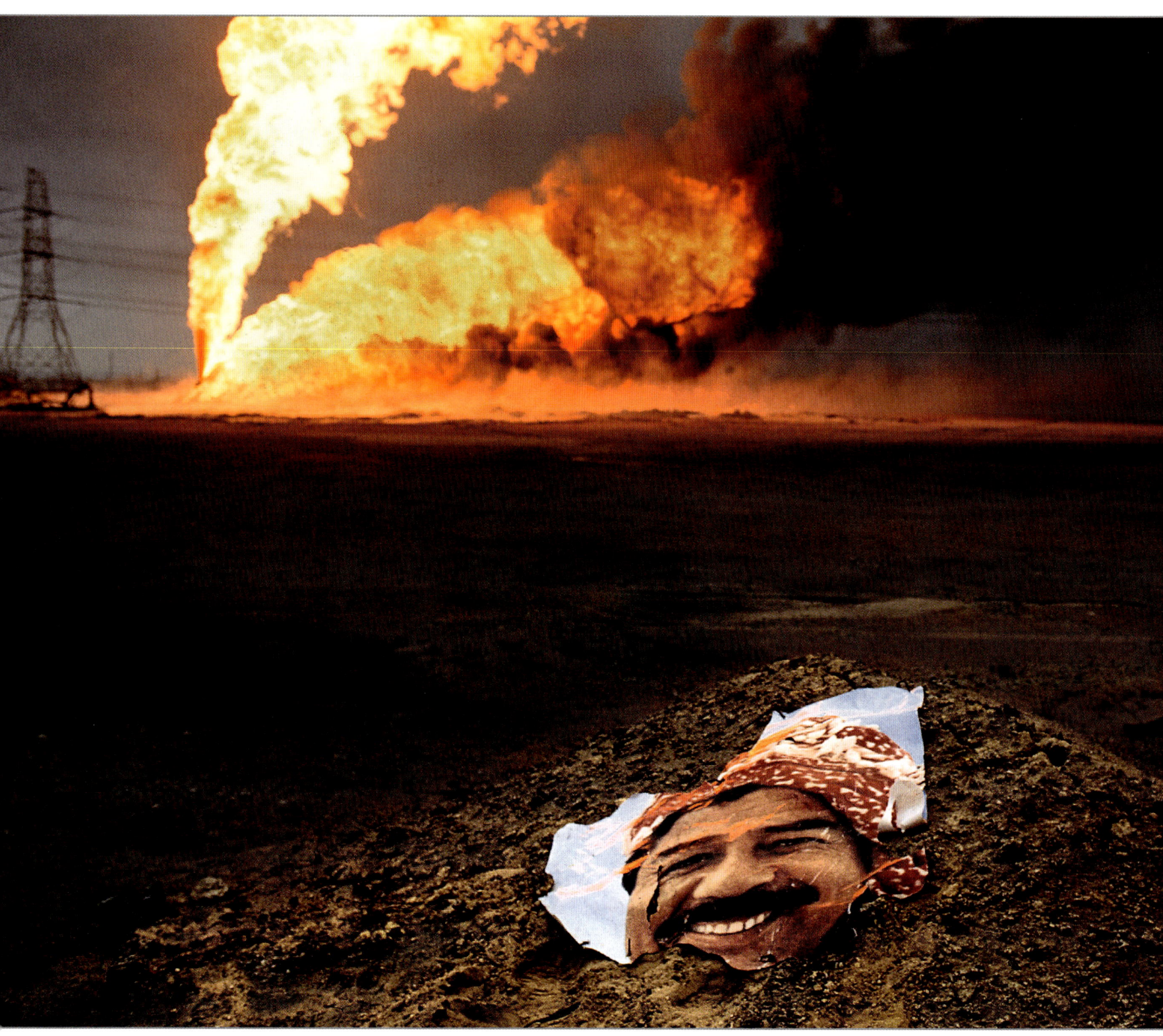

1991 - Kuwait

Columns of smoke rise from oil wells and redden the desert night. Saddam Hussein lies in the dust, smiling on what remains of an old poster. It is difficult to sum up more effectively the First Gulf War. There is oil to conquer and to defend, or to set fire to when there is the risk it might fall into enemy hands; the role of propaganda and the importance of images; the dictator who remains in power despite defeat, and so has some reason to be satisfied.

Everything is clear in the eyes of Abbas Attar, a photographer for the legendary agency Magnum Photos. Although he lives in Paris, Abbas is an Iranian with deep knowledge of the Arab world. After having documented wars and revolutions in half the countries of the world, he chose in 1987 to examine the differing faces of Islam, from the Chinese region of Xinjiang to the Atlantic coast of the Maghreb.

The First Gulf War was not the only subject of his enquiry. He followed it attentively but did not consider it absolutely central, in contrast to European and American media. From August 2nd, 1990, to February 28th, 1991, many media outlets showed every detail of the Allied forces' operation, broadcasting images taken at night with night vision gear, showing explosions seen from above by fighter planes. It was a huge videogame in which death – especially for the Iraqis – lost all sacredness.

Skeptical and disenchanted, Abbas knew that what would go down in history as the "first war of the global village" was only a stage on a more complex journey. He contextualized the episode and looked beyond. His journey among Islamic people would end in 1994, when he published the photographic book *Allah O Akbar: A Journey Through Militant Islam*. The West would discover its prophetic value only after September 11th, 2001.

Photograph by Abbas Attar

Tim Berners-Lee and the Invention of the Web

August 6, 1991 - Geneva, Switzerland

If there is one invention that has changed the way people live in recent times, it is certainly the Internet, the great network which connects us all and eliminates distance. The service most used by many people in the world is the World Wide Web, which allows us to surf a digital treasure house of interlinked information of various kinds (texts, images, music, films . . .). With just a click, you can find what you are looking for, which in its turn is linked to other content and yet other content, ad infinitum.

The inventor of the World Wide Web, or simply the Web, is Tim Berners-Lee, a computer scientist born in London in 1955. After a degree in physics from Queen's College, Oxford, in 1976, and working for a few years with various telecommunications companies, he obtained a contract at the CERN facility in Geneva as a software engineering consultant. He began to develop the idea of hypertext, and of data networks, with the program Enquire, the prototype of the World Wide Web. And on August 6th, 1991, he successfully created the first website: info.cern.ch. In the meantime, he designed the http protocol and the html programming language. He perfected the entire system, and it opened the way to the communication revolution.

This portrait of Tim Berners-Lee's face was made by the American artist Robert Silvers using a photomosaic technique, a process Silvers invented by during his studies at MIT in Boston. The image contains a vast number of small photographs, an intricate work that reinterprets the painting technique of Pointillism in the digital era: it is a style which breaks down the boundaries between art, photography, and technology. That today these fields are increasingly open and interconnected is also due to the genius of Tim Berners-Lee.

Photograph by Robert Silvers

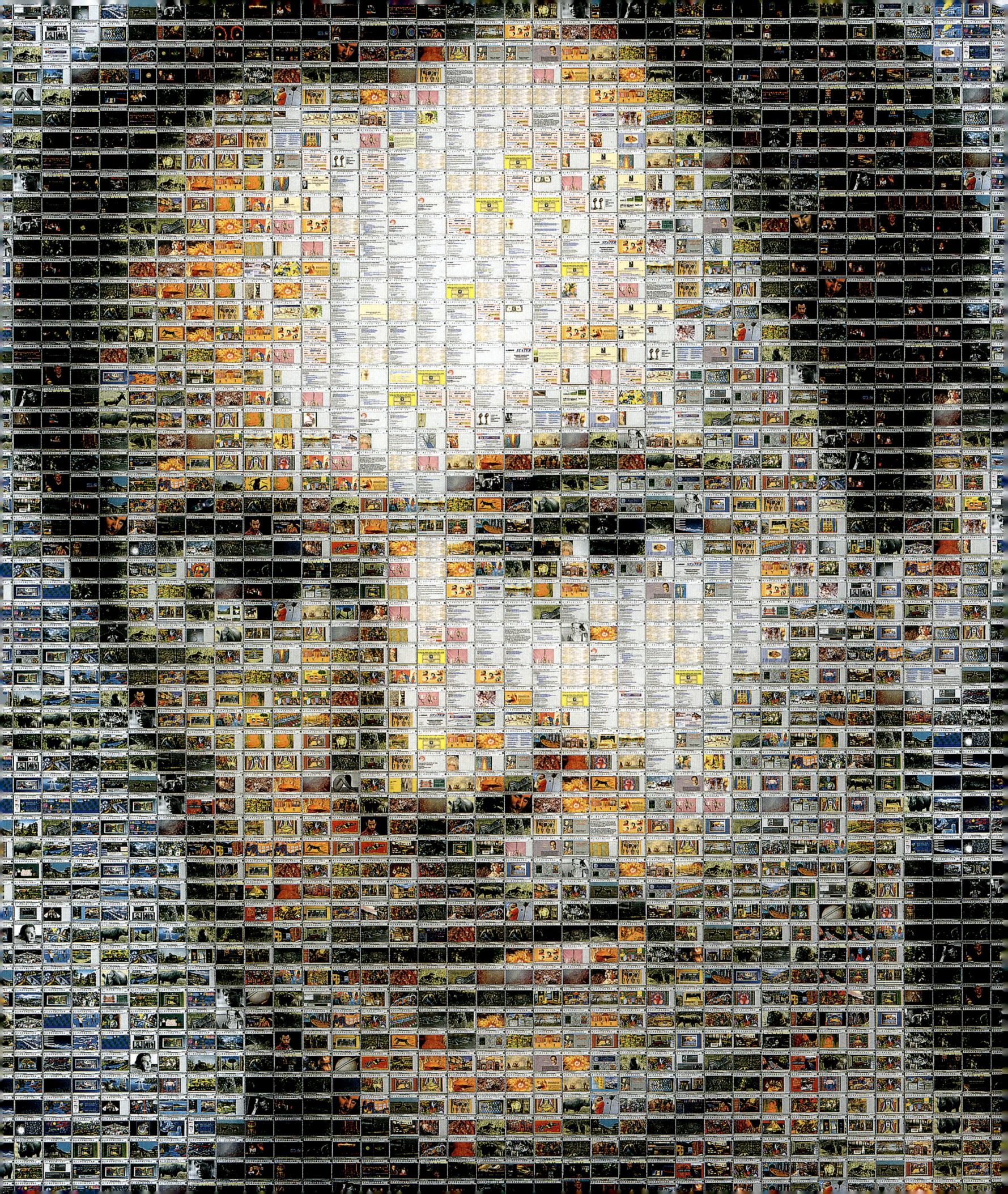

Landing of Albanian Refugees in Bari

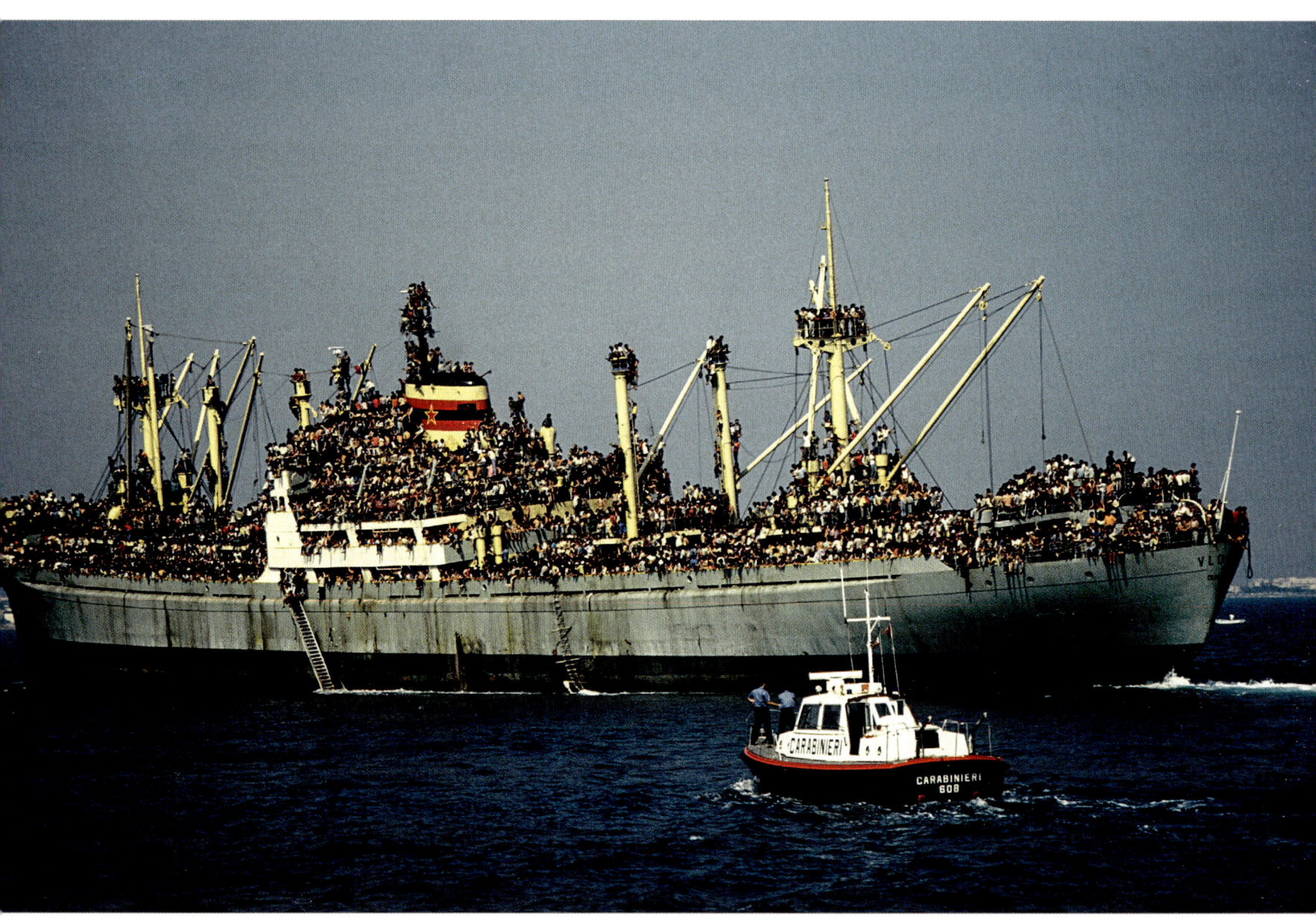

August 8, 1991 - Bari, Italy

An old merchant ship crammed with people fills the horizon. The ship, the Vlora, is about to moor in the port of Bari. The commander is Halim Milaqi, and the cargo he arrives with is crazy and unexpected. A small *Carabinieri* launch approaches the vessel, appearing totally powerless in the wake of this giant. The occupants, who have even climbed up the masts and flagpoles, are mostly adult males, young men and boys. They attacked the ship in the port of Durrës and came on board with no plans and no baggage. They are all of Albanian nationality, but speak Italian, having learned it by watching RAI programs. They are dressed as if they were still in the seventies, but it's August 8th, 1991.

The Puglia sun beats down, and the August humidity is oppressive. The local authorities are on vacation and the beaches are crowded with tourists, while a human wave – almost 20,000 people – inundates the port. Some dive into the sea, while others slide along the ropes. Escaping from Albania was easier than trying to rebuild it. The toppling of the statue of the dictator Enver Hoxha, in February of the same year, signaled the collapse of the Communist regime. Similar events of political and cultural transformation, starting with the fall of the Berlin Wall in 1989, were happening in many places in eastern Europe. Italy and Albania are just 50 nautical miles apart, and the "Country of Eagles" then saw in Italy the Promised Land.

Bari is unprepared but shows the migrants solidarity in every way. The government, however, plans their immediate repatriation: by law, they have no right to political asylum. They are directed to the stadio delle Vittorie, which becomes a place of imprisonment and guerilla warfare. An air bridge is organized to send them home, but the exodus of the Albanian people has just begun.

Vulture Stalking a Child

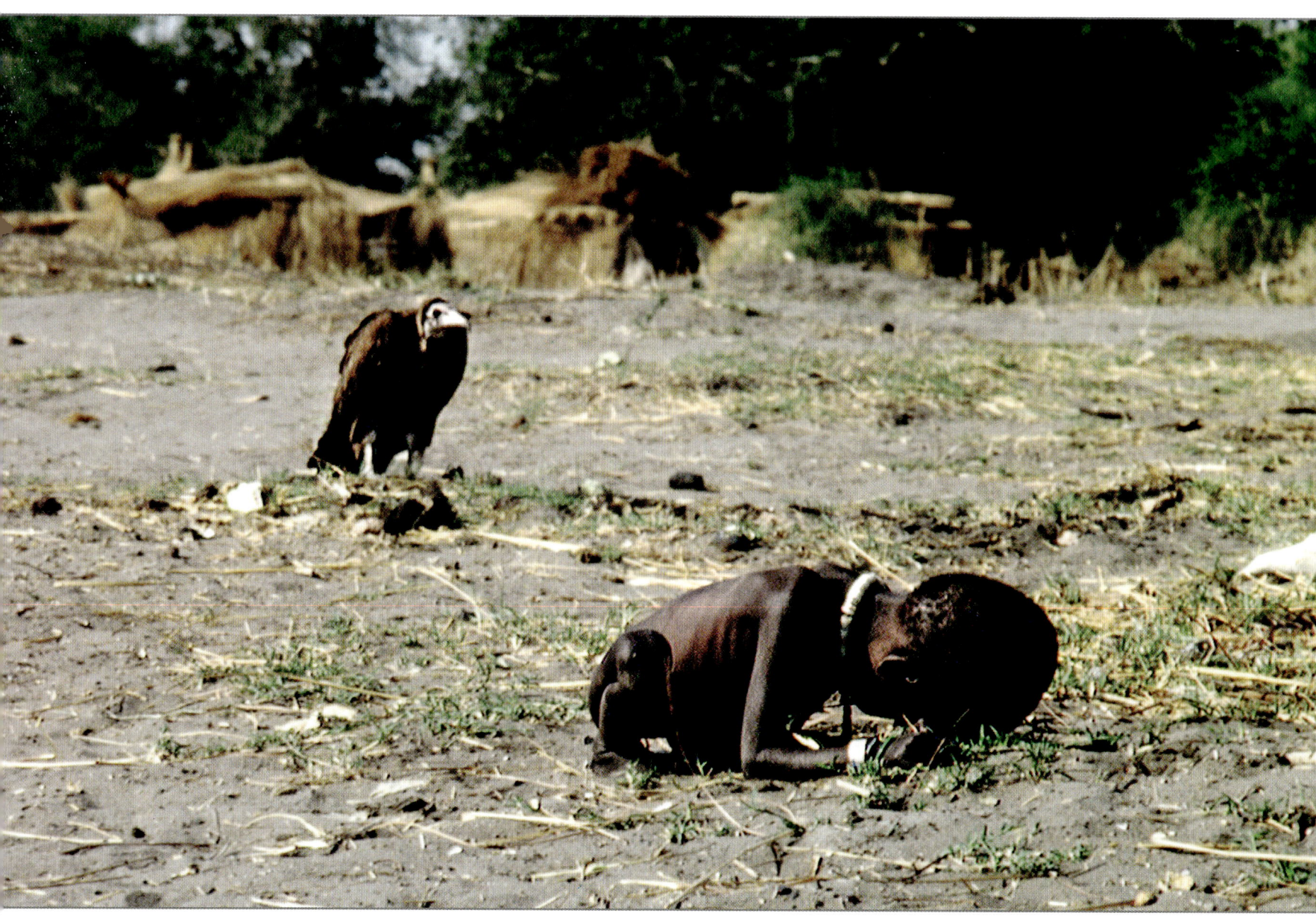

Photograph by Kevin Carter

March, 1993 - Ayod, Sudan

This silent and dramatic photo is almost unbearably painful to look at. It is also a barebones photo, without trickery: two subjects, placed on the diagonal, stand out in contrast to the bare, arid background. The little girl is extremely thin, with no more strength. She is doubled up and dying of hunger. We cannot see the expression on her face, but we can intuit her fatigue and her suffering. Behind her, a vulture waits motionless: we understand that death is near. The angle chosen for the shot, and the diagonal composition of the image, make the bird's next move seem imminent.

Kevin Carter, a South African photojournalist, had documented apartheid and bloody violence in his country for many years. In 1993, he followed a grave famine that was decimating the population of Sudan, a country already scarred by civil war, poverty, and disease. He chanced upon this scene near the village of Ayod, not far from the UN camp distributing food to the starving population. The photograph, which appeared in the *New York Times* on March 26th, 1993, won him the Pulitzer Prize in 1994, but also harsh criticism: he was accused of simply taking pictures while the little girl needed help. Carter never said unequivocally whether, after the shot, he took the girl to safety. Perhaps he did not have the time or lucidity necessary to clarify the situation, to give reasons for his behavior: a few months later, he took his own life. He was thirty-three. Certainly he had never been insensitive to the tragedies framed by his camera.

In the years since, the image of the little girl has become a symbol of the suffering of the entire African continent. This suffering is also a product of indifference: too often the global community not only lacks the initiative to intervene, it lacks the courage to simply look.

Signing of the Oslo Peace Accords

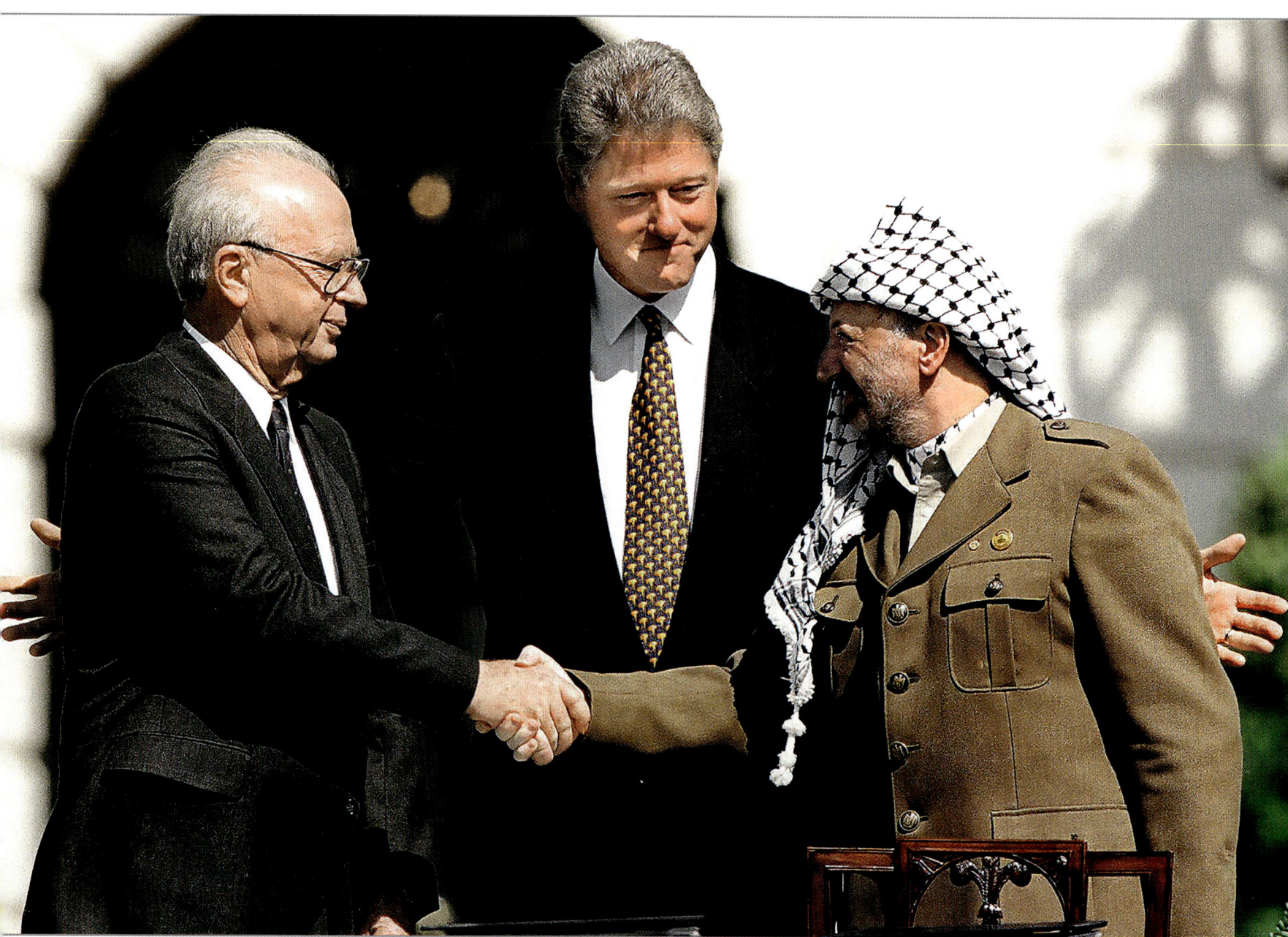

Photograph by J. David Ake

September 13, 1993 - Washington D.C., United States

David Ake is the kind of photographer who is always in the midst of history: when something of global significance happens, there he is, with a lens. The photograph he took on September 13th, 1993, is, for many reasons, the perfect image. It is a triple portrait: in the center, the President of the United States, Bill Clinton; on his right, the Israeli Prime Minister, Yitzhak Rabin; and on his left, the PLO President, Yasser Arafat. It was an historic occasion: the signing of the Oslo accords decreed the foundation of Palestinian National Authority and the beginning of self-government for the West Bank. The treaty ended a long period of violence between the two peoples and laid the foundations for a future Palestinian state and definitive peace in the region: it was the most one could hope for with diplomacy. In fact, the following year, Rabin and Arafat received with Shimon Peres the Nobel Peace Prize.

This image, which became a symbol of the accords, contains all the elements of the official celebration. The first element we note is its symmetry, as in a group sculpture: the two signatories shake hands at the focal point of the photo, while their powerful (and taller) host divides the field into two equal halves. The full light of a late summer day in Washington is at its zenith and leaves no shadowy areas, appropriate for an international treaty which must be clear and transparent in the eyes of the world. The faces of the three figures express great satisfaction, hands meet and clasp each other without hesitation, while the American President opens his arms ecumenically, a symbol both of the power of diplomacy and the status of the United States on the world's stage.

It is impossible not to reflect on what happened in the following decade, both to the treaties and to the three protagonists: their agreements were disregarded, peace was never reached, Rabin was assassinated, Arafat died, and for Clinton they were years of steady political decline. It's a destiny far removed from the promise expressed in this radiant photo.

The AIDS Memorial Quilt

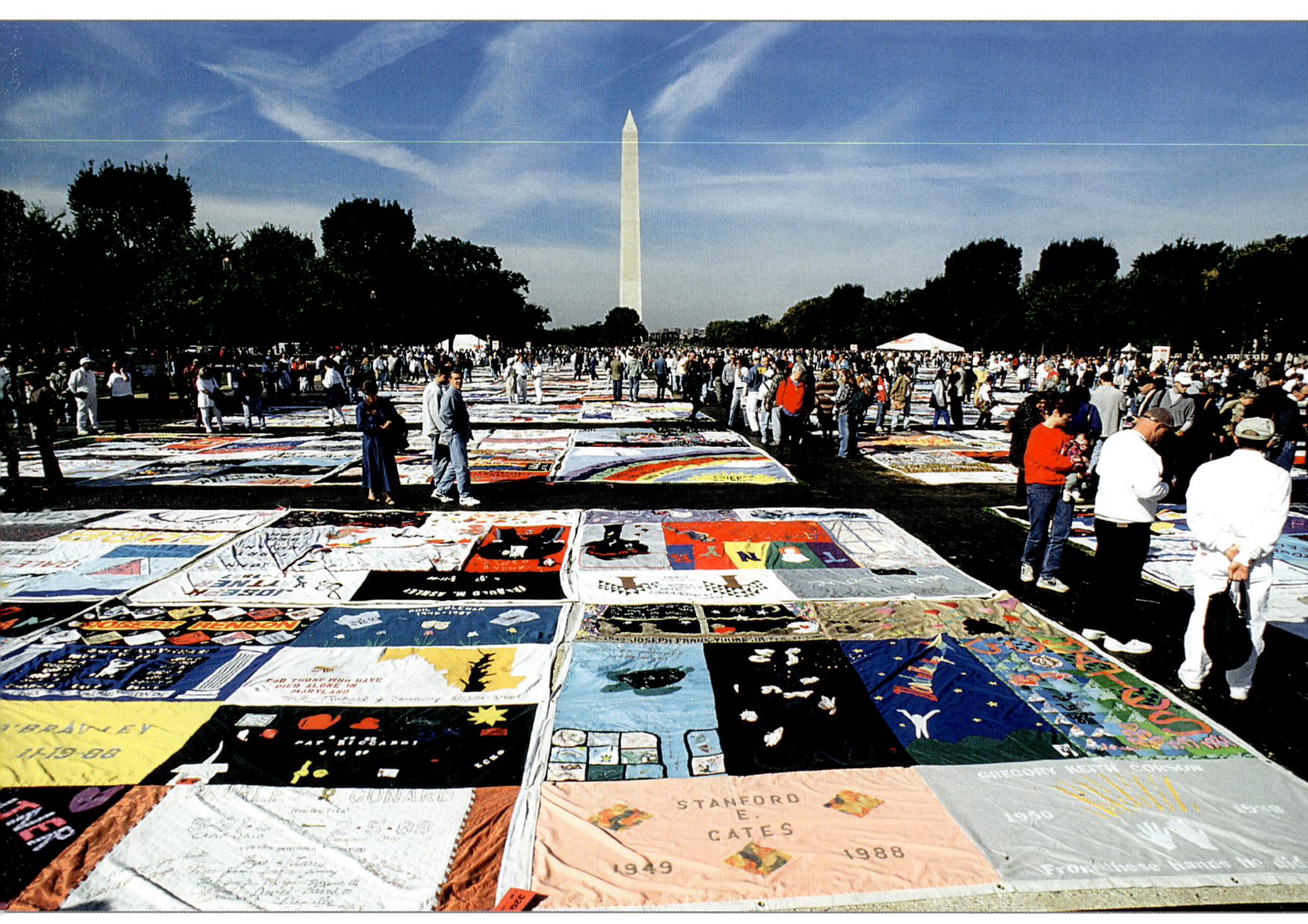

Photograph by Evan Agostini

October 12, 1996 - Washington D.C., United States

While its official name is the *NAMES Project AIDS Memorial Quilt*, the *Memorial Quilt*, as it is better known, is a vast quilt of cloth panels sewn by people in every country in memory of AIDS victims. The project was launched in San Francisco in 1985 by Cleve Jones, a gay activist who asked friends involved in the annual march in memory of Harvey Milk and George Moscone – who were killed for their committment to homosexual rights – to write on pieces of card and posters the names of loved ones who had died of AIDS. At the end of the demonstration, the posters were left on the steps of the San Francisco Federal Building, creating a patchwork effect which inspired the first *Memorial Quilt*: a public work meant to denounce the devastating impact of the rapidly spreading disease. The quilt was exhibited for the first time in Washington in front of the White House on October 11th, 1987, on the occasion of the national march for gay rights. It consisted of nearly 2,000 patches. In 1989 it was a candidate for the Nobel Peace Prize, while in 1996 the whole quilt was exhibited for the last time, also in Washington. On this occasion Evan Agostini photographed a considerable part of it: not all, because it was impossible to get it in the frame without going up in a plane or helicopter.

Today, the *AIDS Memorial Quilt* is the greatest collective artwork in the world: it includes more than 48,000 panels and it is exhibited only in "fragments." Thus the project, in which artistic design and the threads of everyday life meet, has become a powerful visual reminder of how individual experiences intermingle in a single object and memory. It bears witness to those who have fought back, making the space of the disease a space for the body itself. It goes beyond internal suffering by moving it, in order to bear the loss, into collective memory.

The Plight of Kosovo Refugees

May 3, 1999 - Kukës, Albania

At least four different people gently and carefully pass a small child through a barbed wire fence. The child looks frightened, in contrast with the smiling and emotional young woman on the other side.

The barbed wire surrounds the great refugee camp of Kukës in northeast Albania which, during the Kosovo War (1998-99), received thousands of ethnic Albanian Kosovar refugees. The child's name is Agim Shala, and he is only 2 years old. His family members are looking him in the eyes for the first time in a long, fearful time.

The parents and the child are Kosovars and they are housed inside the camp. They have crossed the border to flee the violence committed by Slobodan Milošević troops and the Serbian paramilitaries: Belgrade has decided to destroy the UÇK (Kosovo Liberation Army) and to violently suppress the province's attempt to secede. The grandparents are outside the camp. They have just arrived from another locality in Kosovo, and now they are waiting to be admitted. In the meantime, they cannot help wanting to embrace their grandson.

Carol Guzy, who took the photograph, won the Pulitzer Prize in 2000. She was a photographer for *The Washington Post* and, together with her colleagues Lucian Perkins and Michael Williamson, she spent two months among the refugees to document their living conditions. The diagonal composition makes the scene more immediate and effective: the image is divided into areas of shadow and luminosity. The eye of the observer is immediately captured by the child, both because of the bright colors of his clothing and the light gently touching his face. The sun, too, seems to want to celebrate the triumph of life: barbed wire will not deprive the grandparents of the very human joy of enjoying little Agim.

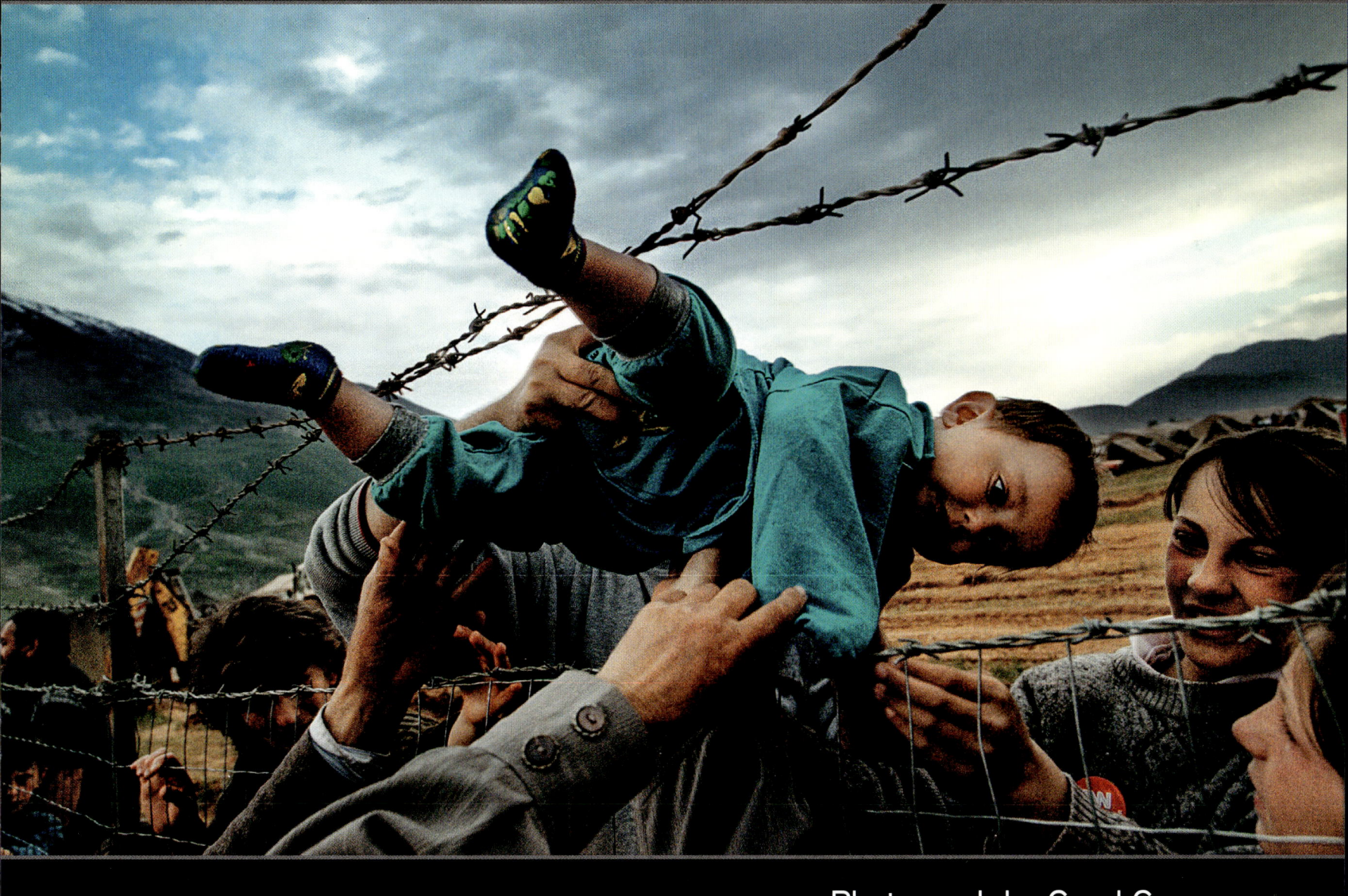

Photograph by Carol Guzy

Afghan Refugee Camp
in Pakistan

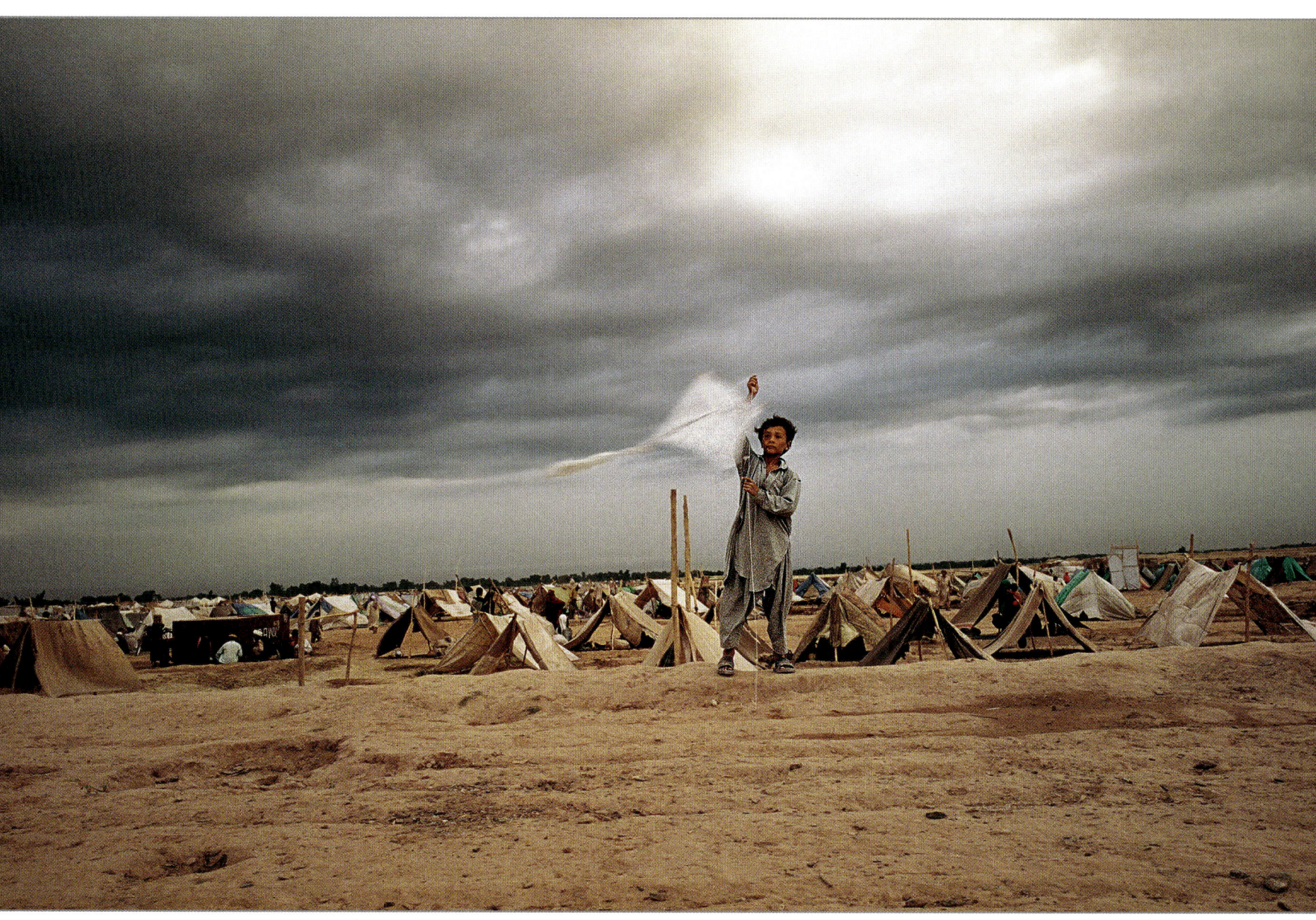

Photograph by Thomas Dworzak

August 2001 - Peshawar, Pakistan

Every child should have the right to play. This was not so in Afghanistan, in 2001, where the Taliban forbade kites and essentially banned the happiness of children. Due to a bloody civil war and a terrible drought, very many of these children, together with their families, were forced to flee their homeland. Little tents in provisional camps became their new homes, offering limited spaces of peace and temporary serenity.

The German photographer Thomas Dworzak, who has long documented the Afghan crisis and lived in the areas dominated by the Taliban, followed the fleeing population over the border, toward Pakistan.

This photo, which was taken in August, 2001, in the Jalozai camp, near Peshawar, shows an Afghan child concentrating on flying his white kite under low clouds on a stormy day. The melancholy expression on his face expresses all the contrast between the normality of the game he's playing and the dramatic situation of life in a refugee camp. The colors are those of a sunless desert: dull, almost uniform. The line of the horizon is slopes at an angle, while the child is stands vertically, in a gesture of resistance against the absurdity of the world.

For the child, this is a world reduced to the area of the little tents behind him, the sand under his feet, and the immense sky overhead. Only the sky, which takes up most of the image, has no limits. And his kite can fly lightly, freely, following the wind.

Ground Zero

September 11, 2001 - New York City, United States

This shot could be a daguerreotype from the early nineteenth century, a scene of frigates in battle at sea. In the center, a single great sail remains standing, while around it rise waves of death and desolation. It is all that remains after the terrorist attack on the Twin Towers in New York: a heap of ruins, surrounded by a cloud of black smoke and dust.

The saturated colors of this apocalyptic scene sharpen the dramatic tone of the shot: multiple shades of black and grey illuminated by amber, the light distilled through the dust.

The photo was taken a week after September 11th, 2001, by the newspaper photographer Chris Corder, who was wandering around in what until a few days before had been the World Trade Center, in the financial district of New York, the most important economic center in the world. In the photograph, he shows the last remnant of those twin skyscrapers: 1,360 feet high, 110 stories of steel, glass, and concrete. There are not any people present in this photo, and yet thousands moved through the place every day; many survived, but more than 3,000 were killed.

It is 8:46 on an ordinary New York morning when the North Tower is hit by American Airlines Flight 11; there are 92 people on board, 5 of whom are hijackers belonging to the terroristic group al-Qaeda. Seventeen minutes later, the South Tower will meet a similar fate. Both will collapse in less than two hours. It is the largest attack on American soil in the modern era.

On the site of the Twin Towers, One World Trade Center was inaugurated in 2014. It is one of the highest buildings in the world, and is commonly called the Freedom Tower, in memory of what happened, and in commemoration of a new era.

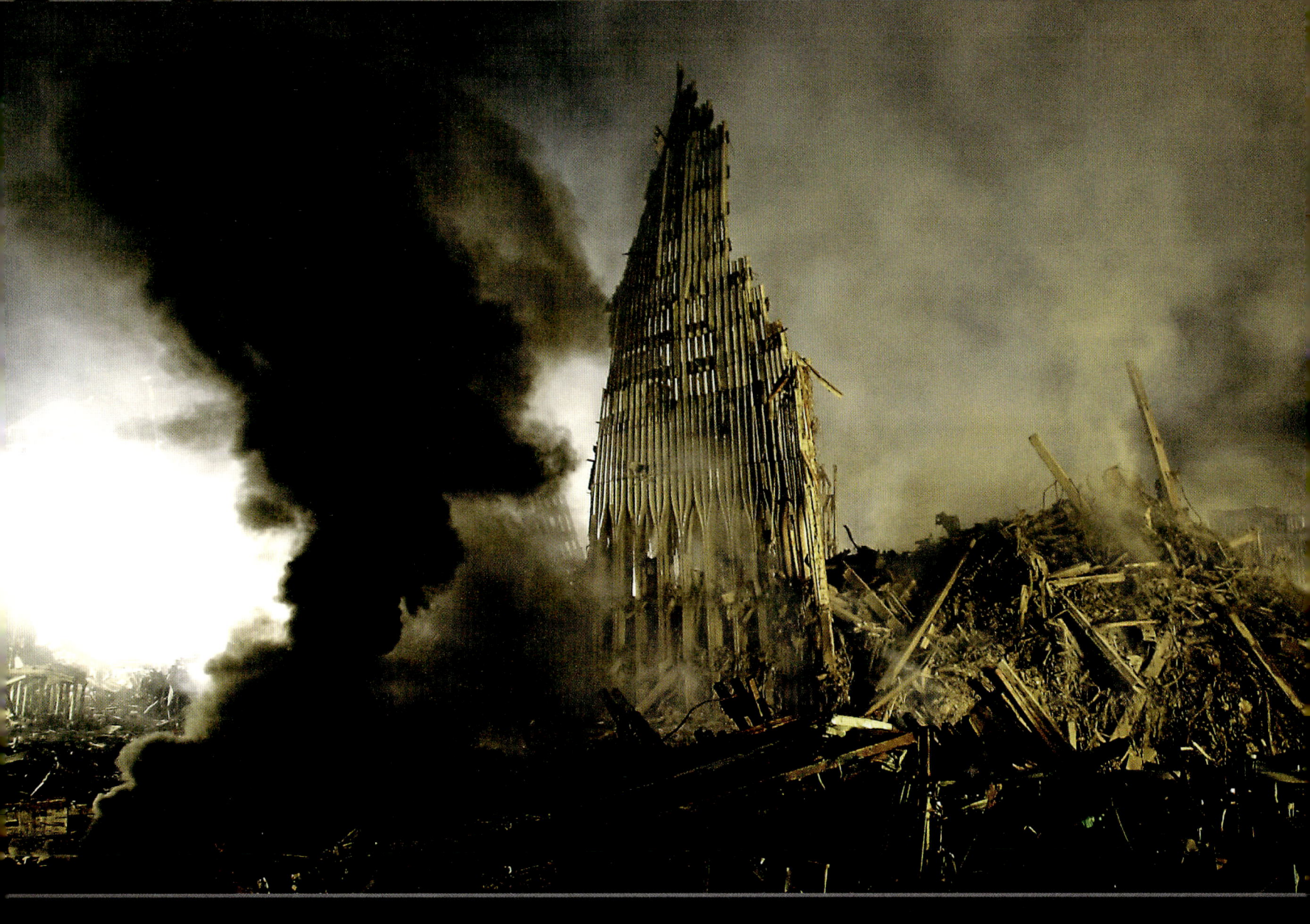

Photograph by Chris Corder

An Iraqi Prisoner with His Son

March 31, 2003 - Al-Najaf, Iraq

A man with his face covered by a plastic hood, in a prisoner camp in southern Iraq, tries to calm his four-year-old son. They have both been arrested by American soldiers. The little boy is terrified, and rests in the arms of his father, who holds one hand on the boy's forehead and the other around his waist. They are surrounded by desert. The tangled barbed wire fence of the camp frames the scene and saturates it with cruelty.

The photograph was taken on March 31st, 2003, a few days after the invasion of Iraq by a multinational coalition aimed at overthrowing the regime of Saddam Hussein. The French photographer Jean-Marc Bouju was in Iraq on behalf of Associated Press, and for about two months he reported military operations following the 101st Airborne Division of the US Army. He was in a camp near An-Najaf, south of Baghdad, when he witnessed this scene. The child had begun to cry and shout when he saw his father being handcuffed and hooded. The American soldiers maintained that they used this practice to disorient prisoners and protect their identity. Later, one of the soldiers took the handcuffs off the man, allowing him to hold his child in his arms. Bouju never managed to learn the name the prisoner or to know his fate or that of the little boy.

The expressive force of the photo is in its simplicity: a few elements that center on the affectionate gesture of the father, in contrast to the cruel theater of war. The image won the 2004 World Press Photo of the Year award. Since then, it has come to symbolize the suffering of children involved in armed conflicts in many places in the world.

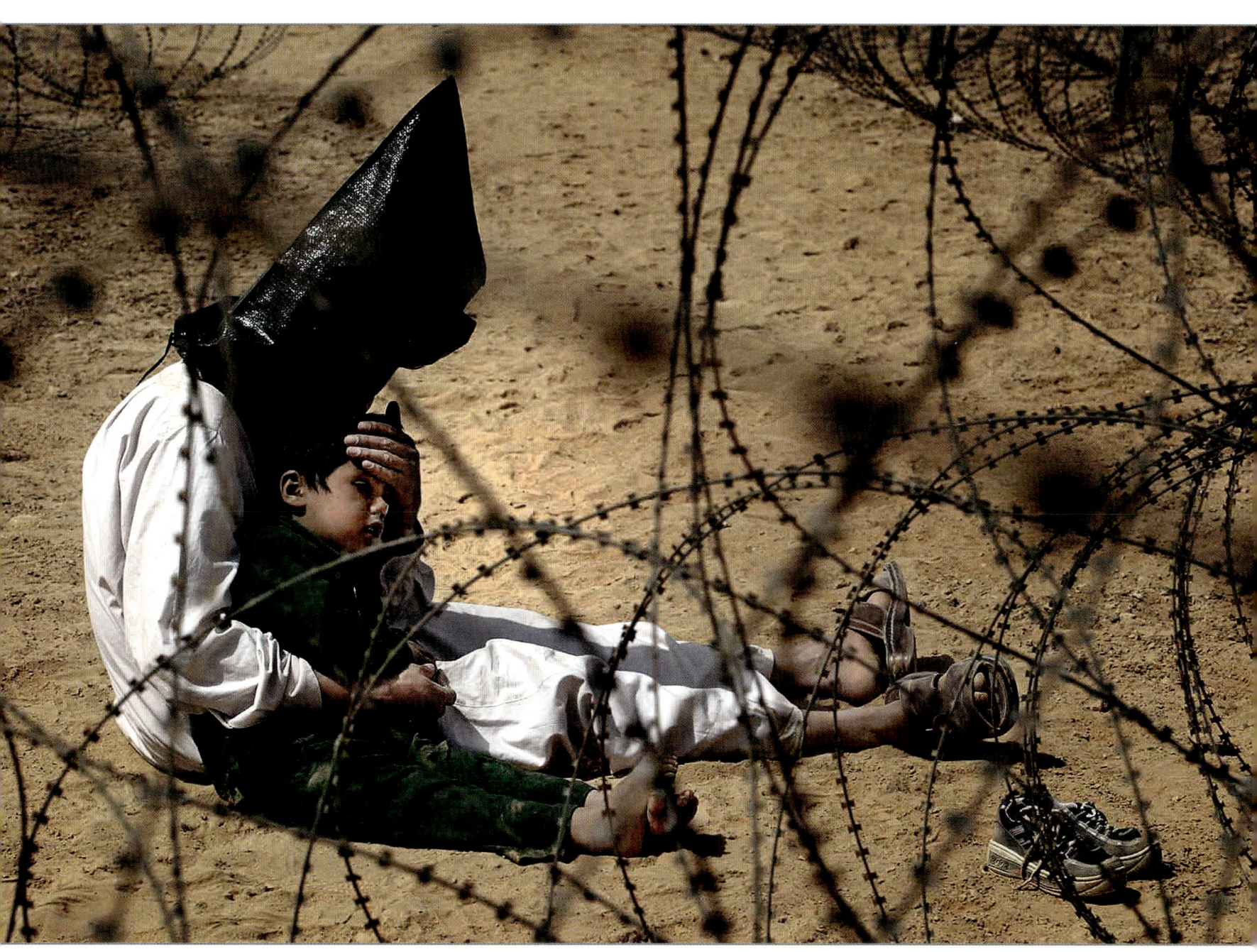

Photograph by Jean-Marc Bouju

The Destruction of the Statue of Saddam Hussein

April 9, 2003 - Baghdad, Iraq

The statue in Firdos Square, in Baghdad, had been inaugurated only one year before, on the occasion of Saddam's sixty-fifth birthday. But on April 9th, 2003, when it was toppled from its pedestal, not many journalists bothered to tell the public. On that day, embedded reporters with US and British troops didn't have to make much of an effort at work, as the hotel where they were staying, the Palestine Hotel, looked onto the square dominated by the giant bronze Saddam.

The official version of the events maintains that the sculpture was destroyed in response to requests from the local population. However, it is very tempting to include the event in the propaganda strategy of the winning army, so much so that the war reporter Robert Fisk described it as "the most staged photo opportunity since Iwo Jima." If the operation was truly aimed at creating an icon for the overthrow of the twenty-year dictatorship, symbolizing the end of the Second Gulf War, we can easily understand why no one dwelled on the history of the monument: contextualizing it, showing its "youth," would have tarnished the unconditional value of the image.

Whatever happened, this photo by Mike Moore, the multiple award-winning British newspaper photographer, shows the preparations preceding the decisive moment: we almost seem to be witnessing the preparations for a public execution. The protagonists are the Marines, who keep photographers and bystanders at a distance, and the crane of the M88 armored recovery vehicle, which cuts the photo diagonally as it puts the statue in a noose. Saddam is relegated to the background, and hardly comes into the photo. He has ceased to be a factor. He is already history.

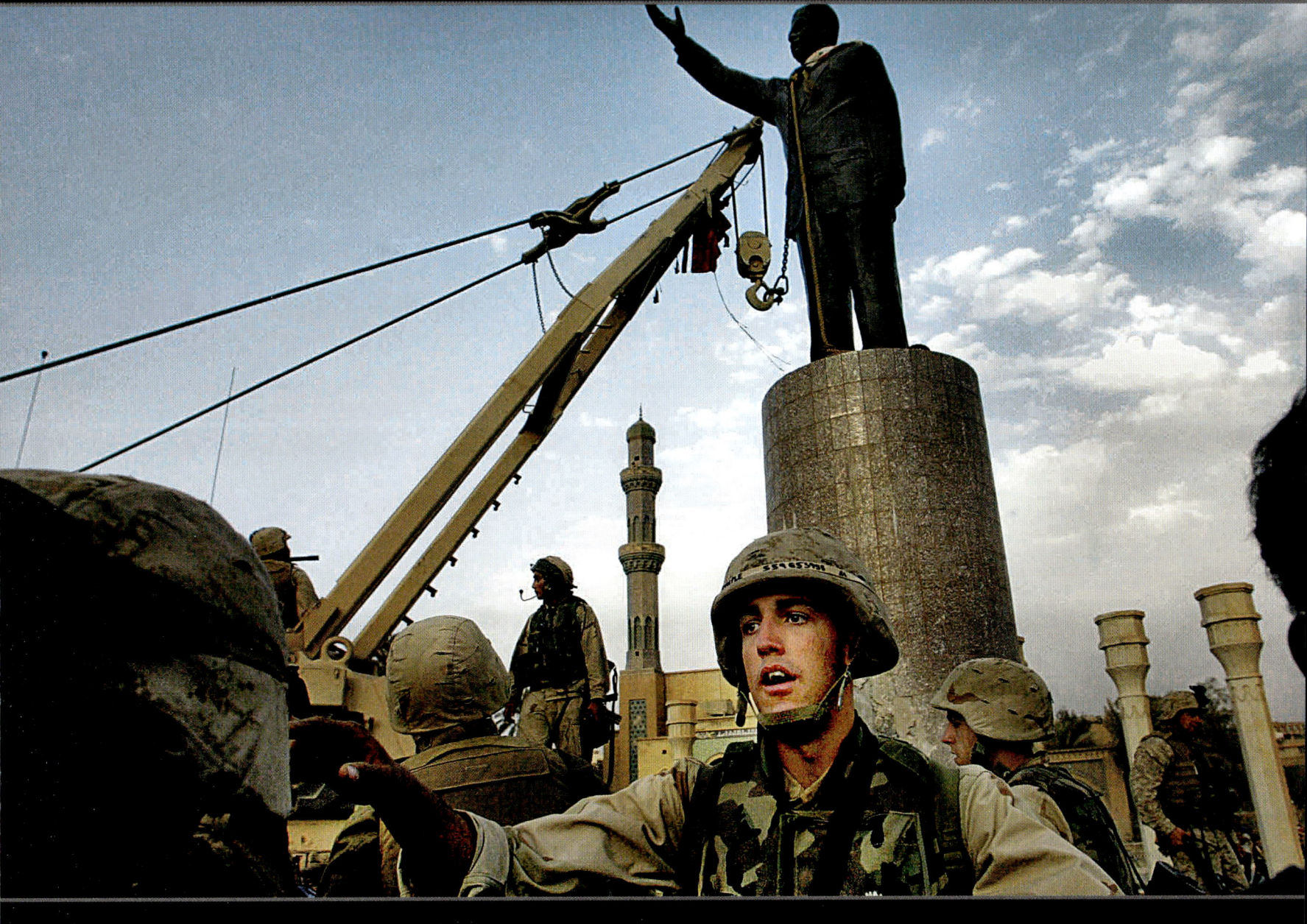

Photograph by Mike Moore

The Wall Street Crash

September 26, 2008 - New York City, United States

"Greed kills." With this sentence around their necks, many people demonstrated in September, 2008, against Wall Street and against rash speculation by banks and finance institutions considered to be at the root of the recession. This photo, by the acclaimed photojournalist Gilles Peress, has considerable symbolic value: it suggests that the strength of capitalism – here personified by Arturo Di Modica's famous bronze bull, in Bowling Green Park in the financial district of New York – has crushed American citizens and destroyed their savings and their hopes for the future. The widespread concern for the economy, caused by the sensational failure of the investment bank Lehman Brothers, was compounded by the strong discontent felt by many at the plan to salvage the banks, which the Bush administration had launched in a desperate attempt to prevent the crisis from worsening. The recession, which exploded in the fall of 2007, would extend to the rest of the world, crippling Europe and numerous banks and financial groups.

Analysts identified numerous causes for the dramatic plunge in the economy, which was considered to be the worst since 1929: among these was the great speculative bubble of the American real estate market, which was linked to defaults on subprime mortgages, which in turn led to the failure of several banks. In the end, the escalating domino effect of these failures destroyed the equilibrium of global markets.

The immediate consequences of the great recession were an increase in unemployment, a deceleration in consumption, and a general impoverishment of the middle-class, which was left, more or less literally, penniless.

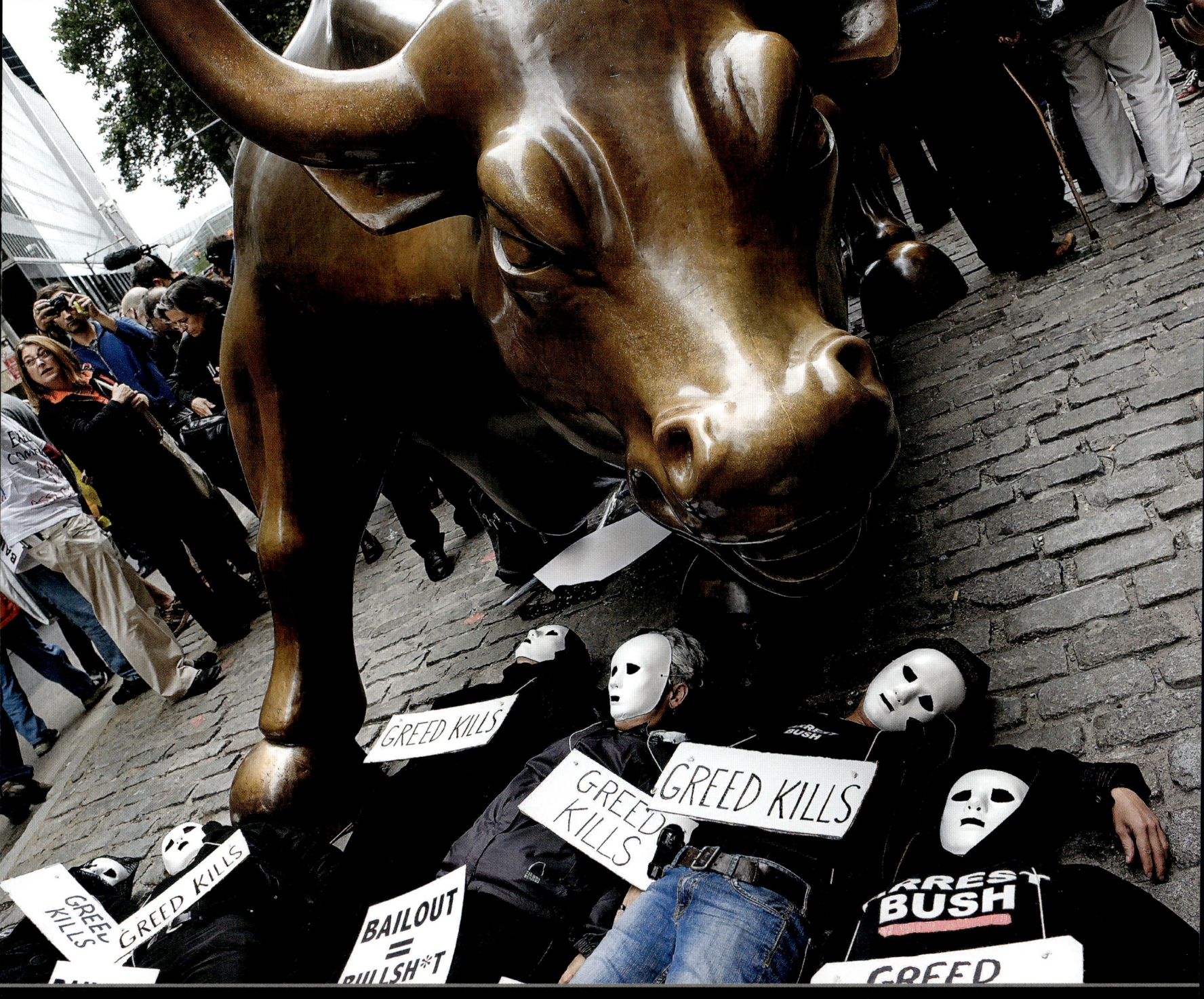

Photograph by Gilles Peress

187

January 20, 2009 - Washington D.C., United States

Barack Hussein Obama was practically an unknown black senator from Chicago when he became the 44th President of the United States of America, the first African American to hold the position of most powerful man in the world. The swearing-in immortalized in this photograph took place on January 20th, 2009, as Obama prepared to succeed his Republican predecessor, George W. Bush. He would remain in office for two terms.

With his right hand raised, and his left hand pressed to the same Bible Abraham Lincoln used in 1861, when he took the oath as the sixteenth President, Obama makes a solemn pledge. In front of him, John Roberts, the Chief Justice of the Supreme Court, reads the words for Obama to repeat. There is a moment of hesitation: Roberts inverts a sentence, Obama is silent, and then begins again. Beside him, almost like a shield, is the First Lady, Michelle. She holds the Bible and, along with their daughters Malia (10) and Sasha (7), watches her husband with pride. Around them, almost 2,000,000 people flood the two miles of the National Mall in Washington.

"All are equal, all are free, and all deserve a chance to pursue their full measure of happiness." From the balcony on the west side of the Capitol, the newly elected President then addresses America, appealing to its traditional values: hard work and honesty, courage and fair play, tolerance and curiosity, loyalty and patriotism. He promises equal rights for all, to sustain balances of peace, to combat climate change, and to end threats of nuclear war. He knows that such objectives will take time and strength greater then he possesses, but it's the direction he wants to take. In less than a year, he will win a controversial Nobel Peace Prize for his "extraordinary efforts to strengthen international diplomacy and cooperation between people." He will be *TIME* person of the year twice. And he is a man who, more than any other in recent times, has succeeded in raising hopes and dreams for a better future.

Barack Obama

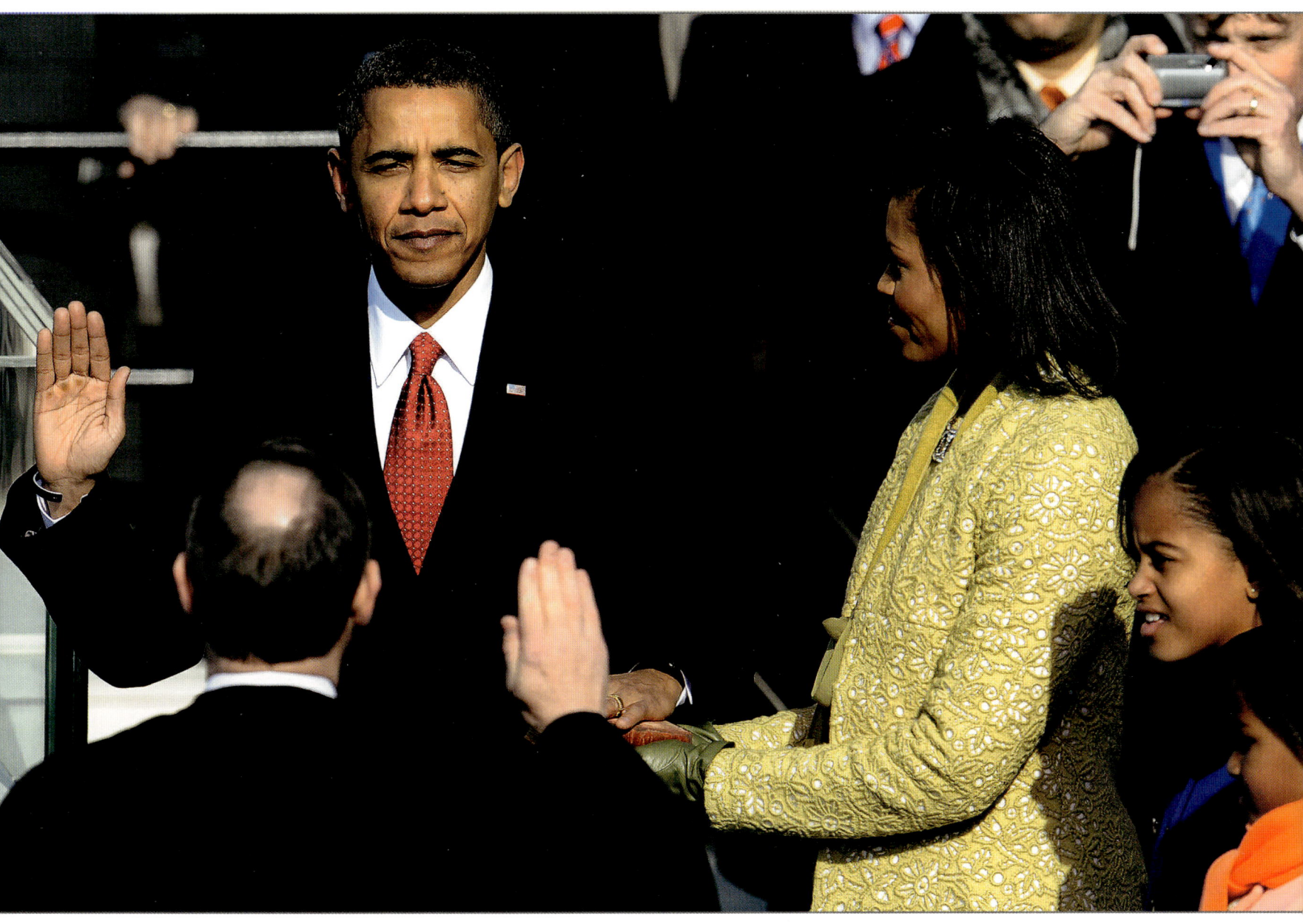

Photograph by Timothy A. Clary

The Arab Spring in Cairo

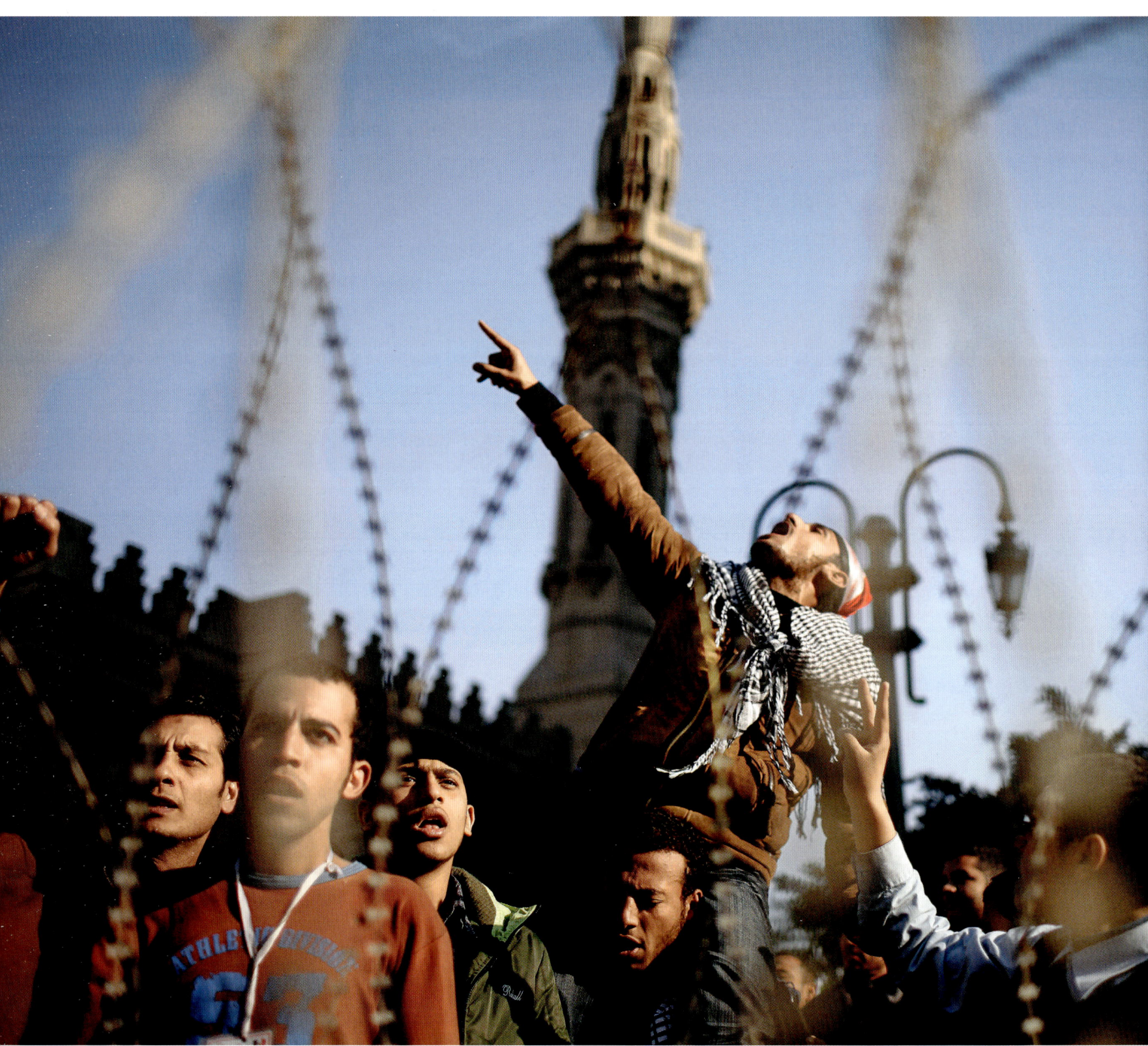

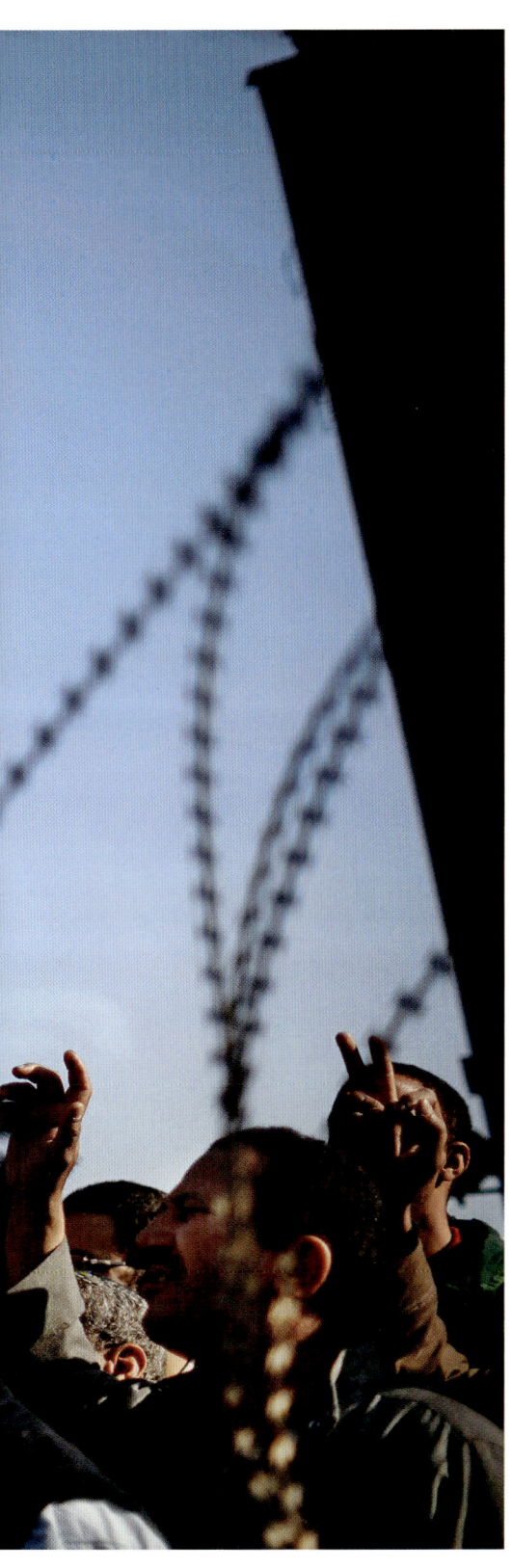

February 9, 2011 - Cairo, Egypt

It took 18 days for the Egyptian people to overthrow the thirty-year-old dictatorship of President Hosni Mubarak. On January 25th, thousands of Egyptians respond to the appeal on the Facebook page "We are all Khaled Said," dedicated to the young man killed a few months before by the Alexandria police in mysterious circumstances. After Tunisia, the wind of the Arab Spring is blowing in Egypt. A crowd of demonstrators pours into the streets of Cairo and reaches, in the city center, Tahrir Square. For days, there is a gathering of young people, students, activists, workers, artists, extremists, Muslims and Christians, men and women, all angry and determined to ask for "bread, freedom and social justice." The regime responds with violent suppression, imposes a ceasefire, and tries to stop communication via Internet.

The photojournalist Moises Saman follows the Egyptian revolution from within, in the midst of the crowd in Tahrir Square. He exposes himself to tear gas and danger to record all the humanity and strength of moments like this. It is February 9th, and the demonstrators fearlessly sing and shout their scorn for Mubarak. A boy with his head wrapped in the Egyptian flag climbs onto another's shoulders to send his cry higher than the others. His finger points to the blue sky, while underneath him timid gestures of victory follow. As in many of the images of the revolution, lines of barbed wire cut through the faces of the young demonstrators, so the observer's point of view is the same as that of the security forces on this side of the barricades. What are they thinking about, while they fight their brothers?

At last, on February 11th, Vice President Omar Suleiman announces that Mubarak has surrendered all his powers to the Supreme Council of the Armed Forces. A wave of joy sweeps the square, which echoes euphorically with the songs and dances of freedom until the morning. Later, everyone will realize that the road to democracy is still very long and painful.

Photograph by Moises Saman

The Anniversary of the Srebrenica Massacre

July 11, 2012 - Potočari, Bosnia-Herzegovina

Continuous lines of identical caskets multiply in an endless array of rows and volumes. Rays of light pierce the darkness, a deep laceration which is as unbearable as the air which smells of death. The echo of grief fills the space about the caskets, but it is silence, emptiness, absence.

On July 11th, 1995, during the war in Bosnia-Herzegovina, horror found its way among the inhabitants of Srebrenica. More than 20,000 refugees, most of them Muslims (called Bosniaks), had taken refuge there because it had been declared a "protected zone," guarded by 370 United Nations troops. However, the Serbian troops of General Ratko Mladić – who was, in fact, born in Bosnia, a little south of Sarajevo – and the paramilitary forces led by Arkan did not meet any obstacles when they decided to occupy the little town and carry out a massacre. Their intention was to complete a deranged plan of ethnic cleansing. The United Nations troops did not intervene; rather, they retreated into their Potočari compound, perhaps because of communication problems with central command, perhaps because they were too small a force and too poorly armed to face an attack of those proportions. In the previous days (and on July 11th itself), they had vainly asked for air support.

Once they entered Srebrenica, the Serbian soldiers and paramilitaries separated males between 14 and 78 years of age from the rest of the population. They killed them

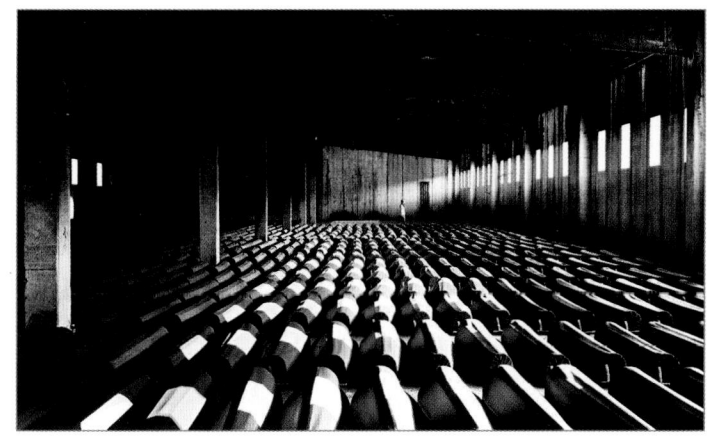

Photograph by Paolo Pellegrin

pitilessly, and then dumped their bodies into mass graves. The result was 8,373 certified victims. Because of the recognition of personal effects, or DNA examination, about 7,000 victims have been identified by first and last name. According to the Bosnian institute for missing persons, 1,200 bodies are still unaccounted for.

Since the massacre, each year in July, the relatives of the men killed return to bury the few remains of their loved ones, which have been exhumed from more than 200 mass graves identified up to now. The caskets are transported and placed in lines at the memorial which was inaugurated at Potočari in 2003, where there was once the headquarters of the UN troops.

At Srebrenica today, only the dead remain, thousands of men and boys asleep in the hill.

In the Potočari Memorial, seventeen years after the massacre, Paolo Pellegrin records, for our collective memory, a horror which has been too quickly forgotten. He photographs the defeat of humanity: those caskets in the silence are reminders of the moral and political vacuum, the lack of response from the international community in foreseeing and opposing the conflict that tore Yugoslavia apart. They tell us that genocide does not end when the killing is over, and perhaps not even with the exhumation of the last victim. Genocide lacerates history, and the future, challenging in countless ways the process of peace.

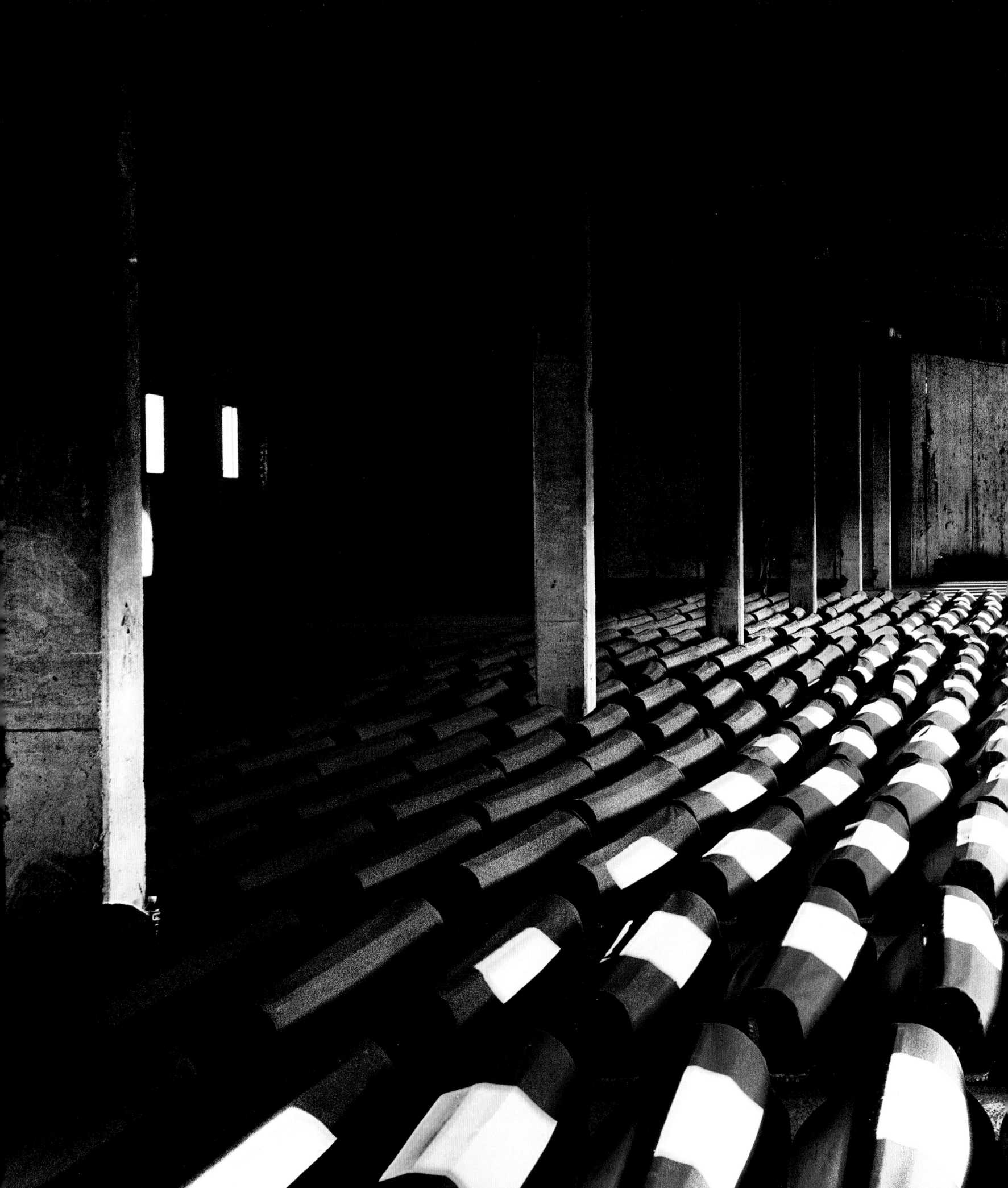

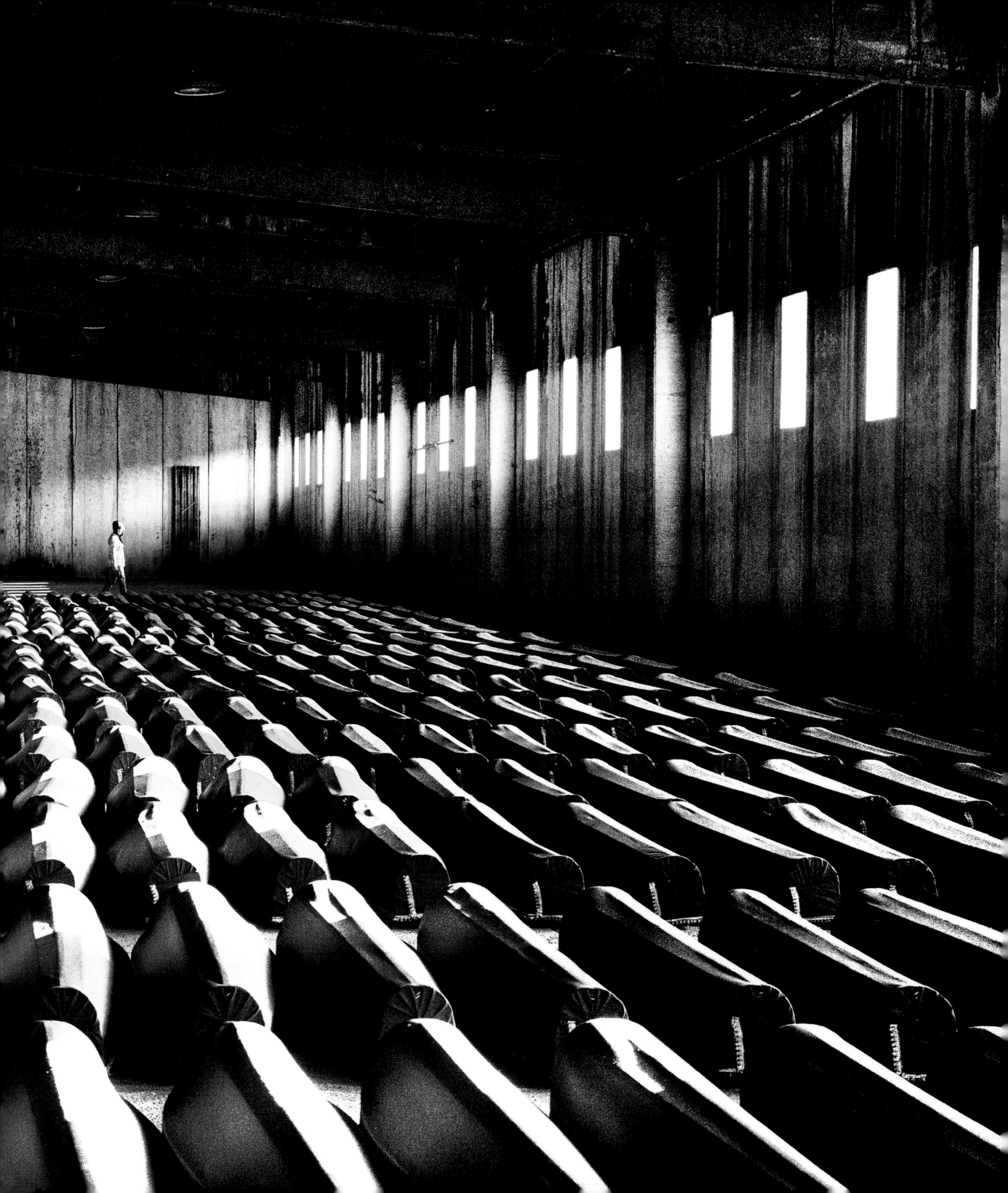

Malala Yousafzai Receives the Nobel Peace Prize

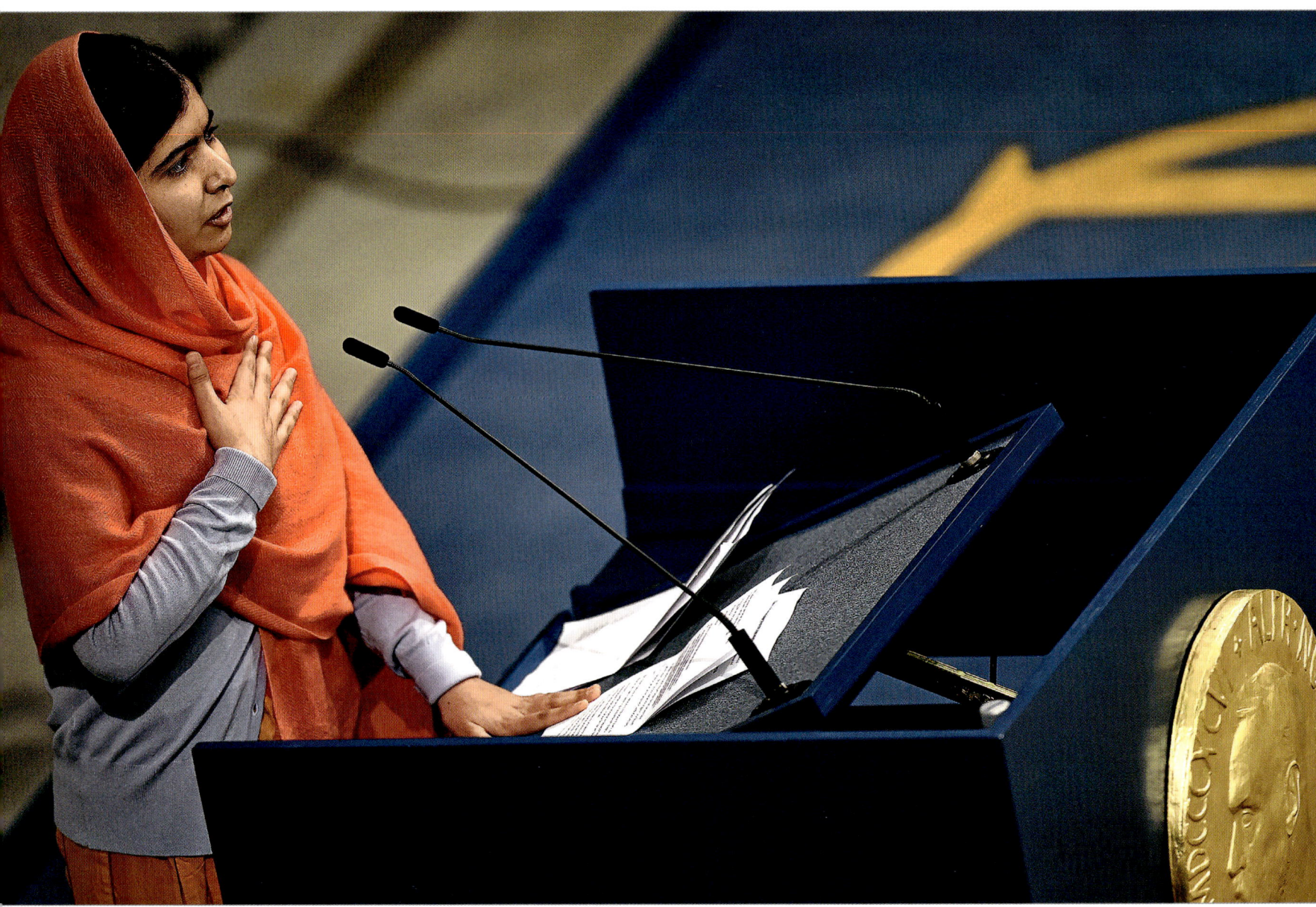

Photograph by Odd Andersen

December 10, 2014 - Oslo, Norway

A young Pakistani woman with a coral red veil over her raven-black hair and her hand on her heart stands on a podium before microphones. She speaks to a crowd of spectators who we cannot see. It is December 10th, 2014: Malala Yousafzai has received the Nobel Peace Prize.

Odd Andersen's photo is taken from above, a photojournalist's shot that, despite the institutional context, conveys strong emotion precisely because of the story it tells. Even before becoming the youngest-ever Nobel Peace Prize winner, Malala was a symbol: the seventeen-year-old, who risked her life by opposing the Pakistani Taliban, embodies the eternal struggle between reason and obscurantism, between freedom of thought and religious fundamentalism. She was born on July 12th, 1997, in Pakistan, and began her career as an activist for women's and children's rights at little more than 11 years old. In the famous blog she wrote for the BBC, she reported daily life under the Taliban regime, telling of its continual suppression of freedom, its enforcement of capital punishment, and of its systematic destruction of girls' schools. In 2012, fundamentalists decided that Malala's expression of her opinions should be stopped, because they considered them "obscene" and responsible for "spreading secularism." Armed men attacked her while she was returning home by bus. They shot her in the head. Unexpectedly, the girl survived, and her voice became still stronger and echoed around the world.

In this passionate speech, Malala emphasizes the importance of the right to education for girls, describing it as an antidote to extremism and oppression. "I had two options," she says. "One was to remain silent and wait to be killed. The second was to speak up and then be killed. I chose the second. I decided to speak up."

The March After the Charlie Hebdo Attack

January 11, 2015 - Paris, France

The satirical weekly *Charlie Hebdo* symbolizes the French libertarian spirit. It is so determined and daring in its frequent use of strong terms regarding the highest political and religious authorities, speaking out against symbols of the various religions, sparing nothing and no one.

On November 2nd, 2011, the weekly was attacked by Islamist extremists because of a cartoon judged to be blasphemous; but the editorial staff was not intimidated. It continued to express its opinions courageously, even those concerning the Islamic world.

On January 7th, 2015, *Charlie Hebdo* was the victim of a much more serious attack. At about 11:30 in the morning, two armed men attacked its headquarters, on Rue Nicolas-Appert, in Paris. Twelve people died, among them the Editor Stéphane Charbonnier, several cartoonists, and two policemen. Eleven others were wounded. The two attackers, brothers Chérif and Saïd Kouachi, French Islamic fundamentalists of Algerian origin, were killed on January 9th, in a shootout with police; on the same day, a third man, Amedy Coulibaly, was shot dead by officers during an attack on a kosher supermarket.

All the world – political leaders and common people, artists and intellectuals – shows its solidarity with the victims of the massacre: "Je suis Charlie" is the sentence

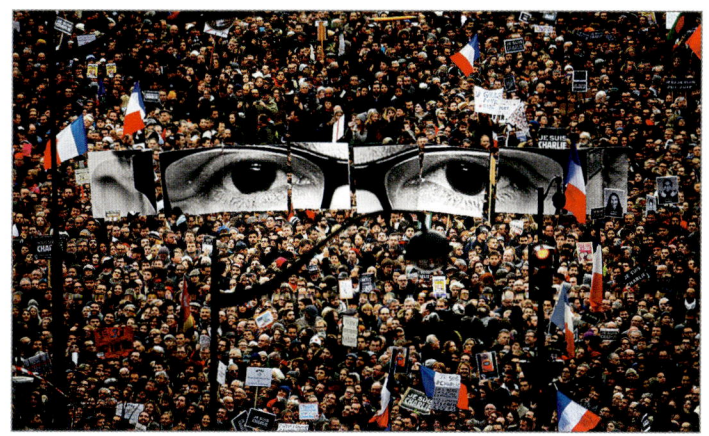

Photograph by Christopher Furlong

which echoes on the social networks and in international media. On January 11th, more than one million people march through Paris to emphasize French unity and to reiterate the value of freedom, considered a foundation of French culture since the Revolution.

The photographer Christopher Furlong captured an image of the procession moving along Boulevard Voltaire: the crowd raises French flags and placards with the sentence "Je suis Charlie." Above their heads, they hold a great photographic mosaic by the French artist JR with the eyes of Stéphane Charbonnier. They are eyes that have faced death in the name of an ideal.

In the meantime, the survivors of *Charlie Hebdo*, hosted in the offices of the daily paper *Libération*, continue to work regularly on the next edition. The week following the attack, on Wednesday January 14th, on the cover of the satirical weekly there's the Prophet Mohammed. He, too, is crying now, holding up the words "Je suis Charlie," while above him appears the sad and sarcastic sentence *Tout est pardonné*, "All is forgiven."

Despite the incredible print run of 3 million copies, edition 1178 of *Charlie Hebdo* sells out in only one day. The digital edition is made available in four languages, among them Arabic.

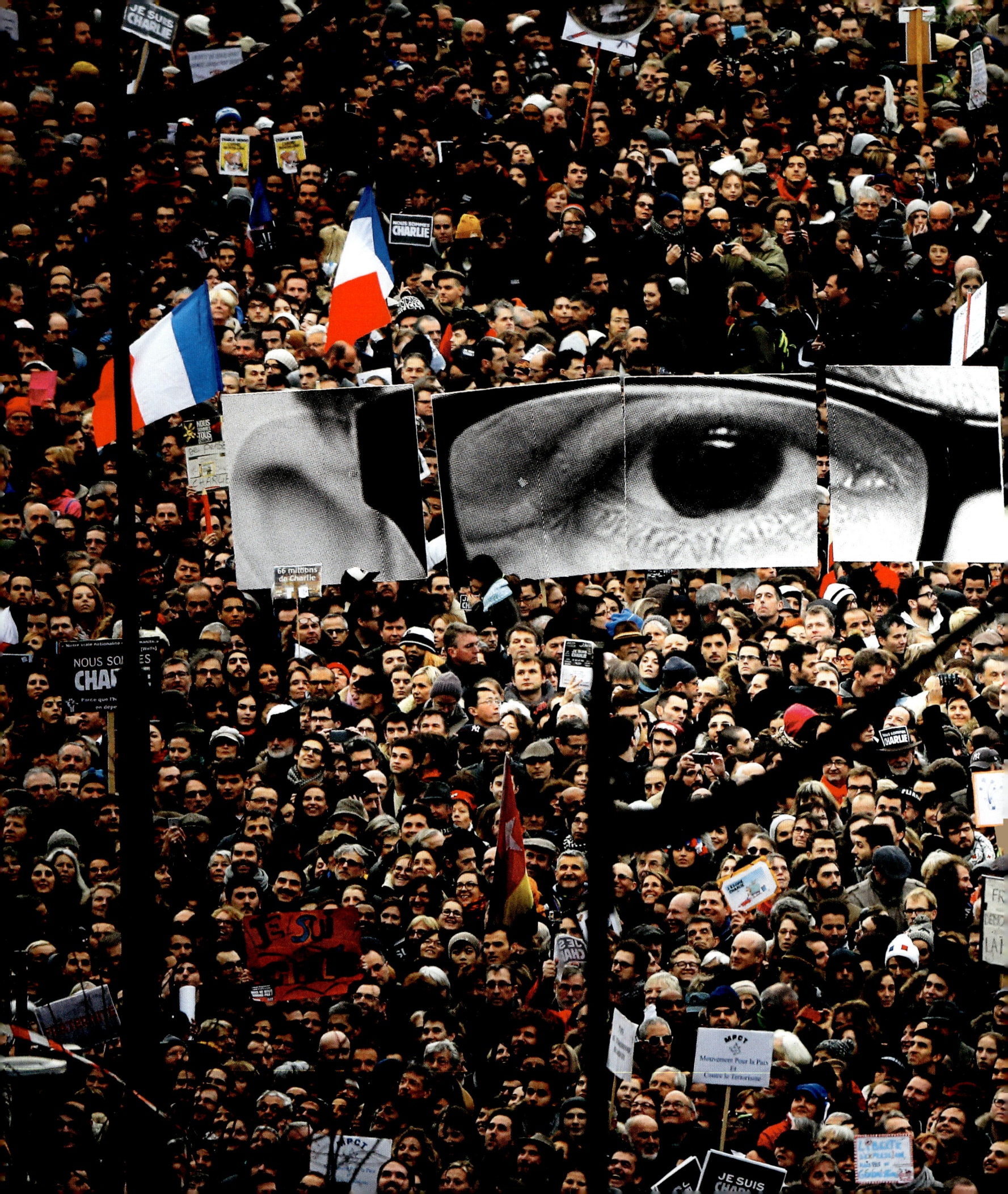

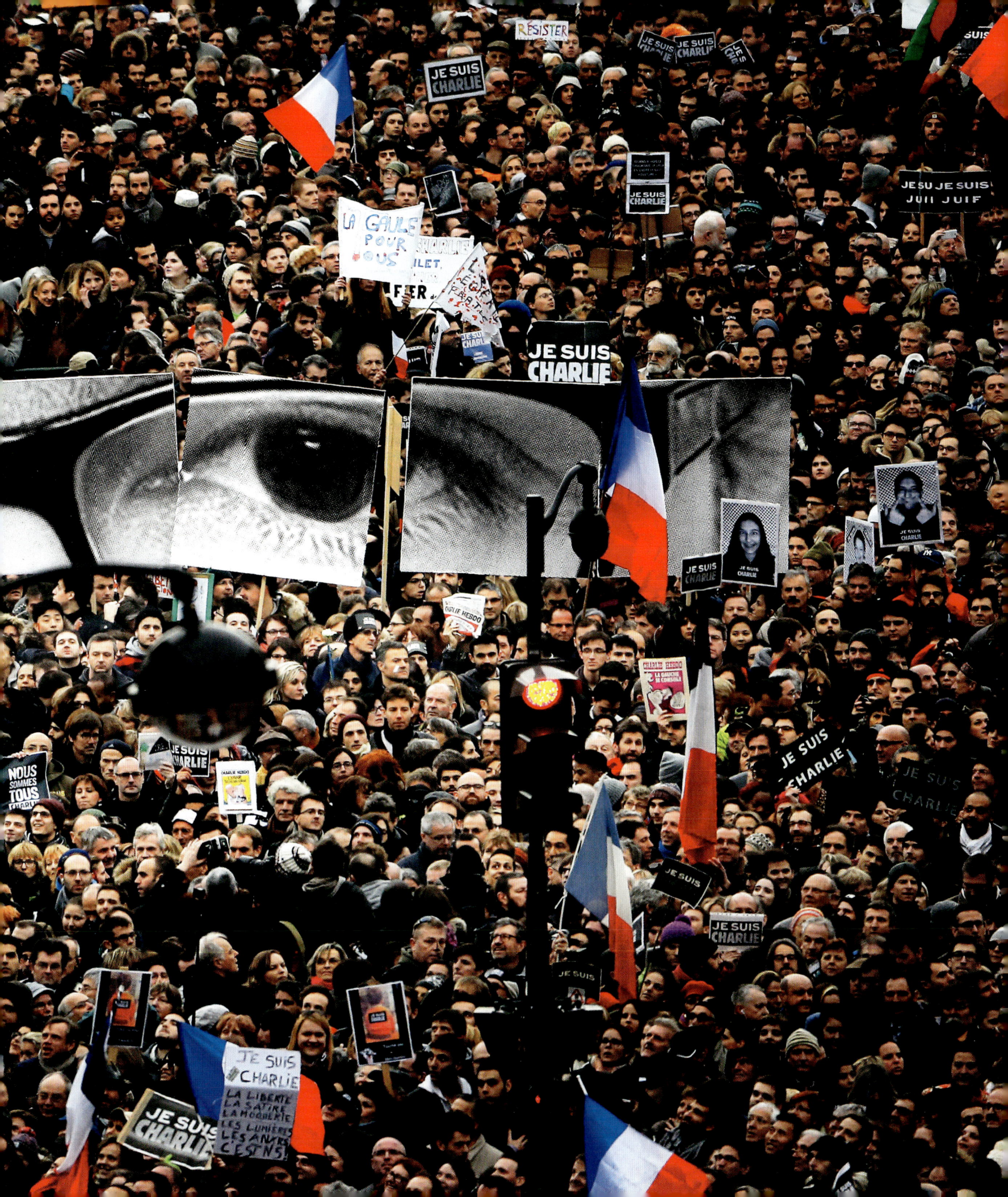

Selfie by Curiosity on Mars

January, 2015 - Mount Sharp, Mars

Here is a mechanical, Martian, spatial, panoramic, robotic selfie. Curiosity, a NASA rover on Mars, took it. With a wonderful name, Curiosity is as big as an automobile, weighs a ton, is powered by solar energy, and is more technologically sophisticated than a microsurgery device. Building and sending it to Mars cost approximately 2.5 billion dollars. Since August, 2012, Curiosity has been strolling about the Red Planet. It makes little holes here and there in the surface (is it called "earth" on Mars, too?), analyzes, studies, and sends information back to Earth. It also takes photographs of the landscape, and occasionally selfies, like this one, which is a montage by the computer of ten shots of the region. Someone, perhaps Curiosity itself, has already named the natural features: Telegraph Peak, the Alexander Hills, the Pink Cliffs, and Confidence Hill. The darker areas on the right and on the left of the photo indicate sand, dust and wind storms.

Curiosity is supplying answers to many scientists' questions: is there water on Mars? Has there been life on Mars in the past? What are the weather conditions like? What is the geology like? Are there recoverable mineral resources? The rover is gathering information for the first explorers from Earth, who are preparing for the interplanetary voyage: it will take about ten months, from spaceport to spaceport, without a stopover. For the moment, there is only a one way ticket, because NASA doesn't yet know how to solve the most complicated part of the adventure: the return to the Earth.

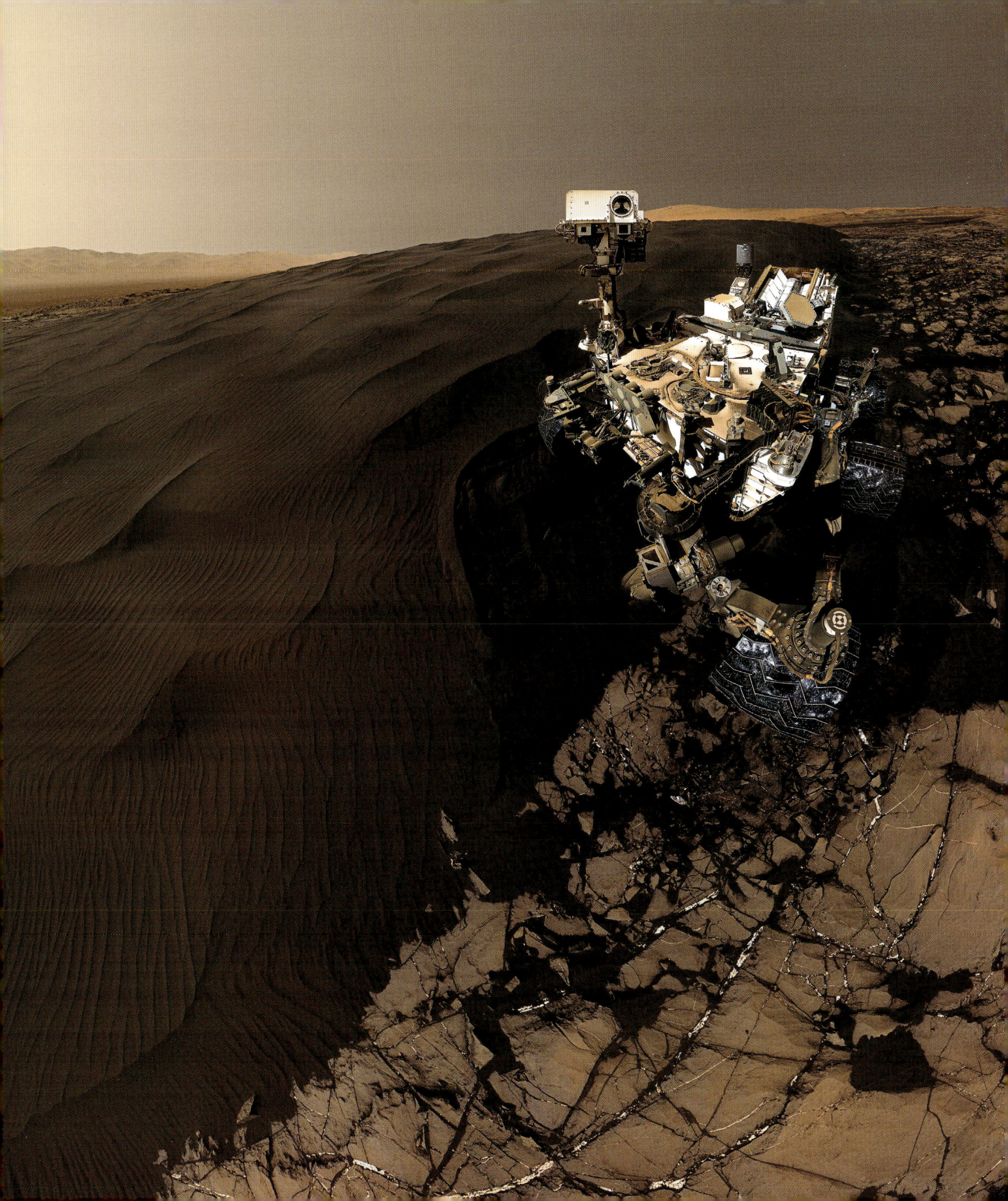

Refugees Landing on Lesbos

October 1, 2015 - Lesbos, Greece

Syria is in flames, victim of a seemingly endless civil war. Many flee from the bombs of the government army, from the atrocities of Isis, and from air attacks by foreign powers; they cross borders illegally, and are willing to trust traffickers in their journey toward safety. Since Syrian citizens cannot legally enter most Arab countries, many try to reach Europe, despite the dangers and difficulties of the long journey, which unfortunately is fatal for many.

In 2015 the refugees' desperation was not a new phenomenon and did not only concern Europe: fewer than 10% of Syrian refugees succeeded in obtaining asylum in the EU. Most of the others remained in camps set up in Lebanon, Jordan, and Turkey. In absolute terms, the numbers are high: in 2014, almost 220,000 asylum seekers arrived by sea, while in 2015 more than 900,000 came ashore on Greek beaches and, to a lesser extent, on those of Italy.

In the final months of 2015, one of the main migratory routes was via the Greek island of Lesbos, the ancient land of the lyric poets Sappho and Alcaeus, off the Turkish coast. Hundreds of thousands of refugees landed on these shores after leaving the Anatolian Peninsula, crossing the Aegean Sea in unsafe inflatable rafts. Following the summer, the whole island was transformed into a permanent reception center.

Among the photographers recording the refugees' landings on Lesbos there were Tyler Hicks and Daniel

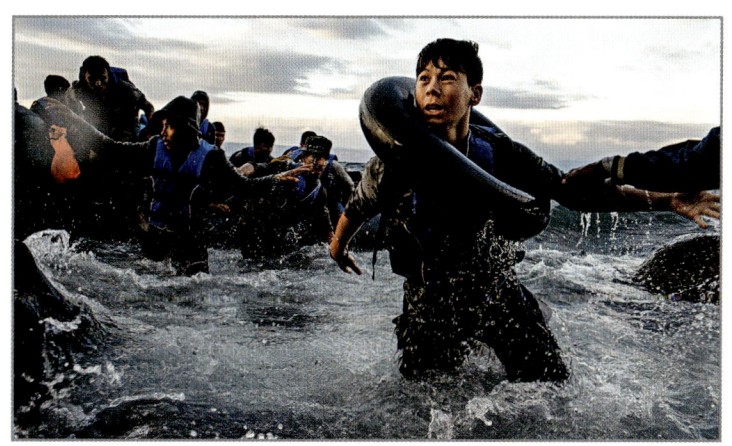

Photograph by Tyler Hicks

Etter, correspondents on the island for *The New York Times*. The same paper sent two other photographers, Mauricio Lima and Sergey Ponomarev, to bear witness to the journey of refugees heading for Sweden through the Balkans. Their collective work, of exceptional journalistic value and emotional intensity, won the 2016 Pulitzer Prize. Hicks, together with the staff of *The New York Times*, had already obtained this honor twice before, once in 2009, and again in 2014, for the photos he took in Nairobi during the attack on the Westgate shopping mall.

What is striking in Hicks' work is his ability to find beauty even in the most difficult circumstances. At the same time, Hicks chooses moments and subjects capable of communicating extreme moods without weak sentimentality. Tiredness, anxiety, strain can be read in the movements of all the men abandoning the inflatable raft that has brought them to Lesbos, at the end of a dramatic crossing. They have survived the Aegean, and their only thought is to reach the beach. One boy, the protagonist of the photo, raises his head and looks up at the sky. He seems to have forgotten his makeshift life belt, and he does not notice either the sprays of cold water or the hand that grasps him, pulling him to safety. He looks toward something we cannot see, out of the shot. It is an incredulous gaze, full of hope, because he realizes that he's made it: at last there's something on the horizon, something different from the nightmares he's left on the other side of the sea.

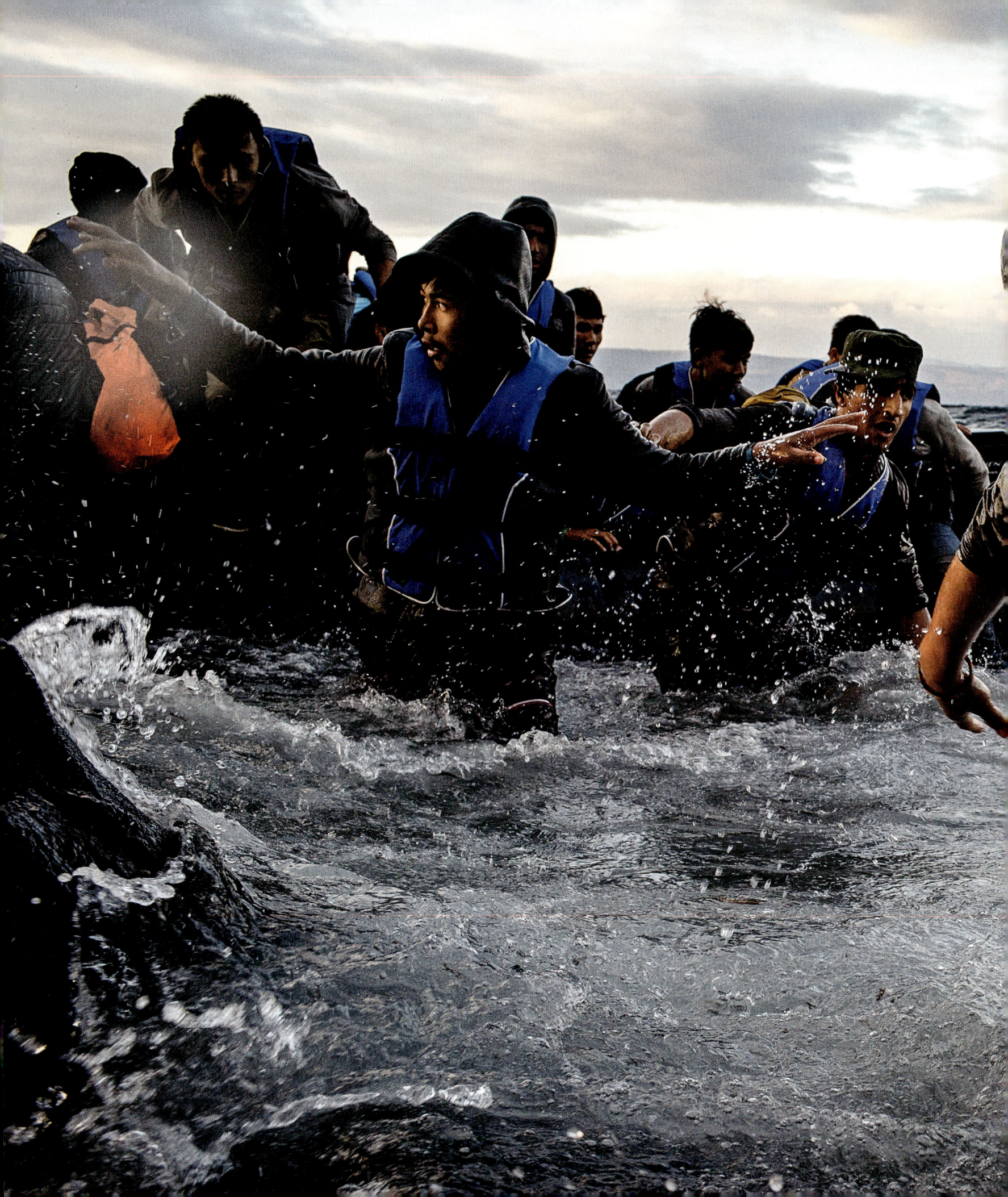

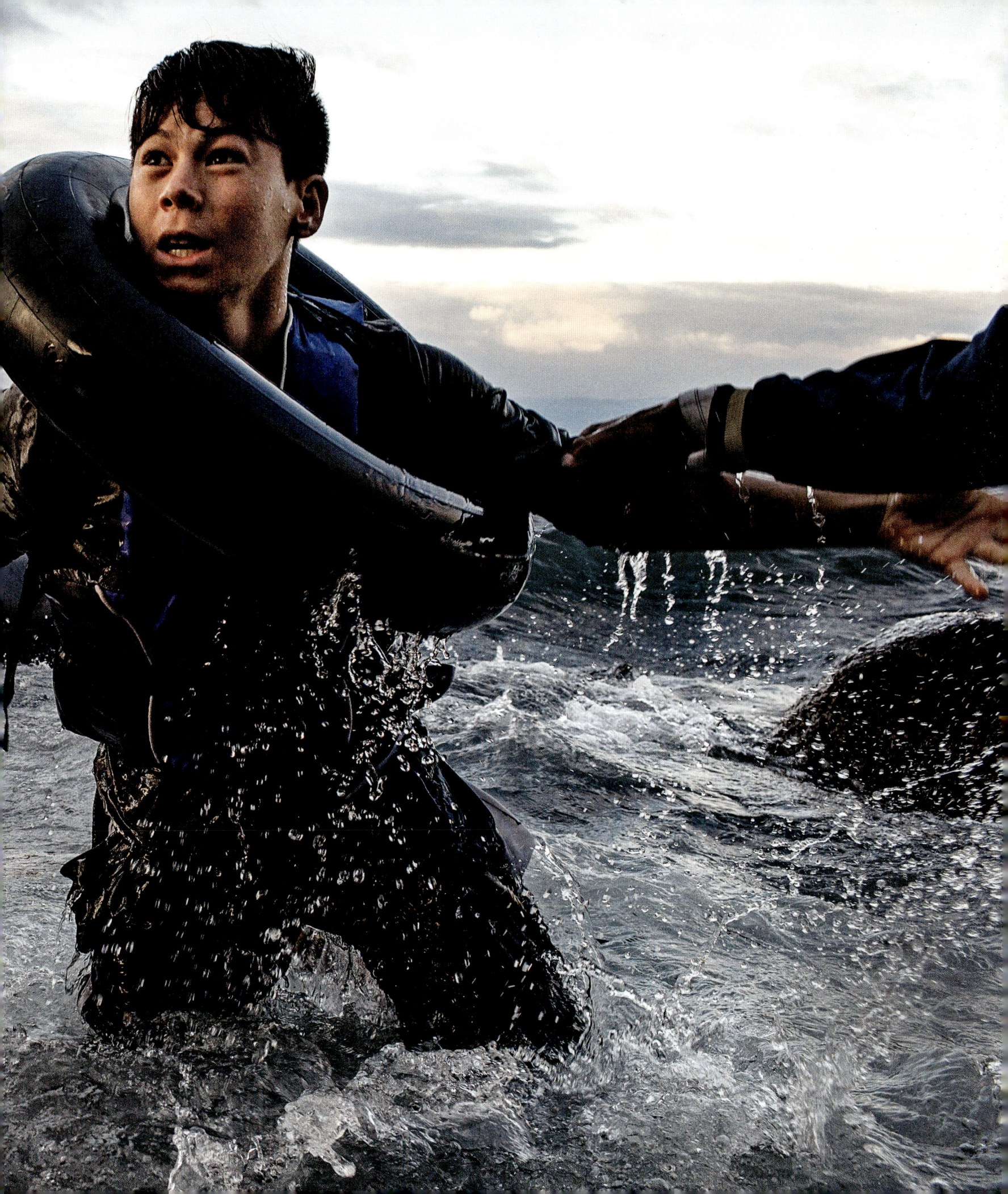

Notre-Dame Burns

April 15, 2019 - Paris, France

The sun was setting over Paris when passers-by noticed smoke rising from the roof of Notre-Dame Cathedral around the scaffolding erected for restoration work on the spire. Soon, the roof of one of the city's most iconic landmarks, a UNESCO World Heritage Site, was engulfed in flames. Tourists and worshippers – mass was in progress – rushed out of the building.

Police closed off access to the Île de la Cité to facilitate the arrival of firefighters. More than 400 firefighters rushed to the scene, but it was extremely difficult to control the blaze. US President Donald Trump suggested in a tweet that Canadair water bombers be used, but they remained grounded. The impact of the water would have caused the building to collapse and the red-hot stones to explode. Fire hoses were used at reduced intensity, with water from the nearby Seine. Relics, works of art, and sacred furnishings were brought to safety, many of which had fortunately already been moved to the sacristy. Operators and journalists arrived on the scene: images of Notre-Dame in agony were broadcast around the world.

Then, the spire collapsed, crumbling onto itself. The situation seemed out of control, as all wooden structures burned. There was the risk that the whole cathedral could burn to the ground. Efforts were focused on saving the towers as the fire was brought under control. Throughout the night, people gathered nearby to watch and pray. The final flames were extinguished the following morning.

The precautions that had been taken – a firefighter always on duty and three inspections under the roof every day – had not been enough. Later investigations revealed that when the first alarm sounded, no one knew where to go to check. By the time a security guard managed to climb the 300 steps to the roof, the fire had already spread. The cause? Likely a short circuit. After extensive reconstruction work, the cathedral reopened to the public on December 7, 2024.

Photograph by Geoffroy Van Der Hasselt

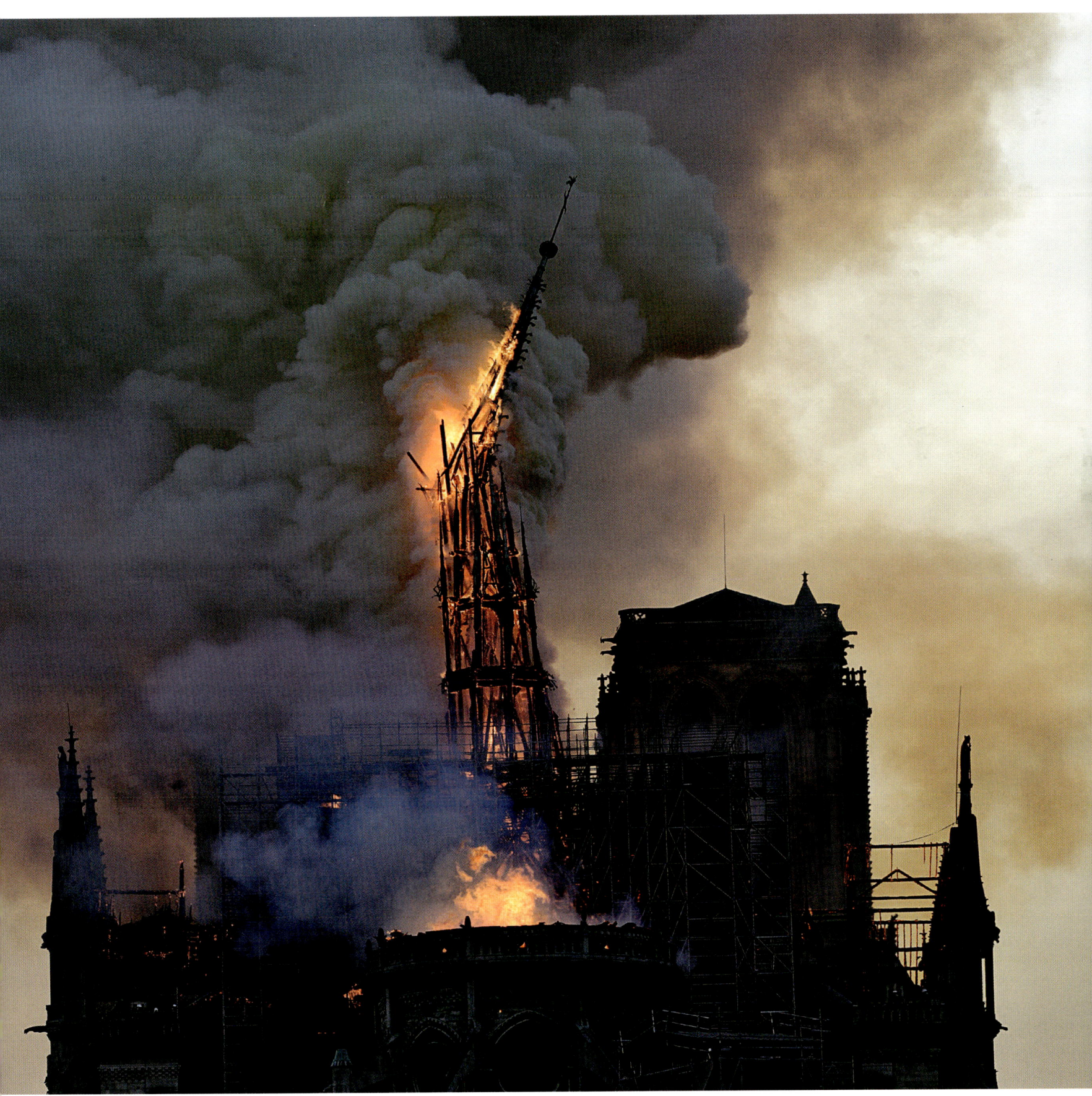

Pope Francis' Covid Prayers

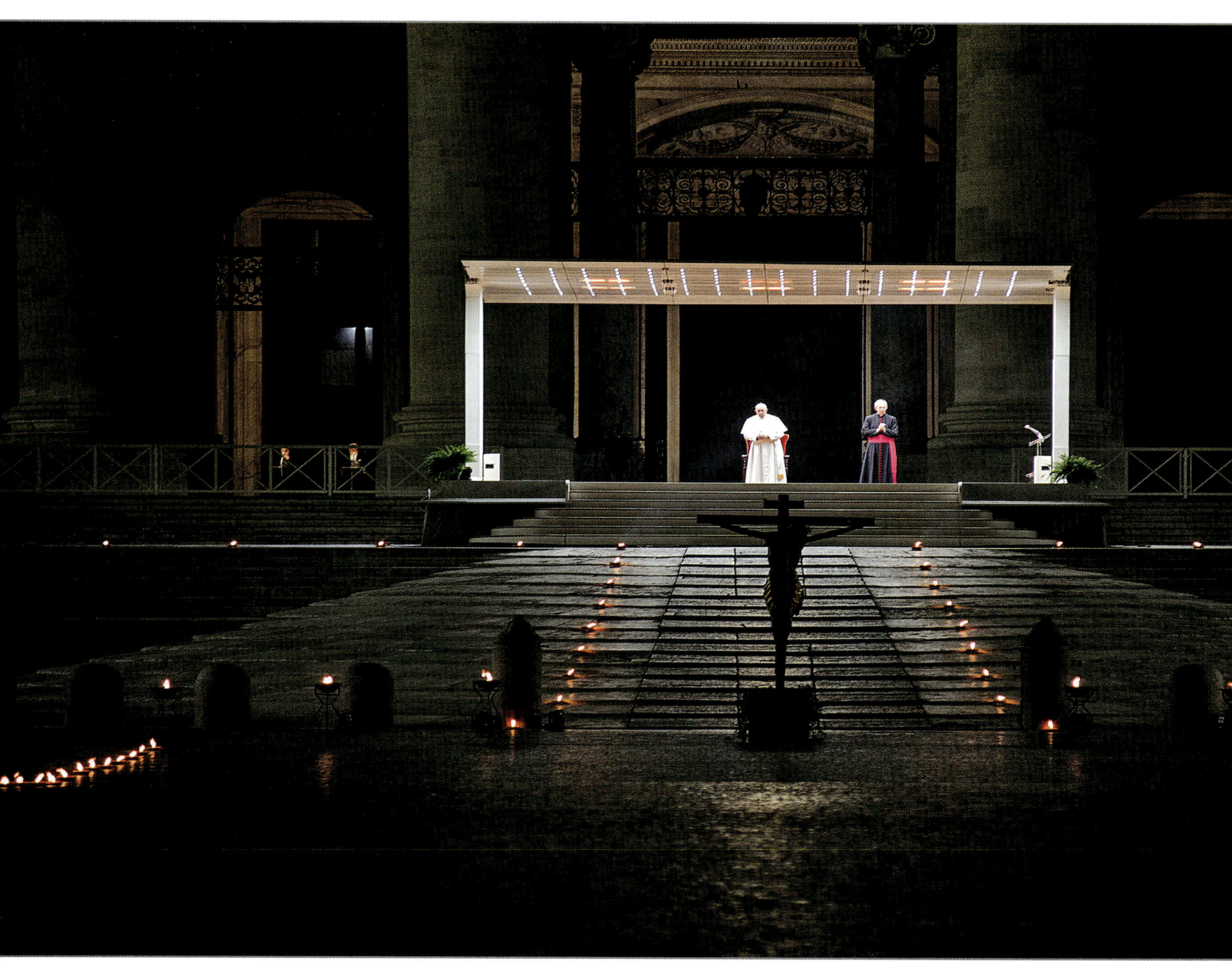

Photograph by Eric Vandeville

April 10, 2020 – Vatican City

In an unusually empty St. Peter's Square illuminated by the soft light of torches, the white figure of Pope Francis stands out, framed by the shadow of the basilica's doorway. In front of him, at the foot of the steps, an ancient crucifix is silhouetted against the light. The almost perfect symmetry is broken by the presence of Monsignor Marini, master of liturgy and the only point of color in the scene, with his purple sash. The pope's slight lean to the left is counterbalanced by that of Christ to the right, suggesting a silent dialogue.

Shaken and sorrowful, Francis was celebrating the Stations of the Cross on Good Friday: the meditation on Jesus' journey from Pilate's court to his crucifixion. That year, the 14 Stations of the Cross were not held in the Colosseum, as is customary, but in the square at the heart of Christianity.

The coronavirus pandemic had shaken the entire world in weeks prior, sowing death and disrupting people's lives and sense of security. Movement and social contact were severely restricted. The future seemed uncertain and threatening, and a return to normality felt very far away. Despondency, the need to reinvent daily life, and forced separation from loved ones opened wounds that were difficult to heal.

On this Good Friday, the Pope prayed for an end to the nightmare. He did so alone, as if to draw upon himself the suffering of all human beings. Doctors and nurses, who had become the unwitting protagonists – and often martyrs – of this dark time, also carried the cross from station to station. They were working extra shifts in hospitals to save those who had contracted a virus for which there was still no cure, putting their own lives at risk. From the balconies of houses where people were confined in an attempt to limit the spread of infection, emotional applause spread through the deserted streets of the cities, merging with the sirens of ambulances.

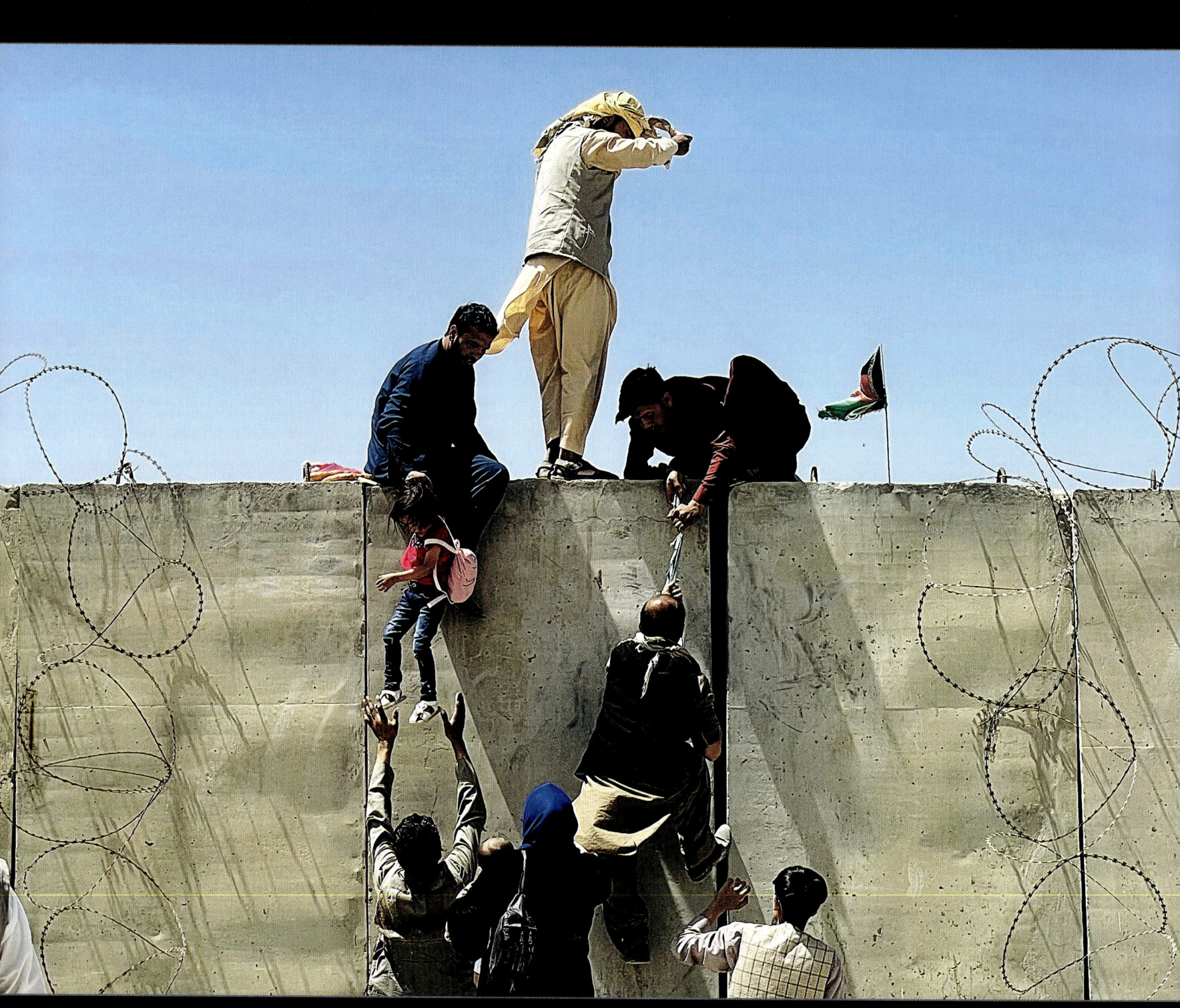

Photograph by Haroon Sabawoon

Escape from Kabul

August 16, 2021 - Kabul, Afghanistan

On August 15th, 2021, Kabul fell back into the hands of the Taliban, 20 years after the end of the Islamist regime that had ruled Afghanistan at the beginning of the new millennium. The NATO contingent had not yet completed its withdrawal from the country, in accordance with the Doha Agreement, and the regular Afghan army had already surrendered to the advancing Taliban, who stormed prisons and freed prisoners. Panic spread among those who had collaborated with the West. Everyone was trying to leave Afghanistan, but the border crossings had been closed: Kabul International Airport remained the only hope of getting out.

That was how the Western presence in Afghanistan ended, with a great escape. It had begun during the presidency of George W. Bush after the attacks of September 11, 2001. The goal was to wage war on terrorism and eradicate the network supporting Osama bin Laden and Al-Qaeda.

Military planes and helicopters took off in a hurry, heading abroad. The US embassy rushed to organize the departure of staff, American citizens, and Afghans working for NATO forces. The following day, amid general confusion, thousands of civilians flocked to the airport in the hope of catching a flight. Some, in desperation, tried to climb over the perimeter wall. Some clung to the wings and landing gear of planes, falling to the ground shortly after takeoff. The crowd was dispersed by US soldiers, who took control of the airport and managed to evacuate over 123,000 people within two weeks.

In Afghanistan, an Islamic Emirate was established and Sharia law was reinstated: arbitrary violence and contempt for human rights resumed with total impunity. The future of the population – especially women and girls, like the one we see dangling in front of the reinforced concrete and barbed wire wall – looks to be full of suffering.

December, 27, 2022 - Bucha, Ukraine

On February 24th, 2022, Russia invaded Ukraine. Suddenly, Europe found itself at war again. Yet the conflict between the two countries has been going on for almost ten years, since the Ukrainian people's desire to look to the West and loosen ties with Moscow led to the Maidan Revolution, which in February 2014 forced pro-Russian President Viktor Yanukovych to flee. The Kremlin's response was the military occupation of Crimea and Donbass, regions inhabited by a large Russian minority. Skirmishes continued for years, confined to peripheral areas, until Russia decided to amass troops on the border at the end of 2021.

By attacking Ukraine head-on, Moscow was convinced it could settle the matter quickly. Instead, unexpectedly strong resistance and Western support for Kiev led to a stalemate. However, missiles and bombs continued to rain down on Ukrainian cities, causing widespread death and destruction. Mariupol was captured after a siege that left the city without electricity or water for weeks. Clashes around the Zaporizhzhia nuclear power plant reawakened the ghosts of the Chernobyl disaster. In Bucha, near Kiev, hundreds of civilians, including children, were massacred by Russian soldiers. When the Ukrainians recaptured the city, the international press documented the recovery of the bodies, executed and abandoned on the streets or buried in mass graves.

In this photo, the violence is modestly concealed. Under an oppressive sky, the long rows of crosses in a makeshift cemetery on the outskirts of Bucha tell a story of silent pain. Hundreds of bodies, many unrecognizable, were buried under those mounds of earth. They are marked only by a number. In the foreground is the yellow and blue flag of Ukraine, which, thanks in part to aid and weapons from Europe and the United States, has been courageously resisting the advance of enemy troops. They wait in vain for diplomacy to bring an end to the hostilities.

Russian Invasion of Ukraine

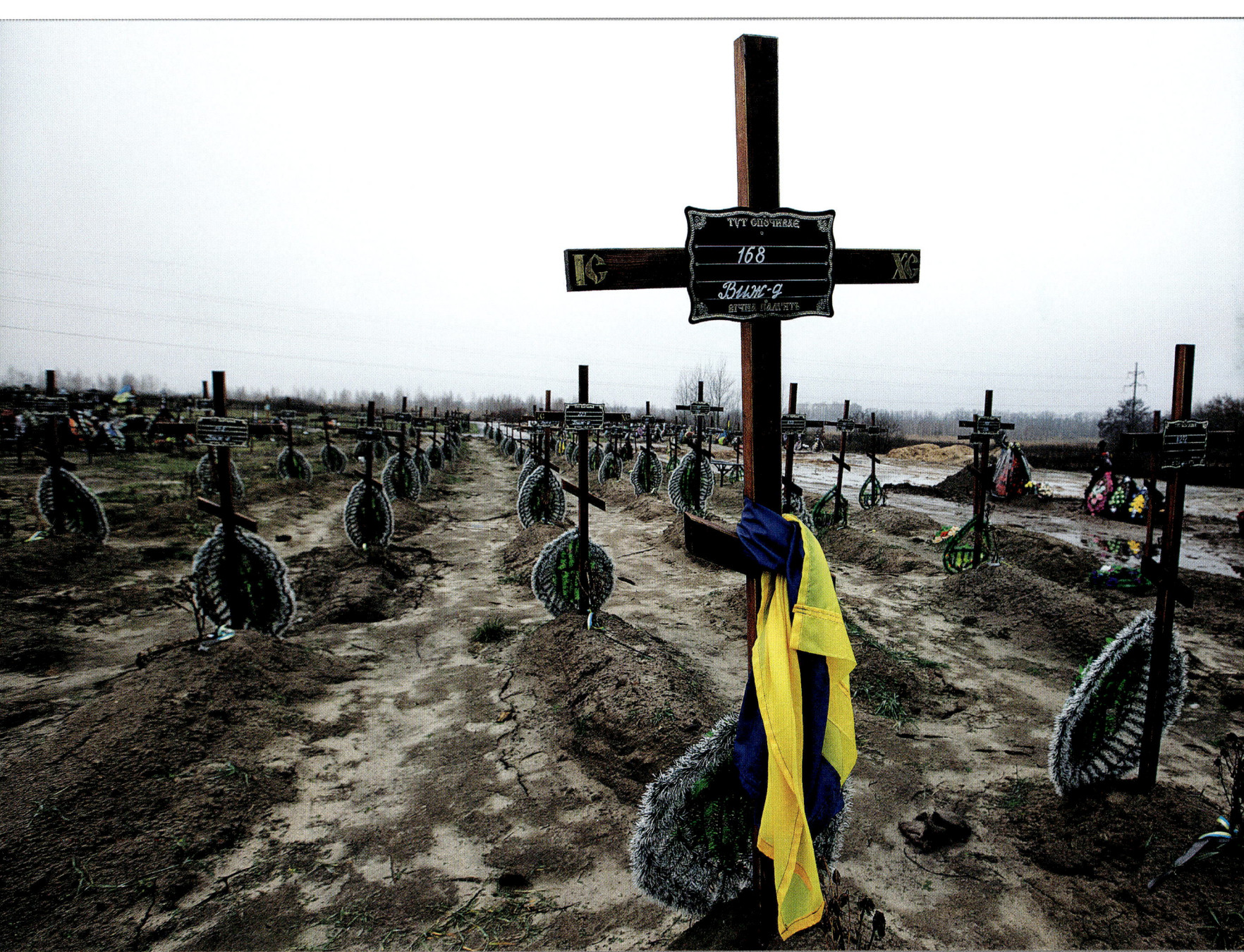

Photograph by Oleksii Chumachenko

New York City Engulfed in Flames

June 7, 2023 – New York, United States

The Empire State Building, along with the rest of New York City, is blanketed by a cloud of yellow smog. The skyscrapers look unusually pale and photos of the famous skyline appear artificially aged by sepia. About a thousand miles north, in Canada, vast forest fires caused the smoke that was then carried down to the city, causing an unusual atmospheric phenomenon. Like a prolonged, surreal sunset, the air, thick with polluting particles, filters the sunlight, allowing only red and yellow waves to pass through, which are shorter than those that normally give the sky its color.

When David Dee Delgado captured it in this shot, New York City had the worst air quality in the world. Public schools suspended outdoor activities, authorities advised people to stay indoors as much as possible, and the few who ventured outside wore masks, evoking memories of the recent pandemic.

The year 2023 had been particularly hot and dry in North America, with prolonged droughts setting the stage for numerous fires. In Canada, there were more than 400, making it the worst year on record. This is just one of the consequences of climate change. Within a couple of days, when the wind pushed this blanket of smoke out over the Atlantic, New York and other American cities most affected returned to normal.

However, the fires continued for weeks, and above-average summer temperatures will continue to cause new ones, releasing tons of carbon dioxide into the atmosphere, a vicious cycle that is difficult to reverse. The apocalyptic landscape captured in the images of those days is a powerful warning. It is up to us to prevent it from becoming a preview of our future.

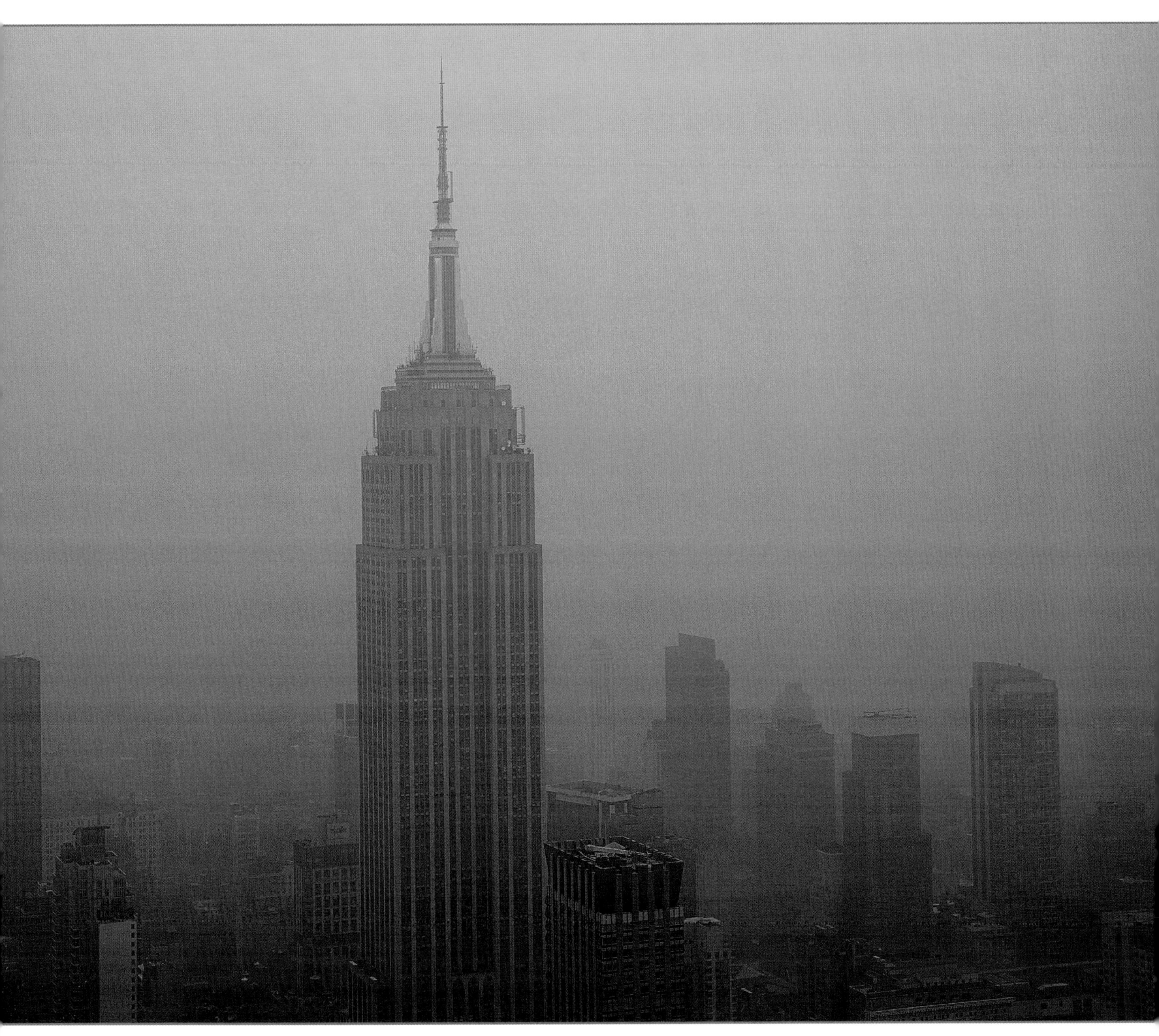

Photograph by David Dee Delgado

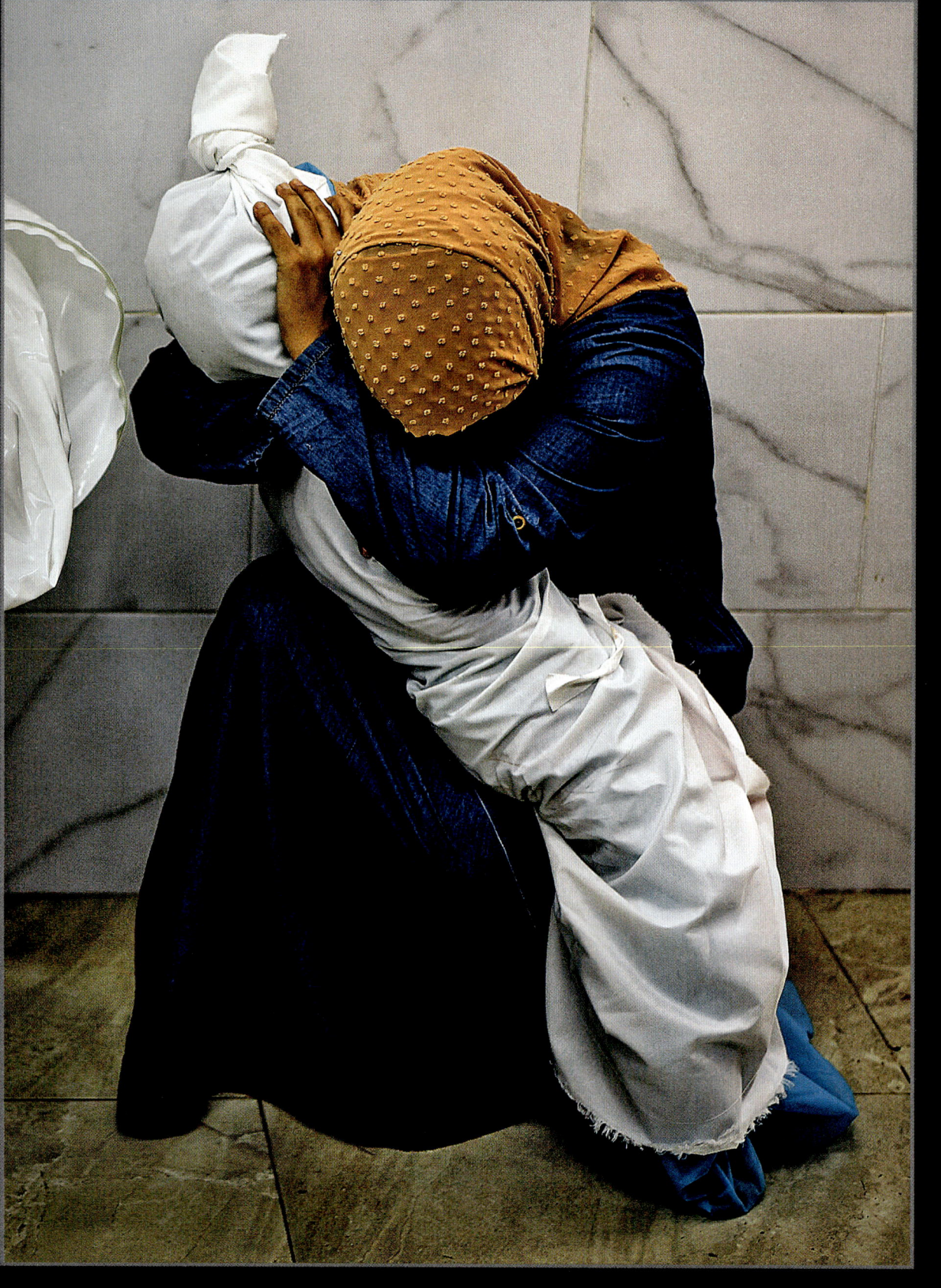

Photograph by Mohammed Salem

Pietà, Gaza

October 17, 2023 – Gaza Strip, Palestine

A crouching woman clutches a sheet that appears to be rolled up. A single hand is visible from the sleeve of her deep blue tunic. Her face is hidden by her head, which is bent forward and covered by an ochre-colored veil. The white shroud resting on her legs envelops the lifeless body of her five-year-old niece, Saly. An Israeli air force missile ripped through the building where she lived, killing her, her mother and her sister. This is the morgue of the Khan Younis hospital, in the southern part of the Gaza Strip, which has been flooded by distraught families rushing to identify and recover the bodies of their relatives, hoping that someone has survived.

On October 7th, a few days earlier, Hamas militants carried out a brutal incursion into Israeli territory, attacking kibbutzim and settlements, massacring 1,200 civilians and soldiers and kidnapping 250. Survivors recount scenes of unprecedented violence and horrific rapes. Prime Minister Benjamin Netanyahu immediately declared a state of war and organized a ruthless and brutal counteroffensive. Electricity, fuel, food and water supplies to Gaza were cut off. Densely populated areas were targeted by Israeli bombing, and on October 26th, a ground offensive began. The civilian population suffered the most: in a short time, most of the buildings were reduced to rubble. Hundreds of thousands of Palestinians were forced to flee in dire conditions.

With this poignant shot, Mohammed Salem, a Palestinian photographer for Reuters, won the prestigious 2024 World Press Photo of the Year award. He and many of his colleagues courageously bear witness to the atrocities of war as they put their own lives at risk on the shores of the Mediterranean, the same sea that bathes southern Europe, which remains indifferent to the deaths of tens of thousands of people, numb to this endless tragedy.

July 13, 2024 - Butler, Pennsylvania, United States

Donald Trump stands with his face bloodied and his right fist raised to the sky, surrounded by bodyguards trying to shield him and keep him safe. Behind them, the American flag waves. Only three colors are seen in this shot: red, white, and blue. Like a wounded but indomitable warrior, Trump angrily shouts a single, short word three times – "Fight!" – oblivious to the danger and chaos around him.

Moments earlier, the former president was rallying his supporters at a rally in a small town in Pennsylvania, historically one of the key states in US elections. The former president was in the midst of his campaign for a second term. Suddenly, rapid gunshots interrupted his speech: a bullet grazed his right ear. The shooter was 20-year-old Thomas Matthew Crooks, who was lying in wait with an assault rifle on the roof of a warehouse about a hundred meters away. He had been spotted and reported as a suspect, but no one had intervened. Snipers killed him instantly.

One of the photographers present, Evan Vucci, rushed towards the stage. His years of experience, including in dangerous war zones, allowed him to react quickly, understand the situation, and act with clarity, taking the almost incredulous agent looking at the camera by surprise. It was later determined that Trump had turned his head slightly just before the shots were fired, a movement that most likely saved his life. In the hours that followed, the photo was shared on social networks and broadcast by media outlets around the world.

Kamala Harris' candidacy for the Democratic Party the following week to replace a weary Joe Biden was to no avail. In November, Trump achieved a resounding victory, riding the wave of the slogan "Make America Great Again," returning to the White House after four years marked by the 2021 storming of the Capitol, numerous trials in which he was the defendant and increasingly virulent political confrontations.

Assassination Attempt on Trump

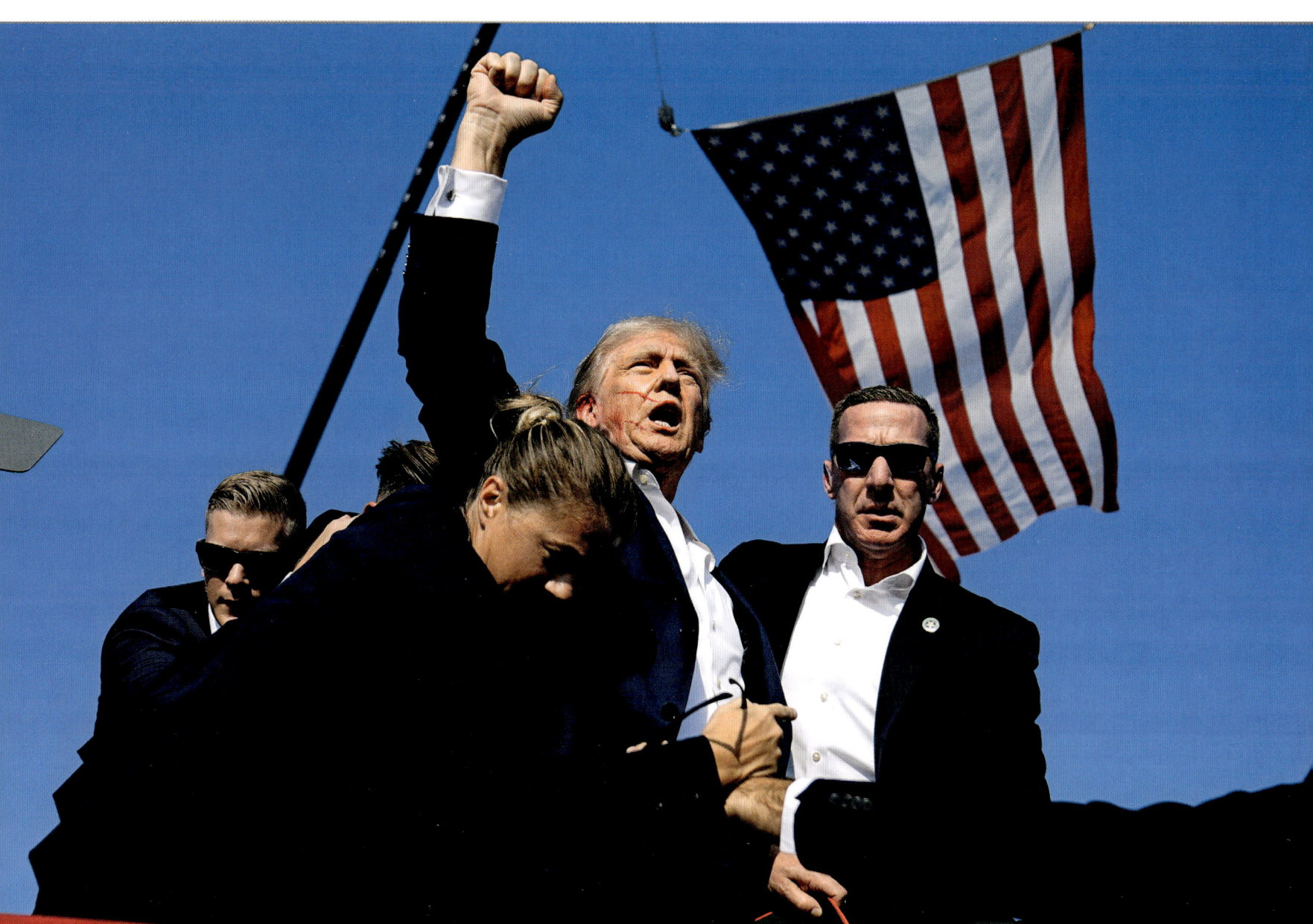

Photograph by Evan Vucci

The photographers

Adams Eddie (1933-2004) American war photographer, he covered 13 conflicts. He worked for Associated Press and *TIME* magazine. In 1969 he won the Pulitzer prize.

Agostini Evan American entertainment event photographer. He works for Invision Agency and has been published in many major magazines and papers.

Ake J. David American photojournalist, covered the 2004 presidential campaign and the White House for AFP. He's now Photo Chief for Associated Press in Washington D.C.

Andersen Odd Norwegian photojournalist, he's AFP Chief Photographer for Germany and Scandinavia.

Attar Abbas (1944) Iranian photographer living in Paris, he's a member of Magnum Photos. He has covered wars and conflicts, and critically investigated great religions.

Avakian Alexandra (1960) American photojournalist of Armenian origin, she has worked with magazines as *TIME* and *National Geographic*.

Barbey Bruno (1941) French photojournalist born in Morocco, he traveled the world in the middle of wars and revolutions. He's a longtime member of Magnum Photos.

Barrington Brown Antony (1927-2012) British photographer, explorer and designer.

Beaton Cecil (1904-1980) British fashion, portrait and war photographer, stage and costume designer. He's best known for portraying Hollywood stars and British society. Queen Elizabeth II made him a Knight Bachelor.

Bosshard Walter (1892-1975) Swiss photojournalist, he reported on Asia, from Gandhi to Afghanistan.

Bouju Jean-Marc (1961) French photojournalist, he won two Pulitzer and the World Press Photo of the Year 2004. He was embedded with US Army during the Iraq War.

Browne Malcolm (1931-2012) American photographer and journalist. When he was Associated Press Chief correspondent for Indochina, he won the World Press Photo of the Year 1963 and the Pulitzer prize in 1964.

Burrows Larry (1926-1971) British photographer, he bore witness to the Vietnam War, where he was killed.

Capa Robert (1913-1954) Pseudonym of Endre Erno Friedmann, Hungarian photographer. He took famous shots of the Spanish Civil War and Second World War. In 1947, he was cofounder of Magnum Photos agency.

Carter Kevin (1960-1994) South African photographer, he covered the famine in Sudan. In 1993 he won the Pulitzer prize and committed suicide the following year.

Cartier-Bresson Henri (1908-2004) French photojournalist, painter, and director, he was cofounder in 1947 of Magnum Photos agency. He worked all over the world. He's considered the master of candid photography.

Chumachenko Oleksii Ukrainian photographer, his photos have portrayed the military conflict that erupted following Russia's invasion of Ukraine in February 2022.

Clary Timothy A. American photographer, works for AFP.

Corder Chris American photographer, works for UPI.

Daniels John T. (1873-1948) American surfman, he took the picture of the first flight of the Wright brothers.

Delgado David Dee Puerto Rican photographer, he works with Reuters, The New York Times, and the The Wall Street Journal. He was a Pulitzer Prize finalist in 2023.

Dominis John (1921-2013) American photographer, he covered Korean and Vietnam Wars and events like Woodstock. He worked for *LIFE* and *People* magazines.

Dworzak Thomas (1972) German photojournalist, he covered conflicts in Chechnya, Afghanistan, Iraq, and Pakistan. He's a member of Magnum Photos.

Eisenstaedt Alfred (1898-1995) German photographer established in the USA, he worked for *LIFE* magazine. He portrayed politicians and celebrities.

Ejzenštejn Sergej M. (1898-1948) Soviet director, film theorist, writer, and filmmaker, he was a pioneer in montage.

Erwitt Elliott (1928) Russian born photographer and director established in the USA. Thanks to Robert Capa, he became a member of Magnum Photos, and then president.

Franklin Stuart (1956) British photographer, he's a member and former president of Magnum Photos. He covered historical events, wars, and ecological issues.

Furlong Christopher (1947) British photojournalist, after serving in the army he's now Chief Photographer for Getty Images. He's specialized in culture and current news.

Fusco Paul (1930) American photojournalist, he's a longtime member of Magnum Photos. He has covered wars and social subjects, as Chernobyl disaster's effects.

Gaumy Jean (1948) French photographer and documentarian, longtime member of Magnum Photos. He has covered many wars and inspected marginalization contexts.

Glinn Burt (1925-2008) American photographer, former president of Magnum Photos and American Society of Media Photographers. He worked in Cuba during the revolution, Russia, and Japan. He portrayed American high society.

Goldstein Grigori P. (1870-1941) Russian photographer, he covered the Revolution for the Muscovite magazine *Rannee Utro*. Then he dedicated himself to cinema.

Gotfryd Bernard (1924) Polish photographer, he went to the USA after surviving a concentration camp. For *Newsweek* he portrayed personalities, politicians, and artists.

Guzy Carol (1956) American photojournalist, she works for The

Washington Post. Winner of four Pulitzer prizes.

Hicks Tyler (1969) American photojournalist born in Brazil. He lives in Kenya and works for *The New York Times*. He hastens to where the story is happening, regardless of danger. In 2016 he won his third Pulitzer.

Hou Bo (1924) Chinese photographer. With her husband, Xu Xiaobing, she was Mao Zedong's official photographer.

Joe Alexander Zimbabwean photographer, he has covered great events for AFP in Africa, from famine in Ethiopia to Mandela's liberation.

Koudelka Josef (1938) Czech photographer, today a French citizen. He became famous with his photos of the Prague Spring, has then made photo features all over Europe.

Lange Dorothea (1895-1965) American photographer, she reported with clarity on the condition of the poor classes during the Great Depression.

Levy Charles (1919-1997) US Army official, he took the photo of the Nagasaki atomic explosion.

Lowe W. George (1924-2013) New Zealander climber, film director, and educator. He's famous for climbing Everest and making a documentary about the expedition.

Lumière Auguste and Louis (1862-1954; 1864-1948) French brothers, founding fathers of the cinema, at first believed an "invention without any future."

Marlow Peter (1952-2016) British photographer, he has been president and vice president of Magnum Photos. In 1987 he founded the London offices of the agency.

McCurry Steve (1950) American photographer, he's especially famous for his portraits. He reported conflicts, dying traditions, and little beauties of daily life.

Miller Henry American soldier, he took photos of Jews' conditions in Buchenwald concentration camp.

Moore Mike British photojournalist, he was the first to embed with the British Army during a conflict (the Iraq War).

Peary Robert E. (1856-1920) American explorer, he was believed to be the first man to reach the North Pole (record then conferred on Frederick Cook).

Pellegrin Paolo (1964) Italian photographer, member of Magnum Photos. He has reported on the conflicts in Yugoslavia and Darfur, Guantanamo Bay and tsunamis.

Peress Gilles (1946) French photographer and documentarian, he's a member and former president of Magnum Photos. He teaches Humans Rights and Photography at Bard College in New York.

Piper Eric British photojournalist of the *Daily Mirror*, he took photos of the Beatles and showed to the world the atrocities committed by the Cambodian regime of Khmer Rouge.

Preisig Dölf (1940-2005) Swiss photographer. He was Chief Photographer of Schweizer Illustrierten magazine. He received an honorable mention at World Press Photo for his shots of the assassination attempt to the Pope.

Riboud Marc (1923) French photographer, he was one of the first members of Magnum Photos. He was also one of the first European photographers to go to China, and became famous thanks to his photos of the Vietnam War.

Roger-Viollet Henri (1896-1946) French photographer from the beginning of the twentieth century. His daughter, who collected his shots, was the founder of Roger-Viollet General Photographic Documentation, one the first Parisian photo agencies (1938).

Russell Andrew J. (1829-1902) American photographer, he covered the American Civil War and the construction of the first transcontinental railroad.

Sabawoon Haroon Afghan photographer and president of the Afghan Multimedia Agency. In 2021, he documented the withdrawal of US troops from Kabul.

Salem Mohammed (1985) Palestinian photojournalist in Gaza, he has worked for Reuters since 2003. In 2024, he won the World Press Photo of the Year award.

Saman Moises (1974) Hispanic American photojournalist, he's a member of Magnum Photos. He covered the Middle East after September 11 for the daily paper *Newsday*.

Sanders Walter American photographer of German origin, he's a longtime member of LIFE magazine.

Silvers Robert (1968) He has become famous for his photographic mosaics. With this technique he portrayed heads of state and celebrities.

Smith W. Eugene (1918-1978) American documentarian photographer. During the Second World War he covered the battles on the Pacific front for LIFE magazine and he was injured by a grenade.

Tracy Evarts (1868-1922) American architect, during the First World War he was Chief of Engineers in the army Camouflage Section.

Ut Huynh Cong "Nick" (1951) Vietnamese photographer who emigrated to the USA, he works for Associated Press. He has won a Pulitzer prize and the World Press Photo of the Year in 1973.

Van der Hasselt Geoffroy (1985) Belgian photojournalist based in Paris, he works with AFP to cover politics, current events, and sports.

Vandeville Eric (1958) French photographer, he has lived in Rome since 1998 and has taken photographs of Vatican architecture, as well as portraits of Pope Francis and Pope Benedict XVI.

Visalli Santi (1932) Italian-American photographer, he portrayed six American presidents and various celebrities. He's especially famous for his urban views.

Vucci Evan (1977) Chief photographer of the Associated Press, he mainly covers American politics. He was part of the team that won the Pulitzer Prize in 2021 for documenting protests following George Floyd's death.

Photo Credits

WS whitestar® is a registered trademark property of White Star s.r.l.

© 2016, 2026 White Star s.r.l.
Piazzale Luigi Cadorna, 6
20123 Milan, Italy
www.whitestar.it

Updated edition

Translation and Editing: Iceigeo, Milano (Jonathan West, Max Rankenburg and Alexa Ahern)

ISBN 978-88-544-2179-0
1 2 3 4 5 6 30 29 28 27 26

Printed in India